FAMILIES, SCHOOLS, AND COMMUNITIES
Building Partnerships for Educating Children

FAMILIES, SCHOOLS, AND COMMUNITIES
Building Partnerships for Educating Children

Second Edition

CHANDLER BARBOUR
Towson University

NITA H. BARBOUR
University of Maryland, Baltimore County

Merrill
Prentice Hall

Upper Saddle River, New Jersey
Columbus, Ohio

Library of Congress Cataloging-in-Publication Data

Barbour, Chandler.
   Families, schools, and communities : building partnerships for educating children /
Chandler Barbour, Nita H. Barbour.—2nd ed.
      p. cm.
   Includes bibliographical references (p.) and index.
   ISBN 0-13-015523-
      1. Home and school—United States. 2. Community and school—United States. 3.
School environment—United States. 4. Students—United States—Social conditions. 5.
Education—United States—Curricula. 6. Child development—United States.   I. Barbour,
Nita.   II. Title.

LC225.3 .B27 2001
371.19'0973—dc21

                                                                    00-020866

Vice President and Publisher: Jeffery W. Johnston
Executive Editor: Ann Castel Davis
Editorial Assistant: Pat Grogg
Production Editor: Sheryl Glicker Langner
Production Coordination: Holly Henjum, Clarinda Publication Services
Design Coordinator: Diane C. Lorenzo
Photo Coordinator: Sherry Mitchell
Cover Designer: Ceri Fitzgerald
Cover art: Stockworks
Production Manager: Laura Messerly
Director of Marketing: Kevin Flanagan
Marketing Manager: Amy June
Marketing Services Manager: Krista Groshong

This book was set in Melior by The Clarinda Company. It was printed and bound by R. R. Donnelley & Sons Company. The cover was printed by Phoenix Color Corp.

Photo Credits: Steven Barbour, pp. 1, 7, 13, 47, 89, 107, 109, 116, 119, 123, 126, 146, 179, 185, 189, 312; Anthony Magnacca/Merrill, pp. 9, 99, 159, 247, 306, 339, 347; Scott Cunningham/Merrill, pp. 16, 82, 173, 292, 315; Ben Chandler/Merrill, p. 21; Anne Vega/Merrill, pp. 24, 55, 74, 77, 112, 176, 193, 218, 251, 282; The Bettmann Archive, pp. 27, 43; Courtesy of the Library of Congress, p. 31; Corbis-Bettmann, p. 35; Todd Yarrington/Merrill, pp. 38, 60, 69, 268; Lawrence Migdale/Pix, p. 51; Michael Mancuso/Omni-Photo Communications, Inc., p. 64; Lloyd Lemmerman/Merrill, p. 93; Courtesy of IBM, p. 96; Jeff Greenberg/Omni-Photo Communications, Inc., p. 131; Barbara Schwartz/Merrill, pp. 135, 150, 155, 208; Scott Haskell/Bangor Daily News, pp. 140, 232, 260; Ken Karp/Pearson Education, p. 143; Shirley Zeiberg/Pearson Education, p. 163; David Young-Wolff/PhotoEdit, pp. 168, 329; Michael Newman/PhotoEdit, pp. 196, 337; Mary Jane Porterfield, p. 206; Belle Kuhn, p. 213; Richard Frear/National Park Service/U. S. Department of the Interior, p. 222; Ian Shaw/Tony Stone Images, p. 227; John Paul Endress/Silver Burdett Ginn, p. 236; PhotoDisc, Inc., p. 241; Keith Brofsky/ PhotoDisc, Inc., p. 263; James L. Shaffer, p. 273; Tom Watson/Merrill, pp. 279, 301; Bruce Johnson/Merrill, pp. 288, 325, 333; Larry Hamill/Merrill, p. 296; Dan Floss/Merrill, p. 321; Berkeley Police Department, p. 344.

10 9 8 7 6 5 4 3 2 1
ISBN 0-13-018552-3

We dedicate this book to the fascinating families with which we are connected, to the challenging schools we have served and from which we have learned, and to the satisfying communities we have been welcomed into and that have provided good settings for our own networks and for our aspirations.
And especially for Victoria Galina—YPA!

Preface

We have 54 million school-aged children in the United States today, and another 20 million preschoolers are growing rapidly in homes, care centers, and communities across our nation. Teachers, social services providers, and administrators, as well as family members, community members, and caregivers of all kinds, have a tremendous responsibility to ensure the most productive education possible for this huge section of the American public who will be the mainstay of society in the future. The responsibility is staggering. However, many critics question our success rate, and some kind of reform or education renewal seems to be on everyone's mind.

In the four years since the first edition of this text, a number of significant events have unfolded, and all have implications for education in America. A burgeoning economy has surrounded us and made life easier for most Americans, but almost one-fifth of our children continue to live in poverty. A national welfare reform plan has been instituted, and while some successes are evident, some regrettable results also are associated with that reform. Brain research findings provide more answers to nagging questions about development, but Judith Harris's book, *The Nurture Assumption,* on the potency of peer groups has startled Americans about parent roles.

Marital statistics have changed considerably: Divorces are less frequent, but so are marriages, and more children are raised in single-parent homes.

At the same time, the proliferation of the cyberworld has created new challenges and opportunities for all citizens. The rapid rise of the Internet in the past few years has overstepped the bounds of all estimates and signals vast changes in the way Americans will communicate, purchase materials, and access information in the future.

In addition to all the new and sobering challenges, old demands are still evident in our postindustrial society. Cultural and ethnic diversity is expanding rapidly in the United States, and concerns about special-needs children grow each year. Our federal government, as well as most state governments, displays more interest in education and seeks to play a more influential role. The effect of this governmental interest and role is perceived differently by educators, parents, and community leaders.

The face of our world can never be the same again, and most people realize that the requirements for citizens in the 21st century are very different from those of a generation ago. All these concerns point to a need to develop education agendas aimed at blending interests, using cooperation to the fullest, and identifying all resources possible for addressing children's educational needs.

Most authorities agree that major changes in the procedures, the curriculum, and the formats of U.S. schools are needed as never before. For many, the greatest changes focus on drawing more partners into the management and handling of children's formal education. A number of educational collaborations and partnership designs have spread across the United States, and they have served as effective bridges in many school districts. This text moves in a similar direction, and the authors support the designs that emphasize the benefits of collaboration among the many agencies and persons working with our children.

A basic tenet of *Families, Schools, and Communities: Building Partnerships for Educating Children* is that schools will always be a primary venue for educating the young child. And educators must be in the forefront of any endeavor to bring about change. However, we stress that to accomplish the tasks at hand, all school districts must develop vibrant partnerships—uniting parents and community members with teachers in educating tomorrow's citizens. Schools are where the action is, but respectful collaboration is the key to success.

Significant steps for improving children's education through collaboration are already at work in schools and communities across the United States. A growing number of research studies, controlled assessments, and personal accounts support new education approaches. These beginning ventures provide intriguing evidence and guides for others to follow. We do not need to reconceptualize our curricula or most of our teaching practices. The big job now is to study and adapt the amazing examples that already exist.

NEW TO THE SECOND EDITION

Building on the success of the first edition, we have rearranged some material and topics to give the text more coherence and usefulness. Since research studies and findings are frequently expanded or replicated, we have updated a large number of references. We have changed the recommended readings section in each chapter to include other media, particularly websites, that we believe will have staying power. We have inserted a new chapter on child care to support the sections in other chapters that could not cover the topic adequately. New and updated figures and tables synthesize information for the reader.

We have inserted more information on special education, although we realize that the scope of this text serves only as a beginning step for this important area of educational experience. Lastly, we have inserted a new section in each chapter labeled "Implications for Professionals," which we hope will help the reader to personalize the chapter material.

ORGANIZATION OF THIS TEXT

We feel it vital for preservice and inservice teachers as well as other social services providers to understand the myriad influences on children's lives and how the structures of homes, schools, and communities affect children's learning. By acknowledging this broader scope of curriculum, teachers in training and other young professionals will recognize the family and the community as crucial educative forces.

We begin this text with an overview of the powerful influences surrounding young children. Along with this, we identify the three primary social settings of home life, school life, and community life and discuss how these settings interplay to affect children's lives. Society does change, of course, and some forces influencing children have intensified in recent years. We categorize these influence patterns to gain a perspective of what exists in the United States today.

Chapter 2 focuses on how responsibilities for children's education have emerged over time and how different ethnic groups in the United States have been affected over more than 3 centuries. We look particularly at the uneven progress of collaborations that have affected schoolwork.

The next two chapters present information on U.S. family life, reviewing various family patterns and recognizing the different ways that families function. Prospective teachers will grasp the range of situations that professionals encounter as they work with children in a diverse society, and our hope is that they will comprehend the logic for establishing collaborations in light of this diversity.

Chapter 5 is a new chapter for this second edition, and it is devoted to the expanding out-of-home care programs for the millions of preschool-aged children as well as young school-aged children. Far more mothers have joined the workforce and must now find adequate care for their preschool-aged children and their in-school children who need care during after-school hours. We discuss the various child care arrangements and practices as well as the agency-directed preschool programs that growing numbers of young children encounter.

Chapter 6 examines the responsibilities of parents and professionals in each of the three social settings. It points out the various educational assignments and expectations that each setting places on the others.

Chapters 7, 8, and 9 deal with curriculum in the three social settings. Curriculum surrounds children, and though we do not always take notice of it, much of what children learn comes from the world outside the classroom.

The reader must recognize that all citizens are educators and that when teachers acknowledge this, an even greater potential for learning exists.

The last four chapters focus on the possibilities for collaboration among the three social settings. In chapter 10, we discuss traditional as well as new ways for teachers, parents, and others to work together. Chapter 11 reviews several model programs that demonstrate partnerships working beneficially. Chapter 12 highlights effective social settings and extends ideas about the ingredients for developing partnerships. Chapter 13 examines the demanding and often difficult process of getting together. In this last chapter, we review the steps required to establish a good partnership. We then use idealized rural and urban school districts to demonstrate how two actual communities are struggling toward collaboration, exploring the typical problems they encounter, and evaluating their progress.

The appendix for the second edition carries an extensive bibliography of children's books to help make the content of this text more pertinent and meaningful.

SPECIAL FEATURES

To assist instructors and students using this text, we have included several pedagogical aids.

Chapter Objectives, Implications, and Summaries. Concise statements of each chapter's main ideas serve as advance organizers for the content that follows. To relate the chapter content to a beginning professional's life and experience, we have placed a brief section near the end of each chapter that urges the reader to reflect upon and personalize the chapter information. This "Implications for Professionals" section is a new element in the second edition and is designed to increase understanding by relating text to self. A chapter summary reviews the highlights of the content in each chapter.

Vignettes.   Depictions of real-life events that the authors have encountered clarify many concepts throughout the text. These personal stories are all from the authors' experiences (except the names used) and give a human connection to the chapter information and purpose.

Suggested Activities and Questions.   Each chapter ends with questions and activities that give instructors another means to make the text applicable to their course outlines and to students' lives. For students, the activities will help apply concepts presented and will stimulate reflection and discussion on the reading as well as their own experiences.

Resources.   In addition to citing extensive references within the text and featuring tables and figures that encapsulate text content, we list a few particular titles at the end of each chapter to allow for a more thorough examination of content. We also have extended the second edition chapters with other resources: (1) up-to-date films and videos to provide another medium for the chapter concepts, (2) lists of key organizations and agencies that relate to the profession, and (3) several websites that will give current status reports for our chapter features.

Bibliography of Children's Literature.   The selections depict valuable examples of children in different family arrangements learning in a variety of settings. This updated bibliography provides instructors as well as inservice teachers and other professionals with curriculum material to illuminate the chapter content. It will be particularly valuable for chapters 3, 4, 5, 7, 8, and 9.

Glossary.   Because the text draws from sociology, psychology, human development, and anthropology as well as from pedagogy and curriculum content, we include a glossary to help readers with specialized terms.

ACKNOWLEDGMENTS

Many people assisted in the writing and assembling of this text. We would like to acknowledge particularly the following individuals: Ithel Jones of Florida State University for developing chapter 5, offering valuable reflections on use of the first edition, and commenting on manuscript drafts; Valerie Mekras for supplying background material and references on special-needs programs; and Audrey Jewett for providing research on materials and retrieval of children's literature topics.

We also are grateful to Cyndi Gostenhofer, Director of First Experiences Child Care Center, and her wonderful team of colleagues for providing support and observation opportunities. Many thanks go to our colleagues, classroom teachers, and parents who willingly supplied photos to illustrate our text. We thank Steven Barbour for supplying numerous photos plus suggestions for illuminating several text sections. Library personnel at the University of Maine and the University of Maryland have been patient, helpful, and supportive in filling numerous requests and supplying materials in a timely fashion.

We wish to thank Ann Davis, our editor at Merrill/Prentice Hall, for her excellent guidance for this text. We also thank Holly Henjum, our production editor at Clarinda Publication Services, and freelance copyeditor Deborah Cady for their many valuable contributions. Several individuals reviewed this text, and we thank them here: Marcia Broughton, University of Northern Colorado; Laurie Dinnebeil, University of Toledo; Janie H. Humphries, Louisiana Tech; and Sandra J. Wanner, University of Mary Hardin-Baylor.

Discover the Companion Website Accompanying This Book

THE PRENTICE HALL COMPANION WEBSITE: A VIRTUAL LEARNING ENVIRONMENT

Technology is a constantly growing and changing aspect of our field that is creating a need for content and resources. To address this emerging need, Prentice Hall has developed an online learning environment for students and professors alike—Companion Websites—to support our textbooks.

In creating a Companion Website, our goal is to build on and enhance what the textbook already offers. For this reason, the content for each user-friendly website is organized by topic and provides the professor and student with a variety of meaningful resources. Common features of a Companion Website include:

FOR THE PROFESSOR—

Every Companion Website integrates **Syllabus Manager**™, an online syllabus creation and management utility.

- **Syllabus Manager**™ provides you, the instructor, with an easy, step-by-step process to create and revise syllabi, with direct links into Companion Website and other online content without having to learn HTML.

- Students may log onto your syllabus during any study session. All they need to know is the web address for the Companion Website and the password you've assigned to your syllabus.

- After you have created a syllabus using **Syllabus Manager**™, students may enter the syllabus for their course section from any point in the Companion Website.

- Class dates are highlighted in white and assignment due dates appear in blue. Clicking on a date, the student is shown the list of activities for the assignment. The activities for each assignment are linked directly to actual content, saving time for students.

- Adding assignments consists of clicking on the desired due date, then filling in the details of the assignment—name of the assignment, instructions, and whether or not it is a one-time or repeating assignment.

- In addition, links to other activities can be created easily. If the activity is online, a URL can be entered in the space provided, and it will be linked automatically in the final syllabus.

- Your completed syllabus is hosted on our servers, allowing convenient updates from any computer on the Internet. Changes you make to your syllabus are immediately available to your students at their next logon.

FOR THE STUDENT—

- **Topic Overviews**—outline key concepts in topic areas
- **Electronic Bluebook**—send homework or essays directly to your instructor's email with this paperless form
- **Message Board**—serves as a virtual bulletin board to post—or respond to—questions or comments to/from a national audience
- **Web Destinations**—links to www sites that relate to each topic area

- **Professional Organizations**—links to organizations that relate to topic areas
- **Additional Resources**—access to topic-specific content that enhances material found in the text

To take advantage of these and other resources, please visit the *Families, Schools, and Communities: Building Partnerships for Educating Children* Companion Website at www.prenhall.com/barbour

Contents

Contents

Contents   xvii

FAMILIES, SCHOOLS, AND COMMUNITIES
Building Partnerships for Educating Children

Chapter 1

Home, School, and Community
Influences on Children's Lives

There was a child went forth every day, And the first object he looked upon and received with wonder or pity or love or dread, that object he became, And that object became part of him for the day or a certain part of the day . . . or for many years or stretching cycles of years.

(Whitman, 1855, p. 90)

🦋

This chapter highlights the many ways in which young children's learning, behaviors, viewpoints, and habits are affected by family members, school personnel, and members of the immediate and larger community. In reading this chapter you will learn the following:

1. How the three social settings—home, school, and community, including children's peer groups—affect children's perceptions and attitudes about learning and schooling.

2. How these three social settings have greater or lesser impact depending on the child's age and stage of development.

3. How various forms of media, including the entertainment industry, exert influence on children and how that influence affects children's learning and behavior.

4. What the impact of special interest groups is on children's learning and behavior.

🦋

Zach was waiting at the child care center for his mother to pick him up. He donned his Power Ranger™ helmet, a gift from his father during their last visit. Zach then picked up his Power Ranger™ toy from his cubbie where he had left it on arriving at the center and approached Kelsey, also waiting for her mother. "I'm warning you, if you don't tell me where you planted the bomb, I'm going to drill a hole in ya," he said in his deepest voice. He pushed his toy at Kelsey. "No, I won't tell. We'll all blow up," giggled Kelsey, entering into the play and holding up her fists to Zach. The children lunged at each other, growling and hissing until Zach accidentally struck Kelsey's head,

and Kelsey began to cry. At that moment, Zach's mother and the teacher entered the room. The teacher, calming Kelsey, said to Zach's mother, "We don't allow aggressive play here at the center. I really wish you wouldn't let Zach bring toys like that."

In spite of Zach's attempt to explain what had happened, his tired mother informed him he couldn't watch television while she got ready to go out. But while he waited for his father to pick him up, he could read. When they reached home, she let Zach select "Three Billy Goats Gruff" and "Max's Dragon Shirt." When Tom, Zach's mother's boyfriend, arrived, Zach asked him to read. As Tom got to the first little goat crossing the bridge, Zach exclaimed, "Oh, let me read the troll part," and pulling the book closer, asked, "Is this where the troll speaks?"

"How did you know?" Tom exclaimed.

Zach replied, "Dad told me," then, in a gruff, "pretend read" voice, demanded, "Who's that tramping on my bridge?" At each goat's passing, his voice got gruffer, and he clenched his fist as he told the goats he was going to eat them up. When the third goat passed, Tom, in character, gave Zach a gentle push, hugging and tickling him as the "goat" pushed the troll into the river. Zach giggled and said, "Let's read it again, and I'll be the goats this time." When Zach got to the third goat part, he butted Tom, who pulled Zach off the couch with him, "falling into the river." A bit of horseplay ensued. Zach then got up and said, "Let's read "Max's Dragon Shirt." You know, I'm gonna ask my dad to buy me a dragon shirt like that. Isn't it wild?"

🦋

All children are constantly developing, and their development is a result of both genetic and environmental factors. Early researchers debated the importance of each factor and attempted to determine which aspect exerted the greatest influence—often ignoring the role children played in their own development. The important role children play in their own development was underscored by interactionist/constructionist theories of development and even extended by cultural/context theories. Bronfenbrenner's bioecological theory maintains there are multiple contexts (physical, mental, social, and historical) affecting a child's growth and development. The interactions between the child, other people, objects, and symbols in these contexts unleashes the child's genetic potential to produce many and varied changes (Ceci & Hembrooke, 1995). Current brain research further supports this transactional process of development (Bruer, 1998). In the preceding vignette, you can see that Zach's development is being influenced by the ways he interacts with the experiences and episodes in his life.

Experiences of one kind or another bombard the perceptual field of any child, constantly influencing learning and development (Sameroff, 1993), for better or worse. Zach's feelings and attitudes toward aggressive behavior, as well as his reading habits, are influenced by his interactions at school, at home, and in his community and by what he witnesses through the media.

The messages children receive from their surroundings aren't always consistent, but all still influence attitudes and values. One can't be sure, for example, exactly what Zach is internalizing. It appears that his attitude toward reading is positive and that he is getting similar messages from those close to him. Reading appears to be fun; people answer his questions about the text and respond to his reactions to the story. Though his mother denied him television that day, she allowed him to select favorite books to entertain himself.

The messages Zach receives about aggression, though, may not be as consistent. Zach's father buys him toys that represent aggression, but the child care center bans them. In spite of the ban, his friend Kelsey seems to share in his "aggressive-acting behavior," at least until she is hurt. The mother attempts to reinforce the school's nonaggressive policy by forbidding television temporarily and by suggesting a more passive activity. Still, Zach finds acceptance for his need to express aggression by reenacting a story with his mother's friend and engaging in mild horseplay.

Children's learning is greatly affected by the attitudes, values, and actions emanating from homes, peers, schools, and communities. Of course, the impact varies according to children's stages of development and amount of contact with these social settings. Children's learning is also extensively influenced by their immediate neighborhood and perhaps even more so by their extended community as communicated to them through the media, including the entertainment industry. Special interest groups will influence policies of schools and community endeavors and thus will have an impact on children's learning. Graham (1993) points out that the school can actually be less effective in educating children than can the cumulative influences of other forces. This is especially true when school messages contradict the impressions children receive from the other social settings. Harris (1995) maintains that the peer group is the greatest influence—especially in the child's developing personality.

As a teacher, you cannot ensure that all the influences children receive are positive for their learning, but you must be sensitive to the idea that children's learning will be affected both positively and negatively by many factors beyond your control. You must also be attuned to your own feelings and reactions, as these, too, affect children's growth.

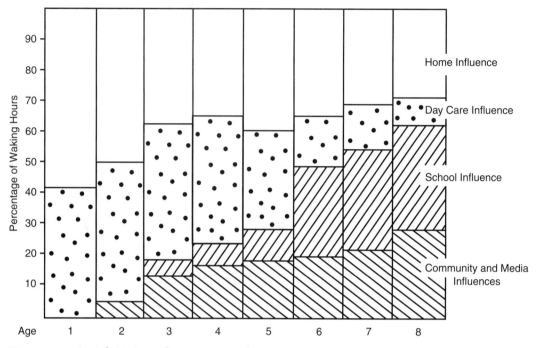

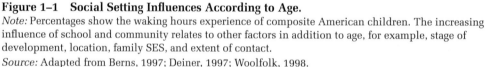

Figure 1–1   Social Setting Influences According to Age.
Note: Percentages show the waking hours experience of composite American children. The increasing influence of school and community relates to other factors in addition to age, for example, stage of development, location, family SES, and extent of contact.
Source: Adapted from Berns, 1997; Deiner, 1997; Woolfolk, 1998.

As you identify the strengths of family, media, and community influences, you should strive to build on these qualities. When outside influences or your own disposition adversely affects children's learning, attempt to counter some of the dissonance and the negative effects. Figure 1–1 shows the relative influence on children of their home, school, and community experiences.

CHILD ATTITUDES

Attitudes determine what individuals attend to in a situation, how they perceive the situation, and even their response to the event. Children acquire certain attitudes by hearing words, observing actions, and surmising the feelings of significant others in their environment. These attitudes then become more firm when children are reinforced for expressing such beliefs. Adult attitudes result from perceptions sustained over years.

Attitudes change, of course, but those demonstrated at any one time affect those children exposed to them. How parents or teachers view their roles will affect the socialization and learning of children under their supervision (Ecksel, 1992). For example, children are aware at early ages of their family's and community's attitudes regarding education, other cultures, racial or religious groups, and roles that males and females play in society (Coleman, 1996; Sadker & Sadker, 1995).

The impact of parental behaviors and attitudes is not linear with regard to children's development. In fact, children are actively involved in their own development. As they change over time, there is a dynamic and continuous process between children and their parents/environment (Deiner, 1997). During the child's infancy, parents begin by responding to the child's perceived need level. As babies respond and develop trust, they begin to sense control over self, and thus interaction patterns are established (Bornstein, 1995). Over time, both parent and child attitudes and behaviors change, and these influences and interactions affect the child's intellectual ability. Clearly, children's early experiences form a foundation for helping them cope with change (Sigel, Dreyer, & McGillicuddy-DeLisi, 1984).

Home Influence on Attitudes

Children's attitudes develop early from home influences. Families communicate to even very young children how they feel about themselves and their neighbors and about their schools and community.

🍃

Mrs. Kohl was astonished when her 3-year-old, Brittany, spat at elderly Mrs. Foster. Mrs. Kohl didn't remember that yesterday, when Mrs. Foster knocked at the apartment door, she had told her husband not to answer, saying, "I'm tired of the old hag coming around, nosing in our business, and always borrowing something. Sometimes I feel like spitting, she annoys me so." When Brittany's mother took her to her room as punishment, the child said defiantly, "I spit. She old hag."

🍃

At this point, it may be just Mrs. Foster that Brittany has antipathy for, but continued negative attitudes expressed by her parents

and others important to her towards elderly persons will affect the child's acceptance and attitude towards older persons' presence, interactions, and authority.

Parental attitudes and feelings will influence their children's feelings about school in similar ways. The annual Gallup/Phi Delta Kappan polls (Rose & Gallup, 1998) over the past quarter century show that on the whole, Americans value their local schools and have confidence in them. But we find vast differences throughout the country in the faith that individuals have in schooling. Parents communicate this faith, or lack thereof, to their children and thus influence how their children react to their teachers, to their learning experiences, and even to attending school.

🍃

A few years later, Mrs. Kohl and her neighbor Mrs. Reed received letters stating their daughters would be in Mrs. Owens's kindergarten. Reactions in the two households differed, and each affected the children's feelings about school. Mrs. Reed was delighted. Turning to her daughter, she said. "Oh, Samm, you're going to love school! Mrs. Owens was my teacher, and you'll just love all the fun things you'll do in class."

Mrs. Kohl, on the other hand, felt quite different. She expressed her thoughts to her husband in her daughter's presence, "Rats, Brittany has that old Mrs. Owens. I was hoping she'd get the new young teacher." It was no wonder the two children reacted differently when they met at the bus stop on the first day of school. Samm jumped up and down and grabbed Brittany's hand as she ran toward the stopped bus, saying, "Oh, we're going to have so much fun." But Brittany pushed her away and refused to get on the bus. No amount of cajoling from the adults could convince her that she should get on. Mrs. Kohl was forced to drive Brittany to school for several days before the child would take the bus with her friend.

🖋

Initially, both children appear to be responding to their parental attitudes as they viewed and responded to schooling. It is also difficult to determine what caused the change in Brittany. School may have been fun, and she may have started to enjoy her teacher. Or perhaps, her peers influenced her thinking on "how one ought to go to school."

Parental attitudes, interests, and involvement regarding such things as home organization, disposition toward work, or attitudes toward reading provide models for children's interests and involvement. Because young children learn by manipulating their environment, we can see that how parents and caregivers organize their surroundings affects children's intellectual development. Researchers have found strong positive correlations between higher IQ scores and child interaction in environments rich with appropriate materials and space (Sigel et al., 1984). Coleman (1991) points out that children whose parents stress the importance of good work habits, punctuality, and task completion carry these traits over into their schoolwork and have greater academic success.

Since Durkin's (1966) classic study of the commonality of influences for early readers, other studies, on the effect of home environment and parent perceptions of literacy development, indicate that parental attitudes and modeling regarding reading with young children are critical factors in children's development. Adults engage in literacy events in nearly all homes (Heath, 1983; Teale, 1986), but considerable differences exist in adults' attitudes towards the importance of books and in the ways in which adults interact around literacy events (Bus & Van Ijzendoorn, 1995; Debaryshe, 1993). Children respond more positively to books when they engage in a greater amount of literacy interaction with adults and when the adults believe in the importance of these interactions (Adams, 1990; Clay, 1991).

School Influence on Attitudes

Parental attitudes affect children's learning and acceptance of school. In turn, school personnel attitudes affect how children learn. Research by the Institute for Responsive Education regarding educators' attitudes toward low-income parents shows that many of these individuals didn't expect low-income parents to be productive participants in their children's education and, in turn, that those parents felt that their participation wouldn't have much effect and therefore often had negative attitudes toward the schools (Heleen, 1990). Children internalize these attitudes of mutual disrespect. Children's self-worth is diminished or enhanced as the children sense how school personnel view the lifestyle and culture of their families, and these attitudes can breed tolerance or intolerance for others.

In the following vignette, Camille and Helen reacted differently to a bus driver's careless words, but both were distressed.

🖋

Camille and Helen arrived at their homes distressed over a comment their bus driver had made. There were empty cans on the bus, and the driver said, "Don't touch them cans. I just drove a bunch of black kids on a trip, and they aren't clean." Camille exclaimed to her mother, "But, I ride the bus every day. Does he think I'm not clean 'cause I'm black?"

Helen's distress was similar, but from a different perspective. "We had to ride the bus after a bunch of black kids today, and they left it dirty. Ugh!" Both Camille and Helen could have misinterpreted the bus driver's words, but their attitudes about self and others were affected by the driver's careless speech.

🖋

How parents organize the home affects children's intellectual development.

Teachers can't prevent what happened to Camille or Helen. They can only be alert to problems and provide an emotional climate that accepts all children regardless of their ethnic or social class standing. They must be cognizant of how their own words and actions can bring to pass the self-fulfilling prophecies noted by Rosenthal and Jacobson (1968).

Rosenthal and Jacobson advance the notion that teachers' expectations of children result in self-fulfilling prophecies and that children who teachers perceive as capable and intelligent will do much better than those children teachers do not perceive to be capable. In this classic study, first and second graders appeared to be most subjected to their teachers' attitudes. Studies conducted in the 1970s, 1980s, and 1990s continue to suggest that children are affected by their teachers' perceptions of them.

Good and Brophy (1972) and Proctor (1984) found that teachers treated children differently according to their perceptions of children's abilities, garnered from sources such as children's background, personality, gender, and physical attractiveness. The children studied tended to react both behaviorally and academically according to their teachers' expectations.

In grade school, girls are likely to do better academically than boys (Tittle, 1986), but by the time students graduate from high school, boys score higher on SAT tests (Sadker & Sadker, 1995). Some researchers suggest that the reason for this is that teachers treat boys and girls differently. Researchers have noted that as early as preschool, girls are inclined to select activities with more rules, guidelines, and suggestions for accomplishing the task, while boys tend to select activities allowing for more open-ended behavior. Being rewarded for such behavior, girls tend to become more compliant, and boys become more assertive (Sprafkin, Serbin, Dernier, & Connor, 1983; Tittle, 1986). As children progress through school, these reinforced behaviors get boys more attention, more opportunities for classroom discussion, and more specific guidelines as to the correctness of their responses. Girls are called on less often than are boys, are asked to raise their hands, are given less feedback on their responses, and are encouraged to listen rather than to participate. Girls tend to be praised for their neatness, while boys receive praise for academic contributions. Consequently, girls get the message that their academic responses are not important (Sadker, Lerner, & Sadker,

1999). Because in elementary school, achievement is often measured on tasks that require skill mastery, girls, reinforced for obeying the rules, can be expected to do better than boys, but as children progress and school success depends more on problem solving and assertiveness, boys, having been reinforced for more aggressive behavior, can be expected to outperform girls (Tittle, 1986).

Teachers also may discriminate against children of different ethnic and ability groups by treating them differently—as a result of their expectations for different children's performance. Teachers are likely to give high achievers and majority-culture children more opportunities to respond, more praise, and more time to formulate a response. Teachers who perceive minority children to be low achievers do not expect them to know answers and do not give them as many opportunities or as much encouragement to respond (Minuchin & Shapiro, 1983). Such differential treatment over time lowers children's involvement in school and may prevent their developing confidence in their abilities (Hrabowski III, Maton, & Greif, 1998; Page & Rosenthal, 1990).

Community Influence on Attitudes

Community influence on children's attitudes varies because of the different perspectives held by the organizations within a community as well as the interactions of individual citizens. Bronfenbrenner (1986) points out that a community's influence on children's growth and development will be from both formal and informal community structures. Influence from formal structures comes from political and social systems, health and recreational services, business enterprises, entertainment, and educational services. The informal structures are the personal social networks that each family establishes with people outside the home. Members of some communities hold attitudes in common toward their local schools, as evidenced by communitywide political support for various activities, in linkages established with other community organizations, and in news coverage by local media.

It is difficult to measure the actual effect of community attitudes on student achievement, but we know that children quickly assimilate attitudes expressed by adults around them. Research suggests that a community's social climate and the personal relationships that children form within the community influence their attitudes about learning (Hoffer & Coleman, 1990). For example, if school sports activities receive thorough media coverage and the teams get money for trips but the school librarian can't buy good children's literature for the library, children soon get the message that being a good athlete is more important than being a good reader. When a community paper publishes the poems, stories, and artwork of local primary school children, children understand that the community values their academic achievements. Primary-age children are

less likely to make such direct connections to community attitudes toward their schools, but they get excited about winning a pizza for reading a certain number of books. Eventually, they get a message that reading is important.

Businesspeople often provide support for various school programs. Sometimes children witness that support and learn that important people value learning. When children hear the local grocer, businessperson, or politician comment on the positive qualities of teachers, they learn that others value the learning experiences these teachers provide.

As a teacher or community worker acting alone, you have minimal opportunity to change the attitudes, feelings, and biases of others that impinge on your classroom. You can, however, become alert to your own attitudes and how they affect the children with whom you work. You can listen to and work with parents who may feel that the school is "discriminating" against their child and assist in a reevaluation of the child's progress. And

As teachers listen to parents, they assist in assuring positive evaluations of children's progress and overcome negative attitudes.

while you cannot change all of the negative aspects of a child's environment, you can provide a supportive school or child care environment. When businesses or other community agencies offer support, you can write letters of thanks. You can also encourage your students (or take them on a field trip) to visit the bank, post office, or other establishment where children's work is on display. Observe and encourage your students and families to note how the grocery store has posted the thank you letters that schools have written to them. By providing curricula and activities that take into account the attitudes and feelings of children's families and community, you help create coherent learning experiences for your students.

AGE LEVELS AND INFLUENCE

Community, home, and school exert a greater or a lesser influence on children's learning, depending on the age of the children concerned. Theorists have described the stages of children's development from dependency to independence and have theorized how children do learn. (See Table 1–1 for a review of selected theories.) In practice, parents, teachers, and community people do not necessarily subscribe to one particular theory, but the decisions they make about children's learning will reflect a stronger belief in one viewpoint. As you develop strategies to promote partnerships for children's education, it is helpful to keep in mind that others may have a different perspective of development from your own.

The Early Years—Strong Home Influence

Early researchers such as Maslow (1970), Erikson (1963), and Piaget (1967) all emphasize the strong need for attachment and environmental support of infants and toddlers. Developing children require a physically and emotionally supportive environment in which their basic needs can be met. Infants must first develop trust in others so that they can venture out and explore their surroundings. According to Piaget, it is this exploration that enables them to construct knowledge about themselves and their world. He states that "the period that extends from birth to the acquisition of language is marked by an extraordinary development of the mind" (Piaget, 1967, p. 8).

Recent brain research substantiates the notion that a child's knowledge develops because of an interactive process, beginning even as the brain develops before birth. Neuroscientists have discovered links between brain structure and brain activity. Heredity may determine the framework of a developing child's brain, but researchers are discovering the many ways that genes, environment, and infant responses interact to develop the connections between the brain cells that account for learning (Education Commission of the States, 1996). Nash (1997) explains that "experts now agree that a baby does not come into the world as a genetically programmed automaton or a blank slate at the mercy of the environment" (p. 52). Such research confirms that the nature/nurture controversy is passe and that both are crucial to development. However, this process is complex, and though the early years are important, the brain is highly plastic and able to reorganize itself (even in adulthood) as a result of enriched environments (Bruer, 1998).

Because of this brain/environment development, a myriad of events will affect growth, some positively and some negatively. The type of housing, the presence of caregivers, and the lifestyles associated with different homes influence children's lives in profound and dramatic ways. Some environments are extremely supportive and nurturing, while others are dominating, negligent, and even dysfunctional. For example, consistent practices, organized schedules, and high-quality nourishment bring support and security to young children (Carnegie Corporation, 1994). Such

Table 1–1 Major Theories of Young Child Development

	Nativism	Behaviorist	Psychoanalytical (Psychosocial)	Interactionist
Basic Premise	Genetics or internal mechanisms as primary force in child's development.	Environment as primary force in child's development.	Sexual energy within humans as force for personality development.	Both internal mechanisms and environment are forces for child development.
Major Contributors	Arnold Gesell (1880–1961)	J. B. Watson (1878–1958) B. F. Skinner (1904–1991)	Sigmund Freud (1856–1939) Erik Erikson (1902–1994)	Jean Piaget (1896–1980)
Stages of Development	Developed sequences of characteristic behavior. Maturational readiness means that child must develop to an appropriate point before training or teaching has an effect.	No stages. Learning happens as a result of conditioning. Classical conditioning and unconditional stimuli result in reflex response, which later becomes a learned response. Operant conditioning. Child learns as a result of receiving positive reinforcers or a reward.	Three structures: Id—Instinctive Ego—Rational Superego—Moral Oral stage (birth–1 yr) need for gratification from mouth Anal stage (2–3 yr) need for gratification from the anal area Phallic stage (4–5 yr) need for gratification from the genitals Latency stage (middle years) repression of sexuality	Expanded on Freud's theories. Basic trust (birth–1 yr) development of sense of inner goodness Autonomy (2–3 yr) development of sense of self and pride of achievement Initiative (3–5 yr) takes charge of own activities Industry (6 yr to puberty) becomes producer and user of things	Children develop by assimilating external stimuli and accommodating new stimuli to already existing structures. Sensorimotor stage (birth–2 yr) use of senses Preoperational stage (2–7 yr) use of mental imagery Concrete operations stage (7–11 yr) logical thinking occurs
Meaning for Parents and Educators	Adult supports development, observes outward behaviors that would indicate readiness for learning.	Adult determines desired behavior and sets up strategies for reinforcing children when behaviors occur.	Adults provide the needed support so that children's instincts are satisfied, but not so much that children do not move appropriately from one stage to the next.	Adults provide a rich and stimulating environment assisting children to interact with that environment as they construct their own knowledge.

secure and nurturing environments allow care-givers to respond to their children by touching, cuddling, talking to, and reading with them. Secure adults are better able to play with their children and provide stimulating experiences. Such emotional support and interactions with the child provide the building blocks for intellectual competence and language comprehension.

On the other hand, the trials of homeless-ness, highly mobile families, and absentee parents often mean that parents are unable to provide positive and secure environments because they lack the skills or support in their own life experience. This lack of responsive environment will affect a child's intellectual, social, and emotional competence. However, the brain is quite resilient, and later stimulation or strong emotional bonds can help the child overcome some of the negative results of early deprivation (Bruer, 1998; Newberger, 1997).

Regardless of family configuration, American society does expect all families to perform certain functions: economic support, psychological support and socialization, family status and role expectations, plus emotional support and intimacy. Nurturing families are those that sustain their infants and toddlers in these major areas. In contrast, negligent or dysfunctional families rarely provide the help in these areas that is crucial for children's positive development.

Economic Support. The dependent infant relies on its mother and significant others for food, clothing, and shelter, all of which require a basic economic foundation. Inadequate nutrition, prenatally and in the early years, naturally affects children physically, emotionally, and cognitively. In many cases, an ill-nourished child becomes unresponsive to adults. When this happens, the mother may alter her attitude toward the child, and vital interactions for healthy emotional and intel-lectual growth become impaired (Owens, 1993). Many families are unable to provide adequate housing, or they may live in unsafe neighborhoods. The results of poverty often cause a family great stress, and children then become the victims of poor health, maltreatment, and inadequate parenting skills, all of which place children at risk of not developing normally. Erikson (1963) summarizes the primary features of economic support, stating that when basic needs are met, children develop a sense of trust that enables them to venture forth and explore their environment. When basic needs are not met, exploration is hampered, and the child's development is jeopardized.

Psychological and Socialization Support. Infants and toddlers begin their socialization process in a family structure when they begin to communicate their needs and respond to their primary caregiver. As their actions are reinforced or rejected, infants and toddlers come to understand what is appropriate social behavior in dealing with others. Infants coo, cry, and gurgle, and nearby adults respond to these sounds as if the baby is trying to communicate (Meadows, 1996). As adults respond and babies' needs are satisfied, babies begin to differentiate the sounds they make based both on intent and on expected response. As they do so, their caregivers adjust their own responses to the sounds they hear, conforming them to what they both understand and desire them to mean.

🖎

Sarah was confident in dealing with her new baby. She maintained she could tell exactly what he needed when he cried because he cried differently when he was hungry, was wet, or was bored and wanted company. Not only did she inform anyone present of her knowledge, but she also told her infant as she provided whatever "he was asking for." Whether

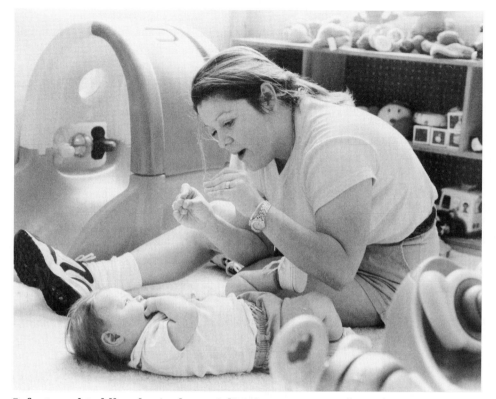

Infants and toddlers begin the socialization process as they communicate their needs and respond to their primary caregiver.

the infant really understood may be debatable, but Sarah and the baby were establishing attachment and communication links.

🦋

This early infant-mother attachment is an important factor in how children develop the socialization and intellectual skills that enable them to function effectively later on with peers and in school.

Family Status and Role Expectations.   Because infants and toddlers are extremely dependent on all aspects of their environment, their status and role within the family and community are not clearly defined. They gradually begin to understand that an important

relationship exists between themselves and other members of the family. This developing understanding will later enable them to function in the larger society. In the following vignette, Susan has incomplete information about roles in her family but has formed some notions.

🦋

Susan, 18 months old, was accustomed to her mother's feeding her juice each morning. Sometimes, when her mother wasn't available, she would accept help from her older sister, calling her "li-ul mamma." The first time Susan was left with her aunt's family, she expected similar treatment, referring to her aunt as "aunt-mamma." But when her uncle tried to feed her juice, she balked at the idea, asking for "aunt-mamma." When that strategy didn't work, Susan looked about in vain, searching for her "li-ul mamma."

Susan, even by 18 months, has some defined role expectations for members of her family and transfers this information in a new situation. She clearly becomes upset when her role expectations are challenged in her new environment. As she interacts in new situations, she will begin to recognize the various roles she and others play in other family units. Parents and significant others are laying the foundation for Susan's understanding of how to behave in socially accepted ways in more than one setting.

Emotional Support and Sense of Intimacy.
Infants and toddlers require emotional support and a sense of intimacy. When significant adults in a baby's environment express joy and delight in the baby as a social being, the baby develops a sense of well-being and responds. As the baby grows older, this basic emotional security leads to a desire to share its feelings and emotions with loved ones. Ecksel (1992), summarizing several studies, states that infants who formed secure attachments to their mothers were more socially competent later in school than were children whose mothers were unable to give their infants a warm, supportive surrounding.

Some families lack the emotional or social ability to provide adequate emotional nurturance. We find some households with problems so great that adults lack the inner resources to manage an infant's many needs. Other families with deficits, however, have support systems to rely on or may know how to use community support systems, such as day care and health and human services, to supplement their own meager resources. Schools and day care providers should always assist needy parents by informing them of available services and reinforcing parents' attempts at meeting their children's basic needs.

Influence of Out-of-Home Care.
Since the 1940s, changes in American lifestyles have been altering the early influences of the home. Today, with 60% of women with preschool children in the labor force (as opposed to 25% in 1940)(Bianchi & Spain, 1996), we find a steady increase in the need for some type of out-of-home care for many children. Many are cared for by relatives or by nonrelatives in a home environment, but increasing numbers are in a family day care or child care center. This change is a concern of today's society, since it means that the development of infants and toddlers is being affected by other social settings at a much earlier age (Carnegie Corporation, 1994).

Since the early Spitz (1946) studies examining whether infants were better cared for by their mothers or in an orphanage, the American public has been concerned that children may not develop emotionally, socially, or intellectually if they have multiple caregivers. However, new research indicates that infants in "quality day care centers" are able to form strong maternal attachments as well as secondary attachments to consistent caregivers (Clarke-Stewart, Allhusen, & Clements, 1995; Honig, 1993). Most studies indicate that though there may be some differences in social development, children who regularly attend day care centers show individual differences in development just as do children raised at home. Other issues such as economic factors, parenting styles, time away from mother, and quality of care do, of course, influence children's development, whether it be in a home or in a child care setting (Berns, 1997). We consider out-of-home care more fully in Chapter 5.

Preschool/Kindergarten Years—Increasing School Influence.
Children developing a sense of autonomy need to learn the boundaries

they can operate within and must learn to identify new ones they will encounter as they separate from home. As parents give their children necessary support, they must also give them freedom to try things on their own. For preschoolers and kindergartners, the significant others in their home setting continue to influence their development as they move from basic trust to autonomy and independence. One's sense of self first develops in the home and then extends into the neighborhood, day care center, and larger family. At school, the teacher and the children's peers begin to alter or reinforce this sense. Children modify their behavior in school in response to different rules and regulations and to perceived teacher and peer expectations.

Many children have school-like experiences in their preschool years. For other children, school as a culture first comes into focus when they enter formal public or private schooling. In the preschool years, children may encounter several different types of school-like experiences. Head Start programs, child care centers, nursery schools, and play schools all demonstrate somewhat different philosophical orientations. Some programs provide rich experiences for children; others provide only custodial care. It is difficult to conduct rigorous studies to determine the influence different programs have on developing children, and such research is always confounded by socioeconomic factors, community support systems, types of curricula, and parental interaction styles. However, we have evidence that quality preschool programs do have lasting positive effects on children's academic growth and on subsequent life skill development (Levin, 1991; Schweinhart & Weikart, 1993).

Primary Years—Growing Community Influence

The impact of the community appears early in children's lives and progresses steadily as children mature; however the effect the community has depends on how families use community resources. The nature of that effect is not simple but derives from the many subsystems within the community (Bronfenbrenner, Moen, & Garbarino, 1984). For example, the family may live in a neighborhood that provides moral and physical support or in a neighborhood where parents are afraid to go out or take their children out.

All families need quality social and health services, and such agencies' ability to help families in need affects children's well-being. Positive interactions between community and family give a sense of security and well-being to all, so that families are better able to provide the nurturing children need. Children raised in communities where there is a great deal of violence can be affected adversely as a result of stress the violence causes. Inattentiveness to schoolwork and hyperactivity are but two of the effects that stress has on academic achievement (Groves, Zuckerman, & Marans, 1993).

As children expand their horizons, the living conditions of the neighborhood and community give them experiences on which to build their linguistic, kinesthetic, artistic, spatial, and interpersonal skills. Children who can visit zoos, museums, libraries, business establishments, parks, and other natural settings are better equipped (than children who can't) to deal with the many mathematical, scientific, social, and language concepts discussed in schools.

Primary-age children are becoming independent and are moving from the preoperational to the concrete operational stage of intellectual development. Traditions, cultural values, community mores, opportunities for recreation, and other social and cultural activities play a part in children's development. Experiences interacting with adults in clubs, sports, and art and music activities open up to children differences in communication styles and offer them a range of experiences. Coleman (1991) calls this type of involvement with

Experiences interacting with adults in clubs, sports, or art and music activities open up to children different communication styles.

adults a child's **social capital** and stresses that this capital is as important as financial capital in determining school performance. Heath and MacLaughlin (1989) point out how these experiences interacting with different adults give participating children greater opportunities to practice their negotiating, problem-solving, and intellectual skills. Steven in the following vignette begins to learn some of these important lessons.

🖎

Steven, in second grade, had joined a riding club but was unhappy because the instructor was "always criticizing" what he did. "I don't even know what I do wrong," he told his mother.

"And what do you do when he tells you something?" she asked.

"I get so mad, I just glare and ride away."

"Are you sure he never compliments you?"

"Hardly ever," pouted Steven.

"Well, why not try an experiment?" his mother suggested. "The next time he even suggests something is good, smile at him and say, 'Oh, that really helps me know what I should do,' and just ignore the criticisms." Steven reluctantly agreed to give it a try.

Two weeks later, a jubilant Steven returned from riding club saying, "Hey Mom, he really does tell me lots about what I'm doing right!" Whether Steven or the riding instructor changed behavior patterns isn't clear, but certainly Steven was learning new ways of working with adults so that he could profit from their instruction.

🖎

Regrettably, not all communities provide healthy conditions for children. Community tolerance for gangs, illicit activities, or promiscuous sexual encounters will have unhealthy and negative influences on the growth and experiences of children. Violence in the streets limits everyone's sense of security. Any opportunity for positive interactions or for the use of community resources to expand children's skills is lessened in disruptive communities.

Peer Group Influence

In ways similar to the community, the peer group becomes an agency of enculturation and development. Even very young children develop a sense of self from their perceptions of important people in their surroundings, including relatives, teachers, and peers. Socioeconomic status, ethnic identity, and the type of work parents undertake affect how families view themselves and the process by which they socialize their children (Bornstein, 1995). Later, as children leave the home setting, their self-perception and socializing skills become influenced by how their peers view them.

Peer groups begin to form early or late, depending on a child's experiences and availability of playmates and on his or her personality and sociability (Parke, 1990). When children move out from the family into child care centers, school, and the community at large, they begin to form attachments, and real friendships emerge later through their play. These relationships influence behavior. Even young infants and toddlers are observed reacting to other infants by touching them, by crying when others cry, and later by offering nurturance or comfort. It is not until around the age of 3 that early friendships begin to form and children's peers begin to have a more lasting influence (Parke, 1990).

Peer influence on behavior gradually becomes more dominant. Children discover that others can share their feelings or attitudes or may have quite different ones. The perspectives of others affect how children feel about their own families. Children usually have a "family" view of their own and of other cultures. When confronted with other perspectives, they often need to rethink their own viewpoints. It is often difficult for children to adjust to the idea that other families can function radically differently from their own and yet hold many of the same attitudes and beliefs and be equally nurturing and secure. The peer group serves as a barometer for children examining themselves and their feelings about self and family.

The peer group also influences development of children's socializing skills. It is from these early friendships that children learn how to negotiate and relate to others in addition to their siblings and other family members. They learn from peers how to cooperate and socialize according to **group norms,** group-sanctioned modes of behavior and thought. The peer group can influence what the child values, knows, wears, eats, and learns. The extent of this influence, however, depends on other situational constraints, such as the age and personality of children and the nature of the group (Hartup, 1983).

In its most acceptable form, the peer group is a healthy coming-of-age arbiter where children grasp negotiating skills, learn to deal with hostility, and learn to solve problems in a social context. In its most destructive mode, the peer group can demand blind obedience to a group norm, which can result in socially alienated gangs with pathological outlooks (Perry, 1987). Harris (1998) maintains that peer groups have an even stronger socialization influence than parents.

MEDIA INFLUENCE

Today, all members of our society are influenced both directly and indirectly by powerful media vehicles, including print, television, sound recordings, cinema, computer CD-ROMs, and the Internet. People have at some point used all of these media to advocate what people should wear, what they should eat, and what values they should hold. Vivid colors and language tell us both what is happening in the world and how to react to the events shown. While our society's media vehicles seem to be dominated by social chitchat, aggression, and violence, they are also sources of education, humor, and nonviolent entertainment. Just remember that the effect of media will vary with a child's age and stage of development.

The different forms of media may be used for information, education, and entertainment. We here discuss what we broadly term the *entertainment industry* in its role as a general society-wide influence on young children. We first discuss two of its primary forms, print and television, and then treat other current media under the rubric of the industry in general.

Print media—such as books, magazines, and newspapers—present content using words and static images. Though both pictures and language convey a message, printed materials do require greater reliance on a reader's language development and life experiences to be understood. As children decode words from the printed page, thoughts generated by these words serve to create images, thus requiring children to rely on their imaginations and interpretations (Singer & Singer, 1992). Generally, this is helpful to a child's developing mind.

Of all media forms, television and the Internet appear to have the greatest impact in terms of memory recall. Input is presented using both sound and moving pictures, and the active images assist children in remembering familiar content (Singer & Singer, 1990). Programs that children have easy access to are not always appropriate for young children and often do little to stimulate children's thinking and imagination. Families can control what children see by selecting programs, but most homes exert less control over television and access to the Internet than over printed media (Van Evra, 1998).

When Meringoff (1980) compared children's reactions to stories presented through television, books, and radio, children seemed to view television events as something not directly associated with themselves, but they appeared to personalize the events in books. Berns (1997) surmises that because the reader is more intimately involved in the book, it is a stronger socializing agent. However, the stronger personal influence of printed materials over television or the Internet also could reflect the manner in which the two are presented to children (Neuman, 1995). Young children first know about books because someone reads to them and interacts with them about the story, whereas more often than not children are left to watch television or to use computer games by themselves. Perhaps children are socialized on how to react to books, thus getting more personal meaning from them as they become readers themselves. Some researchers suggest that when parents or other adults interact with children viewing television or using the computer, those children develop better interactive and processing skills (Neuman, 1995).

The entertainment industry, a powerful influence on life in the United States, engulfs society through print, television, radio, sound recordings, computer networks and games, and live performances (Figure 1–2). These media influence the actions, dress codes, and values of many adults and capture and hold children's interests for a large part of each day. As a teacher or community worker, you must understand that the entertainment industry's influence on children both enhances and inhibits children's growth as human beings. You should not underestimate the effect of this influence, but rather should work to incorporate it into your teaching, helping children to assimilate it in a healthy context with the rest of their education.

Print Materials

Print materials reach the child indirectly, through parents and other caregivers, and

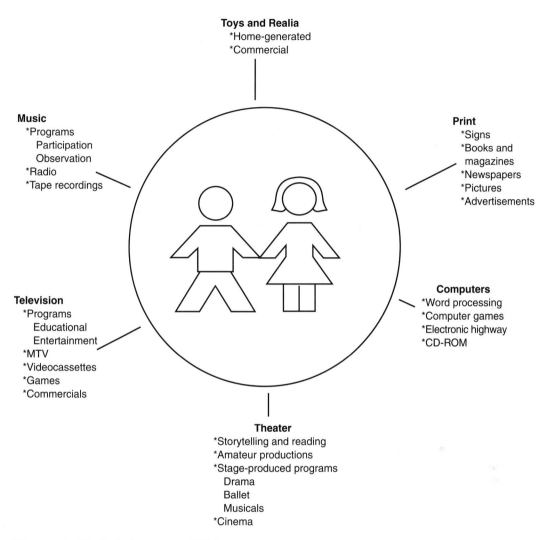

Figure 1–2   Media Influence on Children.

directly, such as when children participate in a presentation or select particular publications. Newspapers, magazines, books, and other print media normally portray different ideas, actions and activities, and subsequent consequences or reactions. What print is available implies the values and philosophy of the community and can influence all areas of education.

Physical Development. Print media affect children's physical, emotional, and intellectual development indirectly through the parents or other significant adults. Books and magazines inform adults how to lead healthy and productive lives and proclaim the dangers of unhealthy practices. Mothers whose reading persuades them to quit smoking, acquire healthy eating habits, and avoid alcohol and other drugs during pregnancy produce for the most part healthier babies. In contrast, parents who believe that teaching young children to play sports gives them a head start on athletic participation may exert pressure too early. This expectation pushes their children to learn tasks for which they may be physically unprepared.

Social Development.   Advertising from both print media and television affects the type of clothes, food, and, especially, toys bought for children. Some toys engage children's imagination and are designed for groups of children playing together. Other toys are more suitable for children playing alone. Children's potential for social development is affected by which type of toy adults are influenced to buy. Both Piagetian theory of development and brain research studies report that children construct knowledge about their world by interacting with materials, adults, and peers in their surroundings (Bruer, 1998; Piaget, 1952). A flexible environment that has opportunities for imaginative play and group interaction enhances children's potential for social development. Environments with fewer opportunities inhibit such development.

Intellectual Development.   The toys and games children acquire affect their intellectual as well as their social development. Some toys have multiple uses and engage children's imagination; other toys have only one use, resulting in less creative play. Thus, adults' choice of toys and games may enhance or inhibit children's intellectual development.

Print media also affect children's literacy development. Studies on early literacy indicate that the amount and types of printed materials that adults have in the home, as well as how adults interact with these materials around children, affect the children's interest and literacy achievement (Adams, 1990). From the books that adults read to children, chil-

dren internalize attitudes, feelings, biases, and perspectives about their own and other cultures. Zach in the chapter's opening vignette had a chance to express aggression in acceptable ways through "Three Billy Goats Gruff." He was influenced in the kind of clothes he wanted by the story "Max's Dragon Shirt."

The kind of books that children read and have read to them influences and supports their emotional, social, and intellectual development both directly and indirectly. Sutherland and Arbuthnot (1991) point out that "to function successfully in society, children must learn to know themselves, to achieve self identity, . . . [to] learn about social interaction and recognize ways in which they are alike as well as different from others" (p. 20). Books, like peers, provide children with a vision of their world that sometimes reaffirms their own lives and sometimes challenges their perspectives.

Television

Television's substantial impact on all growing children began in the 1950s. Today, 99% of American households contain at least one television set. Children start the viewing process early, as young as 2 years of age. In many homes, though the TV is on much of the day, the amount of actual viewing time may be less than supposed, as the youngest often watch only intermittently. However, conservative estimates are that preschool children watch about 2 to 3 hours of TV a day (Gunter & McAleer, 1997). In the 1980s, Postman (1983) found that children spent more time viewing television than they did going to school. In the 90s, television viewing was somewhat diminished because of increased use of computer games and the Internet and also because children are in child care, school, and after-school care programs longer. But TV still occupies more of a child's time than do schoolwork, reading, and playing (Van Evra, 1998).

Television can exert more influence on children than can the school.

Television influences children in direct proportion to both time spent viewing and the overall effect of what is viewed (American Academy of Pediatrics, 1990). Certainly, eating habits, family interactions, and use of leisure time are considerably influenced by television (Arendell, 1997; Leibert & Sprafkin, 1988). Commercials take up 12 to 14 minutes of every hour of television, and in that time, advertisers try to influence viewers about all types of consumerism. Notar (1989) points out how advertisers use the power of imagery to hook both children and adults to their products. "Advertisers view training of children's imagery as all important. Once children are trained to view life in terms of commodities, they have many more years of productive consumption" (p. 67).

Children are especially vulnerable, and television advertising has an effect. Heavy viewers want the advertised products, including unhealthy food products, and they tend to eat more snack foods and be overweight. Social interactions are also affected. Heavy viewers hold more traditional sex-role attitudes, behave more aggressively, are less socially competent, and perform less well in school (Arendell, 1997).

Not all TV advertising is negative. There have been efforts through TV to modify behaviors such as smoking, drunken driving, and poor nutritional habits (Van Evra, 1998). How children are affected by both positive and negative advertisements also depends upon such factors as parent/child interactions, how children are disciplined, and even to some degree on social-economic factors (Gunter & McAleer, 1997).

Advertising, of course, is not the only way television influences viewers. Two major concerns about effects of television are the amount of violence, in both commercials and programs, and the amount of time children's television watching takes away from more creative and intellectual pursuits.

Concern over the effect of television violence resulted in the passage of the Children's Television Act of 1990. In 1995, the Federal Communications Commission (FCC) put some teeth into the act by requiring broadcasters to air 3 hours of educational programming for children each week. Producers and advertisers have begun to recognize the potential impact of television on children and the necessity of sharing the responsibility of lessening the negative impact of advertising and violence (Murray, 1997).

Gunter and McAleer (1997) have summarized 20 years of research on the effect of television violence on children's behavior. They have reported that it is difficult to make direct linkages between television watching and aggressive behavior in children because of the difficulty of isolating television's influence from other violent events in children's lives. However, there does seem to be fairly strong accumulated evidence that television violence affects behavior. Heavy viewing, without adult mediating effects, results in greater child aggression, acceptance of violence as a viable reaction to life's situations, and increased fearfulness that the world is a dangerous place (Murray, 1997).

Of course, not all television programming is violent, and we have some evidence of TV's positive effects. Some researchers indicate that programs depicting positive and altruistic actions also influence children. As a result, children prize such behavior and act in more positive ways toward their peers (Arendell, 1997; Comstock & Paik, 1991).

Research on the impact of television viewing on academic achievement indicates that such influence is complex in nature. Television viewing takes time away from important social interactions, such as conversations, storytelling, imaginative play, and, for primary-age children, leisure reading that promotes literacy. Children who are heavy viewers of television have less practice conversing and reading, but the amount of viewing, the kind of programs watched, IQ, and socioeconomic status are all factors that affect children's achievement (Wright & Huston, 1995).

The Entertainment Industry

Most school-age children in the United States are exposed on a daily basis to entertainment and education delivered through other media besides print and television. Films (in theaters and on videotape), radio, sound recordings on compact disc and audiocassette, computers (most are now equipped with CD-ROM), and access to the Internet are the main sources.

The entire entertainment industry has great influence on American society. Whereas relatively few movie stars, musicians, and sports figures provided role models for generations earlier in the 20th century, the visual and auditory stimuli of the new media bombard most homes and communities today. Some of this exposure is educational, positive, and directed at an appropriate level for young children. But much current fare is violent in nature and is presented in ways unsuitable for children's level of maturity (Van Evra, 1998). With the rapidly expanding information high-

way, young people are exposed more than ever to both good and bad influences.

Producers and advertisers expand successful films and television shows by urging the purchase of associated toys, clothing, soundtrack CDs, and videocassettes. Similar marketing comes from developers of video and computer games. These new forms influence individuals' values, compete for children's attention, and may reduce the amount of reflection and interaction time children have with both adults and peers. While some maintain that such games are opportunities for children to let off steam, others insist there are better ways of achieving this goal.

In 1999, 48% of American households owned a personal computer. A steadily growing number of these (estimates range up to one half) are connected to the vast resources of the Internet, and this means that many American children are now experiencing the wonders, the information, and the dangers of electronic communication around the world.

The Internet is now the world's largest source of information and completely dwarfs even the world's renowned libraries. This is an extraordinary amount of information and resources for today's young people; it also carries great potential for misuse. For example, primary-age children regularly surf the Net and tell about their findings. Pornography is widely available to any child willing to misrepresent his or her age. Even more alarming are the steadily expanding hate-group websites—some designed for children. Filtering systems for Internet use are a must for schools and homes to make Internet use more safe. WebBlocker is installed in many schools (but not all libraries), and Cyber Patrol and Net Nanny are examples of useful filters for home computers. This is a resource that must be harnessed successfully by families, school, and communities if its potential is to be productive.

On the positive side, these media provide children opportunities to practice skills, solve problems, create pictures or figures, and expand their knowledge base (Papert, 1993). For example, some primary-age children use the Internet for practice on chess matches, for e-mail, and for information from Net bulletin boards. Our best strategy when considering the impact of these media on children's learning is to observe how children use them.

When parents and other adults watch videotapes or television or use the computer with children, the children benefit more from the programs and the adults learn more about the children. Adults discover what children know and what interests or bores them and may act to enhance their learning. Adults may introduce children to the original stories from which the programs were adapted, helping them to learn to make comparisons and develop better discrimination skills about stories and presentations. For children to be engaged in positive learning, it seems urgent that schools, parents, teachers, and other concerned individuals develop partnerships for interpreting and dealing with the products of both currently available media sources and those soon to appear in their communities. It is only when this begins to happen that the negative influences of the media industry can be reversed (Murray, 1997).

SPECIAL INTEREST GROUP INFLUENCE

In recent years, the United States has witnessed a steady increase in the number and potency of special interest groups, such as the National Association of Christian Educators, Literature Review Council, Action for Children's Television, and the various pro-choice and pro-life groups, organized to affect everything from legislative matters to informal controls on curriculum topics. These groups can have both direct and indirect and positive and negative influence on children's learning, depending on family, school, and community reactions to their efforts and objectives.

A special interest group usually has a single objective (though some are quite broadly conceived), and many have had considerable success. Some groups have been formed by parents concerned about a particular educational issue affecting children. For instance, in 1968, Peggy Charren, concerned with the amount of violence in children's programs, organized a group of parents to form Action for Children's Television (ACT). This group lobbied for improved television programming and advertising during children's viewing time and worked to educate the public regarding television's positive and negative influences. This action resulted in the Children's Television Act of 1990. Continuing pressure resulted in the FCC's mandating that broadcasters devote at least 3 hours a week to educational fare. As a result, much more attention has been given to better programming (Murray, 1997).

Grassroots efforts by special interest groups resulted in the special education legislation of the 1960s for improving education for all children. As children with special needs were first mainstreamed into regular classrooms, curricula, classroom environments, and learning for all children expanded. Continued pressure by these special interest groups has helped to examine the effects of the laws and to pass additional legislation to better serve special needs children.

The influence of special interest groups is not always viewed as positive. Schott (1989) warns of the danger of such groups as the National Association of Christian Educators who wish to "gain control" of schools to eliminate the influence of "secular humanism." He notes that such groups seek to effect legislation that would permit censoring of books and dictating of particular elements in curricula. In many communities, both schools and libraries have been forced to remove certain books, deemed quality literature by literary critics, because of the views of special interest groups. One teacher was dismissed for teaching such poems as Langston Hughes's "Dreams," material that a special interest group found racially inflamatory (Kozol, 1991).

At the local level, some religious groups have succeeded in banning Halloween activities and even traditional fairy tales that include supernatural events and characters. Other groups have successfully changed units of study in schools about Christmas, Hanukkah, and Easter holidays. Special interest groups have positive influence when they act to initiate dialogue among parents and teachers as to the appropriateness of materials in schools. Their influence is negative when they seek to restrict children's access to humanity's best artistic, philosophical, and intellectual efforts and attempt to deny children's learning about different ethnic and cultural groups and other historical periods.

IMPLICATIONS FOR PROFESSIONALS

Why is it important for you as beginning teachers, caregivers, and family workers to understand these influences that affect children's development? First, if you do understand these influences, you will be able to recognize

Teachers help children develop positive attitudes and interactions as a foundation for learning.

situations where children appear to be strongly influenced. Then you can reinforce or give support for those events that exert positive influences on children. It is equally important to recognize and then offset the negative influences. As suggested throughout this chapter and in remaining chapters, several particular strategies exist that teachers and community workers have used effectively to improve children's experiences.

As you plan for work with children, you will use various media, engage children in group processes, and take children into the community to learn important concepts. Often children will express very different responses to a learning situation that you provide. For example, Zach's teacher attempted to counter some of the influence of the home and peers by "not allowing" aggressive play in the school. This strategy may work well for this teacher. But there are other solutions, such as having a discussion with both children and parents, noting where Power Rangers equipment may be acceptable. Such a discussion might also have been productive in this situation. Good workers try to be attuned to children's and parents' responses. If you follow such a course, you will become more sensitive and adept at responding to children's development when you see manifestations of their needs.

As children enter the primary school years, peers will exert greater influences on each other. When this influence is problematic and harmful, professionals will want to modify it. But counteracting negative peer influence is very difficult. Still, becoming aware of these influences gives you a background while you continue to show an accepting attitude towards everyone and model positive interactions with all persons.

Your job is to provide the foundation for children's developing reading, writing, math, social, and science skills. Understanding the impact of both negative and positive influences on a child's learning makes your objectives and goals easier as you plan for each student's learning.

SUMMARY AND REVIEW

Children become well or poorly educated, depending on many factors that both directly and indirectly influence what they learn and how they learn it. The attitudes, values, and interests that homes, schools, and communities have regarding children's learning can be in concert or in conflict. Young children are usually more strongly influenced by immediate or extended family attitudes, and primary-age children begin to be influenced by peer groups, media, and community mores and traditions. Teachers in many instances have no control over these factors and must study about and be alert to their influence in order to provide appropriate education for children in their classrooms.

According to Coleman (1990), children need many types of support systems to grow into functioning adults. They need what he calls human, financial, and social capital, which provide the nurturing and physical environment in which children learn to cope with their world. Children with little financial capital may still succeed if sufficient social and human resources are available to them. We find that families can compensate somewhat for lack of effective community and school influences on their children, and community and school personnel can exert influence and extend resources to compensate for missing family social resources. However, schools are far more effective in educating children when families, schools, and communities unite their efforts. When these three social settings recognize the influences on children's experience and work together in resolving conflicting issues undermining child development, the best possible circumstances result.

SUGGESTED ACTIVITIES AND QUESTIONS

1. List what you consider the major influences that guided your education. Are they different from those we have noted in this chapter? What influences did your classmates list? Discuss.

2. Watch a televised news program, a situation comedy, a soap opera, and a cartoon and chart the incidence of violence in each program. Identify what you believe could be the effect of such televised violence on primary-age children. Discuss your conclusions with your classmates.

3. Interview a teacher in a local primary school and determine whether any special interest *groups* influence the decisions this person makes with regard to curricula. Do some groups exert positive pressure? If so, how does the person view its benefiting children's learning? Do some exert negative pressures? If so, how does the person view these pressures as limitations for children's learning?

4. Discuss with a primary-age child a list of favorite books, movies, television shows, and entertainers. Find out what the child likes or finds important about these choices. Ask whether the child wants to be like any of the people or characters, and why. Attempt to determine how the media the child is exposed to has influenced these choices.

RESOURCES

Books

1. Beatty, J. J. (1998). *Observing development of the young child* (4th ed.). Upper Saddle River, NJ: Merrill/Prentice Hall.

2. Levin, D. E. (1998). *Remote control childhood? Combating the hazards of media culture.* Washington, DC: National Association for the Education of Young Children.

Films/Videos

1. Cooing, Crying, Cuddling: Infant Brain Development and Laughing, Learning and Loving: Toddler Brain Development. 1998. [2 Videos, 28 min each]. Indiana Public Broadcasting Stations with National Association for the Education of Young Children.

2. Space to Grow: Creating a Child Care Environment for Infants and Toddlers. 1998. [Video, 27 min]. California Department of Education.

Organizations

National Center on Educational Media and Materials for Handicapped Children
Ohio State University
Columbus, OH 43210

Action for Children's Television
(http://hugse1.harvard.edu/~library/act.htm)
46 Austin Street, Newtonville, MA 02160

American Library Association Booklist
(http://als.lib.wi.us/ArrowheadBooklists.html)
50 E. Huron Street, Chicago, IL 60611

Websites

1. http://www.carnegie.org The website entry to the programs and reports supported by the Carnegie Organization.

2. http://www-hpb.scripps.edu/Home.htm　An entry to research on the human brain project.

3. http://www.newhorizons.org/blab.html　New Horizons provides articles and resources on brain research.

4. http://www.superkids.com/ Reviews educational software for young children.

5. http://www.teacherzone.com/ A good one-stop resource for beginners on information about hardware, software, and the World Wide Web.

Chapter 2

Historical Perspectives

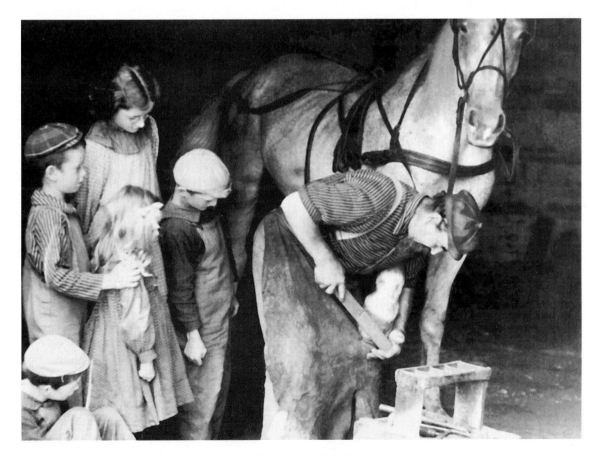

History is the witness of the times, the light of truth, the life of memory, the mistress of life.

(Cicero, de Oratore)

〽

The intent of this chapter is to examine the evolution of roles played by the home, the school, and the community in children's education. In reading this chapter you will learn the following:

1. Historically, the family and the community have always played significant roles in children's education, but at different periods, each setting has had a more dominant role, with the school's assuming leadership at the beginning of the 20th century.

2. Although *partnerships for educating children* is a relatively new term, parents, teachers, and community members have always worked together to some degree for children's benefit.

3. In recent decades, the federal government, in fostering better educational opportunities, has encouraged new procedures for parent involvement in children's education.

4. Since the 1960s, programs for poor children, children with special needs, and children of differing ethnic orientation have focused on the importance of parents as an educating force. However, changes in family lifestyles and recent welfare reform measures have affected the importance of out-of-home care.

5. Although Anglo-European culture has dominated the shaping of American schools, starting with the 1960s, other cultures have contributed to a multicultural emphasis for most present-day curricula.

6. In the 1980s and 1990s, a multicultural perspective in a school meant changes in attitudes, staffing arrangements, content, and interaction patterns.

Partnerships among homes, schools, and communities for children's education is a term of the 1980s and 1990s, yet throughout the history of the United States, we find connections among the functions of these three social settings. At different times, each, as an institution, has occupied a dominant role in children's education while acknowledging the others as important forces helping children to succeed in society.

In colonial times, the family was the major force for educating children, although the community exerted pressure on families not conforming to local codes of conduct. Later, as towns and villages developed, community leaders recognized that some families were not willing or able to educate their children successfully. Taking command in the later colonial period, community leaders gave needed support to families, started to develop laws concerning education, and eventually formed public schools to ensure that children met the goals and objectives of the community.

In the late 1800s, as public schools developed into bureaucracies, professional educators moved to the forefront and took responsibility for overseeing schools and curricula. At the same time, the public mandated a more diverse curriculum, so teachers were required not only to teach academic skills but also to provide programs designed to help children develop socially, physically, morally, and emotionally. At this time, when more blue-collar jobs required technical skills, schools became responsible for teaching vocational skills as well. In the later part of the 20th century, when only a part of the school population succeeded in these extended schools, questions began to arise. Parents and communities became perplexed and displeased about lower success rates, and often alienation set in.

Table 2–1   Historical Events Affecting Family-Community-School Relationships

1600s	**Families Responsible for Children's Education (Community Responsibility)**
1642	Massachusetts Act requiring all families to teach children to read Bible and laws of the land
1687	Old Deluder Satan Law requiring every community of 100 or more to establish schools
1700s	**Community Responsibility for Children's Education (National Influence—State Responsibility)**
1779	South Carolina outlaws education for black children
1785 to 1787	Northwest Ordinances reserved sections of land in the Midwest for the support of schools
1789	Constitution of the United States—no mention of education—assuming education was States' responsibility
1800s	**Education Establishment's Responsibility for Children's Education**
1815	First parent program in Portland, Maine
1835	Massachusetts establishes first state board of education
1852	Massachusetts first to establish compulsory education law
1867	U.S. Office of Education established
1873	First public school kindergarten founded in St. Louis
1888	Federation for Child Study founded
1889	G. Stanley Hall established first child study center at Clark University for studying children and disseminating information to parents about child-rearing practices
1896	Plessy v. Ferguson decision supporting segregation
1897	National Congress of Mothers founded (later became Parent-Teacher Association)
1900s	**Education Establishment's Responsibility for Educating Parents as Well as Children**
1909	First White House Conference on Care of Dependent Children
1912	Children's Bureau established in Washington, D.C.
1916	First parent cooperative founded at University of Chicago
Mid-1900s	**Parent and Community Involvement in School Policies**
1954	Brown v. Board of Education opened the way for desegregation of schools
1956	Ford Foundation grant to New York City to train volunteers to work with teachers
1964	Civil Rights Act mandating desegregation of schools paved way for compensatory education acts that required parental involvement in schools
1965	Elementary and Secondary Education Act; Project Head Start; Title I/Chapter I
1965	First Bilingual Education Act
1967	Economic Opportunity Act follow-through programs
1972	Home Start programs established
1975	Public Law 94-142 Education for All Handicapped Children Act (amended in 1990 to Individuals with Disabilities Act [IDEA])
1984	First National symposium on Partnerships in Education sponsored by the President's Advisory Council
1986	Federal Preschool and Early Intervention Program Act Public Law 99-457 extends PL 94-142 mandating services for preschoolers
1986	Handicapped Children's Protection Act (PL99-372) passed
1988	National Association of Partners in Education formed
1988	Educational Partnerships Act Title VI passed
1988	Family Support Act
1992	Head Start Improvement Act passed extending services to infants and toddlers
1994	Goals 2000: Educate America Act signed into law
1996	Personal Responsibility and Work Opportunity Reconciliation Act (Welfare Reform Act)
1997	Reauthorization of IDEA

In the 1990s, a new trend for developing collaborations (stimulated by researchers and professional educators) became a focus for parents, community leaders, and teachers. In this way, many people came to appreciate the truth in the African proverb, "It takes an entire village to educate a child." As you review this historical overview of relationships among parents, communities, and schools, consider what happens to children as society changes.

In this chapter, we trace the changes and forces that have shaped our present educational condition in the United States with respect to roles played in childhood education by families, communities, and schools from the dominant culture. We also consider attitude changes over the three centuries toward children from minority cultures and other special populations. Naturally, all changes have affected the roles and responsibilities of the three institutions for the education of all children. Table 2–1 lists major American events affecting family-community-school relationships.

FAMILY AS A SIGNIFICANT EDUCATIONAL FORCE

From primitive cultures to modern society, the family has been the most important social setting for educating the child. In all societies, children must learn skills of survival, the rules and regulations of the society in which they live, and the values by which their society functions (Sanderson, 1995). Children learn by following their elders' examples, through direct teaching of important skills by their elders, and by oral telling of traditions, lore, attitudes, beliefs, and values (Frost, 1966).

In the original English colonies, the family was the prime educator, though the community exerted pressure on families to teach what that society deemed important. The education that children received in the colonial period depended on economic status, ethnic background, child gender, and to some extent the section of the country the child lived in.

Early settlers for the most part were able to form cohesive family units, depending on each other for survival. Towns and villages, particularly in New England, were initially established around particular religious groups migrating from Europe. With their religious heritage, early colonists believed that children needed to learn not only the vocational skills necessary for survival but also particular codes of behavior and moral integrity. The more economically advantaged also valued reading and writing for their own children. It was a patriarchal society, and in most cases, teaching was the responsibility of the home, with the father the dominant force. Parents, grandparents, and older siblings were the primary instructors. Fathers taught their sons skills needed to carry on the family vocation; mothers taught their daughters homemaking skills. In the intact homes, children had a profound appreciation and sense of family. They tended to understand who they were and how they were a part of the larger community (Zelizer, 1994).

Puritans in New England were adamant about the need to learn to read and write, and stressed the importance of reading the Bible. Parents assumed this responsibility. In addition, certain women who became more skilled in teaching gathered in their homes children whose parents were unable to teach reading and writing. This practice resulted in the creation of dame schools, precursors of our current primary schools.

In the Southern colonies, wealthy settlers hired tutors to teach their children academic skills plus the behaviors befitting a plantation owner. Poor parents were responsible for educating their children as best they could. For the most part, African Americans were forbidden an education, and because of slavery, black families were often torn apart, so that even parental teaching of basics was hampered (Berlin, 1998; Travers & Rebore, 1995).

When colonial boys needed to learn skills the family was unable to provide, apprenticeships were sought, and boys as young as 7 were sent to live with a master craftsman. They could be apprenticed until age 21. Apprenticeships were the precursors of our later grammar schools, for in many colonies, the masters were expected to teach reading and writing as well as the skills of their trade (Webb, Metha, & Jordan, 1999).

In the English colonies, basic formal education was available to established families, but children of slaves and Native Americans were considered unworthy for teaching. There were, however, notable exceptions to this trend. The Church of England in the South and Quakers in the middle colonies provided educational opportunities for a few African Americans, some Native Americans, and some poor Anglo colonists.

COMMUNITY AS A SIGNIFICANT EDUCATIONAL FORCE

As townships in the colonies became more established in the late 1600s and the 1700s, religious leaders became more dominant in determining the education of children within the community. Thus began the American heritage, extant today, that a community oversees its schools and determines school policy and curriculum.

The Puritans are credited with establishing the foundation of public education in this country because of their belief that all children, no matter their economic status, needed to be educated. They believed that every child in the land should learn the rigid codes of behavior for a religious society and the "meaning of salvation" from Bible reading. As early as 1642, a Massachusetts law

Puritans are credited with establishing the foundation of public education in the United States.

required all parents and master craftsmen to teach reading and writing to children in their care to ensure that children attained "religious understanding and civic responsibility" (Travers & Rebore, 1995, p. 42). There was, however, difficulty in enforcing such a mandate because of widespread illiteracy in the adult population. Consequently, in 1647, the Old Deluder Satan Law was passed which required that townships with 50 or more households provide a teacher of reading and writing for young children in the community. Townships that had more than 100 households were also to provide a Latin grammar school to prepare boys for university study (Cohen, 1974).

Though these laws were not easy to enforce, they were important in establishing a precedent for education as the young nation expanded. First and foremost, the family had primary responsibility for educating a child, but the laws also laid a foundation for community responsibility in assisting families in educating the young. Since communities hired the teachers, they also taxed families on their property so as to have funds to pay teachers (Cohen, 1974).

In the late 1700s and early 1800s, political and economic factors in the young United States again affected the relationships of families and communities in educating children. The advent of the Industrial Revolution meant that families moved from an economy dependent on farming to one increasingly dependent on manufacturing. Now fathers, and sometimes mothers, left home to earn a living, and naturally there was little opportunity to teach children vocational skills or reading and writing in the home. An urban population began to arise, and many families became more isolated from their kin. Thus, the changed circumstances demanded a new response to the country's needs.

The republic was coming into being at the end of the 18th century, and as it unified, the strong influence of religious communities was replaced by the notion of nonsectarian education. Political leaders such as Benjamin Franklin and Thomas Jefferson believed that the new nation needed a literate populace and that it was not sufficient to educate only the wealthy and the strongly religious. Education, they felt, needed to be available to children from different social and economic classes and needed to be more functional. Merchants added their voice to that of politicians, for business interests realized that the nation needed workers with more than rudimentary literacy skills and more practical skills than those provided in Latin grammar schools (Sadker, Lerner, & Sadker, 1999).

If wider schooling opportunities were to be available, something needed to be done to help communities establish schools. The new government responded, and significant pieces of legislation, such as the Land Ordinance Act of 1785 and the Northwest Ordinance Act of 1787, were passed by the Continental Congress. These acts encouraged settlers to move to the Midwest and to set aside land to support schools. Such acts indicated the new nation's faith in education, even though in writing the Constitution the founding fathers did leave the responsibility for education to individual states.

The ideas and practices of European philosophers and educators, such as Comenius (1592–1670), Rousseau (1712–1778), Pestalozzi (1746–1827), and Froebel (1782–1852), influenced educational thought in the United States. These new ideas, however, regarding who was to be educated and where and how did not immediately change American children's education. Community sentiment first had to endorse any practice. Even today, in a general sense, community standards, mores, and expectations are among the strongest determinants of social behavior and participation. We find that community validation continues to be necessary for any substantial change or redirection to take place in children's educational opportunities.

SCHOOL AS A SIGNIFICANT EDUCATIONAL FORCE

The mission of formal schools and support for public education have increased gradually over the more than two centuries of the United States as a nation. In spite of our founding fathers' expressing a need for universal, free, and secular education, it has taken a long time to achieve such a goal for all children.

Even in the early 1800s, the prevailing view was that education was the family's responsibility; any education beyond a family's immediate capacity to give was a luxury. Some communities at that time maintained public schools for their children, and some charity schools existed for the poor. In addition, religious sects continued to provide schooling in some areas for all children, and, of course, there were private schools for the wealthy (Cremin, 1982). But universal education was not yet supported in the United States of the early 1800s.

It was the mid-1800s before the political and economic climate provided fertile ground for the establishment of free, open, secular schools in the United States. On one front, new immigrants were voicing dissatisfaction in not being a part of the political process. Trade unions were forming, and unionists believed that the path to success was through educating their children. Also, humanists and educators, such as Horace Mann (1796–1859) and Henry Barnard (1811–1900), wrote and lectured about benefits of universal and secular education. In addition, population movement from rural to urban areas meant that many families lacked the resources to educate children at home. The time for public education had arrived.

States at this time urged local communities to begin taxing themselves so as to provide public schools for their citizenry. States also started the practice of giving aid to communities needing support. In 1852, Massachusetts began to require compulsory attendance, but it wasn't until 1918 that the last state in the union—Mississippi—enacted legislation requiring children to attend school (Cremin, 1961). With such enactments, parents began to relinquish to schools the responsibilities for educating their children; however, home and community continued to influence many educational trends.

As schools became the major force in educating American children, a professional education establishment emerged that influenced parents as well as local and state government about curriculum. Some collaborations between schools and homes resulted, but often parents and communities were at odds about the specifics of children's education.

As compulsory education took hold in the late 1800s, it became apparent that many children in the United States were not being reared in the manner the dominant culture felt necessary. Poor children in urban communities were often viewed as neglected, and new immigrants from southern and eastern Europe, unable to speak English, had different values and views on child rearing. It became clear that schools with their prevalent Puritan ethic did not meet the needs of many children. Something needed to be done, and parent organizations with strong female advocates were formed to press for action on more comprehensive schools. Schools were urged to provide hot lunches for needy children, and immigrants were taught English so that they could be assimilated into American society (Kagan, 1993).

Philosophical swings in education, from conservative and academic to more liberal progressivism, have resulted from what the American public has perceived as needed in different periods. For example, with new immigrants and a growing urban, industrialized society, a movement emerged in the 1920s and 1930s for more openness in education—with schooling tailored to the needs, interests, and abilities of children. Then, in the 1950s, as the space race captured people's imaginations, U.S. citizens became concerned with the lack of strong academic focus, and a swing to a more rigorous academic curriculum followed. Following the civil rights movement, social issues were of great concern, and again schools were pressured to change to a more responsive curriculum to serve all children. In the 1980s and 1990s, Japanese economic successes had people worried that American graduates could not compete with their Japanese counterparts. Once again pressure from parent groups and communities forced schools to promote greater academic achievements.

Parent Involvement in Schools

At the turn of the 20th century, as society brought pressure on schools to change ways of operating, similar forces were directed at parents. No longer were parents viewed as knowing the best way to rear their children. Psychology as a science came into its own at this time, and young children quickly became a focus of study. Many theories were advanced on child development and the best ways to rear children.

In 1815, the first parent education program was held in Portland, Maine, to instruct parents in proper child-rearing practices. Through the efforts of Elizabeth Peabody (1804–1894), a follower of Froebelian programs, kindergartens were established, first by church societies and settlement homes and later as part of public schools. Besides providing moral and religious training and a safe and healthy environment for children, the kindergarten was a way to reach immigrant families and influence them in rearing children according to the beliefs of mainstream society (Weber, 1969).

In the late 1800s and early 1900s, interest in the plight of children in urban settings became a focus for some early childhood educators. Armed with new knowledge on the importance of good nurturing and proper training in the early years, child care centers and family child care programs were established as extensions of the kindergarten programs. Many of these programs were directed at poor families in which mothers worked outside the home (Seefeldt & Barbour, 1998).

Early parent involvement meant educating parents as well as involving them in supporting school activities. The National Association of Parents and Teachers, later to become the Parent-Teacher Association (PTA), was established in 1897 for this very purpose. Community involvement in parent education came in the form of women's organizations, such as the Society for the Study of Child Nature (1888), the American Association of University Women (1882), and the National Association of Colored Women (1887). These organizations sponsored lectures and conferences and published magazines promoting parent education and stressing the importance of parents' taking an active role in children's education (Schlossman, 1976).

Child study in the late 1800s became a focus at colleges and universities as a result of the work of G. Stanley Hall (1844–1929). Many universities established laboratory schools for preschool-age children where educational theories and child-rearing practices could be tested. Supported by federal and private funds, these schools provided courses in child development and parent education and practice for teachers and researchers, and disseminated information on their research (Schlossman, 1976).

Perhaps the zenith of early parent involvement came with the founding of parent cooperatives at the University of Chicago in 1916. Founded by 12 faculty wives to provide quality care for their children and parent education for themselves, these programs were modeled after the nursery school program in England founded by Margaret McMillan (1860–1931). Though McMillan founded her school for the poor, nursery schools and the first parent cooperatives were adopted in the United States by middle-class parents, and parent involvement became entrenched. An open, play-oriented curriculum was emphasized in both nursery schools and parent cooperative programs as they developed. However, not all the newer nursery school programs were committed to total parent involvement, as were the parent cooperative programs. Parents of children in cooperative programs were decision makers for the schools. They hired teachers, approved the type of program, served as assistants in the classroom, and planned the parent education programs (Taylor, 1981).

During the first half of the 1900s, parent education became viewed as vital to the welfare of society, and professional educators began to feel responsible for providing this service. Parents, even though no longer considered experts in child upbringing, were still viewed as essential components for children's success in school and later in life. Experts felt that parents needed help in seeing how they could support their children's learning and thus benefit society (Taylor, 1981). A rather popular belief, at least among the middle class, was that the mother should be at home raising her children and learning from the experts how to raise these children. But with urbanization, there have always been mothers working outside the home, and they needed child care services.

The Works Progress Administration supported day care for families in poverty during the 1930s.

There have been periods in history when more emphasis has been placed on the need for society to help provide child care. In the 1930s, the Works Progress Administration (WPA) had a program providing full day care for families in poverty. Then, during World War II, day care centers were set up in factories so that women could help in the war effort. Great attention was paid to training teachers about child care development and in developing curricula. However, parents were seen not as collaborators but rather as being in need of support and education.

In the late 1990s, with large numbers of mothers again in the workforce and welfare mothers required to return to work, quality child care services became very important as a buttress for all parents. National child care organizations like National Association of Education of Young Children established guidelines for quality care in the late 1980s, and the Welfare Reform Act of 1996 stressed the need for such care if mothers were to leave the welfare rolls.

Federal Government Involvement

Following the establishment of the U.S. Office of Education in 1867, the federal government took particular interest in families. The first White House Conference on Care of Dependent Children in 1909 sparked interest in child welfare throughout the nation, and in 1912, the Children's Bureau was established as a follow-up. Following that period, educational opportunities abounded through university courses, lectures and conferences, school programs for parents, magazine articles, and books. Later, television programs were developed instructing parents on how to educate their children. Benjamin Spock's book *The Common Sense Book of Baby and Child Care* (first published in 1946) and Burton White's *The First Three Years of Life* became popular guides in child-rearing practices, es-

pecially for the middle class (Schlossman, 1976). A proliferation of such materials continued at the end of the 20th century with even more information available through computer services and the Internet.

As society has become increasingly urban, decision making regarding children's education has become more complex. The federal government has become influential by granting monies for projects or by withholding the same from states not complying with federal mandates. State educational offices have also developed curricula and issued mandates regarding what should be taught in schools. Also, to qualify to receive state monies, local school authorities in recent years have begun to dictate certain educational requirements, and teachers have felt obligated to respond. At times, strong parent and advocacy groups also have attempted to influence what should be taught. The end of the 20th century was marked by disillusionment over the quality of American education. The federal government has taken a somewhat different focus and now requires that the states take more responsibility. Through establishing goals and then financially supporting schools by block grants and special funding for specific goals, the federal government continues to play an active role in influencing educational issues.

Goals 2000

The Goals 2000: Educate America Act, signed into law in March 1994, signaled a change for federal involvement in educational practice. Goals 2000 was presented as a new face for the federal government—where the federal role was to be one of support and facilitation to improve schools for all children. The act established very general goals as incentives and then gave support to states and communities as they worked to meet those standards and objectives (Riley, 1995). The legislation, incorporating eight national education goals (which emerged from 1990 legislation by the Bush administration) (National Education Goals, 1993), is summarized as follows:

1. All children in the United States will start school ready to learn.

2. The high school graduation rate will increase to at least 90%.

3. U.S. students will leave grades 4, 8, and 12 having demonstrated competency in challenging subject matter, including English, mathematics, science, history, and geography; and every school in the United States will ensure that all students learn to use their minds well so that they may be prepared for responsible citizenship, further learning, and productive employment in the modern economy.

4. U.S. students will be first in the world in science and mathematics achievement.

5. Every adult American will be literate and will possess the knowledge and skills necessary to compete in a global economy and to exercise the rights and responsibilities of citizenship.

6. Every school in the United States will be free of drugs and violence and will offer a disciplined environment conducive to learning.

7. The nation's teaching force will have access to programs for the continued improvement of their professional skills and the opportunity to acquire the knowledge and skills needed to instruct and to prepare all American students for the next century.

8. Every school will promote partnerships that will increase parental involvement and participation in promoting social, emotional, and academic growth of children.

Following establishment of Goals 2000, President Clinton added the America Reads Challenge in 1996. Recognizing that reading is a skill developed not only in school but also in the home and community, the initiative called for schools to involve community organizations and homes to help ensure that all children would read by the end of third grade (Mitchell & Spencer, 1997).

Partnerships and Collaborations

Partnerships in education is not a new concept, if we consider the various groups and interests that have worked together with our schools. As we have pointed out, families and community leaders have great input into the functioning of schools. The question arises as to how these would-be partners for the professional education establishment view their roles and how they assume responsibility and leadership.

In the 1950s and 1960s, the American public, for the most part, viewed all education as the responsibility of schools, and parents were expected to support teachers and their programs. However, the community school movement also developed at this time, and for those subscribing to the movement, the purpose of schools was more comprehensive. Community school advocates felt that schools, as well as serving young children, could serve the larger community by providing various resources for the public within the school facility (Kagan, 1993).

Educators took an active and strong role at this time, often advising parents on their roles and responsibilities. There was prosperity in the United States and a belief that through education the United States could provide equal opportunities for all citizens.

Schools needed support to meet this goal, and volunteer programs sprang up as a result. In 1956, the Ford Foundation granted money to the Public Education Association in New York City to recruit and train volunteers to teach reading and to assist children who did not speak English fluently. In the beginning, these volunteers were primarily nonworking mothers. But as the programs expanded and spread to other areas, retirees, college students, and businesspeople also began providing volunteer services (Merenda, 1989).

Parent, school, and community relations found a new impetus for collaboration in the 1980s as businesses became concerned with the quality of education in the United States. Some government officials recognized that ed-

ucational problems could not be solved by the public sector alone. Thus, an Educational Partnerships Program was established under the Educational Partnership Act of 1988. The purpose of the act was to encourage community organizations, including businesses, to form alliances to encourage excellence in education (Danzberger & Gruskin, 1993).

Partnerships no longer involved just the basics of establishing good relationships with

Businesses have become involved with schools, including assistance in shaping school policy.

parents and using the resources that a community provides. Businesses became involved in schools in a variety of ways. Partnership arrangements grew to include such supports as volunteers for the classroom, incentives for children to improve skills, internships for teachers, mentors and tutors for particular areas of study, visits to a business enterprise, special projects sponsored by businesses, provision of new technology for classrooms, and assistance in shaping school policy. The "business for education" movement grew from 17% involvement in 1983 to include around 40% of all schools by 1989 (Heaverside & Farris, 1989). The notion continued to prosper in the 1990s, with the 21st Century Community Learning Centers Act being introduced as a part of Title 20. Communities were encouraged to use public schools as a basis for uniting the many services within a community so as to deliver education and human resources for all members of the community.

CHILDREN WITH SPECIAL NEEDS

Major social events in each generation result in social policy changes that affect children. In the 1930s, the Great Depression resulted in Franklin Roosevelt's New Deal programs. In the same vein, political movements in the 1960s resulted in sweeping changes for American education and in the corresponding roles of parents, schools, and communities. The civil rights movement resulted in the Civil Rights Act of 1964, which acknowledged that children in segregated schools received an inferior education. Whereas middle-class white parents have generally felt themselves a part of their children's educational process, many parents in various minority and low-SES (socioeconomic status) groups felt disenfranchised prior to the landmark legislation of the 1960s. Parental involvement for all, regardless of heritage and economics, became highlighted in this era and continues to be an important issue.

Children in Poverty

In the 1930s, social welfare programs were seen as a way to help the poor. Aid to Families with Dependent Children was just such a program that existed at first primarily to assist unmarried women in providing for their children. Even with a rising economy after World War II, large numbers of children were still living in poverty. Such children entered school with many problems that affected their ability to learn. In 1965, President Lyndon Johnson launched the War on Poverty. Children raised in poverty were now to be given assistance before entering school and thus a greater chance at success in society. The Elementary and Secondary Education Act of 1965 (PL 89-10) was the largest grant ever made by the federal government to aid education. Educational programs such as Chapter I (originally called Title I), Head Start, Home Start, and Project Follow Through were designed under this act to compensate for the lack of early education by children living in poverty. The Head Start project was perhaps the most comprehensive. In addition to receiving educational experiences, children and families were provided with health, nutritional, and psychological services. Parents also were to play important roles as volunteers, paid aides, and instructors in their children's education. Parents became a part of Head Start advisory boards, thus acquiring decision-making powers both in selecting teachers and in making curriculum decisions (Lazar, 1977). Teachers in these programs were expected to make home visits, and the curriculum used was expected to reflect both the experiences and the cultural heritage of the diverse children. By implementing the federal guidelines, these programs provided an early model for family-school-community involvement.

In the 1990s, Americans began to believe that though Head Start was ultimately deemed successful, the War on Poverty had somehow failed. In spite of many welfare programs, child poverty increased over 60% from the early 1970s to the 1990s (O'Hare, 1996). In an attempt to change this course of events, the Family Support Act of 1988 stressed education and job training for welfare recipients. Mothers on welfare who returned to work or enrolled in education programs were guaranteed child care assistance and coverage for health insurance through Medicaid.

After some degree of success, there were new proposals in the 1990s to modify the act considerably. The 1996 Welfare Reform bill replaced child care entitlement programs with a single federal Child Care and Development Block Grant (CCDBG) and gave more responsibility and decision making for administering and funding to the states. This bill required all child care funds to be administered from one lead agency, thus avoiding overlap of programs. Other aspects included the following: (1) a limit was placed on how long a family could receive welfare; (2) persons receiving welfare were required to get at least a part-time job or receive job training; and (3) mothers with a child under a year old were exempt, but only for one child (Blank, 1997). The funding stressed improving the quality of care for children and providing education for the parents, though child care was not guaranteed (Hagan, 1998).

Children with Disabilities

As the federally supported programs developed, parents realized they had more power in determining their rights to educational opportunities for their children. A group of parents in Missouri, concerned about how their children with disabilities were being treated, united with a civil rights organization to focus on rights for children with disabilities. Thus, the Education for All Handicapped Children Act (PL 94-142) emerged in 1975. This act ensured a free and appropriate education to all children with disabilities, and in 1986, the Federal Preschool and Early Intervention Program Act (PL 99-457) extended rights and services to 3-year-olds. In the 1990 amendment, the title of the act was changed to Individuals with Disabilities Education Act (IDEA), and the term *handicapped* was changed to *disabled*. In keeping with this legislation, the Head Start Act was amended in 1992 by the Head Start Improvement Act, with services extended to infants and toddlers. In 1997, the act was reauthorized with modifications in the delivery systems, requirements in placement of students with discipline problems, and provisions for professional development. IDEA became such a comprehensive law that it was divided into three parts: Part A describes the extent and policies of the law, Part B points to the rights and benefits for the 3- to 21-year-olds, and Part C (formerly Part H) is for infants and toddlers (Turnbull, Turnbull, Shank, & Leal, 1999).

Under the preceding acts, parents are given rights of due process; they have the right to be involved in the entire process of their child's evaluation, placement, and educational objectives; and if there are differences of opinion, they have rights to the services of a mediator. Children placed in special education programs now must receive an **individualized education program (IEP)** prepared by a school team, including parents, and an **individualized family service plan (IFSP)** for families with infants or toddlers with disabilities.

An important aspect of the law has been that children are to be placed in the least restrictive environment. Except for extreme cases, this means that they are to be included in the regular classroom setting with resource persons and support services available to assist the regular teacher. When a child's behavior is disruptive to others in the classroom, the child may be placed in alternative placement, but only if the behavior is a manifestation of the child's disability and not of the child's ability.

Over the years, interpretation of the law has often caused much controversy. At one point, the term *mainstreamed* was used, and more recently, the term *inclusion* has been used. Neither term has been used in the mandate that declares that school districts are obligated to provide an education for children with disabilities alongside able-bodied children to the maximum extent possible. Removal is allowed only when the severity of the disability is such that even with special aides and services the regular classroom cannot provide an appropriate education (Yell, 1998).

Parents have the right to accept or challenge any school decision and to examine all records the school keeps on their children. Parent involvement is assured in these procedures, and the acts have actually had the effect of forcing parents and educators into partnership relationships.

In many instances, parents and educators have collaborated successfully in educating children with special needs. They have also used the resources of the community in different ways, including having volunteers work one-on-one with children. However, not all school personnel and parents have agreed on the most appropriate education for particular children. Since the laws have been enacted, the number of children classified as having disabling conditions has risen steadily (Webb et al., 1999). Half of these identified children are now classified as learning disabled, and a disproportionate number are African American and Hispanic children. Concerns about inappropriate placement or mislabeling of children have appeared as the number of children classified as learning disabled has risen. It is understandable that some parents have used their due process rights to sue schools for inappropriate placement. With such pressures, it becomes vital for schools to find new ways to work successfully with parents and to use community resources for improving education for all children.

Minority Populations

The history of parent-community-school involvement has taken a different course for other families. Some individuals of diverse racial and ethnic backgrounds have integrated, through education and employment, into mainstream American culture and have gained greater educational opportunities and material benefits. Others, reluctant to forego their own culture, have sustained problems in opportunity. Still, for many groups, assimilated or not, discrimination and denied opportunities for equal education are continuing problems.

The history of the United States is a story of waves of immigration. In the 1600s and 1700s, West Europeans came to colonize different parts of the United States—crowding out Native Americans and bringing slaves from Africa. In the 1800s, as a result of famine in northern Europe and with the acquisition of Mexican lands by the United States, new minority groups became a part of the American fabric. Then, in the early 1900s, other groups from central and southern Europe and Asia came to the United States seeking new opportunity. In the later part of the 1900s, as other countries sustained internal strife, a large number of immigrants came from Latin America, Asia, and the Caribbean seeking refuge from conflict and persecution. By the mid-1900s, three quarters of each year's immigrants were from Asia and Latin America (DeVita, 1995). All of these immigrant groups have had an impact on American culture, but still at the beginning of a new century, the dominant culture in America has remained Anglo-European.

The early minority groups were assimilated in accordance with how much they were able or willing to adapt to the majority culture. This usually worked for Europeans but rarely with other ethnically different populations. Today, Native Americans, African Americans, and Hispanics make up large ethnic groups in the United States and, in spite of civil rights legislation and affirmative action, have higher poverty rates than whites (O'Hare, 1996). Throughout the history of the United States, these particular groups have been denied easy and equal access to quality education, which means that their chances of moving out of poverty are less than those of their white counterparts (O'Hare, 1996).

Minority Populations and Families. During the colonial period, the two major nonwhite cultures were Native American and African American. For these two groups, the family, in conjunction with its ethnic community, was the primary means for educating children.

A communal ethic has always prevailed in Native American communities. Historically, community groups helped parents educate children and teach them economic skills, their cultural heritage, and spiritual awareness. The community expected all women to teach necessary homemaking skills, and boys as they matured were taught by various elders to hunt, survive, and fight. Through rituals, ceremonies, and oral traditions, the tribal elders passed on the religious beliefs and cultural heritage to young Native Americans (Szasz, 1988).

African Americans have lived in the United States since 1619, when the first individuals appeared as indentured servants at Jamestown. By the 1700s, most African Americans were slaves, and plantation owners exercised complete control over them. Though there were few opportunities for formal education in slavery, African Americans formed a distinct culture. It was the family and plantation that taught the children values, community behaviors, and as much of their native customs as possible. In some instances, the children learned reading and writing as they played with their owners' children (J. M. Rich, 1992). But during these early years, the sanctioned education for African American children was limited to the necessary skills for working and living within the plantation community.

Minorities and the Community. As the American expansion began, conflicts arose among the Anglo-American settlers regarding the education of non-Anglo persons. Some colonists believed that Native Americans should be annihilated and that African Americans should be kept from getting an education so as to avoid revolts (Berlin, 1998). Others, whether from religious zeal or from practical considerations, maintained it was necessary to acculturate minority children about Anglo-European culture through education. In different parts of the country, religious groups established schools and missions to convert Native Americans. They found that they had to teach reading and writing before they could teach Christianity. In the Southwest, priests and nuns taught Native Americans farming practices, vocational skills, and the Spanish language (Kidwell & Swift, 1976). Still, the major emphasis at that time was that all groups should accept the Caucasian conquerors' religious teachings and behavior codes.

In the South, despite laws forbidding education for African Americans, some plantation owners did teach the children of slaves to read and write so that they could become skilled workers and read the Bible. Later, some of those literate African Americans formed their own clandestine schools (Weinberg, 1977).

Despite these modest efforts to provide education, the majority community made no effort to work with Native American and African American children and their families. The Euro-American community dictated the rules of conduct irrespective of the values and culture of other groups. For many minority groups, these early practices were the beginnings of alienation between schools and families. Such practices of disrespect have resulted in serious alienation problems and further discrimination of minority-group members.

Minorities and the Schools. In the 1800s, as schools became the major force for educating children of the dominant culture, schools were seen as the way of melding the increasing number of immigrants in American society into one cultural group. But Mexican Americans and Asian Americans migrated to the United States in increasing numbers in the 1800s, and these groups created more variety in ethnic grouping and therefore more controversy. Differences that existed in earlier periods regarding how society provided schools for minority groups reappeared in the 1800s. The controversies continue in some areas today.

Native Americans.   To ensure better acculturation of Native Americans, boarding schools were established in the late 1800s, and children were taken from their families and tribes.

Some schools were established on reservations, but the Bureau of Indian Affairs, not the tribe itself, was in charge of them. Anglo-American-style schools were established to teach Christianity, English, basic skills, and some vocational training to young Native Americans. No sense of partnership on education existed, and each Native American community was expected to submit to the type of education provided by the majority culture (Szasz, 1977).

African Americans.   The aftermath of the Civil War offered greater chances for formal education for many African Americans. "Freedman schools" were established in the South in which former slaves and their children, along

The aftermath of the Civil War offered greater chances for formal education for many African Americans.

with some impoverished white children, were taught the curriculum of the New England common schools. Reading, writing, math, geography, moral development, and industrial education became the curriculum so that these students would be ready for the labor force (Gutek, 1996). There was, however, so much resistance from Southern whites after Reconstruction that until 1954, African American children were educated in segregated schools. The landmark case of <u>Brown v. Topeka Board of Education</u> (1954) precipitated action by African American leaders and some whites that led to the Civil Rights Act of 1964, forcing school desegregation (Bullock, 1967).

Hispanic Americans. Family, school, and community attempts at partnerships have had a history more of alienation than of cooperation for the Hispanic American population. When America gained possession of the northern half of Mexico in 1848, the Spanish-Mexican-Indian population was expected to become American. Attitudes of most Americans at that time were that Mexican Americans were inferior and could be denied their rights (J. M. Rich, 1992). In spite of negative attitudes and unequal treatment throughout the era, migration of Mexican Americans to the United States has continued to the present.

Other Hispanic groups from Central America and the Caribbean have migrated to the United States, especially since the 1960s. Some new emigres were affluent and had few economic and educational hardships, but this situation did not exist for the great majority. Presently, over 60% of Hispanic Americans in this country are Mexican American and, together with Puerto Ricans, experience the most discrimination (Sadker, Lerner, & Sadker, 1999).

From the beginning, the concept of assimilation in American public schools created great conflicts with Mexican American populations. English was the language of instruc-tion, and newly enrolled children were expected to abandon Spanish as well as their culture. Though no legal segregation existed for Hispanic Americans, de facto segregation did, and most Mexican Americans over the years attended separate and inferior schools or were placed in separate classes. They usually had fewer well-prepared teachers, and fewer monies were spent on their education. Classrooms were monocultural—reflecting Anglo traditions, learning styles, and value systems.

These circumstances often alienated Hispanic parents, who saw no purpose in education that destroyed their family lifestyles (Weinberg, 1977), even though early political leaders in the Hispanic community urged assimilation to avoid trouble. During the civil rights movement of the 1960s, new leadership appeared for Mexican Americans. Parents and political leaders joined forces in making demands for better schools and more equal treatment. Some gains came in a curriculum more responsive to their cultural heritage, instruction in Spanish, and culture-free IQ tests (Weinberg, 1977). The Bilingual Act of 1968 and subsequent acts provided non-English-speaking children with instruction in both their native language and English. Much controversy regarding the best way to teach non-English speakers still persists. In 1986, then Secretary of Education William Bennett changed the role of the federal government in bilingual education. States were given the responsibility of determining the type of language instruction for their students.

In states with large Hispanic populations, bilingual programs were popular. In these programs, children received at least some academic instruction in their native language. Many believed that these programs delayed Hispanic children's progress in English and denied them academic opportunities. In 1998, California voters replaced their extensive bilingual programs with structured English immersion (SEI) programs. Children in these programs are immersed in English in schools and get assistance as needed, and their own language is used only as it helps to clarify points (Baker, 1998). This has practically eliminated bilingual education in California.

Asian Americans.   Asian Americans, an extremely varied group, are relatively late arrivals to this country. Chinese workers first came to the western United States in the 19th century in connection with railroad building. The first Japanese came at the beginning of the 20th century, and Southeast Asians immigrated in the 1970s and 1980s as they fled their war-torn countries. Though Asians have been discriminated against and have experienced hardships adjusting to living in the United States, they have been, as a group, more academically and economically successful. However, like other emigres, Asian Americans have been expected to put aside their languages, cultural mores, and customs and adjust to Anglo-European culture. Because there are many different Asian languages, schools struggle to find the best types of bilingual education programs for Asian children. As with other minority groups, Asian American parents have often been alienated or confused by school expectations and by mainstream American culture. This problem makes good parent-school-community relations difficult to maintain.

MULTICULTURAL EMPHASIS

Adjustments for minority groups with regard to educational opportunity has changed dramatically in recent decades. As federal legislation has guaranteed educational opportunities for all children regardless of race, color, or national origin and has given a voice to parents, a change in attitude towards cultural diversity has also taken place. From an earlier melting-pot thesis, American schools and communities in general have moved in recent decades to a position of valuing multicultural education. As this type of education gains dominance, we find parent and community involvement more prominent in schools. Multicultural education requires substantial change—in attitude, staffing patterns, curriculum and materials, and interaction patterns—from the techniques of the monocultural curriculum that has always dominated education in the United States.

Attitude Change

At the beginning of the 20th century, the dominant attitude in the United States held that minority groups and new immigrants should be assimilated. The children from different groups were to learn behavior codes, values, and cultural expectations of the majority culture. This attitude of assimilation continued into the 1950s and 1960s, making the tacit assumption that "something was wrong with the other culture" that assimilation could fix. *Cultural deprivation* was the term used during the War on Poverty and in the initial bilingual programs. Officials believed that children needed compensatory programs to make up for this deprivation (Stein, 1986). The healthy dimension in the legislation of this period was that parents became included as decision makers. This important step required teachers and parents to communicate and work together, thus affording all a chance to grow.

As parent-school-community partnerships became established in the 1980s and 1990s, attitudes gradually changed toward ethnic groups and people of different heritages. Instead of the monocultural curriculum, multicultural education has been implemented in many American schools. In schools adhering to principles of true cultural pluralism, attitudes have changed so that children of diverse cultures and their parents are viewed as having strengths that contribute to and expand the education of all children.

Staffing Patterns

Historically, American thinking has been that if children were to be acculturated, it was important that teachers and administrators be from the majority culture so that children would have "proper" role models. In earlier periods, teachers who were recruited from minority groups were always sent to training schools that would educate them for the dominant culture (Gutek, 1996), thus continuing the ideas of monoculturalism.

As multicultural education gained ground, it became apparent that the staff in any school needed to have special training in cultural sensitivity, members working as a team, and representation from different cultures (Kagan & Neuman, 1997). Such diversity of staff is important, as it provides positive role models for children from different ethnic groups. All teachers can emphasize their own cultural heritage as they invite parents and members of diverse cultures and backgrounds to collaborate in providing richer classroom experiences. Using their own experiences, teachers from different minority groups can now help others understand different nonverbal behaviors and learning patterns.

Curriculum and Teaching Materials

Early publications and all curriculum materials were based on an Anglo-European world view. White children were the main characters in stories where people lived in pleasant homes surrounded by nice lawns. There were two parents, the father working hard and the mother lovingly tending the children. Extended families were rarely depicted. Individuals with different lifestyles were often portrayed as somehow wrong, to be pitied, or quaint (Stein, 1986). Moral lessons, based on Puritan ethics, were often taught along with reading and writing. History and geography were taught from the Anglo-European viewpoint, and the contributions of other cultures

to society's development were largely ignored (Garcia, 1993).

Our newer multicultural curriculum presents materials from several perspectives. People of all cultures are viewed in a variety of situations, and children study the major contributions of numerous cultural groups. Customs, rituals, and traditions of different cultures are explored so that students may appreciate both similarities and differences. Teachers can now begin to view minority-group parents as a vital link in communicating aspects of culture to all children. However, textbook companies have, at times, yielded to "political correctness" pressure from ethnic groups and have at times distorted both history and cultures in an effort to "be fair" (Stille, 1998). Teachers need to preview materials to be used with children for their accuracy and currency. When pressure groups exert so much influence that a skewed view of history, different cultural expectations, and literary quality hinder children's educational development, teachers must seek support in finding more appropriate materials (Elkind, 1995).

Interaction Patterns

When minority-group children were first educated in public schools, teachers assumed they learned in the same manner as children from the dominant culture. If they responded in an unfamiliar way, the teacher assumed they were being impolite or were not very bright (Stein, 1986). Official America had a correct way to rear children, and minority-group parents were expected to learn these ways or doom their children to failure. Competitive, individualistic, and aggressive learning styles have always been rewarded in traditional American schools, and cooperative learning, until recently, was seen as cheating.

Schools that now sponsor multicultural education recognize different learning styles and understand the need to employ different strategies to accommodate different children.

In multicultural classrooms, children learn to accept differences.

In multicultural classrooms, children learn about these different patterns and learn to accept these differences. One can see that the family becomes an important part in providing a bridge from the family's cultural patterns to the more diverse patterns found in a multiethnic and multicultural society. With proper opportunities, we find that all children can learn to be conversant with more than one culture (Banks, 1998; Garcia, 1993).

IMPLICATIONS FOR PROFESSIONALS

As you become immersed in study about various aspects of teaching and about children, the concerns of the present can often cloud your thinking and objectivity. Every generation has

its problems and successes in educating children. Understanding the major issues at different historical times helps you view current events in a broader light. In studying this chapter, you have seen that home, schools, and communities have always affected how children learn, but recognition or use of this knowledge by educators has varied. Family structure and societal expectations, as we move into the 21st century, are very different from those at the beginning of the 20th century. Because of these changes and the complexity of society, there are no easy solutions for how to work and deal with the families of today. But some things haven't changed, and how parents, families, and communities were viewed in the past can be beginning points of how to work with parents today.

Look at the picture at the chapter beginning in which children are observing a process that was a part of their lives—shoeing a horse. Now look at a modern picture—the girls at the tidal pool, for example, in chapter 7. The girls, too, are observing a process important to their lives. Adults in the two pictures realize the important educative process of the environment, but, how each adult handles the learning will depend on the times and the culture. Understanding how the relationships among parents, teachers, and community members has changed in different generations gives you a broader perspective as you learn the expectations of your particular community.

SUMMARY AND REVIEW

Parents, communities, and schools have always assumed significant roles and responsibilities for the education of children in any society. At different times in American history, each of the three social settings assumed greater leadership and responsibility than did the other two. And in most periods, we find some instances of parent-school-community cooperation and collaboration. At other times, conflicts appeared when one institution seemed to dominate the way children were educated.

In colonial times, the family was responsible for educating children. The Puritans of New England are credited with the notion that the community at large should oversee education, and early laws in that colony regulated the teaching of academics, behavior codes, and moral development. By the 1800s, communities became the strong voice in organizing schools, hiring teachers, and taxing themselves to support these schools. Professional educators gained dominance over curriculum decisions in the 20th century.

Parents, communities, and schools have, of course, collaborated from time to time. Not until recently, however, have we seen any sig-

nificant joining of forces. By the 1980s, it became clear that strong parent-school-community relationships were necessary if schools were to be responsible for educating all children. Various partnerships for educating children have been formed since then.

Though free and compulsory education has been a tenet of American educational theory for many years, most communities still have not extended equal opportunity to all cultural groups. From the 1800s to the mid-1900s, most minority-group children attended segregated schools or de facto segregated classrooms with fewer educational opportunities. As desegregation became more prevalent in the 1950s and 1960s, federal programs provided special programs for children living in poverty. Initiators of these federal programs recognized that to be successful, they must involve parents and the leaders in the community where these children live. As a result, many minority-group parents acquired decision-making powers over their children's education—a situation that had been absent for generations.

In the 1980s, Americans began to realize the importance of multicultural education for all children. Attitudes continue to change, school staffs have become diverse, and curriculum materials now present topics from a multicultural viewpoint. Many educators have started to value differences and, in the process, include parents as valuable partners in the curriculum.

At the end of the 20th century, in spite of many federal programs, the numbers of children in poverty had increased. American children seemed to lag behind academically, and more mothers needed out-of-home care for their children. The federal initiatives to solve problems that arose from these changes have been varied but have included welfare reform, establishment of national goals, and growing support for schools to develop home, school, and community partnerships.

SUGGESTED ACTIVITIES AND QUESTIONS

1. Interview a senior citizen and determine whether he or she thinks family influence patterns have changed since his or her childhood.

2. Identify a federal law affecting education in the United States. Interview a teacher, a parent, and a local businessperson to assess their feelings about the law and how it affects them personally. Compare your findings with other classmates. What laws did these different groups dislike?

3. Visit a primary-school classroom in your area. Interview the teacher to determine the amount of parental involvement the teacher feels he or she has at present. Ask the teacher whether this level of involvement has changed over his or her career.

4. Examine a primary-grade curriculum guide (or textbook) from the 1950s. Compare the amount of multicultural material you see with that found in a current guide (or textbook). Make a chart or list of these changes.

RESOURCES

Books

1. Corsaro, W. A. (1997). *The sociology of childhood.* Thousand Oaks, CA: Pine Forge.
2. Mills, K. (1998). *Something better for my children. The history and people of Head Start.* New York: Dutton.
3. O'Neill, D. M., & O'Neill, J. E. (1997). *Lessons for welfare reform: An analysis of the AFDC case-*

load and past welfare-to-work programs. Kalamazoo, MI: W. E. Upjohn Institute for Employment Research.

Films/Videos

1. *Include us.* (1997). [Video, 33 min]. Shows various children's disabilities with acceptance, independence, and friendship. Tift Hill Productions, Sioux City, IA.
2. *New faces on Main Street.* (1998). [Video, 60 min]. Presents interviews with community members where new immigrants have settled. Focuses on problems, prejudice, and hopes as integration takes place. University of Wisconsin—Green Bay.

Organizations

Children's Defense Fund
   (http://www.childrensdefense.org/)
25 East Street, NW, Washington, DC 20001

Council for Exceptional Children
   (http://www.cec.sped.org/)
1920 Association Drive, Reston, VA 20191

Websites

1. http://www.negp.gov Gives information on the National Education Goals and what different states have accomplished in reaching these goals.
2. http://www.intac.com/-washington/sped1.htm Contains essential information regarding special education for teachers, parents, and administrators.
3. http://www.doe.gov/ Site for U.S. Department of Education. Contains comprehensive outlines of federal legislation and initiatives, such as Goals 2000, IDEA, and Drug-free schools.

Chapter 3

===== 🌿🌿🌿🌿 =====

Viewing Family Diversity

🌿🌿🌿🌿

When you start measuring somebody, measure him right, child, measure him right. You make sure you've taken into account the hills and valleys he's come through before he got to where ever he is.

Lorraine Hansberry, Raisin in the Sun, *p. 145*

🦋

American families vary immensely in makeup, and if you talk with several colleagues, most likely all will have somewhat different descriptions for what "family" means to them. Chapter 3 focuses on the demographics and the diverse nature of families we find in the United States today. In reading this chapter you will learn the following:

1. American children are reared in many different types of households and family groupings.
2. Many social and economic factors affect family life.
3. Racial, ethnic, and language differences affect the structure, status, and functioning of families.
4. Religious factors, cultural expectations, and conditions of disability have an impact on family life.
5. Families are always in a process of change from one stage or condition to another.

The following vignette points out some not so uncommon changes that unfolded in one American family as the members progressed through several years of living.

🦋

Five-year-old Jana had just entered Mrs. Thompson's multi-age classroom. Mrs. Thompson found her a happy child who came from a "nice family." As did other mothers in the neighborhood, Jana's mother walked her to kindergarten. At noon, her mother met her, and they walked to Gramma's to tell about Jana's day at school. In the evening, Jana bubbled away at the dinner table, telling her father and older brother all about her day. Jana was secure and snug in her world where love abounded. But Jana's world was about to change.

Her mother became very ill that fall and was often hospitalized. Gramma came to take Jana to school on most days, though the child sometimes was angry with her. But then Jana became worried that Gramma would not be close by.

Jana's mother died within the year, and the following year, Jana's life was filled with adjustments. Gramma and Grampa came to live at her house and take care of her, and that helped. Jana sometimes missed her mother taking her to school, for now she had to go to school with her older brother, who wanted to be with his friends, not with her. Her dad, always involved in his work, just didn't seem to be there every evening as she would have liked. Jana, however, worked hard in school and enjoyed the consistent routine Mrs. Thompson provided over the three years Jana was in her class.

At age 8, Jana's world shifted again. Her father remarried, and now she had an extra older brother and an older sister. Her own older brother became a "pain" when he looked after her while her father and stepmother were out. Sometimes when that responsibility was shared by her brother and stepbrother, the two boys quarreled, and it was awful. Jana tried to tell her side of the story, but it seemed to her that her stepmother always became angry and then unresponsive. Jana's father tried to comfort her in her room after the quarrels, but he felt Jana should cooperate more and help become a part of this new life. Gramma and Grandpa had moved away that year, and this seemed to delight Jana's stepmother, who felt they interfered.

When Jana was 10, a new baby was born into the family. At times Jana enjoyed the delightful baby, but she became jealous when the baby got a lot of attention. Jana did begin to develop a more accepting, although shaky, relationship with her stepmother— they especially enjoyed cooking together and taking special packages to neighbors who were sick or in need.

🖋

What is a family? Family can mean different things at different times. Jana, in this opening vignette, was always part of a family, but the configuration changed several times in her growing-up years.

The term *family* describes particular household groupings that occur in all human societies. Historically, the designation indicated a specific home grouping, but in today's world, sociologists argue that "family" denotes a variety of clustered adults and children (Bianchi & Spain, 1996; Fine, 1993). For some families, the cluster remains relatively constant; other families, like Jana's, evolve into different arrangements over the years. Whatever the cluster, the family is a dynamic and ever-changing force in a child's life.

Though family composition may not have actually changed a great deal over the years, cultural concepts of what constitutes a "proper" family and the percentages of different family clusters have altered considerably. In the late 19th century, Victorian society in Britain and the United States idealized the family as consisting of two doting and proper parents with several adoring and capable children at their knees. Of course, this was far from universal even then, but through literature and folklore, people accepted this picture of what ought to be the situation in their towns, cities, and neighborhoods.

Changes in family composition and arrangement in the latter part of the 20th century certainly were dramatic, and we now find many variations in family structures.

Family arrangements became a highly charged political issue in the 1990s, and the notion of "family values" received extensive media coverage during election campaigns. Actually, this foment paved the way for much more study and analysis of American families, and our population appears more knowledgeable today about the social, economic, and political upheavals that precipitated much of the change.

Traditional and idealized American family forms are obviously diminishing, and other arrangements grow more commonplace (Bianchi & Spain, 1996; Carnegie Corporation, 1994). While the total number of households expanded 11% between 1980 and 1996, the nuclear family (with two parents plus their biological children) decreased from 31% of all household units to only 17%, and in the same time period, single-parent families increased more than one fourth (U.S. Bureau of the Census, 1998a).

While there may be distinct advantages to the traditional nuclear family, labeling it as the only "good" or "positive" family form is risky, to say the least. Many other family arrangements have proved coherent and viable (Coontz, 1997). Human service professionals need to be aware of subtle and unsubtle prejudices toward nontraditional families. It is all too easy for teachers to value or feel comfortable with only those configurations that approximate their ideal family unit. The important thing to remember is that many arrangements work quite well, and over time most young children will experience changes in their own family structure. As you learn about interacting with families, be sensitive to differences and carefully search out ways to support, value, and work with all the differing types you encounter (Fine, 1993; Hildebrand, Phenice, Gray, & Hines, 1996).

The family is the organizational arrangement recognized by society as foremost in protecting, nurturing, supporting, and mediating for children in their growing years. The term *family* in Western culture connotes married adults. Our definition in this text does not require marriage, for many stable and prospering family units involve unmarried adults. And while some partners have been married to others, they have reconstituted a family singly or with a new partner without the formality of marriage.

As the 21st century begins, recognized family groups in the United States are very different and vary more from traditional arrangements than ever before. However, it is important to remember that more than one half of all American households do not have children. Statistics on family makeup cited in this text are based on families with children in the household. See Figure 3.1 for the breakdown of household units and note that our categories include only the first two bars of that graph.

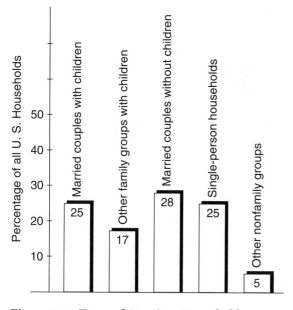

Figure 3–1   Types of American Households in 1997.
Source: U. S. Bureau of the Census, Current Population Reports P20-483 & P20-509, 1998.

Most families, like Jana's in the chapter's opening vignette, are dynamic. Family structure is never permanent; members form a particular configuration for only a brief time and then change comes about. For example, when Jana was in eighth grade, her teacher asked her to draw and label two pictures: one of her family when she was in kindergarten and another of her family now. Jana's explanation shows her grasp of family changes.

In her kindergarten picture, Jana drew and labeled, "my real mom, my dad, my brother, and me." In her eighth-grade picture she drew herself in the center with other people in clusters around her. Closest to her were figures labeled "dad and my older brother." On the other side but distanced from her were four people labeled "my stepsister, my stepmom, my stepbrother, and my little sister." In the right corner she had drawn a circle for four people and wrote, "my aunt, my uncle, me, and my cousin." When her teacher asked her to explain her pictures, she said, "This first picture is me and my family before Mom died. Dad remarried, so now I have a stepmom and a brother and sister and a little sister. These people," she added, pointing to the encircled, "aren't really my family, but I stay with them a lot, so sometimes they feel like my family."

Public schools in the United States must (at least initially) accept all children in a community, with whatever orientations and experiences they have. This means that any one classroom teacher relates to and interacts with representatives from several different family types. The backgrounds, values, and experiences vary from one child to the next, and teachers and other community workers must accept and value all families as they communicate and work to enhance programs. Sensitive and responsive interactions are the only base for healthy home-school-community relations.

In any description of family lifestyles it is impossible to include all configurations, but as a prospective teacher or community worker, you will want to ascertain the makeup of homes in your community and assess how they function. Chapter 4 discusses family functioning in depth.

DIFFERENT TYPES OF FAMILIES

Nuclear Families

From shortly after World War II through the early 1970s, media producers in the United States presented what they considered to be the typical American family. That image of the nuclear family with a father breadwinner and mother homemaker was viewed throughout the United States as the all-American, *Leave It to Beaver* model family. It appeared in film, on television, in books and magazines, and in advertisements of all types.

This model, two-parent home with children usually was presented as stable, thrifty, economically secure, and very happy. Of course, individual situations varied with regard to health, social status, and problems encountered for the sake of plot or to meet current marketing needs. The archetype has been part of American and British (and, to a lesser degree, continental European) culture for generations. But the nuclear family, and particularly that version with the breadwinner father, is much less predominant today.

A **nuclear family** is one in which the parents are first-time married, the children living with them are their biological children, and no

Nuclear families are much less prominent today than in earlier generations.

other adults or children live in the home. This arrangement is true now for only 48% of U.S. families with children (U.S. Bureau of the Census, 1998). A minor variation is the home where the children are legally adopted rather than biological offspring.

Role redefinitions for males and females, social pressures, changing economics, relaxation of marriage requirements, and reconsidered family functions have all affected the nuclear family's dominance. Census Bureau statistics show that in 1995, only 26% of children in the United States lived in a two-parent *Leave It to Beaver* family with a breadwinner and a homemaker, and *American Demographics* magazine noted in April 1998 that only 17% of American households were of this type. This significant demographic change for this type of household implies concurrent changes for other types. Figure 3.2 shows this demographic distribution as of 1998.

Extended Families

The multigenerational family unit resembles the nuclear family but with additions, usually adult relatives. The identifying feature of an **extended family** is that the reference person, head of household, or wage earner is the adult with young children. Older relatives or other adults are appended to this nucleus.

The extended family arrangement is typical for agrarian societies. Many farms in such communities have three generations of a family living together. In the United States, many individuals who were born in the earlier part of the 20th century can remember living as part of an extended family. Intergenerational families have advantages over nuclear ones: The "extra" adults can provide care and nurturing for the young, to say nothing of helping with farm chores. The extended family was common in Europe in the 19th century, and immigrants to the United States brought the practice with them when resettling (Bailyn et al., 1997).

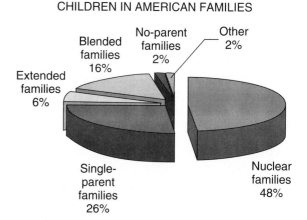

CHILDREN IN AMERICAN FAMILIES

Figure 3–2   Where American Children Lived in 1998.

Note: Adopted children, foster children, and children in subfamilies are included in one or another of the categories. *Source:* Adapted from 1998 census projections: U. S. Bureau of the Census, Current Population Reports, P20-506 & P20-509.

Extended families survived in urban areas for different reasons than they did in rural areas. The practice fit the need to economize, the cottage industries, and the social situations in which newcomers found themselves. Extended families became less common in American culture after industrialization, but the configuration has been retained in many minority-group homes (Webb et al., 1996) and sometimes temporarily in single-parent homes, as in the case of Jana in our vignette. Economics alone can dictate a need for sharing a dwelling when families are pressed. Heritage, the need for security, and the sharing of materials all combine to make the extended family a logical arrangement for many groups.

An extended family can occur in any of a number of combinations. Typical are the following:

1. Mother and father with children, plus one or more grandparents.

2. Mother and father with children, plus one or more unmarried siblings of the parents or other relatives.

3. A divorced or separated mother or father with children, plus grandparents or siblings or other relatives.

It is easy to see that extended families can be quite large, often including several related adults and children. But the decline in number of extended families continues. Children's Defense Fund (1997) indicates that approximately 6% of American children live in this type of family.

Single-Parent Families

Single-parent families, in which one parent lives with her or his children, have always been present. The death of a spouse was not uncommon as a disrupter in the lives of our ancestors. Surviving spouses in earlier periods often remarried soon after the death of a partner, creating stepfamilies. In recent years in the United States, divorce and separation, rather than death, have precipitated the increasingly large number of single-parent families. The rising number of out-of-wedlock births creates even more. DeVita (1995) notes that 25% of white babies are born to unmarried mothers while one third of Hispanic babies and two thirds of Black children are in this category.

For a variety of reasons, the single-parent family is becoming one of the most common family groupings in the United States today. Census reports for 1998 show 26% of families with children are now single-parent (Annie E. Casey Foundation, 1998). This contrasts with 1970, when there were 11%. Projections also show that between 50% and 60% of all children born after 1987 will spend part of their minor years in a single-parent family (Bianchi, 1990; Eitzen, 1992). Cohabitation of adults confounds some of these statistics, for some children are born (estimates range up to one third) into the homes of unmarried mothers and fathers. The arrangements are far less stable than married couples (Bianchi & Spain, 1996).

The single-parent family has several structural variations:

1. Single mothers—divorced, widowed, or never married—living alone with their biological children.

2. Single fathers—divorced, widowed, or never married—living alone with their biological children.

3. Single parents (male or female) divorced, widowed or never married living alone with adopted children.

4. Male or female parent living alone with children and spouse incarcerated, deserted, or moved away.

Single-mother families are by far the most common (87%) of one-parent families, but fathers raising their children alone are found much more often—1.4 million in 1995—today than only a few decades ago (Levine & Pittinsky, 1997).

Blended Families

Most divorced and widowed persons remarry, and different kinds of family units emerge from remarriages. In some cases, a single adult joins an already existing single-parent family to form a stepfamily, and in others, an adult with his or her own children joins a partner with children to form a **blended** or **reconstituted family**. Each year about one-half million children in the United States experience a remarriage of their custodial parents (Hetherington & Stanley-Hagan, 1995; Reid & Crisafulli, 1990). Several studies near the end of the 20th century (Edin & Lein, 1997; Mason, 1998) reported that this family form is destined to soon be the most common in America when we include cohabiting couples with children. The following are typical arrangements in blended families:

1. Parent with children remarries a single adult to produce a stepfamily for the new partner.

2. Two parents, each with children, remarry to produce stepchildren for each other and step siblings for the children. At least one half of such new marriages produce children who are half-siblings for the existing children (Bianchi & Spain, 1996).

3. Common-law families, which are similar to numbers 1 and 2, but without marriage.

Not all parents seek marriages when realigning their living arrangements. Blended families can easily be formed without marriage, functioning exactly as married blends would. The Census Bureau in 1996 revealed that of the 3,958,000 unmarried couples sharing a household, over one third have children under 15 years of age (U.S. Bureau of the Census, 1998a). Figure 3.2 shows only blended families derived from marriages.

Adoptive Families

Most **adoptive families** function as nuclear ones, except that some of the family's children are not biological issue of either parent (though they may be related to one parent). Many families include both biological and adopted children. Adoptive families can also be single-parent—divorce occurs in adoptive families—and sometimes a single adult chooses to adopt children while foregoing marriage. In addition, some single-sex (gay and lesbian partners) families adopt children. Almost 3% of American children are adopted, and over 2% of " couples with children" fall into the adopted family category (DeVita, 1995).

Subfamilies

Though certainly not a new phenomenon, some family groupings, referred to as **subfamilies**, reside in other households for economic or protective reasons. Perhaps the most common is the young unwed mother who takes up residence with her parents or other family members. The condition is much like the extended family, except that the parent with young children is appended to and is not the central family figure in the household. For tax purposes, these units qualify for head-of-household status. We also find communal arrangements, in which two or more family groups choose to live together for economic and other support reasons (Cohen, 1992; Edin & Lein, 1997).

Foster Families

Families with **foster** children have been in existence for centuries. Dickens and other novelists allude (frequently in poignant terms) to foster home arrangements. The arrangements, both legal and informal, exist today in the United States and are increasing in many urban areas as social welfare agencies try to find suitable living quarters for orphaned, unwanted, abused, and neglected children. While sources vary in numbers of foster children, the Children's Defense Fund (1997) records 470,000 children, or a little less than 1% of our children, in foster care. At times, childless couples elect to become foster parents for children, but more frequently it is the nuclear family that extends itself to accommodate additional children. The Child Welfare League of America (1994) advances the argument that kinship must be considered first in any foster care arrangement to preserve a child's culture and family heritage.

Arrangements for foster care are most often financial contracts by which a family agrees with a state agency to accept one or more state wards for a stated remuneration. Time elements vary from several weeks for newborns, who will be placed for adoption, up to 18 years for other children. In the 19th century, foster care was often without remuneration, and families accepted children for humanitarian reasons as well as economic objectives, such as for securing help for farms or households.

Other Family Groupings

As noted, the family types discussed here occur in many specific configurations. It is also true that some children, as Figure 3.2 shows, have no organized family, living in institutions or boarding facilities that serve as a family substitute. Other family groupings involve children living in homes not headed by a parent. Significant numbers of young children live with grandparents, aunts, uncles, cousins, and even nonrelated adults. Census Bureau reports show that in 1996, over 1% of American children were in such arrangements (U.S. Bureau of the Census, 1998a). Other informal living arrangements involve runaways and abandoned children who have escaped social agency notice and have adapted to temporary homes that provide the basics. These arrangements are always fragile and extralegal.

The family types discussed in this chapter all exist to some degree across the United States, and while quality of child rearing varies with individuals, all family structures can be viable. It is more than likely that you know people who belong to several of the above-noted patterns, as perhaps you do yourself. Economics and social pressures in our country ensure that diversity in family arrangements continues, and transformations from one type of family to another occur daily in thousands of homes, as happened in our opening vignette. One positive result of this continuing transformation is the acceptance now found in our society for a multiplicity of forms, which was not present a generation ago.

Diversity also is a challenge for professionals working with families. As an educator, you must come prepared with knowledge, communication and interaction skills, and an ability to accept differences. Think of how you will work for consensus with the myriad groupings as you help your community educate its children.

SOCIAL FACTORS RELATING TO FAMILIES

Ethnic and Cultural Factors

Physical characteristics, language, and cultural factors distinguish some families from mainstream culture in the United States and may give them a different identity. Though racial awareness has a long history in our nation, "race" labels are often unproductive, inaccurate, and meaningless (indeed, the very existence of "race" itself has come to be questioned by some). The Census Bureau still uses four "racial" categories (plus "Other"), but in 1990, when respondents had a write-in blank for "race," they wrote nearly 300 different ethnic group labels (O'Hare, 1992)! This clearly suggests that current labels provide inadequate information, but with continued reliance on census-based formulas for distributing federal aid, ensuring minority election districts (being challenged in U.S. courts now), and tracking racial discrimination, the United States seems destined to use them for some time yet.

In this text, we use the term *ethnic* to refer to the general complex of cultural and physical individual and group characteristics and use the term *cultural* to refer specifically to that complex of created, linguistic and societal, nonphysical characteristics that distinguish societies and groups. We feel that reflecting on ethnic identification instead of focusing on "racial" lines and characteristics is more productive because it more accurately represents the wide demographic palette in the United States. This focus is certainly more helpful for educators and community workers whose task is to support all children's development. Table 3.1 gives statistics for the major ethnic groups in the United States.

Until the 1970s, American schools and communities operated mostly on the basis of assimilating different cultural and ethnic minorities and language groups into the mainstream Anglo-American culture (Tiedt &

Table 3–1   U.S. Population by Race and Ethnicity in 1998

Total U.S.	270,933,000
Non-Hispanic White	195,474,000
African American	32,791,000
Asian & Pacific Islander	9,892,000
Native American & Eskimo	2,007,000
Hispanic	30,769,000

Source: U.S. Bureau of the Census website
www.census.gov/population estimates/May 1999.

Tiedt, 1998). Since the 1970s, the concept of cultural pluralism (discussed in chapter 2) has taken root. A large number of schools and communities currently subscribe to the idea of recognizing the positive contributions and qualities of the numerous cultural groups in the United States and using them to build a stronger society. Most professionals accept the notion that diversity can produce strength (Gonzales-Mena, 1998; Hildebrand et al., 1996).

Applying this acceptance notion in communities and schools means emphasizing a multicultural curriculum that promotes positive multiethnic relationships among children, school personnel, parents, and community. As a teacher, you must be prepared to occasionally alter your curriculum to accom-

Schools are stronger when teachers recognize the contributions of different cultural groups in our society.

modate special cultural characteristics and qualities and to make adjustments in discussions and interactions with parents. Among these are minority versus majority ethnic/cultural status and the presence in your class of children belonging to bilingual and interethnic families.

Minority Status

The United States, whose population was once predominantly of West European Caucasian (white) ethnic derivation, has expanded swiftly in the past century to include numerous ethnic and cultural groups. At the beginning of the colonial era, the Eastern seaboard colonists were mostly Europeans, with a tiny minority of African Americans. A large group of Native Americans, indigenous to the continent, existed as a separate and parallel cultural complex.

The minority population in the United States reached 27% in 1995 and is growing rapidly (DeVita, 1995). Minority families are common in all but a few of the 50 states. In Figure 3.3 you can see that African American, Asian, and Hispanic minorities will grow much faster than the Caucasian population in the decades ahead. Minority children currently account for over 30% of our total school population, and 22 of the 25 largest city school systems have over 50% minority students. Census projections indicate that by 2030, one half of our school-age children will be minorities. We will soon need a descriptive term to replace *minority*.

The concentration of minorities across the United States is very different. Hispanic, Native American, and Asian families are concentrated more heavily in the western and southwestern United States; African Americans are concentrated in the southern United States and in urban areas nationwide. Six states have arrived at or are nearing a 50% minority population (U.S. Bureau of the Census, 1998a), which means that Euro-Ameri-

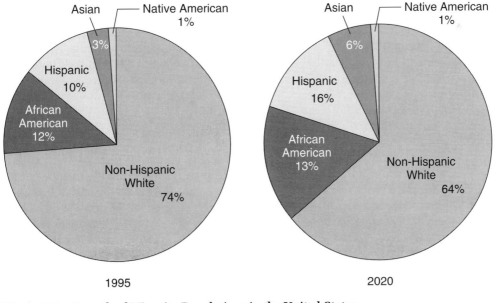

1995   2020

Figure 3–3   Growth of Minority Populations in the United States.
Source: U. S. Bureau of the Census, Current Population Report P25-1104 and projections, 1995.

cans are approaching minority status in some parts of our country.

Educational orientations, expectations, and learning styles vary within all families, and many minority families have favored and even encouraged different learning strategies (Hrabowski et al., 1998; Webb et al., 1999). Schools and communities must recognize that people have different ways of knowing and acknowledge that some differences are beneficial. As a teacher, you will be called upon to accommodate these different cognitive styles. Chapter 7 includes more information on different learning styles.

Bilingual Families

Bilingualism and linguistic differences are far more common for American children than is generally perceived. Almost 32 million people in the United States speak a language other than English at home, and over 14 million "do not speak English well" (Federal Interagency Forum on Child & Family Statistics, 1998). Bilingual school programs have been developed in response to the growing numbers of linguistically different children. In recent years, bilingual education has been most closely associated with teaching Hispanic minorities, but programs exist for over 90 other minority groups in U.S. schools (McNeil, 1996).

Approximately 3.6 million students in the United States show a need for special linguistic assistance in order to participate in a public school curriculum. But less than 10% of that figure actually are in bilingual programs (McNeil, 1996). These statistics are significant for communities and schools where concentrations of non-English-speaking families live and work. Particular problems in communication and general acceptance do appear, and since English is the language of instruction in most schools, children with less than full fluency are in some ways handicapped. During the 1990s,

we found a backlash against bilingual instruction and funding for the programs (Rose & Gallup, 1998). For example, California in 1998 approved a referendum that virtually bans bilingual education in that state. One of your challenges will be to support children and families with different language backgrounds. This challenge forms another basis for school-home-community discussion and action.

Interethnic Families

Since interethnic and intercultural marriages are becoming more common, more children with parents of different ethnic backgrounds attend American schools today. *Population Today* (Intergroup Married Couples: 1998, 1999) notes that 5% of all U.S. married couples are of different racial/ethnic groups. One frequently finds in the popular press descriptions of the changing racial diversity in the United States, and this indicates a gradual homogenizing of our population. This notion is supported when one finds 4% of all births nationally as "mixed race" and much higher proportions for Asian and Hispanic groups (DeVita, 1995). One new magazine, *Interrace*, published in Atlanta, is aimed particularly at this increasing group of Americans. More than anyone else in recent years, Tiger Woods, the young golfing phenomenon, drew attention to multiracial backgrounds by labeling himself "Cablinasian."

Since different ethnic groups generally hold differing cultural expectations, interethnic families will have different perceptions about culture and their child's participation in school and community. Through adoptions, some families are rearing children from a culture different from that of the adoptive parents, and many of those parents are interested in preserving features of the adopted child's heritage. Other families will have a multiethnic makeup as a result of remarriage or combinations of parent and child ethnicity.

Culture and ethnicity are family characteristics. As the United States becomes more culturally and ethnically diverse, professionals need a stronger grasp of the range of multicultural interests. The history of race relations in the United States has seldom been positive, and most minority-group children have felt the stings of racism and ethnocentrism. If children from our various ethnic groups are to succeed, they need to know and feel that schools and communities want them to succeed.

SOCIOECONOMIC STATUS OF FAMILIES

While the United States is reputed to be a classless society, most sociologists point out that indeed we do have a several-tiered system in our country that defines a social class structure closely related to socioeconomic status (SES). Social classes are not easily portrayed, because there are overlaps, but in general, class standing is based on the occupation, income, education, and values of the parents in a family. Figure 3.4 diagrams the social classes generally used to show the organization of American society.

Historic Class Descriptions

The upper class in the United States parallels the aristocracy in other societies. These families have inherited wealth and a close-knit circle of friends, family, and colleagues. Children from upper-class families normally attend exclusive private schools and prepare for careers in a family enterprise or in public service,

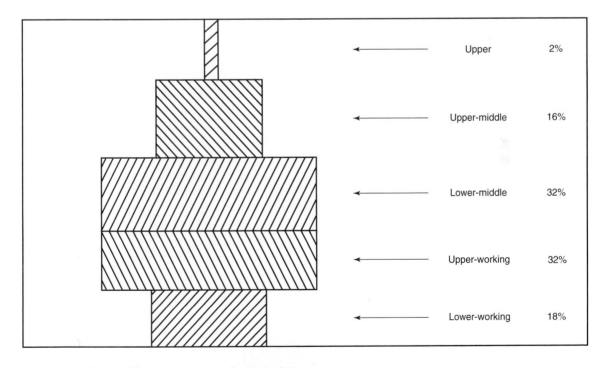

Figure 3–4   Social Class Structure in the United States.
Source: From *Society and Education* (8th ed.) (p. 7) by D. U. Levine and R. J. Havighurst, 1992, Boston: Allyn & Bacon. Reproduced by permission.

such as in politics or with social help organizations. Family heritage and "proper rearing" are very important in this class, and children are expected to conform to established standards of behavior, etiquette, and education.

Middle-class families have arrived at their status through vigorous pursuit of education and industry. Upper-middle-class American families are affluent, hardworking, and achievement oriented. They are often the community's leaders, physicians, lawyers, and successful businesspersons. A defining quality for these families is the practice of delayed gratification; children are reared from an early age to exercise self-discipline, to avoid conflict, and to wait for rewards. Families are often nuclear and closely knit. Middle- and lower-middle-class families are much the same as those of the upper middle class in ex-

pectations and desires. Less highly paid professionals are in this category, as are many successful businesspersons. This is "middle America," which enjoys many social advantages and good-quality living standards.

Upper-working-class families represent skilled tradespersons, factory workers, and other hourly wage earners. Members of this class emphasize hard work but hold education to be less important than do members of the middle and upper classes. Working-class children are encouraged to expect a life of wage earning. Economic ups and downs often affect working-class families, who are more likely to deplete their available resources. Child raising is more direct, and parents often dominate their children and frequently use physical punishments. Archie Bunker in the 1970s television series *All in the Family* made stereotyp-

In some homes, children at a young age are expected to care for younger siblings.

ical behavior attributed to this class well known to the rest of the viewing public.

The lower working class is made up generally of unskilled laborers, who are susceptible to layoffs and at times must depend on welfare for subsistence. Male and female roles are definitely shaped in this section of the scale, and males dominate most family decisions. Families in this class will often live in substandard housing and have poorer diets and marginal health practices. Children of lower-working-class parents are expected at an early age to develop responsibilities for taking care of their siblings and doing chores. Cramped living quarters is a trademark of those living in cities. The class is most at risk in an economy of the future, since the emerging information age has minimal opportunities for people with manual or nontransferable skills.

The Underclass—A New Dimension

Sociologists and demographers now recognize an expanding group (although not represented in the classic diagram), previously merged with the lower working class, that occupies the lower margin of our economic and social scales (Benson, 1997; Blau, 1992). The underclass comprises individuals and families locked into a debilitating cycle of poverty and despair from which they can find little escape. Underclass families subsist primarily on welfare or other government assistance, live in inferior housing or on the streets, and face lives racked by crime, deprivation, chemical dependency, and abuse. Since most individuals in this class possess little education and limited experiences, the culture of poverty spirals onward. This perpetuation of economic and social dislocation gives individuals and families little chance for working out of the chain of burdens.

Many at-risk children are in the underclass, which means that nutrition and health care are minimal and illness, disease, and abuse are common. Minority families are highly represented in this expanding group (Children's Defense Fund, 1997). The dilemma of how to help the underclass is perhaps the greatest challenge we face in our efforts to eradicate poverty (Mayer, 1997; O'Hare, 1996).

We have considerable evidence that persons move from one socioeconomic or social class group to another via education, personal improvement efforts, or successful investments. While upward movement for middle-class Americans seems almost assured, options for the underclass seem far less promising in the future. Education levels and minimal experiences as well as the neglect by mainstream America represent a fixed ceiling for this group. With welfare reform spreading across America since the mid-1990s, many families suffer more hardship (Children's Defense Fund, 1998).

Economics and American Families

The economic base of a family is extremely important for its members. It determines the family's quality of life, health care, nutrition, and living conditions as well as level of self-worth and ability to function in a community. While a majority of U.S. families maintain a high standard of living compared with the rest of the world, we find increasing numbers of families in poverty. Industrial jobs are rapidly being eliminated and are being replaced by lower-paying service employment. The effect is that real wages for most families fell 14% between 1973 and 1986 (Eitzen, 1992) and the buying power of a majority of households was even less in the 1990s (Federal Interagency Forum on Child & Family Statistics, 1998). Downward mobility, rather than upward movement, has become the pattern for more Americans in this generation. Note in Figure 3.5 that the lowest 20% and the middle 60% of households are receiving less and less of the total income distributed in our country. Dis-

Figure 3–5   Distribution of American Household Income 1974–1994.
Source: U. S. Bureau of the Census, Current Population Report P60-197, 1998.

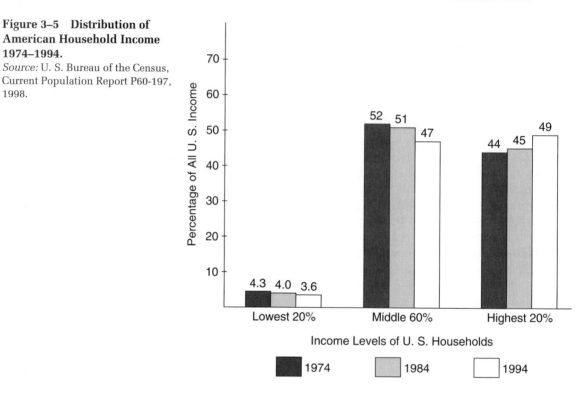

couraging as it appears, we seem destined for more bipolar economic situations.

In an attempt to ward off declining living standards, more nuclear families now have both parents working. This condition has negative implications for quality of life in these families as well as for their participation in their schools and communities. Economics correlates with risk factors; almost always, the lower the income, the higher the risk. However, we do find "**at-risk**" children in middle- and upper-income families, and teachers and other helping professionals must be alert to the frequently disguised risk factors.

Middle-Income Families. The American dream has been to achieve a middle-class style of life. The middle class are supposed to enjoy full employment and the esteem that society places on the engine that propels the nation.

For many, this scenario is true. In 1996, over 28 million families enjoyed an income above the median, one that permitted them to enjoy a better-than-average lifestyle (U.S. Bureau of the Census, 1998). However, we must keep in mind that real earnings slipped badly in the 1970s and 1980s, so to remain in the middle class, many of these families have moved to the dual-income plan in order to maintain the features of suburban living, recreational opportunity, and college education for their children (Leach, 1994).

Middle-income families often hold to traditional values. Child-rearing practices are in line with status, featuring reasoning with children in lieu of physical punishment. Communication is valued. Middle-income families are more easily involved in school and community activities, and the parents' education level usually makes communication easier. Parents' volunteer work can be considerable, and since their participation has a history, minimal instruction or organization is necessary. Members of this group can make valuable contributions to a school program in sharing talents, giving presentations, or managing projects. But time may be scarce with middle-income parents, and new demands—especially with dual-income families—can result in time constraints.

Working-Class Families.   Values in working-class families often differ from those presented in schools. While we need to draw all families into school and community service, professionals need to be prepared for communicating and interacting with people who want productive lives for their children but do not always understand school and agency strategies or objectives.

Working-class families fit well into school and community programs where tasks are carefully defined and arranged. Family members here consider themselves as "doers" and normally are willing to work avidly on specific projects or use other means to support a school or agency.

Underclass Families.   As discussed, the United States has for generations contained an underclass of families with limited education, limited employment, and a history of subsisting on government and institutional assistance. In addition, financial reversals and economic deterioration in some locations have resulted in poverty for previously working-class American families. In the closing years of the 20th century, the number of families in the United States at or below the subsistence level was growing. In 1994, statistics (O'Hare, 1996) showed almost 40 million people, or 15% of our population, below poverty level and another 25 million poised on the brink of poverty. This figure does not count the numbers in welfare-directed institutions. O'Hare

(1996) goes on to note that 22% of our children live in poverty. Minority children under the age of 6 have the highest rate of poverty, with figures ranging up to 46% (Edin & Lein, 1997). (Refer to Figure 3.5.)

Poverty is a risk factor associated with numerous negative outcomes—particularly for children. In the 1980s and 1990s, poverty became more permanent because of difficulties individuals have in breaking out of menial task jobs. The United States appears to now have a permanent underclass (poverty figures have remained almost static for over two decades), and two expanding groups at this level are homeless and itinerant families.

Homeless Families.   Some families suffering economic hardships surrender their homes, others have a history of wandering from state to state, and changes in mental health regulations in many states have resulted in previously institutionalized persons' being left to their own devices. These persons and their families make up our homeless population.

Because they have no permanent address, homeless families spend increasing amounts of time in shelters, in automobiles, or on the street (Edin & Lein, 1997). Welfare reform will undoubtedly push more families into homelessness when benefits expire in the near future (Lindsey, 1998).

Whereas the typical media image of the homeless person is the unemployed male who abuses substances and wanders the streets, statistics show that over 25% of the homeless in the early 1990s were family persons and two thirds of that number were small children (Blau, 1992; Nichelason, 1994). Numbers of homeless are difficult to ascertain, and estimates differ sharply. Conservative figures show that 200,000 American children are homeless in the course of a year (Blau, 1992; O'Hare, 1996). Edin & Lein (1997) indicate that 2.3 million children experienced some form of homelessness during the early 1990s.

Many of the parents in homeless situations are employed but work in low-end jobs that pay insufficiently for housing. Some children from homeless situations manage to attend school, although usually only part-time. Clearly, such circumstances offer a challenge to communities and schools working together to produce basic health and nutrition services for our neediest children (Swick, 1999). One positive example is the U.S. Office of Education's validating the efforts of Sandra McBrayer by naming her 1994 Teacher of the Year for her work with homeless students on the streets of San Diego. Another inspiring example is the B. F. Day Elementary School in Seattle, with special provisions for homeless children (Quint, 1994). See chapter 7 for one unexpected benefit of shelter life for some children.

Itinerant Families. Some families are highly mobile because of erratic work availability and the unsettled lifestyles of the parents. Living conditions for families in this category are normally poor, and many family members suffer from serious health problems (Educational Research Service, 1992; Morse, 1997).

Migrant workers constitute a significant block of both U.S. citizens and resident aliens who move up and down the continent during harvesting seasons. Many families are without a permanent home—children are in one location for several weeks and then move to another. Life for these children has little security, health care, or stability, and this group has greater likelihood of infant mortality, disabilities, and chronic illness of any cohort in the nation (Culatta & Tompkins, 1999). This situation poses a particular problem for schools and teachers. Children are forced into new situations every few weeks and thus have little continuity in school or community experiences. The progress in cognitive growth for migrant children is often minimal, and such children frequently become socially alienated simply because they cannot feel a part of any school or community (National Commission on Migrant Children, 1992; Tao, Khan, & Arriola, 1997). Even Start programs are attempts to bolster educational opportunity for the young children of at-risk families, and 5% of Even Start funds are earmarked for migrant families (Tao et al., 1997).

Effects of Economics

The economic foundation of a society governs in large part the socioeconomic status (SES) of individuals within that society. Financial resources for families become the most important variable in determining class status and opportunity; money governs diet, place of residence, access to health care, and chances for the future. Naturally, children's achievement in school is affected tremendously by these factors.

Early studies by Coleman (1966) showed a strong correlation between family SES and children's cognitive development and achievement. More recent studies qualify those findings. Mayer (1997) points out the importance of the psychological environment at home for child learning. Hrabowski et al. (1998) find a similar pattern, noting that parental behaviors toward children are more strongly predictive of cognitive growth than are SES variables. We may thus hope to keep alive the chance for upward mobility and improvement for economically disadvantaged populations if we can deliver to these families intervention in the form of educational programs. If parent attitudes and behaviors represent those characteristics that can be affected by education and training (Ramsey, 1998; Walberg, 1984), schools and communities have the best chance for engaging parents in the process of educating their children.

FAMILIES WITH CHILDREN WITH SPECIAL NEEDS

Special education of children with disabilities involves a large number of diverse families with children whose disabilities range from physical impairments to severe mental retardation. In spite of a generation living under regulations requiring the inclusion of persons with disabilities in all aspects of American schools, individuals and families frequently encounter conditions of discrimination and segregation. All professionals must seek to acknowledge all children according to their abilities rather than disabilities.

During the 1994–1995 school year, 5.5 million children and youth from age 3 through age 21 were served under federal programs for children with disabilities (Turnbull et al., 1999). This is a significant population (12% of children in that age bracket, according to U.S. Census Bureau statistics) and places considerable challenge and pressure on available assistive time and resources. When you work with schools and communities, you need to understand not only particular disabilities but also those problems and pressures that affect both the family and the child. Professionals must be both sensitive and supportive when working

Children with special needs are a part of all communities and cut across all socioeconomic groups.

with families of children with disabilities. (Note the legacy recounted in chapter 2.)

Families with special needs are a part of all communities, and since disabilities cut across all socioeconomic groups, affected children will be present in most schools. Diversity is always a challenge for education professionals, but often the special-needs families require more school-home-community planning to realize the most positive outcomes. While major physical disabilities are evenly distributed across SES groups, milder disabilities (called *school-identified disabilities*) occur much more frequently in poor and disadvantaged families (Educational Research Service, 1992). Poverty, lack of health care, and particularly lack of prenatal care are responsible in large part (Argulewicz, 1983; M. Wagner, 1995) for the disproportional number of disabilities in minority families.

RELIGIOUS ORIENTATION

Ethnic origin, SES, and the presence of disabilities are demographically identifying family characteristics. The family's religious affiliation is another. In their attempt to follow the letter of the constitutional requirement of "separation of church and state" in the United States, schools often try to ignore or deliberately overlook the religious affiliation of children and their families. However, religious affiliation and commitment affect how children feel about school activities, rules, and the behavior of others. Religious practices may affect interaction and participation, holiday observances, foods eaten, and gender roles. Remember that 90% of Americans indicate a religious preference (Hoge, 1996), so it is important that school and community professionals know and respect the tenets of the different religions represented in community families. A school's ability to accommodate different religious practices directly affects whether the school's work with children,

their families, and particular communities will be successful.

The religious landscape in the United States is in constant flux, as one would expect in a country where religious tolerance abides. New faith traditions emerge frequently, and membership in established congregations moves up and down (Lindner, 1998). The major faiths represented in the United States are Christian, which includes Protestants and Catholics; Jewish; and Islamic. Much smaller representations of Hinduism, Buddhism, and other beliefs are found in major U.S. cities also. All major faiths are divided into smaller sects and denominations, which vary considerably. For example, within the Protestant Christian faith are dozens of denominations, ranging socially and politically from liberal to conservative. Catholic subgroups include Roman Catholic and Eastern Orthodox. Jewish groups range from conservative Hasidic sects to liberal Reform synagogues. The rapidly expanding Islamic affiliations in the United States include Black Muslim groups and Near Eastern aggregations as well as immigrants from East Asia. Mosques are now becoming much more common in U.S. urban landscapes.

Religion helps many persons find purpose and meaning in their lives. While socioeconomic success does not seem to be linked with any particular faith, some researchers indicate a correlation between religious commitment and moral behavior (Gorsuch, 1976; Hoge, 1996). This statistic should be comforting, considering that 90% of Americans profess to having a religious attachment! However, attendance at religious services rarely exceeds 20% of the population in any one community.

The *Yearbook of American and Canadian Churches 1998* (Lindner, 1998) catalogs the religious affiliation of approximately 240 million persons in the United States indicating a religious connection. Of that figure, the membership percentage for the predominant groups is as follows: Protestant Christians, 57%;

Catholic Christians, 26%; Muslims, 4%; Jews, 3%; no religion, 9%; and other, 1%.

These figures affirm a dominant Protestant religious heritage in most areas of the United States. This stems from a strong Protestant affiliation during the colonial era of the country.

Religion directly influences how families rear children as well as how they conduct their affairs and relate to a community (Hoge, 1996). Even though the U.S. and State Court decisions (case law) carefully separate church and state, one finds a great deal in legal codes and the common law of the United States resting firmly on a Protestant ethic (Uphoff, 1993).

Applications of Religion

All religions deem sacred certain ideas, objects, or aspects of the natural world, and these dictates have implications for observance within those groups. Even though many children are only casually acquainted with the practice of their religion, it is still a background feature in their lives, and their behaviors and reactions will demonstrate that. The following are points to consider as you collaborate with parents and community members in educating children.

Observance of Holidays. Most religions have selected, faith-specific holidays. Christians celebrate Easter and Christmas; Jews celebrate Rosh Hashanah, Yom Kippur, and other holidays; Muslims celebrate Ramadan and other holidays.

Codes. Religious groups have codes relating to sexual behavior as well as to the observance of marriages, births, and deaths. Many religions have dietary laws, and children will seek or avoid specific foods at certain times or during particular occasions.

All religions have a moral code, and when we compare religious practices around the world, many aspects of the different codes re-

semble one another. Differences are in such features as locus of control. For example, Protestant groups hold that human beings are individually responsible for their behavior, but other groups teach that it is loyalty to the group that counts and that individuals must adhere to acceptable practices as defined by the religion or its authorities.

Educators and other professional community workers must adhere to the following points regarding religion (Uphoff, 1993):

1. Ascertain the religious affiliations of associates, clients, schoolchildren, and community members.

2. Learn to value all religious practices and encourage people to share information about their faiths.

3. Learn about the larger community endeavors that focus on religion or feature religious holidays.

4. Learn how to use the various religious links in the school and community to educate children and to help them develop tolerance for others.

CHANGES IN CONTEMPORARY FAMILIES

Even though the concept of family has been with humanity for millennia, we still find gradual changes in form and function of this basic unit. The focus of this text is on families in the United States at the beginning of the 21st century, but in this section we consider family evolution over the past two centuries. The comparisons will help explain how we arrived at our present situation.

From its inception to the mid-1800s, the United States was primarily an agrarian economy, and its population was mainly rural. This circumstance produced a typical farming family structure across the United States. This land-based family was often extended and often included three generations of members.

Children were considered valuable assets to families at this time, since farmwork involved numerous tasks calling for extra hands.

With the advent of the Industrial Revolution in the late 1700s and early 1800s, American economy and social structure changed rapidly. Urban centers expanded, and whole new classes of jobs in manufacturing and commerce became available. Changes in the economic situation brought changes to families. A large working class emerged. A whole new ethic was injected into family life. Roles in the home changed. The need for many hands in the home diminished, since children of factory workers did not participate in the work of parents. Homes changed from places where child rearing was linked with acquiring adult skills to environments where only child rearing took place. Education was no longer passed from older to younger family members but became something taught in "schools" as children's need for literacy and calculation skills moved beyond parental expertise.

At the beginning of the 19th century, the urbanization of the United States was well under way. Industrial and commercial development continued in rapid strides until World War II. Following the westward expansion movement in the 1880s and the general availability of railroad transport, relocation became relatively common for American families, especially after the early 1900s. Some families became isolated from relatives as they tried to establish roots in other communities and regions (Bailyn et al., 1997). It is during this period that the extended family diminished and the classic model of the nuclear family, typified by the smaller family of children living with their parents in an individual house with mother as homemaker and father as breadwinner, became more prominent. After World War II, mobility intensified as large groups moved to different parts of the country to find better living conditions. This activity and reorganization increased the prevalence of nuclear family features.

Of course there were many exceptions in early 20th-century households. Death often left single-parent families in its wake. Single parents clearly had a difficult task, so remarriages and, consequently, stepfamilies occurred frequently. Divorce was rare during this time, but foster care was not.

With World War II, new shifts in economics, a rise in minority populations, and changes in social habits had great impact on families in the United States. These changes included increasing numbers of women in the workforce, instability in marriages, a rise in divorce rates, increased mobility for families, and the rise of an influential peer group culture (Bailyn et al., 1997).

Women joining the workforce became more independent, redefined family roles, and changed attitudes for both males and females. Many couples chose separation, remarriage, and different styles of living when they found they now held different expectations of family life. Female heads of households became more common, and there were fewer adults in a family unit (see Figure 3.6).

One drawback to this phenomenon was the loss of what Coleman (1991) calls "social capital" in families—meaning adults' attention to and involvement with children's learning at home and nearby.

After a decade of legislation and social challenge with the civil rights movement, American social behavior took an even greater turn in the 1960s and 1970s. Younger Americans challenged an older order and experimented with different types of living arrangements. The more informal relationships, more flexible marriage and living arrangements, and new lifestyles of the 1990s were outgrowths from this period.

The postindustrial era arising in the United States at the beginning of the 21st century brings new directions and implications for families. The rise of massive service and communications industries shows that the im-

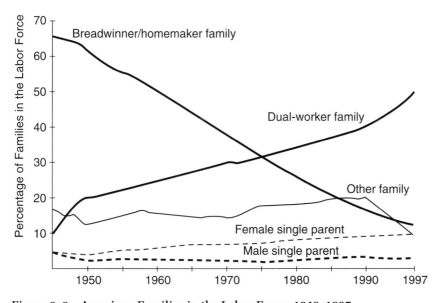

Figure 3–6   American Families in the Labor Force, 1940–1997.
Source: From "Family Members in the Work Force" by H. V. Hayghe, 1990, *Monthly Labor Review, 113*(3), 16. Reproduced by permission. And extended with information from the following: U. S. Bureau of Labor Statistics, Bulletins 2217, 2340, & 2307; plus U. S. Bureau of Labor Statistics, *News*, USDL97-195, June 16, 1997.

portance of physical labor as known to previous generations has lessened considerably. In lieu of high-energy occupations, more U.S. workers now direct their attention to service of equipment, service of living conditions, and transmittal of information and processes. More and more employees work at home and in a variety of locations (Goodman, 1993; Vosler, 1996). Thus, the notion of a constant skill for employment or an established workplace diminishes.

At the same time that the information age and the service industry blossom in the United States, we have a more noticeable differentiation in economic haves and have nots. Blue-collar workers are finding physical labor less in demand. Automation and robotics increasingly replace manufacturing jobs, and large segments of our skilled labor forces are witnessing the end of their vocations. Younger members of this force find themselves inherit-

ing a decreasing number of available jobs, while others are moved to depend on welfare. While the information age has brought acceptance of different lifestyles, it has produced abrupt economic demands that leave Americans scurrying to find new ways to cope. All of these changes have immense implications for family and home situations.

As we move into the 21st century, new attitudes concerning sexual behavior have also emerged, and cohabitation without marriage has become socially acceptable. Interethnic marriages are more common, and out-of-wedlock births appear less controversial. Communal living arrangements are more accepted, as are same sex partnerships and adoptions. Though flexibility and tolerance are key requirements for new lifestyles, educators must appreciate the need for a far more sophisticated education of all younger people. The demand on literacy, problem-solving, and negotiating skills is higher for youngsters, who as adults will be very mobile and less constrained in living arrangement and who will face frequent job changes and must constantly learn new methods for accomplishing things.

In the midst of all these changes in conditions and societal attitudes, children from various families will continue to arrive at schools and to participate in communities. The new conditions and family configurations may be very stable and supportive for young children, or they may precipitate difficulty. As in all family and community changes, children are expected to adapt to new circumstances. They usually do, but they can also suffer. Living arrangements affect children's academic participation. Teachers and other service personnel need to acknowledge such conditions and circumstances when planning for the next steps in each child's educational endeavor.

IMPLICATIONS FOR THE PROFESSIONAL

Our population landscape is changing socially, ethnically, and economically, and it will change more in decades to come. Think of this as a chal-

lenging but interesting time for you to foster healthy change in educational opportunity as you go about school or community work. It means you must figure out what the children and families in your district have to work with and where they come from. Peter Benson (1997) in his ambitious book *All Kids Are Our Kids* presents a fascinating "asset-building" vision that helping professionals will want to consider for school and social service careers.

The information in this chapter forms a base of information for the strategies you use in working and interacting with the diverse families you will come in contact with. The essential element to grapple with is understanding and accepting the wide variety of family groupings in our towns and cities. The following chapters will extend your knowledge of strategies and resources for communicating and for making curriculum decisions. But before moving on, evaluate yourself on the major foci in this chapter.

1. Language tolerance. Your attitude about persons who speak a different language or use other forms of English is important. Develop a tolerant ear for the range of English forms spo-

Teachers help celebrate diversity by joining in activities of communities different from their own.

ken in the area where you work. If possible, identify persons who use local language and arrange for them to help you with communication and with cultural differences; it helps you to avoid misunderstandings.

2. Lifestyles. Your ability to value other lifestyles is another key item. Can you see quality in other than traditional relationships and how they work for the benefit of those other individuals? Consider how you will extend the information you acquire in this chapter about different work styles, ways of earning a living, entertainment modes, and religious practices in your assigned community.

3. Diversity. Stretch yourself to see through different lenses and celebrate the diversity you find by joining the activities in a different community. For example, help plan a craft show for the neighborhood, attend different religious ceremonies, or volunteer in a classroom or on a farm. The main point is to adopt a multicultural ethic as soon as possible.

SUMMARY AND REVIEW

Family, though undergoing radical change in many communities, is still the primary social unit in the United States. Families vary in cultural, ethnic, religious, economic, and educational features, but all parents contribute in some way to their communities and to the schools where their children seek instruction and guidance.

The diversity of American families is said to be their strength. That fact can be generally interpreted as meaning that different heritages, values, work styles, and habits give a character to the American landscape that is both stimulating and an incentive for production. However, members of some of these diverse groups are in dire need of help and special support services.

Families have changed over the history of the United States and will continue to change. Ethnic proportions are constantly changing,

mobility will change, values will change, and even socioeconomic status will change. In the past, each generation has had its special problems and its particular successes. With this dynamic base, schools and communities must shape programs that can involve all participants fully and productively. Indeed, you will find in chapters 11 and 13 that many such programs have already begun.

SUGGESTED ACTIVITIES AND QUESTIONS

1. Discuss with several colleagues the family structure in your home. Has it changed over time, or has it remained constant during your lifetimes?

2. Take a quick survey of the cultural and ethnic demographics in your school or center neighborhood. How do your results compare with the overall U.S. population?

3. Have the children in one group draw pictures of their families and then tell you about the persons portrayed. How much information do you receive about the types of families these children have?

4. Find out why children that you meet in your fieldwork are identified as disabled. Was a school or center involved in referrals? Did diagnosis come through a clinic, a family physician, or another source?

RESOURCES

Books

1. Banks, J. A., & McGee-Banks, C. A. (Eds.). (1993). *Multicultural education: Issues and perspectives* (2nd ed.). Boston: Allyn & Bacon.
2. Benson, Peter L. (1997). *All kids are our kids: What communities must do to raise caring and responsible children and adolescents*. San Francisco: Jossey-Bass.
3. Consult Appendix I for a sampling of many useful children's books that focus on family diversity.

Films/Videos

1. What rights has the child? 1990. [16mm film, 20 min]. Exploration of basic rights for children worldwide. United Nations Publications, New York.
2. Our families: Our future. 1994. [Video, 58 min]. Hosted by Walter Cronkite. Visits to six family support programs. Filmmakers Library, New York.

Organizations

Council for Exceptional Children
(http://www.cec.sped.org/)
1920 Association Dr., Reston, VA 20191

National Council on Family Relations
(http://lists.ncfr.org/)
3989 Central Ave., NE., Minneapolis, MN 55400

Stepfamily Foundation.
(http://www.stepfamily.org/)
333 West End Ave., New York, NY 10023

Websites

1. http://www.census.gov The primary web address for extensive information about your own state as well as national statistics. In 2001, the information will change from projections to actual tallies from the 2000 census.
2. http://www.prb.org Population Reference Bureau entry website for objective demographic statistics and analysis of U.S. and world population studies.
3. http://www.childabuse.org National Committee to Prevent Child Abuse website. Offers services and makes connections for teachers, social agencies, and interested citizens.
4. http://curry.edschool.Virginia.EDU/go/multicultural A University of Virginia resource for educators and students interested in cross-cultural learning and information sharing.

Chapter 4

Parenting the Child

We may not have a final solution, we may not be right on all counts, but at least we know now that we cannot rely on. . .dicta about "what parents should do." Parenting practices must fit the child, the parents, and the culture.

Robert A. Hinde, 1995, in foreword for *Handbook on Parenting, Vol. 1*, p. xi.

❦

Differences in customs, modes of interaction, parenting styles, and outside influences affect the nurturing practices in all family situations. Chapter 4 discusses how these qualities and conditions affect the parent role and the outcomes of parent practices. In reading this chapter you will learn the following:

1. Parents are key persons in providing the nurturance needs of young children.

2. Parents assume particular roles in children's upbringing, and these roles have changed in recent years.

3. Although there are commonalities in parenting practices, child rearing varies among different ethnic communities in the United States.

4. Researchers have determined that parents have different parenting styles and that these styles affect children's participation in school and community life.

5. Some forms of stress affect child-rearing practices, and in recent decades, new and intensified stressors have had a great impact on American families.

All families, irrespective of the ways they are constituted, share in community life and in school life, and most of the diverse household arrangements are workable settings. Although some arrangements may be more vulnerable or sensitive, when considered against the dynamics of a particular community, each family can and does make positive contributions to children's development.

When we consider how families function, we find different customs, different priorities, and even somewhat different values. Of course, the differences signal the unique arrangements in our diverse society, but at the same time, those very different elements fuse in most families to provide coherence and stability for members in the household.

In spite of the differences, we find some constants that exist in all families with children. The first constant—the nurturance of children—precedes all others. Nurturance is followed by defined family roles, cultural patterns, interaction styles, and family experiences. Additional characteristics, such as child care arrangements, poverty, and divorce, can emerge as stressors that have an impact on the parenting quality of some family units.

NURTURANCE IN FAMILIES

Generally, **nurturance** means providing the basic necessities of life for children, but in a wider sense, it denotes general support and cultivation for the growing child. In other words, nurturance is "parenting."

Few adults are actually trained for nurturing roles, but our society anticipates certain minimums of support and effectiveness as parents rear children. The assumption is that nurturance in its general and wider sense, has been modeled by our forebears and is refined by an individual's experience and participation in society. But do these qualities exist in all U.S. homes? The range is wide indeed.

Range of Child Rearing

The nurturer accepts responsibilities not only for giving children basic physiological care, guidance, and value but also for stimulating a child's investigations of the world. The nurturing parent is one who is grounded in humane practice and who has a vision of what children can become.

Abusive behavior in families moves parenting toward the antithesis of nurturing. While few parents are so disordered in outlook as to carry out destructive acts with children, a significant number suffer lapses in judgment and vision that result in psychological and physical abuse. But even families with less desirable child-rearing habits frequently have positive qualities, such that through education, counseling, and network support these families can learn to modify detrimental practices.

Indifferent child care practices, which become a different form of abuse, stem from self-centered and impersonal temperaments. We find these qualities in persons who lack a vision and sensitivity about human relationships and who do not or cannot sense their responsibilities.

These categories represent a wide span, and within each domain we find various levels of nurturing competence. This text does not focus on the pathologies that accompany abuse and indifference; rather, we have chosen to consider the range of positive nurturance that is featured in the great majority of U.S. families. In spite of highly publicized accounts of dysfunctional family situations, the norm in all communities is that parents are nurturing and concerned for the welfare of their youngsters.

Communities and schools inherit the parenting or nurturing practices occurring in their localities, including the differences that exist within them. All families are linked with particular cultural groups, and each group will possess particular values and mores. In a community with two or more cultural groups, we find somewhat different viewpoints and probably different practices. Just because a community contains different cultural groups, however, does not mean that antagonism is present. On the contrary, quite different child-raising patterns can easily coexist and interact positively.

Features of Positive Nurturance

Maslow (1970) provided a paradigm (Figure 4–1) that shows, in ascending fashion, the scale of human needs. When related to the lives of young children, the levels of the pyramid clearly imply the need for positive nurturance. It is easy to associate the early nurturing practices of parents—and these are almost universal—with the hierarchy developed by Maslow.

Addressing Physiological Needs. Food, warmth, and shelter are bare necessities for survival, and all parents provide them, except in rare cases when families are caught in physical distress, dislocation, or mental illness. In spite of positive intentions, some financially stressed families find difficulty in providing these basics. Cold or hungry children cannot respond to any educational program. At the same time, unhealthy living climates can lead to reduced functioning, and improper food choices can lead to obesity and other nutritional problems. Teachers and other service providers must be alert to problems and deficiencies and try to arrange referrals.

Ensuring Physical Safety. The next level of Maslow's hierarchy involves safety. Ensuring a child's safety is almost instinctive with parents, and we expect this attention to be provided carefully and lovingly. While most parents are alert to dangers from natural disasters (such as earthquakes and storms), it is all too easy to overlook hidden dangers such as leaded paint, polluted areas, and unsafe objects and locations.

Providing Love. Giving emotional support and providing love are features of nurturance that occur naturally in typical families. Families express these feelings in different ways. Expressions of love range from nonverbal signals and understated expressions to effusive expressions of affection. Differences in discipline practices are linked with this area of

Figure 4–1   Maslow's hierar-chy of needs.
Source: From *Psychology for Teaching* (9th ed.) (p. 270) by G. R. LeFrancois, 1996, Belmont, CA: Wadsworth. Reprinted by permission.

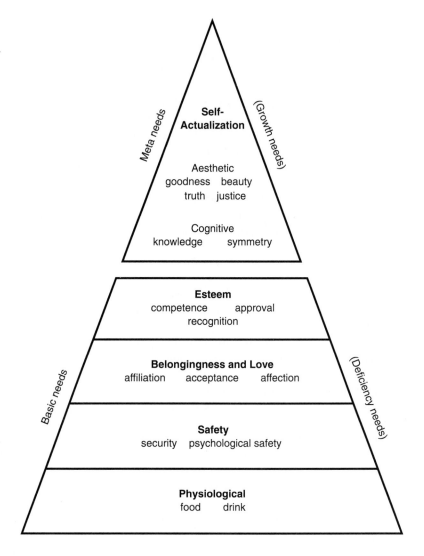

nurturance as well. Some families use physical punishments, while others depend on verbal reprimands and discussions or explanations to rechannel behavior. All practices can be effective under particular circumstances. Occasionally, parents overdo their support role and encourage dependency and immaturity in their child. Overconcern and hovering often have undesirable consequences.

Promoting Esteem, Success, and Achievement.   Families vary greatly in how they foster esteem and support the achievements of their children. Some parents campaign vigorously with and for their children while in action or at work, while others gently encourage or deliberately withhold praise until the end of an activity or a task. Parents sometimes hold children to adult standards in playing games, conversing, or socializing. This expectation can be problematic if children do not succeed, for their aspirations may be deflated. Adult encouragement and delight in partial success normally provide a foundation for children to lift their levels of aspiration.

Self-Actualization. The final level in Maslow's hierarchy is an adult level of competence, but families foster readiness for self-actualization by supporting children's growing independence and sense of responsibility and by encouraging problem solving and decision making at children's appropriate levels of growth.

FAMILY ROLES

The family at the beginning of the 21st century has crucial roles to perform. Because society evolves, these familial roles vary from those of a century ago. Lifestyles are different now, circumstances have changed, and new expectations have emerged. However, certain basics and constants of family roles, such as providing economic support, rendering emotional support, arranging socializing influences, and supplying educational underpinnings for later life, do remain.

Fulfilling these functions varies from family to family, depending on circumstance. When parents fail, other persons and agencies may assume parental capacities and duties. In all cases, the family roles are complemented by the efforts of teachers and various community agencies.

Economic Support

We recognized in chapter 3 that some families in the United States live on a few thousand dollars per year while others enjoy extraordinarily high incomes. This variable determines the type of shelter and quality of food and clothing the family acquires, as well as other family living conditions.

Even though one or more family members are employed, we find at the present that some families are challenged to meet economic minimums and must depend on government assistance and private charities to supplement the basics. Even with a robust U.S. economy, keep in mind that 23% of U.S. children under the age of 6 live in families with incomes below the poverty line (Children's Defense Fund, 1998).

Almost all families do manage their economic responsibility, marginal as it may be at times. Although many U.S. families are subsidized, most do have adequate shelter, food, and clothing. Most families also have reasonable choices in how they allot their finances. But poverty is exacerbated for families struggling to make appropriate choices, and even with meager resources, some choose fads, get manipulated into credit buying, and fail to recycle goods. In other words, the economics of parent education is not solidified. A more desperate circumstance emerges for the underclass, where the basic levels of the Maslow hierarchy are often threatened.

Social agencies are established in communities to guarantee economic basics for all families. The success rate is reasonable, but communities must pursue even more aggressively the task of monitoring and guiding basic economic practices. Welfare reform measures, while making for political happiness, have made this job more difficult. Parent education is a first step in guaranteeing better living conditions, and it is a focus that integrates well with collaborations among communities, schools, and families.

Emotional Support

Even though most parents have little training or instruction in psychological support roles,

Emotional support begins with the bonding between mother and child soon after birth.

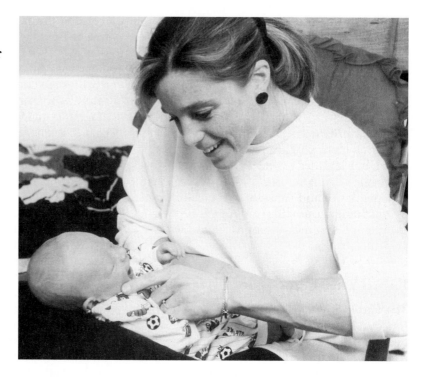

emotional nurturance for offspring appears to be a natural response. Emotional support begins with the bonding between mother and child at birth and continues as both parents seek to ensure happiness and security for their child. Most new parents emulate the parenting skills they observed and experienced in their own childhood (Bornstein, 1995). A growing problem with our present generation is that smaller families, dual-income families, and, especially, single-parent families provide noticeably less modeling of parenting behavior for their growing children (Bianchi & Spain, 1996). Where, for example, do children in a single-mother home observe fathering behaviors?

Parenting classes and clinics are available (and needed) for young mothers who are skeptical and anxious about ways to nurture their new children. Again, community policies must ensure availability of the resource and stimulate its use.

Socialization

While many agents, such as the school, the peer group, the church, and the media, are involved in socializing children, the family has the primary responsibility for beginning the process. Socialization involves values, beliefs, attitudes, family ethnic and religious identity, and gender roles. Though most families carry out this function quite readily in the preschool years (Bigner, 1998), competition for the child's perception and attention becomes more intense once school and community life become significant (Berns, 1997).

Parental impact on children's socialization was more significant in earlier periods of history. More isolated communities, less mobility, and the virtual dominance of parent figures helped values, beliefs, and attitudes become quickly inculcated in children through example and statement. In addition, earlier communities in the United States were highly idealistic in orientation, and role expectations were similar for everyone in the more restricted venues.

Patterns differ today. We have less general agreement in the United States on social mores as a result of the heterogeneous communities in which we live. Families must work harder to establish the socialization roles for their children. One successful mother determined that her children would have a better life than she had as a child. Later, explaining her success, she declared that the television shows *Leave it to Beaver* and *The Donna Reed Show* were her salvation. "I watched those shows and figured out how to manage and help my two girls." Although today we view these shows as less than realistic, this woman recognized her need to find acceptable ways to socialize her children for middle-class interactions.

Values, Beliefs, and Attitudes. Parents rarely plan to teach about values and beliefs. They do, however, model via their behavior what they value and prize and what they are willing to accept. This practice has both positive and negative aspects. If a parent rushes to help a stumbling neighbor, the idea is passed on to children; if a parent models lying, that habit is passed on. Recall that one part of Jana's story in the opening vignette in chapter 3 was the way Jana's stepmother modeled "helping neighbors." Today, Jana is raising her own children and responds to neighborhood difficulties by preparing and donating food.

In today's world, with virtually all homes bombarded by television and other forms of entertainment, many beliefs and values accrue to children just from viewing such programs (Singer & Singer, 1990; Van Evra, 1998). Parents, of course, can monitor and watch programs to discuss actions and make comments, but few take the time or show an inclination to do this. As we noted in chapter 1, the risk is the effect that influence peddlers can have on family values.

Gender Roles. Inculcating gender roles is more complex in our modern age. Both gender and parenting roles in today's society are quite different from those for earlier generations. While gender-related expectations are less rigid in many U.S. homes, most parents do seek to steer their children toward gender-appropriate behaviors.

Fathers are still, in most U.S. families, the primary economic mainstay, but that role is changing. Today, just over 60% of mothers with children under 6 are in the labor force, and 75% of mothers with children between 6 and 17 are employed (Bianchi & Spain, 1996). In many dual-career homes, mothers and fathers now contribute equally to the economic support. In addition, mothers are the breadwinners in most single-parent homes. Thus, the notion of associating economic support with one particular parent is ambiguous for many children.

Beyond economic dimensions is the changing character of family duties in the household. Historically, roles were that mother was cook and general homemaker while father was in the field or away at work. In the modern home, duties are not so clearly defined. It is still a small percentage, but some fathers now have major responsibilities for meal preparation and cleaning in addition to child monitoring. Fathers now attend childbirth and parenting classes along with their wives and take responsibility for infant care. Attempts to eliminate sexism in today's world have surely recast gender roles for U.S. society. Many quality children's books, noted in the appendix, now portray up-to-date gender roles.

All roles are disrupted when a family separation occurs. Gender roles realign when one parent or the other (or both) has custody of children. Single-parent families function in very different ways—which can be confusing for children who travel between homes periodically—and again gender role becomes more ambiguous.

Cultural and Ethnic Identity.   Children become aware of cultural and ethnic differences by age 3 or 4 (Katz, 1976; Ramsey, 1987) when they encounter differences in their communities, but family is the primary source of information. Preserving cultural heritage and learning about one's ethnic identity are very much on the minds of most minority parents today (Banks, 1996).

Disparagement of a minority heritage typically is initiated by individuals in the dominant culture. Such disparagement leads, as in U.S. history, to many minority families' denigrating their own heritage. For example, Butler (1976), in reviewing ethnic preferences in literature, found that up through the 1960s, African American children across social and geographical settings preferred White dolls and White playmates. Since 1970, however, research findings have changed, and in most studies (Butler, 1976; Cross, 1987; Ramsey, 1987), African American children now show preference for Black characters. Ethnic identity and validation are clearly in the province of the family, and feelings about self depend on accurate information and sensitive guidance (Ramsey, 1998). Some minority homes provide support and foster pride in the family culture and give training on how to overcome derogatory messages. But responsibility for enhancing heritage goes beyond family efforts. It must be supported throughout the community.

A positive feature of multicultural education efforts now practiced is that cultural and ethnic heritages are featured in schools, in communities, in museums, and in the mass media. Families celebrate differences now, and few are opposed to sharing stories about their cultural background and traditions in schools or in community programs.

Much of a family's cultural history comes in the form of stories shared and passed down through generations. A fine example in adult literature is *Roots* by Alex Haley (1976). Another is *Daughters of the Dust* by Julie Dash (1992), a story of Gullah families in Georgia's outer islands. Children's literature has many examples as well (see Appendix I).

Educational Underpinnings

As we noted in chapter 2, parents in previous centuries assumed a major role in all aspects of educating their children. Even in the 1800s, many families still attended to basic lessons for living and vocational preparation for their children. As the 1800s moved into the 1900s, however, schools expanded rapidly in scope and assumed most of the role for educating children in literary skills, calculation, and sciences. They even acquired the job of developing work habits; moral training and health education were added quickly thereafter. Today's school has expanded to include sex education, health and recreation training, vocational training, and other educational aspects formerly a family's responsibility. It appears that only the early educative tasks are retained by families in the modern United States.

The regrettable outcome of this transfer of educative roles is that most parents have lost a perspective, as well as participation, in role directing for their children about essential responsibilities. We realize that demands on today's homes are immense, but parents are still answerable for 75% of their children's waking hours during the typical school week (Robinson & Godbey, 1997). This figure on parent supervision carries a responsibility for educating, in the broad sense, that is too often overlooked.

Families can provide the support, the critical demonstrations, and follow-up for a child's learning opportunities if they are mindful of (1) the parents' logical status as guide,

(2) their intimate knowledge of the learner, (3) the influence parental status provides, and (4) the many chances for translating text material to everyday life. In fact, many parents are doing just that by home schooling their children. Chapter 7 provides more detail on home learning and on home schooling.

Changes in Functions for the 21st Century

As we have suggested, U.S. families are diverse and will continue to be. Roles for family members in the information age are still evolving, and certainly changes will continue to appear. One can only guess how different the typical family roles will be in another few decades.

Some changes in recent decades that show increased momentum are that fathers are more involved in early education, and this benefits children; mothers are more involved in sports and recreational activities, and this benefits children; but extended families continue to decrease in contact and impact, and this does not benefit children (Hoffer & Coleman, 1990). Single parenting, while normally less advantageous for children, is likely to continue at a similar pace. School responsibilities are still increasing, but efforts to share and exchange responsibilities are more in evidence (see chapter 11 for particular models of cooperation).

Children of the 21st century face a very different socializing environment from previous generations. Less constancy is found in family matters, and more and different adults are involved with children's experiences. Peer-group influences have expanded, to say nothing of the explosion in influence of the media and entertainment industries. All human service personnel must work for more joint efforts among homes, schools, and communities, where well-reasoned decisions about roles will enable families to produce quality experiences and opportunities for their children.

CULTURAL PATTERNS AND FAMILY FUNCTIONS

We are made up of increasingly different ethnic backgrounds in the United States, and we thus find differences in the ways groups perform tasks, establish values, and relate to one another (McGoldrick, 1993). Different ethnic groups frequently have varying cultural features, but we also find multiple cultures within the various groups (Bullivant, 1993; Hillis, 1996). This makes for an interesting cultural mix in our nation, and one that professionals must study and reflect on.

Ethnic background refers to the national origin or "race" of individuals, whereas **cultural** background refers to the attitudes, traditions, and customs of a certain group of people. Simply stated, culture is how a group survives in the overall society (Bullivant, 1993). Ethnicity and cultural identity frequently overlap; for example, many Native Americans continue to identify themselves by ethnic background, and culturally, these people are separate from mainstream U.S. culture. We also find groups of people with similar ethnic backgrounds who differ culturally. For example, in English-speaking regions, Appalachian Americans are very different from Oregonian ranchers or Connecticut commuters, even though they have similar roots. Their traditions, values, and attitudes place them in different cultural groups.

For simplification, we differentiate in this text between the Euro-American (White), English-speaking majority, and the main minorities in the United States, even though each contains more than one ethnic group. Table 4–1 presents the proportions of these primary ethnic groups as of 1998. While census charts include Hispanic Americans in other totals, our figure divides the population into Hispanic and non-Hispanic, then calculates totals from those two categories to avoid counting Hispanic Americans twice.

Table 4–1   Major Ethnic Groups in the United
States, 1998

Ethnic Group	Percentage of Population
African American	12%
American Indian/Alaskan	1%
Asian/Pacific Islanders	4%
Euro-American	70%
Hispanic Americans	11%
Other minorities	2%

Note: Persons of Hispanic ancestry may be of any race but
are separated from other groups for this table. *Source:*
U.S. Bureau of the Census, Statistical Abstract of the
United States, 1998.

Different ethnic groups have different patterns and different ways of communicating. It is important for professionals to examine and learn about these patterns to help when conducting discussions, when planning, and when making decisions for children.

Cultural groups are far more wide ranging than are ethnic groups, and, of course, cultures overlap. In this section, we use examples to suggest different patterns in parenting (Table 4–2). We urge readers to investigate specific cultural situations occurring in their communities.

In addition to the basics of child rearing, certain variables enter into cultural parenting. Gender roles will be important in the practices of some groups, and social class will have an effect on all parenting. Because occupations influence the actions and goal aspirations of most groups, this feature also affects parenting activities.

The values of any culture are transmitted primarily through adult modeling, directions and instructions given to children, pressures from the cultural group, and reinforcements

Table 4–2   Cultural Differences in Parenting

Group	Physical Contact	Authority	Infant Care	Family Interaction
Euro-American	Less intimacy, aggressive play encouraged.	Shared between mother/father	Babies held less. Allowed to cry it out.	Independence prized. Child does challenge. Distance from nuclear group.
Mexican American	Accepting of contact. Use of physical punishment.	Father	Babies kept close to mothers.	Solidarity with family. Feel obligated to family.
African American	Contact is encouraged. Lots of physical handling.	Mother	Babies fed on demand.	Nonverbal, minimal words used. Extended family focus.
Asian American	Restrained contact.	Father	Babies fed on demand. Constant mother/child contact.	Respect of elders. Care for family.
Native American	Close contact. No physical punishments.	Father	Continuing contact for mother and child.	Nonverbal signals. Distance is valued.

for certain serendipitous actions that each
child displays. However, you must bear in
mind that values and attitudes for many children are influenced more and more by media,
schools, and peers.

Parenting Features in Various Cultures

Child-raising practices in the United States
changed considerably during the 20th century.
We now find great variation from one cultural
group to another within the society as a whole.
The socioeconomic status (SES) of different
families within one cultural group indicates
that other differences exist as well.

For Euro-American groups, behaviorism
was valued in the early years of the 20th century, and many parents at that time valued
the principles of reinforcement and extinc-
tion popularized by psychologists. A child-
centered phase bloomed in the middle years
of the century, but in recent decades, the
swing has been toward a middle ground.
Most minority cultures in the United States
have retained their traditional child-raising
practices much more than have Euro-American families, but the proliferation of ideas in
the mass media has altered some of their
practices as well.

The following lists enumerate general parenting tendencies that sociologists and anthro-
pologists have determined exist, to some degree, within selected ethnic groups. These are
examples only; you could easily find a family
in one of the groups displaying very few of the
features noted for that group. These behaviors
are adapted from Berns, 1997; Janosik & Green,
1992; McGoldrick, 1993; and Sadker, Lerner, &
Sadker, 1999.

Mexican American

Solidarity and importance of family is
primary.

Children play with siblings rather than
with peers.

Mother is the primary caretaker and affection source.

Displayed affection is frequent and prized.

Father is the authority figure and is dominative.

Children adapt to conditions around them.

Children are accepting of others' wishes.

Family is close to extended-family members.

Children feel obligated to family.

Children are obedient and respectful to
parents.

Cooperation is emphasized more than independence.

Gender role is important.

Physical punishments are used more than
reprimands.

Parents emphasize appropriate behavior.

Children learn by observing others and
through reaction of others to their efforts.

African American

Babies are normally fed on demand.

Children relate to numerous people of the
household.

Closeness of family relationship is emphasized.

More emphasis is placed on involvement
with people than with things.

Body contact is expected and encouraged.

Mothers are physically close to children.

Nonverbal communication with young is
common.

Mothers communicate directions with few
words. Tasks are broken into small units
with brief instructions for each.

Vigorous physical movement and activity
encouraged.

Excitement and enjoyment are encouraged.

Signals, head movements, and laughs are all meaningful communication.

Mother frequently is a dominant force in the family.

Time elements (schedules, engagements, deadlines) are flexible.

Asian American

Child raising has a permissive quality.

Infants are seldom allowed to cry.

Mother has constant contact with child in early years.

Babies are fed on demand and are weaned late.

Children often sleep with parents.

Nonverbal communication is often used.

Verbal communication is not as strong in early as in later years.

Affection is indirect—love is shown in ways such as adult's sacrifices for child.

Discipline in later childhood is more strict.

Child actions are known to reflect on the home.

Father is the family disciplinarian.

Respect for older members in family is emphasized.

Native American

Children are socialized by extended as well as nuclear family.

Great respect is given to elders.

Strong bonds exist between family members.

Brotherhood, sharing, spirituality, and personal integrity are emphasized with children.

Respect is taught by example as well as by instruction.

Cooperation is highly valued, and competition is not seen as positive.

Modesty and moderation are stressed: Children are encouraged not to boast or to show emotion.

Children are not expected to be perfect but only to do what they are capable of.

Failure is not a valued concept.

Approval is given through smiles, a pleasant voice, or a pat.

Child is corrected by parent's lowering his or her voice.

No physical punishment, no verbal praise.

Frowns, shaming, withdrawal of affection are controls.

Group pressure is effectively used.

Time elements (schedules, engagements, deadlines) are flexible.

Euro-American

Overall, contemporary Euro-Americans are quite susceptible to current theories and depend less on folklore and tradition than they did in prior generations. Thus, cultural child-raising practices vary considerably over time. However, the following are observed in many Euro-American homes.

Parents prize independence in children. A downcast demeanor or shrinking behavior is criticized.

Aggressive and competitive behaviors are commended.

Parents are eager for child to make a first step.

Parents prize taking turns and being fair but also prize winning.

Children are encouraged to challenge situations and overcome problems of environment or situation.

Parents encourage children to move beyond family, to make other friends.

Gender roles are more merged; fewer gender-specific tasks or play situations are seen.

Euro-American children are encouraged to challenge situations and activities.

Mothers and fathers share more roles in family raising.

Emotional distance and private space are prized.

Less intimacy is found between parents and children.

Babies are not held as much and are allowed to cry it out.

Time elements are crucial. Heavy emphasis on speed and being on time.

Parents value verbal skills and explanations.

Parents talk through situations rather than use physical action.

You can see the differences that exist among ethnic groups, although we restate that these are general characteristics only. One can easily find homes displaying few of the practices noted in the preceding lists. Keep in mind that all these patterns serve the cultural households very well. You will note the logic if you take time to become familiar with different cultural practices.

Parenting is complex, and often factors other than a family's general orientation can influence child-rearing behaviors or any one outcome. Birth order of children, the child's age or gender, parental experiences, and parent temperament will all have an impact. All parents use a mixture of child-rearing practices, and impressions and information from other sources influence their behavior. In general, the higher the education level of parents, the more variation in practice you will find.

"Parenting involves a continuous process of interaction that affects both parents and children" (Berns, 1997, p. 141). The requirements are not always easy to meet. The numerous decisions parents must make regarding the conflicting forces that surround all homes in busy America—media, entertainment, peer culture, and other attractions—increase their responsibilities.

INTERACTION STYLES WITHIN FAMILIES

Research tells us about patterns of child behavior. We also find that child-rearing practices pertain to children's behavior as we observe it in schools and communities. The studies discussed in this section demonstrate connections between parenting and observed child behavior.

Baumrind's Classification

In Baumrind's (1968, 1971) classification, parenting styles are placed along a three-part continuum.

Parent Behaviors

1. Authoritative (democratic). Controlling, demanding, but warm. Rational and receptive to child's communication.
2. Permissive (child-centered). Noncontrolling, nondemanding, and relatively warm.
3. Authoritarian (autocratic). Detached, controlling, somewhat less warm.

In her classic study, Baumrind (1968) found that most children of authoritative parents showed independence and were socially responsible. These parents took into account their child's needs as well as their own before dealing with situations. The parents respected children's need to make their own decisions, yet they exerted control. They reasoned with their children and explained things more often than did other parents.

On the other hand, Baumrind found that those children of permissive parents frequently lacked social responsibility and often were not independent. She concluded that parents who looked at all behavior as natural and refreshing had unrealistic beliefs about young children's growth and socialization.

Baumrind found that children of authoritarian parents also showed little independence and were less socially responsible. Such parents feel children need restraint and need to develop respect for authority, for work, and for traditional structure.

The following summary illustrates the adult behaviors that produce Baumrind's authoritative style. To foster socially responsible and independent behavior in children, parents

- Serve as responsible and self-assertive models.
- Set standards where responsible behavior is rewarded and unacceptable behavior is punished.
- Are committed to the child in a way that is neither overprotective nor rejecting.
- Have high demands for achievement and conformity but are receptive to child's rational demands.
- Provide secure but challenging and stimulating environments for creative and rational thinking.

Maccoby and Martin (1983) reviewed literature on parenting styles at a later point and in general supported the findings of Baumrind. Clark (1983) also produced similar findings. His "sponsored independence" style is consistent with Baumrind's authoritative style. Later studies measuring the long-term effects of the authoritative style produced more evidence that it engenders positive adolescent behavior (Holmbeck, Paikoff, & Brooks-Gunn, 1995; Steinberg, 1991)

One caveat is needed concerning this research. Baumrind used white, middle-class parents in her study, and later, Maccoby and Martin (1983) in their replication studies found that Baumrind's conclusions did not always translate directly for poor, minority, and single-parent families. However, Clark (1983) found that the authoritative or sponsored independence behaviors in Mexican American and African American homes often made the difference between success and failure for minority children in schools.

White's Study

White (1971), in his Harvard preschool project, investigated the development of competence in children and then related his findings to their parents. White categorized the children in his study as A, B, or C, according to competence:

- A children knew how to hold adult attention, how to use adult resources, and how to express affection and hostility. They got along with others, were proud of achieving, and wanted to be grown up. They used language well and understood other points of view. They were able to concentrate on tasks and plan out activities.

- Bs were less competent than As in all the skills.

- Cs were deficient in the social and work skills, even lacking ability to anticipate consequences.

When White and Watts (1973) looked at the homes of the subjects, they found notable differences between the behaviors of the parents of As and Cs. White concluded that a parent's style of child-rearing registered an effect on children as young as ages 1 and 2.

The main differences White and Watts (1973) found among parents were in interaction, attitudes, and attending to environment. The A mothers made themselves available to children, were eager and enthusiastic about helping children, and were tolerant of messes. They set limits and were firm and consistent. The C mothers were not as involved, even when they were in contact with their children. Some were disorganized and overwhelmed by home tasks, and most restricted their children by using playpens.

Bernstein's Work

Language is a primary avenue through which a child learns to understand and function in the world. Children tend to develop language on a predictable developmental scale, but different parental language styles and interactions affect children's socialization and literacy development. Bernstein's (1972) classic study of family language patterns produced two general linguistic codes used in many homes. He termed these very different patterns: *restricted* and *elaborated*. The codes reflect two quite different styles: the position-oriented family and the person-oriented family.

Position-oriented families use a restricted code, and the family role system is positional, or object oriented and present oriented. In contrast, **person-oriented families** use an elaborated code, and the family role system is personal, or person oriented and future oriented. The following example will illustrate.

In the space of three minutes, two attractive family groups approached a traffic-light-controlled crosswalk at a busy intersection. One mother and her preschool son approached hand in hand, talking freely. Within a few feet of the crosswalk, the mother leaned down toward her son and said, "See, the light there, it's red, and we have to stop. See the cars still coming this way? We need to stay right back here, 'til we get the flashing walk light, OK? You watch and tell me when to go."

The second family, a mother, father, and little girl, approached the crosswalk and stopped. Suddenly, the mother noticed the child, who was slightly ahead, starting toward the crosswalk and yelled, "Stay here!" The girl continued to advance, and the mother screamed again, "Stay here, I said!"

The father leaped and yanked the girl back beside him. "Just stand!" the mother said, and the family waited silently for the signal to change—bodies rigid, the parents holding tightly to the child.

The second family here is position oriented and has a prescribed role system. Members have little choice, and roles are assigned according to family position. According to Bernstein, their communication is object oriented and present oriented. Aspects of restricted language code appear, characterized by syntactically simple sentences and concrete meanings. The parents communicate one thing only to the daughter—to obey a single command. There is no explanation, and sentences are simple and direct.

The open quality of the mother and son in the person-oriented family, on the other hand, permits discretion in learner performance. Communication in the open system includes judgments and reasons, and children learn to cope with abstractions and ambiguity. The elaborated language code accommodates this type of content. The mother chats with her son about the crosswalk, explaining what is happening. She engages the child in the decision making.

Teachers must know that children from a closed or position-oriented family must depend on the school and the larger community to help them in acquiring elaborated language. As a teacher, you can become a vital communication model for children from families using restricted codes, as can other children. Older children may often help their teacher communicate with new children not familiar with school language and culture. We find this situation in the following vignette.

🌾

Ms. Dansky, a White teacher, wasn't successful in getting Philip, an African American 5-year-old just entering school, to join other children in a circle. She had used a polite invitation to call all the children. When Philip didn't move,

she gave a sterner and more specific command to Philip. Then Greg, a seasoned African American 8-year-old, raised his hand and asked quietly, "You want me to get him for you, Ms. D?" Upon receiving a polite "Yes, thank you," he yelled to Philip, "Boy, get yo'r butt over here, yu' hear!" When Philip came immediately to sit beside Greg, Greg leaned to him and continued, "When she say, 'Boys and girls join me,' she mean 'come here.' And when she say, 'Philip, it's time for circle!' she mean, 'Get yo'r butt here (pats a spot beside himself) NOW!'" (Seefeldt & Barbour, 1998, p. 340)

🌾

Greg had learned not only the correct language patterns of the school but also the politeness rules. He used language and tonal patterns familiar to Philip, and he skillfully switched between the two patterns to explain what their teacher's words meant. One can appreciate the advantages that elaborated codes have in the broadening requirements of the information age.

Hart and Risley Study

Hart and Risley (1995) also concentrate on language development and demonstrate that quality of parenting and richness of linguistic environment are not necessarily bound with economic status or ethnicity. In their study of homes representing three SES levels, they discuss the linkages between young children's language development and meaningful experiences. The longitudinal study convinces us that the type and amount of interaction between parents and children results in significant differences, irrespective of SES.

According to the study, the quality of interactions in everyday parenting will center on the following five variables:

1. Amount and richness of vocabulary. The parent deliberately uses various terms,

Parents increase children's vocabulary as they verbalize terms for clothing as children dress themselves.

labels, and expressions and models their use when talking. "Yes, these are all clothes—pants, shirts, socks."

2. Sentence usage. Parents make a connection between objects and events when responding to children. "Yes, it is a doll—and it's Cindy's, so you need to give it back."

3. Discourse function. Quality of utterances used is important when parents give choices or directions to prompt child behavior. "Did you remember to hang your coat?".

4. Adjacency condition. This variable centers on the relation between parent and child behavior when the parent listens or initiates for child. Child: "Soup's good!" Parent models by: "Yes, it's *delicious*, isn't it?"

5. Valence of communications. The emotional tone given to interactions is important whether parent tries to be pleasant or not. Simply smiling and repeating a child's word: "That's right, *juice*!" has positive valence.

The positive dimension of this study shows us that parenting behaviors leading to

increased child performance can be learned and practiced. Hart and Risley assert that parents who purposely concentrate on the meaningful differences are being "social partners" with their children.

Even families that use more elaborated code systems have cause for alarm if the amount of substantive interaction does not happen (Fitzpatrick & Vangelisti, 1995). With the busy work schedules in many homes and the amount of television viewing by the entire family, substantive dialogue—which does not include directions, commands, or reprimands—between parents and children is becoming rare. Some dramatic and startling figures command our attention. Schwartz (1995) points out that in far too many homes, fathers average only 8 minutes per weekday in meaningful conversation with their offspring, and working mothers only 11 minutes! Weekend interactions aren't much better (Richards & Duckett, 1994).

Teachers alone cannot compensate for important adult-child interactions. But as you work to establish strong home and school partnerships, you can help parents become aware of this necessary area for skill development.

No two families are exactly alike, and parents have diverse ways of managing. The various features of parenting make family behaviors very complex and difficult to understand. However, we can examine general patterns of parenting, and we can relate these patterns to children's behavior. Investigators noted above, i.e., Baumrind, Clark, and Maccoby and Martin, find that neither extreme of the parenting pattern—referred to respectively as *permissive* and *dominative*—is ideal for children. Some combination or modification appears more beneficial.

Parenting styles are influenced by more than basic orientation. Professionals must be alert to the major influence of family size, family SES, levels of stress in the home, and different community characteristics.

EXPERIENCES OF FAMILIES

The life experiences of children establish a background for their performance and their contributions in their school and community. What children see, do, and sense creates a foundation for their communication patterns, perceptual styles, and modes of thinking. Children learn within the context of learning about life to comprehend messages or understand objects within the environment (Elgin, 1990; Ramsey, 1998). Likewise, children's understanding of encountered images frequently depends on explanations and connections made by nearby adults. Culture and experiential background make a significant difference in how a child learns, communicates, and participates. In addition to basic nurturing, family histories of interactions, experiences, and practices will enhance or detract from children's development potential (Scarf, 1995). When stress or problems arise, some families are resilient and display an ability to explain changes and modify problems; others are ill

equipped and cannot cope (Werner & Smith, 1998). Some adults even lean on their own children for support (Garbarino, Dubrow, Kostelny, & Pardo, 1998). Such resilience or its absence derives from many aspects of family experience. The communication style and parenting style noted earlier have an effect, but we should also consider the skill levels of parents and the type and degree of family mobility.

Skill Levels and Experience

Most parents and caregivers have extensive knowledge about their world—how to operate within society and how to evaluate their surroundings. Adults in families always pass on some bits of this wisdom to their children, some in particularly beneficial ways.

Homemakers know their living quarters and what it takes to live in a particular home. Parents have experiences in food shopping, preparation, and serving, and some have added skills with nutrition and food presentation. Involving children in food management can be realized easily in all homes and contributes a basic foundation for healthy living.

Using tools to build or repair household objects is common in many homes. Some parents have woodworking or metal-finishing skills and perhaps have home workbenches. Almost all parents have interesting experiences involving tools, and many take pleasure in their use. Adults can easily transfer these skills to interested children through demonstration (Voss, 1993), through home projects, or by children's books, such as *The New How Things Work* (Macaulay, 1998).

Some families invest a great deal of time in gardening for relaxation or for summer vegetable acquisition. The growing of green things fascinates most youngsters, and it is the beginning of a basic science that children encounter during their school years. A child's home is a nice place to meet gardening, and any growing project provides a healthy venue for discussion and interaction between adult and child. An example of "gardening" learning was demonstrated when our neighbor Melissa involved her 3-year-old son, in a very natural way, with her regular gardening, singing, and reading activities.

🌱

Having just received Inch by Inch *(Mallett, 1995) from the community's Growing Up Reading Project, Melissa and Adam immediately opened the new treasure and looked at the end pages with pictures of vegetables. Adam saw a picture of a carrot and exclaimed, "That's a carrot". "Yes," said Melissa," we've just gathered those from our garden, haven't we. See any more vegetables we have?" Adam thumbed through and found a huge beet. "Beet, yum, yum!" He turned to the end pages again and with a scooping motion began to "pick up" the imaginary vegetables, named them, and pretended to stuff them into his mouth. In the next few months, Melissa and Adam often played the "Garden Song" tape that accompanied this new book and sang the song together. It was a delight to see Melissa and Adam in the garden together the next spring weeding. Adam trotted along the rows singing, "Inch by inch. . .make my garden grow. . .inch by inch, make my garden grow." Then he stopped to pull a "weed," exclaimed, "A carrot! No, a beet! Yum, yum."*

🌱

Many games feature family interactions, and by using games as entertainment, parents can provide children with involvement in group activities, experience in strategy development and planning, positive use of aggressiveness, and practice in cooperative activities. Games are fundamentally simulations of life experiences, and children with extensive experience with various games internalize approaches for living and considerable amounts of strategy for facing interactive situations (Jones, 1988).

Storytelling plays an important part in children's growth. A large part of language development comes through stories. In families where stories are used for recreating family history, for entertainment, or as examples, listeners grow in appreciation of language and of their culture and of their family's experiences and identity. One very important manifestation is the story in book form. In a book, the story belongs to someone else, but it gives much the same satisfaction to the young child.

Parents' skill levels in these and other aspects of daily life can and should be passed on to children in the family. All community life and school programs must reinforce these practices. Given the right conditions, home management and repair, gardening projects, game playing, storytelling, and other family-oriented experiences represent marvelous resources and a worthy heritage for parents to relay to their children. Most parents are not skilled instructors but can be very successful in teaching home activities and projects. When a caregiver is engaged with a single child on a topic of mutual interest, most classroom "teaching" demands are not present. Instructor and student can go directly to the task of transferring a particular skill to the learner. Most parents are successful at this natural process, and most yearn to pass on their culture when an opportunity presents itself.

Mobility of Families

Another feature of experience that may greatly affect children's emotional and academic progress is the mobility that families have in and around their community and farther afield. Americans move more than people in other countries. On the average, between 16% and 20% of our population moves in a year (McFalls, 1998), but a great deal of that relocating is for young adults moving out of the home for work, education, or marriage. However, we

Parents' skills in daily life are passed on to their children.

find that almost 25% of the persons moving in 1996 were children under 5 (U.S. Bureau of the Census, Current Population Report P20-497,1998), and this has an impact.

High levels of residential mobility can foment social problems for adults as well as children—if the move is accompanied by significant change in quality of home life. African American and Hispanic Americans move more often than Whites because their residences are often rented (McFalls, 1998). For most relocating families, mobility comes in two forms: forced and voluntary.

Forced mobility for families produces images of migrant work, homelessness, coping with unemployment, and escaping hostile ac-

tions or trouble. Forced mobility (apart from job-related transfers) is always a reaction to undesirable conditions and contributes to erratic lifestyles for parents and their children. Isolation is implied, for forced mobility signifies that a family lacks connections or community linkages that could provide help. Whatever the conditions, a family's forced move to a new environment presents different but rarely positive learning experiences for children. Little pleasure comes with a transfer from one area to another under duress.

On the other hand, voluntary travel and relocation, local or distant, frequently connotes an improved socioeconomic situation for the family or vacation time. The important distinction is that voluntary travel involves the positive expectation of new encounters, and all family members view it as a learning experience.

Local travel can mean short trips to the country or seashore for scenic views, sports, or other recreation or trips to a museum or zoo. Arranging for the travel is a learning experience, too, for families can involve everyone in the preparations. Getting to a destination involves a certain amount of investigation, map reading, negotiating bus schedules or checking driving requirements, and anticipating difficulties. Family members learn together, and these social and educational values are important.

Voluntary long-distance travel, while involving many of the same skills, joys, and learnings, has another level of enrichment that is hard to duplicate locally. Transnational or international travel brings a family in touch with other cultures. Travelers need to adapt to new conditions, different foods, and a different sense of space. Such travel is expansive, and families gain psychic income and social capital.

The ways that families exploit surroundings, relationships, agencies, and even challenges show facets of their child-rearing practices and socializing acumen. Some families use their experience with great facility, while others do not. Such use of experience may be a function of SES, as economically privileged families have the means to do more nurturing of this type (Coleman, 1966; Jencks et al., 1972). However, we find instances of modestly endowed families enriching their children's lives through carefully developed experiences (Clark, 1983; Monroe, 1997), and some affluent families neglect needs for family interaction and experience (Metz, 1993).

OTHER INFLUENCES ON PARENTING

Parenting needs to be examined and analyzed in the context of culture and community. As noted earlier, numerous variables affect family life and may be external factors of community and environment as well as internal factors of cultural background, family demographics, and economics. Following is a brief discussion of some of these other dimensions.

Child Care Arrangements

With extended work schedules for most American families, a huge number of parents now must cope daily with requirements for temporary care of their children. At one time, when most mothers were homemakers, child care was merged with the family condition. Mothers attended their preschool-age children, welcomed their children home from school, and supervised most at-home activities.

As the new century begins, the situation is far different: Welfare reform has pushed more persons into the workforce, dual-income families grow every year, and fewer extended family members are available to share the load. For most of the 1990s, about 60% of mothers with children under 6 were in the workforce (Children's Defense Fund, 1998). This means that a huge number of young children, whether from single-parent or dual-income homes, are in some type of child care arrangement for part of every workday. It is also not uncommon for very young children to be watched over during the day by babysitters or cared for by slightly older siblings.

Preschool day care and after-school care for young children are now facts of life for most communities and will intensify as programs nationwide seek to push more welfare families into the workforce. Most day care programs have waiting lists for children who need this service, and added requests will intensify the problem. A number of schools now operate their own after-school care programs to meet some needs. We consider the topic of out-of-home care more fully in chapter 5.

Stress in Families

Adversity creeps into all families; it is a condition of living in a social matrix. Some stressors resulting from adversity are more damaging than others, but some families, through coping skills and resources, are better able than others to handle problems. While a few stressors are self-inflicted, many are unavoidable or are developed through conflicts and economic pressures and through racist, elitist, and sexist practices.

Accumulated stressors lead to at-risk situations, and policymakers, educators, and others must be mindful of this possibility. The effects of risk on the intelligence measurements of preschool children (Sameroff, Seifer, Barocas, Zax, & Greenspan, 1987) are instructive (see Figure 4–2). As the figure shows, most children seem able to cope with low levels of risk, but an accumulation of more than two risk factors jeopardizes their mental development. The message is clear: We must either prevent or compensate for accumulated risk factors.

Before ending our discussion of family functioning, we review in the following paragraphs the concerns and risk factors that cause stress in families. But bear in mind, strategies exist to deflect or accommodate stress arising from these factors.

Divorce.   As noted earlier, divorce has become common for U.S. families in recent decades and becomes more accepted with each passing year. In the 1980s, between 11% and 12% of U.S. children under 18 experienced a divorce or separation in their families each year (Hetherington & Camara, 1984; Schwartz & Kaslow, 1997). That rate continued to increase somewhat during the 1990s. We have a situation in America now that shows that 60% of our children will live in a single-parent home at some point during their minor years (Bianchi & Spain, 1996; Bigner, 1998).

Liberalization of divorce laws in most states permits couples to separate more easily and more amicably. Most family members cope reasonably well with separations, but the situation does invite risk factors as parents strive to make adjustments. Separation changes all roles in a family and alters the way a family functions. Responsibilities for the custodial parent (85% are mothers) increase

Figure 4–2   Effects of multiple risks on preschool intelligence. *Source:* From "Intelligence Quotient on Scores of 4-Year-Old Children: Social-Environmental Risk Factors" by A. Sameroff, R. Seifer, R. Barocas, M. Zax, and S. Greenspan, 1987, *Pediatrics, 79,* p. 347. Copyright 1987 by the American Academy of Pediatrics. Reproduced by permission from *Pediatrics,* Vol. 79, page 347, 1987.

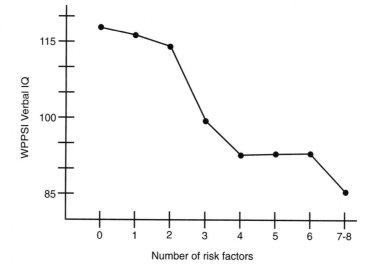

dramatically, particularly with regard to child care arrangements. There are more household tasks to care for, and financial obligations are heavier than before.

Financial Aspects of Divorce. Mothers are most often given custody of children in a divorce, but this often has dire consequences for the resulting single-parent family. Bianchi & Spain (1996) note that children in mother-only families have a 1-in-2 chance of living in poverty, contrasted with a less than 1-in-10 chance for children living with both parents. It is a fact in the United States that women in the workforce earn less than men do. And even though child support judgments are made in divorce cases, fathers frequently do not pay, and mothers must seek employment and suffer even greater management problems. Schwartz & Kaslow (1997) stress the financial problems for women after divorce: Divorce improves the economic position of men but reduces that of women and children left with their mothers.

Other Consequences of Divorce. Increased work hours for custodial parents are typical after divorce, and decreased social interaction with children results (Emery, 1988) This means less parenting. Children in the home will face increased responsibilities and less time with either parent and less emotional support after separation. A serious long-range effect of divorce is the removal of marriage models for children affected.

Behavioral changes for youngsters often result from divorce and separation. A considerable amount of research shows that the negative effects for children of divorce are sadness, fear, aggressiveness, and disobedience (Hetherington, 1988; Schwartz & Kaslow, 1997; Wallerstein, Corbin, & Lewis, 1988). But Olson and Haynes (1993) point out that many studies are slanted toward "what's wrong with single-parent families" (p. 260). They go on to demonstrate that single parenting can be successful and that strengths do exist in single-

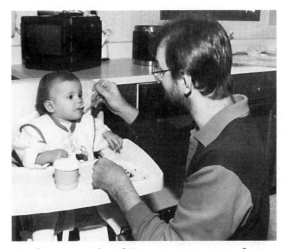

Single parent families grow stronger when healthy parent-child relationships are built.

parent homes when compared to a predivorce situation: happier environments, better custodial parent-child relationships, more commitment to a wider community, and better-run households.

Negative stereotypes continue to affect single parents and their children (Fuller, 1986; Leach, 1994). For example, teachers have a tendency to assume that problems in school are related to the single-parent home. In the foreseeable future, large numbers of young and school-age children will experience their parents' separation. Therefore, school personnel and community workers must find ways to accommodate the extra needs these individuals will have.

Support groups are available to help families after divorce through the period of adjustment, which is always one or more years. Children's literature, when sensitively read and discussed, can also help children who are caught in a family upheaval. See Appendix I for recommended titles.

Dual-Income Families. Management of household life in the dual-income home produces stress at times. While the double income enables a family to enjoy a higher standard of living, it has drawbacks, such as less time for family interaction, tighter schedules, increased dependence on child care, and fewer choices in recreation. Statistics show that 62% of children living with both parents have mothers and fathers in the workforce, and the trend increases each year (Bianchi & Spain, 1996; Center for the Study of Social Policy, 1989). In addition, over 7% of American working men and women hold two or more jobs (U.S. Bureau of the Census, 1998a), which could mean a total of four jobs for some dual-income families. Time for family interactions is of course minimal in such situations.

Poverty.   Poverty restricts many positive experiences for children and their families, because financial resources dictate quality of housing, diet, clothing, and amount of health care, to say nothing of entertainment and recreation. Most of all, poverty lays a veil of despair on families, and aspirations and a sense of self-worth become hard to elevate. Of all the stressors present in U.S. families, poverty is perhaps the greatest, and it is expanding in the lower-income brackets (refer again to Figure 3.5 in chapter 3).

Children's Defense Fund (1998) shows that in 1996 over 14 million, or 20%, of U.S. children were living below the poverty line. In addition, the record demonstrates little change in the amount of poverty in the United States during the 1990s—even with a robust economy! Other figures show that Hispanic and African American minorities dip even deeper into poverty—one third of the U.S. Black and Hispanic populations live below the poverty line (O'Hare, 1996). Figure 4–3 gives a geographic portrayal of American poverty.

Poor families are burdened with the need to survive, and their lives are punctuated with stress brought on by lack of money. Family members are frequently ill, they sustain injury more often, and they encounter hostility from numerous sources. Lives become saturated with despair, and each new plight adds to family discouragement (Benson, 1997; Dash, 1996; Polakow, 1993). The buildup of stress in poor families is extensive. Housing that is affordable to families below the poverty line tends to be in crime- and drug-ridden areas where children and many adults lead lives of sheer terror (Garbarino, Kostelny & Dubrow, 1998; Kotlowitz, 1991). Cramped living and meager diets result in illnesses that precipitate even more stress. Reversing the state of poverty in the United States requires strong community action and large investments in federal, state, and private aid to provide job training, child care, adequate housing, and health facilities to help rebuild families in besieged areas of society. Recommendations outlined in *S.O.S. America* (Children's Defense Fund, 1990), though now a decade old, continue to serve as a good starting point. Leach (1994) in *Children First* reemphasizes this challenging prescription.

Abuse and Illness.   Abuse and illness are associated with, although not limited to, the condition of poverty. Because families in poverty are in dire straits and services are meager, abuse rises in concert with the frustrations and anxieties of needy families (Bigner, 1998; Gersten, 1992; Pipher, 1996). Most abuse occurs where conditions are unpleasant and where frustrated parents and youth are in frequent conflict with other individuals, agencies, and conditions around them (Barth, 1983; Perry, 1997). Children's Defense Fund (1998) reports that between 2 million and 3 million abuse cases are reported each year, with about one third of the cases substantiated. However, caseworkers assert that only a small fraction of abusive situations is ever reported (Osofsky, 1998).

Abuse also occurs at higher SES levels; it is not restricted to the poor. Physical and sexual abuse occur at all levels of society, and

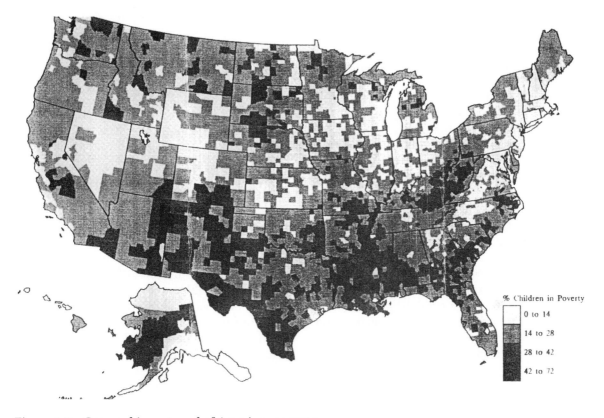

Figure 4–3   Geographic portrayal of American poverty.
Source: S. Friedman & D. Lichter, 1998. *Population Research and Policy Review,* Vol. 17(2), April 1998, p. 6. Copyright 1998 by Kluwer Academic Publishers. Reprinted with kind permission of Kluwer Academic Publishers.

although more often disguised in middle-class families, it is no less a source of stress to family members. Abuse is insidious and continues in the fabric of families for generations—too many abused children become abusive adults or victims of other abusers later in their lives (Scarf, 1995; Zeanah & Scheeringa, 1997). Abuse is an infection coloring the feelings and attitudes of families, and it destroys normal relationships for the entire family.

Illness also is a stressor in families. When a family member becomes injured or ill, numerous interaction patterns must cease or be modified. The amount of family communication can be limited, and attention to those who are not ill becomes restricted. Realignment of

the priorities in family functioning is a consequence of long-term illness. Illness of a wage earner has even greater consequences for the family. And if inadequate health care is the cause (which is the situation for one seventh of the nation's population), this particular stress gives rise to others.

Family Size.   The size of a family can actually be a stressor for the family. Children are considered a boon for most families; most mothers and fathers anticipate them eagerly. However, having too many children can have the opposite effect, and an unwanted pregnancy can become a source of frustration and contention in some families (O'Hare, 1996).

Consider Figure 4–4, which shows that poverty risk increases steadily as the number of children increases.

Large families can provide for increased peer contacts and more extensive interaction, but at the same time, the parents have fewer interactions with each child. Competition among children occurs frequently in large families, and household relations can suffer (Belmont & Marolla, 1973; O'Hare, 1996).

Children and families all are resilient to some degree. We find situations that appear depressing and even disastrous, but children survive intact and view the traumatic events in their lives, such as death, divorce, and hardship, with objectivity (Comer, 1988) and even with humor at later periods (Buchwald, 1994). This demonstrates that most children are not so fragile and impressionable that they must succumb to their problems. As a teacher, you must be mindful that as long as reasonably positive experiences and interventions punc-

tuate the lives of developing children, their outlook and perspective can be ultimately optimistic.

COMPETENT FAMILIES

Families function in a variety of ways and possess different attributes. If permitted to pursue their individual courses, most families, given reasonable conditions, develop along healthy lines and rear children who respect a home culture and get ready to meet the world. Though most are competent, many need the help and support of friends, community, and other services.

At times, stresses are too great, and a combination of cultural differences, poverty, and family problems causes family dysfunction. If this occurs, professional aid via the community is the first level of response. It may be possible that school professionals can help by advocating for the family, talking

Figure 4–4   Poverty rates of families by number of children, 1997.
Source: From Population Reference Bureau analysis of U.S. Bureau of the Census 1998 Current Population Survey, 1999.

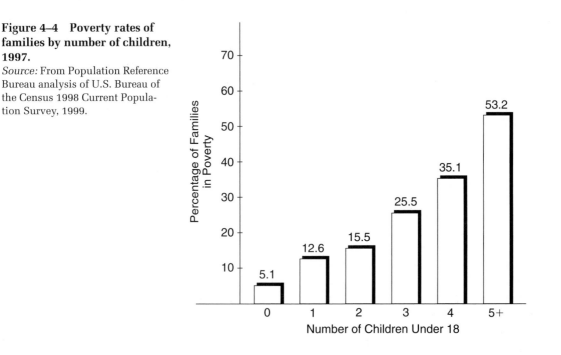

with family members, counseling the family, and listening to family members to show support. Recall the dramatic graph Sameroff et al. (1987) (Figure 4–2) provided. We can demonstrate the likelihood that problems will emerge, if risk factors continue unresolved.

Teachers need to know their students' families as well as their situations, for teachers are in a unique position to explain community to families, and vice versa. It is imperative for school personnel to take time to learn about family functioning to find out about values, ways of doing things, and methods of care that work for them. When you obtain this information, you may then find ways of integrating schoolwork with the home situation.

What is a competent family? The competent family does not require affluence, extensive education, any particular culture, or a particular setting. It will, however, display most of the following characteristics:

1. Understands and acknowledges cultural background and values that produce a heritage.
2. Views children as persons with rights and able to make valuable contributions.
3. Values open communication and constant participation among all members.
4. Clearly establishes standards, values, and expectations.
5. Values all experiences and explains situations and conditions using everyday tasks.
6. Confronts and minimizes stress.
7. Monitors children's use of time, space, and material.
8. Maintains adequate child care.
9. Maintains a "sponsored independence" style for children.
10. Manages financial resources to be above the poverty line.
11. Shows involvement and interest in children's work and activity.
12. Praises all family members' achievements and successes.

IMPLICATIONS FOR PROFESSIONALS

The parenting behaviors you have just read about are, of course, going to have an impact on the youngsters you will work with. Since there is a broad spectrum of parenting behavior and competence, you are going to find yourself working with an equally wide range of child attitudes, behaviors, and skills coming from these diverse homes. And you'll have to address what you find.

It's therefore good to understand the different parenting styles and ways that families function; such understanding will help to explain the situation of children you work with. Then, you must be prepared to understand your own attitudes toward parent dispositions, plus parents' modes of guiding and overseeing their children. This will help you adjust your own responses so that different children can feel a part of your classroom and adapt to different expectations.

Remember that many family arrangements are possible and most can be productive. Understanding the positive aspects of different lifestyles can open your own views and prevent judgmental behavior. Stereotyping children because of practices or behaviors of the family is not productive or solution oriented. Welcome all kinds of children, but understand their modus operandi and the home interaction. When you do, you will better serve them.

As you work with communities and families in any of several social settings, you will come face-to-face with the problems and stressors mentioned in this chapter that confront so many individuals. It is important to understand these and respond—though your responses may be expressions of empathy, guidance to community services, or even reports to authorities about abuse or illness. Teachers can refer persons to social agencies; community workers can refer clients to tutoring services, after-school programs, or other services that some children and families may need.

SUMMARY AND REVIEW

U.S. families are diverse in cultural and ethnic orientation. Rather than being a problem, diversity provides a richness for society and produces numerous benefits. The United States is an unusual nation today, for nowhere else on the planet do such diverse ethnic and cultural groups work together so productively. Our ethnic relations, though far from perfect, are certainly well beyond the horrific contests seen elsewhere in the world.

Different styles of interaction exist for all families. Research shows that the authoritative parent style usually produces better results for most parents and their children than does either a permissive or an authoritarian pattern.

Experience defines a family's quality of life, and some families show greater command over their environment than do others. All families pass on their culture and attempt to instruct children in profitable ways. Some families have natural gifts for instructing the young about tasks, thereby giving them added command of their lives. Mobility is one avenue for enhancing experience; another is manual work skills.

Handling stress is a mark of a family's ability to cope with surroundings. All families encounter stress, but processing and managing it are hallmarks of well-adjusted families.

Unified support and collaborations among homes, schools, and communities pay large dividends when cooperative spirits are willing to work together.

SUGGESTED ACTIVITIES AND QUESTIONS

1. Name three basic responsibilities that parents have for their children. Speculate about how you see them manifested in one child with whom you work.

2. Consider the home environments of children appearing in the vignettes in the text to this point. Deduce the parenting style of each family and discuss with colleagues why you selected the styles.

3. Select two families represented in your classroom or community setting. What appear to be the social and cultural influences affecting them? Are there differences? What do you infer about the education of children in these families?

4. Observe a parent interacting with his or her child in a library. Observe a similar situation in a supermarket. What circumstances do you think account for any differences you see?

RESOURCES

Books

1. Bigner, J. J. 1998. *Parent-child relations: An introduction to parenting.* 5th ed. Columbus, OH: Merrill/Prentice Hall.
2. Vosler, N. R. 1996. *New approaches to family practice.* Thousand Oaks, CA: Sage Publications.
3. Consult Appendix I for a sampling of useful children's books related to parenting.

Films & Videos

1. Step Program video package with resource guides, handbook, and videos. 1998. Examples: *Understanding yourself and your child; Listening and talking to your child.* American Guidance Service, Circle Pines, MN.
2. *I am your child: The first years last forever.* 1997. [Film, 60 min]. Produced by GMMB & A, Washington D.C.

Organizations

1. National Association for the Education of Young Children.
   (http://www.naeyc.org/)
   1509 16th Street, NW, Washington, D.C. 20036
2. Family Resource Coalition
   (http://www.frca.org/)
   230 N. Michigan Avenue, Chicago, IL 60601
3. American Association for Marriage and Family Therapy (http://www.aamft.org/)
   1133 15th Street, NW., Washington D.C. 20036

Websites

1. http://www.Ed.gov/NCES/ National Center for Education Statistics. General information on status of education in the U.S.
2. http://megaskillshsi.org/ Dorothy Rich's link to thousands of ideas and activities on home and school projects.
3. http://family.com/ Family Network home page with resources on most family concerns.
4. http://www.talkingwithkids.org A website that encourages parents to talk with children earlier and more often about sex, violence, and substance abuse. Sponsored by Children Now and Kaiser Family Foundation.

Chapter 5

Preschool Experiences and Out-of-Home Care

Ithel Jones, Florida State University

Today parenting is seen as shared not only between mother and father, but also with other caregivers.

(Elkind, 1995, p. 12)

🖋

Out-of-home care has become the customary experience for over 60% of U.S. children today. This chapter examines the need, scope, and effects of out-of-home care on children and their families. In reading this chapter, you will learn the following:

1. The need for preschool and child care services has grown, and securing quality child care is critical for families.

2. Quality child care makes a significant difference for young children and their families.

3. Different preschool and child care options are available for families, each reflecting different purposes, although these options are limited by cost, location, and availability.

4. Though state regulations govern the operation of child care centers, considerable variation exists in the quality of out-of-home care.

5. Many factors exist that promote quality in a child care program.

6. The preschool and child care curriculum is enhanced when collaboration exists between homes and child care centers.

🖋

Mr. McGee, Tina's father, is a bit surprised not to see Mrs. Holden in her office as he enters the child care center. The assistant smiles a welcome and says that Mrs. Holden is with the infants because an extra lap is needed. On the way to the 3-year-old room, Tina urges her father to stop and watch the fish in the tank. A mother watching the fish exclaims, "We've been stopping here lately, too. Just watching seems to help Janda relax before starting the day. Mrs. Holden did tell me what a boon this tank was, and I can see it."

Upon entering the classroom, Tina notices that Billy is crying loudly! Martha is holding him and saying, "Mama is coming to the phone, and she'll talk with you." Tina goes over to Billy, pats him, and says kindly, "It's okay!" She then puts her coat in her cubby and hurries over to her friend Claire at the water table to do some pouring. In the meantime, Billy's mother is on the phone, and her voice appears to be quieting Billy. As Mr. McGee waits to talk with Martha, he smiles at Felicity, who is seated on the floor with two other children reading. Several children are working at the table while Miranda pours juice. Martha turns to Mr. McGee, who asks if all is okay. "Oh, yes. Billy does take change hard. His dad brought him today for the first time, and now he seems uncertain about his mama. I got her on the phone, and she's reassuring him."

"Good," replies Mr. McGee. "I just need to remind you that Tina's grandmother will be picking her up this afternoon. Tina knows this, and I put it on her chart."

"O.K. Just remember to let them know at the office on your way out."

Mr. McGee kisses Tina goodbye, saying, "Remember, Grandma will pick you up this afternoon 'cause Mommy has to work late."

As Mr. McGee leaves the building, he greets the toddler teacher starting her first outing of the day. Five toddlers are happily seated in their cart for an excursion along the sidewalk to look in the shop windows. Mr. McGee thinks, "I remember how Tina enjoyed those cart rides. This is such a wonderful center. The staff is so great, and everyone seems to enjoy the kids. Boy, we were lucky to find such a center so near home."

🖋

Quality child care makes a difference for families, and the McGees reflect the changes now taking place within American families. Tina's parents are both professional and believe it important that Mrs. McGee continue her career. They represent what Elkind (1995) calls the post-modern family, in which most parenting for very young children is provided by the mother, sometimes with the father's assistance, and by other caregivers. Since Tina's arrival at this center, Tina's family has been blessed. Though the cost of care is high, this center has provided a consistency of caregivers and a safe environment. Many families use the center even into the school years, since it has extended-day programs.

Most families needing child care are not so fortunate. *Kids Count Data Book*, (Annie E. Casey Foundation, 1998) states that a University of Colorado study in 1995 reported that of 400 child care centers studied, only 14% were rated developmentally appropriate, and 40% were deemed a potential threat to children's health and welfare! Yet quality care is a must for parents who rely on others to assist in the care of their children, as it is for society in general.

The number of children being educated and cared for outside the home has increased dramatically over the past 25 years. In 1973, about 30% of children under the age of 6

Quality child care is reflected when children enjoy excursions to view shop windows.

needed child care, and now approximately 65% of children under 6 participate in some form of nonparental child care or early childhood education program (Children's Defense Fund, 1998). This growth trend in out-of-home care has been driven by increases in numbers of women in the workforce, changes in family structure, and parents' desire to provide children with preschool educational experiences. In turn, obtaining high-quality affordable child care is critical for families today, since raising children has become a collaborative effort between parents and other caregivers (Elkind, 1995).

Out-of-home care includes many different arrangements—family day care, home care, center care, nanny care, babysitting, preschool education, and after-school care. These different terms relate to the age of the child, the setting where care is provided, and the purpose of providing out-of-home care. (*Day care* and *child care* are perhaps the most frequently used terms by parents and professionals to describe out-of-home care practices.) These various out-of-home care options all have the potential to provide critical experiences that can positively support children's growth and development.

In chapter 5 we trace the changes that have led to increases in the number of children being cared for outside the home. In addition to discussing the extent of out-of-home care, we outline the varieties of child care arrangements. We also consider the various regulations that affect the cost and quality of child care and discuss the components of quality care. Further, we demonstrate that child care arrangements provide a curriculum of learning experiences and that collaboration between the home and preschool or day care center enhances those experiences. Throughout the chapter, we make references to the effects of out-of-home care on the education and well-being of young children and their families.

HISTORY OF CHILD CARE

Out-of-home care is not a recent phenomenon. Historically, some form of shared child care has always been practiced in the United States.

In the early years of our country, extended families lived together or nearby. When mothers found it necessary to go to work, they usually arranged for the child care to be done by some female relative (Scarr, 1998). Since most of these caregivers had some commitment to the well-being of their relative's child, quality of care was rarely a concern. In the early part of the 19th century, industrialization changed all this. As families moved from rural areas to cities and immigrants flooded into this country to work in factories, women needed to work to help support the family. Child care centers were opened in Boston, New York, and Philadelphia in the first half of the 19th century to provide care for children during the long hours their parents worked (Seefeldt & Barbour, 1998). Most of these centers were custodial in nature, providing the basic needs of food, shelter, and some supervision; some centers did provide instruction for both children and families. Certainly the purpose of the centers was to provide support for needy families (Berns, 1997). Such care continued into the 20th century as a result of the Great Depression and World War II. In 1933, under the Works Progress Administration (WPA), day care centers were funded both to provide care for children whose parents went to work and to create jobs for unemployed school personnel.

Then during World War II, the need arose for industrial workers. Because men were away at war, women left their homes to work in factories. This effort was supported by the federal government and defense factories by creating child care centers. Under the Lanham Act, nearly 300,000 children were enrolled in child care centers. When the war ended, however, most working mothers returned to their homes, and the child care centers closed.

During the 1950s, the nuclear family was much more common than it is today. The usual family arrangement at that time was for the father to work outside the home while the mother cared for the children. Thus, exclusive parental care of infants and young children was particularly common.

The economic boom of the 1950s increased consumer demands for goods and services, and in turn, this left many jobs open to women. Gradually more women became employed outside the home. Then, as new attitudes concerning the roles of men and women at home and at work emerged during the 1960s, the trend for women to enter the workforce increased. The trend continues to this day.

During the 1970s, as increasing numbers of families searched for child care, there was little support from either the government or the private sector. It was true that Head Start, a federally supported early childhood development program, was a new initiative serving almost 400,000 low-income children. At the same time, people expressed concern regarding the quality of child care centers that did exist. Concerns ranged from the lack of training and low wages for child care providers to inadequate health and safety standards (Children's Defense Fund, 1998; Keyersling, 1972). Indeed, this is a concern that has continuously been expressed to this day.

During the past 20 years, there have been significant increases in support for families needing outside child care. This support comes in the form of partnerships between parents, the public sector (federal, state, and local governments), and the private sector, including businesses and charitable organizations. A major initiative of the late 1980s was the Act for Better Child Care, which established what is known today as the Child Care Development Block Grant (CCDBG, 1990). Under this program, the federal government in 1995 invested over $935 million in child care needs. These funds were used for child care services for low-income families and for activities to improve the quality of child care.

Government support for child care also comes in the form of tax-based subsidies. For example, since 1976, a federal tax credit has allowed families to recoup some out-of-home care costs for their children. These tax-based subsidies are designed to assist individuals in covering the costs of child care and encourage employers to address child care needs. The largest tax-based subsidy for child care is the Child and Dependent Care Tax Credit, and it is estimated that in 1995 it provided $2.8 billion to working families. This amount far exceeds federal spending on other programs such as the Child Care and Development Block Grant.

In the 1990s, Head Start continued to provide child development, early education, social, health, and nutrition services to low-income families. At present, Head Start serves approximately 800,000 children at a cost of over $3.5 billion. In addition, the Early Head Start program provides comprehensive child and family support services to families with infants and toddlers. Despite the significant increases in federal resources devoted to child care, Children's Defense Fund (1998) emphasizes the urgent need for increases to support adequate and affordable child care.

Recent legislation (PL 104-93) modifying welfare reform has further highlighted the need for child care. Under the 1996 Personal and Work Opportunity Reconciliation Act, welfare is no longer an open-ended entitlement. Essentially, this law eliminates the guarantee that child care help will be provided to families on welfare (that really need such support) to participate in work or job training. The Temporary Assistance for Needy Families (TANF) block grant repeals Aid to Families with Dependent Children (AFDC) by increasing the ability of states to mandate work for mothers who receive public assistance. Essentially, this legislation gives states discretion to choose which families to assist and what services to provide. Clearly, this legislation will result in dramatic increases in the number of working mothers, thus increasing the demand for preschool education and out-of-home care.

A potential consequence of this legislation is that more families will participate in education and training activities and enter the workforce. In turn, this could lead to increases in the number of children needing care. A related possibility is that reduced child care funding could lead a large number of families to rely on relatives or friends for informal child care, although this is not a feasible option for all families.

Currently, an increasing number of states are developing child care policies so as to allow poor mothers to work. Several states, including Illinois, Wisconsin, and Colorado, have allocated additional funds for child care assistance by guaranteeing child care assistance to all families below a particular income level. In some states, where funds are not available, persons qualified for assistance find themselves on waiting lists. Professionals need to be concerned that providing states autonomy to make decisions regarding the needs of children will not necessarily lead to improvements in the

Federal legislation has stimulated development of services and programs for infants and toddlers and their families.

availability and quality of out-of-home care (Annie E. Casey Foundation, 1998).

Other federal programs that provide significant sources of income for child care and early education are the Individuals with Disabilities Act (IDEA, 1990) and Title I of the Improving America's Schools Act. IDEA established an entitlement for special education services to children ages 3 to 21. Under this act, preschool grants are provided for children ages 3 to 5. Furthermore, grants for infants and toddlers can be used to develop and implement early-intervention services for children under age 3 and their families. Gradually, these services have become part of the mainstream child care and early education system.

NEED FOR OUT-OF-HOME CARE: AN AMERICAN DILEMMA

In about three weeks, Renata and her partner Gregg anticipate the birth of their third child. They are excited about the prospect of having another child and have been preparing for their new arrival. Yet they are feeling anxious, too, because they wonder how they will cope with the additional financial burden. Renata currently works as office manager for a legal firm. When she is working, her 18-month-old daughter Evelyn is cared for by a kindly, grandmotherly neighbor, Mrs. Carlson, at a cost of $75 per week. Her 4-year-old son Josh attends a nearby church-affiliated day care center at a cost of $80 per week. Neither facility is licensed, but both are in the neighborhood and are supervised by caring personnel.

Renata and Gregg have carefully considered their options. "If we have to pay out another $70 a week for child care," suggests Renata, "it'll hardly be worth my while going out to work. I'm not sure Mrs. Carlson will want to take both the new baby and Evelyn, and the

center at church won't take Evelyn until she's potty trained!" Renata said.

"Yeah, but we need the extra money, and you really like what you do," replied Gregg. Renata is unsure, though. She ponders for a moment and thinks to herself, "What with paying out over $200 a week for child care, we're only going to have a little bit left over! I may as well stay at home and look after the children myself. Boy, we really do have some tough decisions to make."

In a recent survey of America's cities, child care was listed as a pressing need for children from birth to age 5 by 74% of all respondents (Meyers & Kyle, 1996). Unlike the past, when a parent at home provided child care, the current situation is that most families leave their children in the care of someone else. And like Renata and Gregg, families often find themselves in a dilemma when quality care is expensive and hard to find.

Though there are many and varied reasons for seeking out-of-home care, we next discuss three major reasons and the accompanying dilemmas for primary caregivers.

First, many families, like Renata and Gregg, rely on incomes from both parents. In some cases, mothers and fathers work outside the home to increase their standard of living, or the family structure has changed and single moms are the sole supporters of their children. According to a 1990 report, almost two thirds of mothers work to keep their families out of poverty (Scarr, Phillips, & McCartney, 1990). Welfare reform since the late 20th century is making this demand even greater. Renata and Gregg already find they must rely on two different types of care: a kindly neighbor who earns a little extra money and church-related care. Although both types of care can be excellent, many like them are only custodial; that is, the children are supervised and their basic needs are met, but the needed social and cognitive stimulation that most children require may not exist.

For some working mothers, a career is important, and the dual role of homemaker and worker is very satisfying. Further, for many women, leaving a career to care for young children can lead not only to loss of income but also to limited promotion prospects and decreased opportunities for advanced training. (This happened to Carla, a mother contemplating returning to welfare, described in the vignette later in the chapter.) Increasingly, mothers report that they are satisfied with their multiple roles. For many parents, having a rewarding and satisfying career helps them in becoming better parents. We should remember, too, that those who choose to work to advance their careers often have more options. They have a greater income, and like the McGees, they can afford a variety of child care situations for their children.

A second reason for increases in demand for child care is based on the premise that the infant and preschool years are important times for cognitive development. Recent brain research has emphasized the importance of appropriate stimulation during these years for young children's development (Education Commission of the States, 1996). Many parents want quality child care programs to give their children such educational opportunities. A widespread belief is that increasing emphasis on physical, social-emotional, and intellectual education in the child care setting provides a better start for future schooling. In centers that are certified, programs are required to have not only a healthy and safe environment but also one that assures intellectual and emotional stimulation. Staff turnover is expected to be low and well-trained personnel to be present.

The third reason for extra demands for child care is to intervene with problems of economically disadvantaged children. A number of programs are based on an **intervention** approach and offer comprehensive care in the form of education, health, and social services for at-risk children. Such programs usually offer parent education classes on such topics as nutrition, infant care, and discipline in addition to classes that teach reading and math skills. Head Start, Even Start, and Early Intervention programs all provide such offerings free of charge to families who meet the poverty or special needs guidelines. However, few of these programs offer full-day care, and when welfare families cease to qualify for benefits, they are faced with trying to find affordable care for their children as a substitute for the intervention program.

NATIONAL DATA ON PRESCHOOL EXPERIENCES AND OUT-OF-HOME CARE

According to the National Center for Educational Statistics (NCES, 1996), in 1995, the United States had 21 million infants, toddlers, and preschool children under the age of 6. Of the 21 million children, about 12.9 million, or 60%, had working mothers. The child care arrangements for the 12.9 million children were as follows: 30% were enrolled in center-based programs, 21% were in family child care programs, 17% were cared for by grandparents, and 9% by other relatives. The remaining 22% were cared for by one or the other of the working parents (Casper, 1996). Figure 5–1 shows this distribution as of 1995.

The percentage of children receiving nonparental care increases with the age of the child. Forty-five percent of children under age 1 were in some form of regular child care. In contrast, almost 78% of 4-year-olds and 84% of 5-year-olds were in child care on a regular basis (Casper, 1996).

Current data highlight some other interesting trends concerning child care arrangements. For example, the number of children receiving nonparental care increases as household income increases. And, of course, chil-

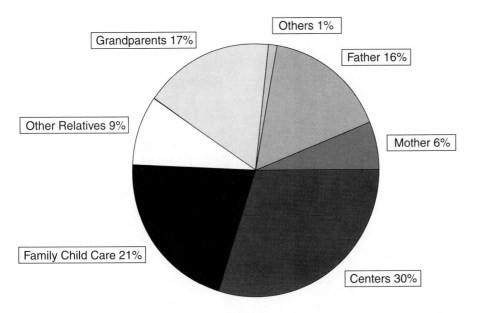

Figure 5–1   Primary child care arrangements used by families with employed mothers for preschoolers.
Source: Who's Minding Our Preschoolers? by L. M. Casper, 1996, Washington, DC: U.S. Bureau of the Census, Current Population Reports, P-70, no. 53.

dren are more likely to receive out-of-home care when their mothers are working. Eighty-eight percent of children whose mothers work full-time and 75% of children whose mothers work part-time receive regular care from persons other than their parents. This contrasts with only 32% of children whose mothers are not in the workforce.

A significant trend in out-of-home care over the past 30 years has been the shift from home to center-based care. In 1965, only 6% of U.S. children were cared for in centers. By 1993, this had increased to 31%. During the same period, there was also a gradual decline in the use of relatives, sitters, and parents. By 1993, of families with employed mothers, approximately 20% of infants and 25% of children from 1 to 2 years of age were enrolled in child care centers. Similarly, approximately 40% of 4-year-olds attended child care centers on a regular basis.

Other trends concerning out-of-home care are associated with family income levels and the mother's educational level. In general, participation in out-of-home care increases as family income increases. For example, only 50% of children in families with incomes of less than $10,000 receive care from persons other than their parents. In contrast, 77% of children from households with incomes of $75,000 or more are cared for by persons other than their parents. Similarly, children whose mothers graduated from college are more likely to be cared for by persons other than their parents than children whose mothers did not complete high school.

Clearly, economic factors play a role in the type of out-of-home care selected by parents. Those families, like the McGees, with sufficient income are able to afford quality center-based programs. Families whose income is below poverty level will receive subsidies for

Some families are fortunate to have sufficient income to afford quality center-based care for their children.

child care, and they are eligible for programs such as Head Start or Even Start. Carla, in the following vignette, provides an example of the benefits that quality subsidized care can offer low-income families. Later, however, she becomes a victim of a system that gives few options and produces a real dilemma.

🖋

Carla's sons Tommy and Cody both attended Head Start, and Carla became an active program participant. She gained skills and confidence in herself. As a result, 2 years ago, with Tommy in school and Cody in Head Start, she took a job as a part-time administrative assistant. Her employer, pleased with her work, helped her continue her education and job

training. With her salary added to her husband's part-time work, the family got off welfare, provided for their children, and even started medical insurance.

Suddenly, things changed. This year, Carla's husband left her and provides no financial support. Carla's employer wants her to work more hours, get more training, and become a full-time employee. To continue her training and career path, Carla must find partial child care for her children. Such care is hard to find and expensive. Carla's salary increment is good, but it no longer covers her insurance payments and child care while still meeting basic needs.

Carla would be eligible for child care supplements, but when she applies, she is told

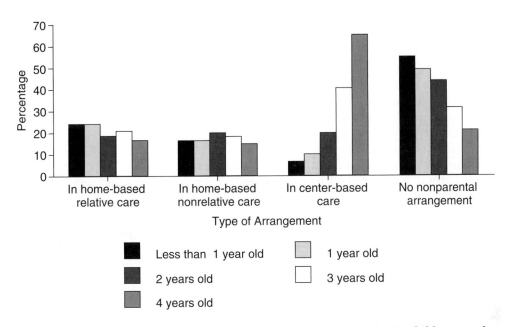

Figure 5–2   Percentage of children under 5 years of age participating in child care and early education programs on a regular basis, by type of arrangement.
Source: From U.S. Department of Education, National Center for Education Statistics, National Household Education Survey, 1995.

that all new applicants are placed on a waiting list. As Carla seeks solutions, she is told she could go back on welfare since she hasn't used up all her allotted time. Presently working full time, she makes too much money to receive any welfare support. If she works only part-time, she can get welfare benefits plus Medicaid; but her employer needs a full-time person. Her job, career training, and future employment are all in jeopardy. Carla is seriously considering going back on welfare until both children are in school full-time, but she is afraid that by then, the skills she has gained plus her employer's goodwill will have vanished.

One can see that those families whose income is above the poverty level but below $25,000 are less likely to be able to afford center-based care, as is the case with Carla in the preceding vignette. In short, these families have fewer options available to them when it comes to selecting appropriate out-of-home care for their children.

Out-of-home care is also related to a child's age. Older children are more likely than infants or toddlers to be enrolled in a center-based program. Two-year-old children are more likely to be cared for in the home of a relative or nonrelative. At the same time, we have seen gradual increases in the participation of infants and toddlers in center-based programs. The distribution of young children's regular participation in child care and early education programs is illustrated in Figure 5–2.

CHILD CARE ARRANGEMENTS

At first glance, we find many options for child care and early education available for working mothers. Yet parents have to be flexible and somewhat inventive nowadays in selecting the appropriate care for their children. And families will usually look for what they need. For example, some prefer a part-time program over a full-time program. Other parents may show a preference for an educational program over a custodial one. In all cases, however, the pressing need for working families is to ensure safe, nurturing care for their children. The various options available for parents are described in the following sections.

In-Home Child Care

In-home care allows the child to remain in the familiar surroundings of the home and community. Usually the provider is a nonrelative (though not always) and is often referred to as a sitter. Although the sitter may have received some training in child care, no regulations require such training. Qualifications are determined by the parents who employ this person. Another approach to in-home care is to hire a **nanny**, a person, usually registered with an agency, who comes with a set of credentials that indicate training in the care of young children. Often, the nanny provides live-in care for the family. Another option is to hire an **au pair**, a young person from another country who exchanges housework and child care for room and board. The au pair is usually sponsored by an agency that determines the qualifications needed by a child care provider and screens parents to ascertain the stability of a family.

Family child care is in-home care provided in the home setting of the child care provider. The provider usually is a nonrelative but may be a neighbor or a friend. In this type of arrangement, the providers adapt their own residence to accommodate usually up to six children. All states have child care licensing requirements, but not all states require family child care homes to meet these requirements.

Still, in many cases, parents will have chosen this type of arrangement because of the home-like environment. Furthermore, the fact that family child care is usually less structured than center-based programs is appealing to many parents.

Child Care Centers

Child care centers refer to out-of-home care provided in special centers that service young children from infancy to school age and even into extended-day care. However, a specific center may specialize in a particular age group or may even espouse a certain programmatic philosophy such as Montessori, Reggio Emilia, or Weikart's High Scope. Most quality centers meet the standards of a developmentally appropriate curriculum established by NAEYC criteria.

Usually, the child care center will have multiple classrooms, each arranged for a particular age range. Child care centers can be housed in a variety of locations, including community centers, church basements, and purpose-built centers. Sometimes they are sponsored by a religious organization, a public school, or a family service agency. Often, they operate as a profit-making business.

Unlike family day care programs, center-based programs provide some form of educational curriculum and staff training. Typically, child care centers are open all day, five days per week, year-round. Some of these centers provide multiple programs, including half-day nursery-like programs for 3-, 4-, or even 5-year-olds, and will do extended-day programs for kindergartners through 9-year-olds. Some centers provide transportation to and from the public schools in the neighborhood. Their long hours of operation, plus flexibility of hours, policy of serving families with multiple children, and provision of care from infancy on, are particularly convenient and appealing for differing family lifestyles.

Child care centers, providing programs from infancy to school age, are convenient and appealing for different family lifestyles.

Some parents have the option of having their children in a child care center at their place of work. These particular centers are child care facilities operated by businesses for their employees and housed in the company's building. These centers are particularly convenient for parents who work for the company and may even be part of a benefit package the company offers. Additionally, some of these centers provide space where mildly ill children can be cared for when needed and parents can visit on breaks or during lunchtime.

Before- and after-school programs offer child care services during those hours before and after school when parents are still at work.

As previously mentioned, many of these programs are a part of a child care center's options. However, in many communities, public schools are helping to meet the need for after-school child care. Other sponsors of such programs include for-profit corporations and nonprofit organizations.

No matter where they are housed, programs vary. Some after-school programs provide specific activities and such extracurricular activities as Girl Scouts, sporting activities, and even dance, art, or music lessons. In other places, after-school care is more of a babysitting service where groups of children are supervised by a few adults.

Preschool and Nursery School Programs

Preschool and nursery school programs are educational programs for children 3 to 5 years of age and are sponsored by different organizations, such as churches or community groups, as well as by private individuals. Thus, there are both for-profit and nonprofit preschool and nursery schools. Typically, these programs have a limited schedule, usually a half day for three days per week. In addition, many nursery schools operate for only part of the school year.

Parent Cooperatives. Parent cooperatives fall into the preschool category, but they differ in that parents form the governing body for these programs. Parents set policy, hire staff, and determine the curriculum, and all members are expected to contribute time on a regular basis, volunteering to do various jobs to maintain the program. Parent cooperatives, historically, are one of the preschool types of programs, with half-day play—but education-oriented—programs. Some cooperatives and nursery schools have their own centers, and often they rent space in churches or public buildings.

Laboratory Schools and University Preschools. Laboratory schools and university preschools usually serve two distinct but related purposes. First, they operate to provide child care for university students and employees. They also serve as professional centers where students and other professionals studying child care and child development can obtain firsthand experiences with children. The original laboratory schools are disappearing, often being replaced by a child care center on university property that collaborates with campus programs. Many of these centers hire students who are studying to become professionals in early childhood education or a related field.

Public Prekindergarten Programs. Some public schools offer half- or full-day programs for 3- to 5-year-old children. Prekindergarten programs are typically designed to reduce the risk of academic failure. Often they are modeled on the Head Start model but differ in that they may be open to children from a broader economic base. Some of the programs are aligned with a local high school's family planning and child development courses, and students in these classes do internships as aides in the classrooms. These programs may also be aimed at helping teenage parents remain in school while their children have a safe and caring environment. The parents not only finish their schooling but also learn parenting skills.

Head Start Programs. These programs were created in the 1960s to serve at-risk 4-year-old children and their families. The Head Start program offers educational, health, and social services for low-income families and frequently coordinates with services such as dental and health care. It also requires parents to become actively involved in their child's education; thus, the center contributes to parent education. Most Head Start programs provide half-day programs.

Other Programs

In our postmodern era, with new parents often separated from extended family and close neighbors, private and public organizations now offer a wide variety of child care/educational programs. Three such representative programs, noted in the following sections, demonstrate different purposes.

Mother's-Day-Out Programs. A mother's-day-out program is designed to offer a few hours of child care each week for mothers who need time to themselves. Such programs are often sponsored by religious organizations or other community groups. The children's program focuses on play activities and emphasizes socialization skills.

Drop-In Child Care.   Some child care programs provide a child care service for parents with part-time jobs or flexible schedules and for those parents who simply need somewhere to leave their children for a short period of time. These centers are often conveniently located in places such as shopping centers. They operate on a more casual basis, allowing parents to drop children off for short periods, and provide safe supervision in a play environment.

Infant/Toddler Programs.   As schools and communities assume more responsibility in assuring children's readiness to learn, service organizations and schools are developing infant/toddler programs. These are a combination of play groups for the youngest children and parental education for the adults. They also serve as a networking service for parents. As we discuss in other chapters, an important component of effective parenting is the "social capital" a family establishes, and these programs help young mothers establish important support systems.

CHILD CARE REGULATIONS

All 50 states and the District of Columbia have regulations concerning the operation of child care centers. In most cases, a child care center cannot operate unless it is licensed by the state. The licensing regulations are minimum standards designed to protect the safety and well-being of children, and the procedure includes regular inspections to ensure that centers are operating according to the guidelines. Licensing laws cover a multitude of issues, such as the ratio of adults to children, health, safety, and building codes, and staff qualifications. Somewhat surprising is the considerable variation across states in child care regula-

tions. Staff-to-child ratios can vary from 4 to 13 children per caregiver from one state to another. Similarly, teacher training requirements vary from state to state.

Some child care centers go beyond state licensing requirements by participating in voluntary accreditation with the National Association for the Education of Young Children (NAEYC), which administers the nation's largest voluntary accreditation system for early childhood centers. Indeed, accreditation is considered an indicator of child care quality. It is a process whereby child center administrators, staff, and parents collaborate with other professionals to determine whether the program meets nationally recognized standards of excellence.

According to NAEYC, a high-quality early childhood program is one that "meets the needs of and promotes the physical, social, emotional, and cognitive development of the children and adults—parents, staff, and administrators—who are involved in the program" (NAEYC, 1998). The following criteria address many aspects of the early childhood program:

- interactions among staff and children
- curriculum
- administration
- staff qualifications and development
- staffing patterns
- physical environment
- health and safety
- nutrition and food service
- program evaluation

The accreditation process represents a professional judgment as to whether the center substantially complies with the accreditation criteria. Centers are usually granted accreditation for a period of 3 years, during which time annual reports have to be submitted. You can see that accreditation for a child care center is an indication of quality.

FEATURES OF QUALITY CARE

Despite great diversity in child care arrangements, as well as the variations in state regulations governing their operation, there is agreement among early childhood professionals concerning quality of child care. From the parents' perspective, what is important is ensuring that their children are cared for in a safe, healthy, and nurturing environment. Consequently, child care professionals are constantly seeking ways to bring quality to their industry. Features of quality care include process and structural qualities, strong curriculum practices, positive parent involvement, and a dedicated professional staff. The following sections discuss these elements.

Process and Structural Qualities

Typically, child care quality is defined by two distinct but related components: process quality and structural quality (Kontos, Howes, Shinn, & Galinsky, 1995).

Process quality refers to the experiences children have in the child care center. *Process* refers to aspects such as adult/child interactions, children's exposure to materials, and how children interact with these materials. Parent and staff relationships are also important aspects in process quality. You can see that these components are most critical because they directly affect children's behavior and learning experiences in the child care setting. Seefeldt & Barbour (1998) summarize the important components that relate to process quality in child care programs:

1. A foundation for cognitive and language learning.

2. A foundation for developing self-esteem, self-confidence, and excitement about learning something new.

3. A foundation for developing a healthy body and physical ability.

4. A foundation for developing effective relations with peers and adults.

Structural quality refers to aspects of the child care environment, such as adult-child ratio, staff training, experience, and policy concerns. Structural quality also relates to the amount of floor space per child, amount of outdoor space, appropriate toileting and diaper-changing areas, kitchen facilities, and similar objective items. Structural quality is important because it is a precondition for favorable process conditions. That is, the structural conditions do establish a foundation for optimal process conditions.

Curriculum

Given the importance of the early years for children's physical, social, emotional, and cognitive development, it is important for child care centers to have a well-planned curriculum. The curriculum should include specific activities that meet the needs of children of all ages. In short, the curriculum offered should be broad and balanced and designed to promote children's cognitive, social, emotional, and physical development.

Each type of child care arrangement offers a curriculum that can extend the cognitive and socialization processes that have been nurtured by children's families. Such a curriculum consists of all the experiences children have while under the supervision of their caregiver, and it normally is a combination of curriculum of the home and curriculum of the school (discussed in chapters 7 and 8).

In some types of arrangements, children's experiences take on a formal nature by emphasizing the development of specific skills and concepts. All types of preschool and out-of-home care arrangements, however, provide an informal curriculum of values and attitudes that stem from the philosophical orientation and organizational arrangements of the center.

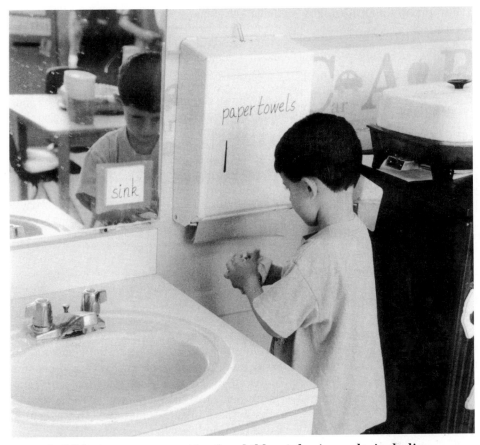

A good child care center provides for children's basic needs, including toileting and cleaning up.

Furthermore, out-of-home care is where many children first learn to interact with other children and adults, and this marks the beginning of community socialization.

Despite the fact that the various out-of-home arrangements demonstrate somewhat different philosophical orientations, we find some common curricular considerations. For example, a good child care center will provide for the basic needs of children, including times and places for eating, sleeping, toileting, and cleaning up. An inviting environment with an abundance of appropriate resources such as furniture, equipment, supplies, and toys is also important. Beyond the physical qualities of the environment, it is important that staff interact with children in a warm, caring manner. That is, the caregivers should help children create attachments by building relationships with other children as well as with their families. The extent to which caregivers engage children in conversation, ask questions, and respond to them when they speak seems to be related to a child's acquisition of cognitive and language skills (NICHD, Early Child Care Research Network, 1997).

It is particularly important for child care to provide for children's needs at each developmental stage. A preschooler will become frustrated if toys, materials, and activities are not age appropriate. Similarly, a school-age child won't feel comfortable in a preschool setting. Infants, on the other hand, need good physical care as well as continuous affection and sensory stimulation. Finally, toddlers' need for active involvement should be supported and encouraged.

Most quality programs are organized around an appropriate daily schedule. This is important so as to provide children with a sense of security. A sample schedule that might be used with preschool children is shown in Table 5–1. A well-organized schedule will provide opportunities for structured and unstructured activities, quiet times, and active play. Providing a predictable daily schedule enables children to make good use of their time, helps children feel comfortable, and thereby prevents potential discipline problems. A clear set of guidelines and simple rules is also effective in promoting and maintaining appropriate behavior.

Parent Involvement

Effective child care programs recognize the importance of parental involvement, and directors usually adopt strategies to bridge the gap between the home and the center. Most families have a strong need to be fully informed about their child's program and their child's progress within that program. In many cases, child care providers see parents as their partners. Collaboration between staff and parents facilitates continuity of experiences for young children and, in turn, enhances the potential for meeting the children's needs. Chapter 10 discusses both traditional and innovative strategies for establishing positive relationships between child care workers and parents. The following paragraphs cover some

Table 5–1   Sample Schedule of Preschool Day

7:30	Arrival	12:00	Lunch
8:00	Breakfast	12:30	Story time
8:30	Free play in learning centers	12:45	Nap time
9:00	Music time	2:00	Free play
9:30	Small-group activities	2:30	Stories and singing
10:00	Snack time	3:00	Snack time
10:30	Free play in learning centers	3:30	Outdoor play
11:15	Cleanup time	4:30	Small group activities
11:30	Story time	5:00	Cleanup
11:45	Toilet and hand washing	5:30	End of day

main points to highlight with regard to parent involvement.

Parents can become involved in their child care program in many different ways. For example, they can volunteer in the classroom or assist outside the classroom. They can become involved in such tasks as assisting with children's activities, managing paperwork, or perhaps helping to set up materials in the center. By becoming involved, parents will feel more committed and supportive of the program. Caregivers can also encourage participation by inviting parents to attend special events, such as potluck dinners or fund-raisers. What is important is that there is effective two-way communication between the home and the child care program. Some effective communication strategies include newsletters, notes, memos, and telephone calls as well as parent-teacher conferences.

Formal meetings between parents and child care providers should be scheduled on a regular basis, for such contact provides stability between home and center. These meetings provide an opportunity for caregivers and parents to exchange information about the child's progress and to discuss any concerns. It follows that if caregivers regularly communicate with parents, they will ensure that they maintain detailed records concerning children's overall progress.

Quality child care programs will keep records of children's developmental achievements as well as daily notes on a child's general well-being in such areas as sleeping, mealtime, and toileting. Some centers use checklists to record achievements, and others keep samples of children's work as the basis for periodic evaluation of progress. The information collected through observation and sampling can then be shared with parents on a regular basis.

Professional Staff

Successful child care programs rely on a team of dedicated professionals. Indeed, a well-trained professional staff is essential when it comes to quality of child care. It follows that child care staff should continue their professional growth by attending conferences and workshops, reading professional literature, and sharing ideas and information with their colleagues. In doing so, they are more likely to become committed to their profession, more satisfied with their work, and more sensitive to children.

Most quality child care programs include similar components of structure and process, curriculum, parent involvement, and professional staff, as well as a number of other characteristics. Kinch and Schweinhart (1999) report that exemplary child care programs share the following characteristics:

- *Financial resources.* Uses financial resources beyond parent fees, such as subsidies for low-income families and donations from individuals and foundations.
- *Creation of alliances.* Forges a variety of alliances with organizations to bring in additional resources. For example, a center might collaborate with a community organization on fund-raising efforts.

- *Parent education.* Seeks ways to educate parents about the value of early childhood education. In so doing, parents become better consumers and are more likely to support programs.
- *Staff benefits.* Directors seek additional salary and other benefits for their staff. In addition, they secure adequate planning time and arrange opportunities for professional development.
- *Establishment of advisory committees.* Strengthens relationships with the community by establishing a board of directors or a community advisory board.
- *Parental involvement.* Maximizing parental involvement ensures that families share information and become partners with caregivers.
- *Recognition of family needs.* Recognizing family needs and stresses and working flexibly with families make a program viable for parents.
- *Institutional structures.* Quality child care programs have institutional structures in place to promote quality, compensation, and affordability and to guarantee their future existence.
- *High standards.* High standards for quality are conveyed through established policies and clearly written standards on mission, philosophy, and educational approach.

The preceding indicators of child care quality serve to remind us that out-of-home experiences, whether at a family day care or a child care center, do provide encounters that can positively influence a child's development.

THE EFFECTS OF OUT-OF-HOME CARE

Research indicates that the quality of child care for young children is important for their cognitive and language development as well as their social and emotional development (NICHD, Early Child Care Research Network, 1997; Scarr & Eisenberg, 1993). Yet, as previously indicated, the costs of quality out-of-home care can be prohibitive for many married and single mothers. Our greatest concern, therefore, for many of our youngest children in the 21st century is not that they will be cared for at a young age by nonparental persons but that they will receive substandard child care. One can see that this means an increased number of at-risk factors for our youngest children because they get less attention and fewer chances to be read to, played with, or stimulated intellectually in low-quality centers. Negative effects of poverty can be exacerbated through child care, for though

children are in out-of-home care so that the mother may work, the mother then has the added burden of working and caring for both home and children. The added frustrations can mean that the chance of child abuse increases.

Conversely, quality care can have positive influences, for it means that children receive loving, nurturing, stimulating care and attention. Quality centers provide this care and have other positive characteristics, such as low child-staff ratio and low staff turnover, which increases the chances of strong adult/child bonding. Staff members in quality centers collaborate with parents regarding developmental issues such as eating habits, toileting, health, and peer interactions as well as

Quality centers provide stimulating activities for experiments and intellectual pursuits.

the child's general intellectual and emotional development (NAEYC, 1990).

Out-of-home care certainly influences children's lives by the quality of care provided, but it also influences parental caregiving (NICHD, 1997; Scarr & Eisenberg, 1993). For some parents, such care means freedom to pursue a career or an education. It also guides parents regarding aspects of child health services, nutrition, and importance of social and intellectual stimulation. Good care provides parents with a sense of greater security and peace of mind, and in some cases, it even alleviates stress that can invite child abuse and neglect. With parents more comfortable with quality care, a community benefits from a more committed workforce (Berns, 1997).

The finding that high-quality child care during the first 3 years of life does not place children at a disadvantage in terms of their cognitive development is particularly important (NICHD, 1997). Indeed, these and other findings suggest that children who regularly attend child care centers actually outperform—on tests of language and mathematics—their peers who stay at home with their mothers.

QUALITY, COST, AND AFFORDABILITY OF CHILD CARE PROGRAMS

After years of research, it seems that quality programs are directly linked to positive outcomes for children. Yet, we find considerable variation in the quality of child care centers. In general, quality of child care programs ranges from excellent to very low, with most being mediocre (Helburn & Howes, 1996).

The Cost, Quality, and Child Outcomes in Child Care Centers study examined over 400 child care centers and found that only 14% of children are in high-quality family- or center-based child care (Helburn 1995; Galinsky, 1994). The study also reported that 12% of children were in poor quality child care arrangements that could potentially harm their development. The majority of centers (74%) were judged mediocre.

The situation for infants and toddlers is even worse. Only 1 out of 12 infants and toddlers is in a developmentally appropriate classroom, and 40% of the classrooms are deemed potential threats to children's health and safety (Young, Marsland, & Zigler, 1997). Research on family home centers and relative child care is equally sobering. A mere 9% of such care offered sufficient quality to positively influence children's development, 56% were considered adequate, and 35% were deemed of such poor quality that children's health and development were endangered. (Galinsky, Howes, Kontos, & Shinn, 1994; Hofferth, 1991)

The low availability of quality out-of-home care is further compounded by the high cost of quality care. Though working parents may have a great variety in the types of out-of-home care from which to choose, they are limited by several factors: (1) the availability of these services in a particular community, (2) the location and operating hours of child care services, and (3) the cost and affordability of care.

In general, center-based care is more expensive than family child care homes, and the most expensive option is child care in the working parents' home. Parents can use only child care arrangements they can afford because the cost of child care can substantially reduce the parents' income (recall Renata and Gregg's situation). As a result, many parents often report that child care costs influence their employment decisions.

The average cost of child care for all families is around 8% of their income, and this is a relatively small proportion of the budget. In reality, the cost for families varies in relation to family income. Low-income families spend approximately 23% of their income on child care, whereas high-income families spend only 6%. One can see that cost in relation to family income is a major factor influencing many families' child care arrangements. We know that children from high-income families and those from families on welfare are more likely to be enrolled in child care centers. This is because high-income families are more likely to be able to afford center-based care and because children from families living at or below the poverty line can receive subsidies for child care or benefit from the services of a Head Start program. One can see that the result of this situation is the emergence of a two-tier child care system (Scarr, 1998). Both affluent and poor families have access to higher quality child care, but middle- and lower-income families are less able to afford the high-quality child-care services. As a result, many child care professionals and child advocates now campaign to make quality child care available for all working families.

IMPLICATIONS FOR PROFESSIONALS

As the preceding pages have established, most preschoolers are cared for by someone other than their parents; therefore, providing quality preschool experiences is important for both children and their parents. Early childhood educators and other professionals will want to assist and guide parents in finding the best care possible for their children.

Because of the lasting effects of the care children receive outside the home, implementing high standards for child care is essential for those of you who work with children in educational settings. It is particularly important for you to know what constitutes a quality child care program. You should then use this knowledge to collaborate with parents and other early childhood educators to implement higher standards for child care. When opportunity arises, you should support initiatives to improve child care as well as efforts to improve training and compensation for caregivers.

Finally, one of the key contributors of success at the preschool level is collaboration between families, communities, and early childhood professionals. As someone who will likely work with young children, you should consider how you will establish a relationship with parents. Communication and collaboration with the parents and families of the children you work with can enhance a program's positive impact on a child's development.

SUMMARY AND REVIEW

Child care is essential to family life in postmodern America. National surveys indicate that an increasing number of children are being cared for outside the home by someone other than parents. Children are also being increasingly cared for in formal arrangements such as child care centers.

The purpose of out-of-home care is to enable mothers to work outside the home and at the same time to enhance a child's development. Child care arrangements can range from basic custodial to highly educational. Options available for working families include in-home care, family child care, child care centers, preschools and nursery schools, Head Start programs, and parent cooperatives, among others.

Considerable variation exists in the quality of child care services, and the quality of care can influence a child's development. The operation of child care centers is governed by state regulations, and some centers strive to maintain quality by participating in an accreditation process with professional organizations such as the NAEYC. Current research suggests, however, that a large percentage of child care centers and family child care are of a mediocre standard.

Parents' choices for out-of-home care is limited by the cost and availability of services in their community. Affluent families can afford more expensive and usually higher quality care for their children. Poor families often qualify for public support for child care. Middle- and lower-income families, however, will often find it difficult to pay for high-quality child care. But quality care is essential if American homes, schools, and communities are to meet the challenge of raising healthy children in the postmodern world of the 21st century.

Quality of care is marked by both process and structural components. Quality of interaction between adults and children, a well-equipped classroom, a developmentally appropriate curriculum, a committed advisory board, and fully staffed and trained personnel are characteristics of quality out-of-home care. These traits provide the intellectual, social, and emotional environments necessary for young children's development. We have a pressing need for more quality child care services in most parts of our nation.

SUGGESTED ACTIVITIES AND QUESTIONS

1. Interview several parents who use child care services. Try to find out what they like and don't like about their child care arrangement.

2. Find a copy of your state's child care regulations. Evaluate the regulations. What are the permissible ratios of children to adults? Do the caregivers have to be qualified, and what teacher training requirements are there?

3. What are some key factors that parents should consider in making child care arrangements? Develop a checklist that would assist parents in selecting quality child care.

4. Observe a child care provider interacting with a toddler. Determine how this interaction influences the child's acquisition of cognitive and language skills.

RESOURCES

Books

1. Beherman, R. (Ed.) (1995). *The future of children: Financing child care.* Los Altos, CA: The Center for the Future of Children. David & Lucille Packard Foundation.

2. Booth, A. (Ed.) (1992). *Child care in the 1990s: Trends and consequences.* Hillsdale, NJ: Erlbaum.

Films/Videos

1. *Techniques in child care: Planning and operating quality family day care.* 1990. [Video, 49 min]. Day Care Video Programs, Boston.

2. *Let babies be babies: Caring for infants and toddlers with love and respect.* 1998. (Set of six videos totaling 2 hr plus guides.) Demonstrates best caregiving routines. Family Day Care Association of Manitoba, Winnipeg, Manitoba.

Organizations

1. National Child Care Association (http://www.nccanet.org/) 1016 Rosser Street, Conyers, GA 30012

2. National Association for Child Care Professionals (http://www.naccp.org) 207 W. Main Street, Suite 1, Christiansburg, VA 24073

3. National Association for Family Day Care (http://www.nafcc.org)   525   S.W.   5th Street, Suite A, Des Moines, IA 50309

Websites

1. http://nccic.org The website for the National Child Care Information exchange.

2. http://childcare-experts.org This website helps parents and employers access information about child development, child care, early education, family supports, and dependent care resources from experts across the country.

3. http://careguide.net A website that includes a child care directory.

4. http://www.acf.dhhs.gov/programs/ccb/ The website of the Child Care Bureau—dedicated to enhancing the quality, affordability, and supply of child care available for families.

Chapter 6

Responsibility for Educating Children

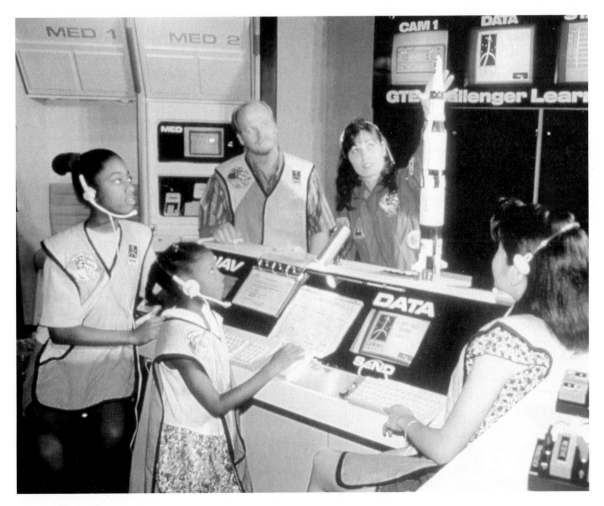

Children cannot know what is inside our art galleries and libraries if we do not take them, anymore than they can know what is in our conscience if we do not tell them.

(Leach, 1994, p. 24)

✍

Many have stated that our greatest resource is our nation's children, and more believe there is urgency in making certain that this resource is carefully and humanely developed. In chapter 6, we consider the obligations for educating American children and the people and agencies that bear the responsibility for carrying them out. In reading this chapter, you will learn the following:

1. Societal traditions convey responsibilities to families, schools, and communities for educating the young.

2. Legal requirements exist for all social settings and hold families, schools, and communities accountable for providing different aspects of education for children.

3. Society in general expects the informal or nonacademic curriculum to be arranged and fulfilled by homes and communities.

4. The formal academic curriculum, though overseen by the community, is largely the responsibility of school personnel.

5. Overlaps and even disagreements occur regarding responsibilities and obligations for some aspects of children's experience.

6. The impact of one social setting on children's education can at times run counter to the expectations of another.

7. Even with conflicts, partnerships among homes, schools, and communities are the best means for providing meaningful experiences for children.

✍

Maria had been annoyed with her son's school for a month. Tony kept bringing home from his second-grade class paper after paper with instructions for Maria to go over and practice with him. Maria felt the teacher couldn't be doing her job, because Tony never seemed to understand what the assignments were all about. One day when Tony brought home a math paper, a reading paper, and a social studies assignment, Maria had had enough. She stopped working on the meal she was preparing for her six children and gathered up a basket of jeans and sweatshirts that needed laundering and mending. With the pile of laundry and Tony, she marched the three blocks to school. Maria entered Ms. Srichan's classroom and plunked the laundry basket on the teacher's table. "You expect me to do your work? I think you should help me with mine," she remarked angrily and then marched off with Tony in tow.

✍

Whose responsibility is it to see that Tony learns his math, reading, and social studies concepts? In our opening vignette, the teacher and parent obviously are not in agreement and probably are not communicating at all.

In chapter 1, we assert that young children become what their world provides and that they learn skills to the degree that surroundings guide, entice, or motivate them. The influences and forces affecting children at the beginning of the 21st century are numerous and constant. Children encounter them in all three of our fundamental social settings: family, school, and community. As you prepare for a career in teaching or community work, it is important for you to identify and understand where and how persons in each setting assume responsibility for children's learning. You also need to understand that each institution can work in tandem or in conflict with the other two, as seems to be happening in Tony's case.

Societal expectations in the United States imply that families, schools, and communities have responsibilities for both formal and informal education and enculturation of children. Responsibilities range from instructing in basic social skills and hygiene practices to teaching the skilled manipulation of equipment to awakening children's aesthetic appreciation and reasoning ability.

Surrounding each child is a formal and an informal curriculum propelled—and also moderated—through the three social settings. Responsibility for accomplishing the objectives will overlap at times, and representatives in each setting may contend at times concerning whose prerogative it is to accomplish a particular task or objective.

In the following sections, we examine the educational responsibilities associated with each of the three social settings. We view these responsibilites both from a legal standpoint and as traditional and cultural practices found in communities in the United States. We discuss the following: (1) who determines appropriate content and experience for children's learning, (2) where we find nurturance and support for that curriculum, and (3) who governs, coordinates, and evaluates children's education.

YOUNG CHILDREN'S LEARNING

An academic curriculum is provided for children enrolled in many different types of school environments: private and public schools, preschool, and child care. A formal school's academic curriculum is constantly affirmed by school personnel as well as by laypersons, and its purpose is, in general, to help children accumulate knowledge and skill. Much of what children learn, however, actually comes from the experiences, associations, and interactions children have outside and beyond scheduled school activities. This is the unplanned, the covert, or hidden, curriculum that teachers and parents often forget about or overlook. This second curriculum is a dominant part of any child's life, and it must be related to the formal curriculum as prepared and implemented by schools (Apple, 1995; Dreeben, 1970; Giroux, 1978).

Children's interests and stage of development determine what is meaningful for children, and the stimuli and experiences that result in learning come from many forces within each child's life (Bronfenbrenner & Weiss, 1983). When we consider who is responsible for children's education, we must ascertain who has the most substantial and direct access to children's time, minds, and interests. We must take into account all of the forces bombarding children with information and experience. For example, a definite curriculum of the home exists, although we do not label it as such. It starts at birth and continues to be dominated by primary caregivers for children's earliest years. The community begins to affect children by the time they are toddlers; these stimuli increase dramatically through early childhood. School programs will begin as early as age 3 for some children, and by age 5, almost all children are involved with school curricula. Williams (1992) summarizes by pointing out that a child's knowledge comes from his or her observation of society and through playful imitation of the life the child sees around him or her.

While much of the informal curriculum is random and incidental, following normal living patterns in particular homes and communities, we find cases where some parents impose an almost academic curriculum, with definite ideas on what their children are to be exposed to and how. For instance, some parents obtain materials for teaching their children letter recognition at age 2, have prescribed reading-to-baby times, program all play with "educationally valuable" toys, and arrange selected private lessons with specialists in the arts. While the extreme of this idea invites comparisons to laboratory conditions, the underlying attitude is very much the orientation of some middle-class parents wishing to "prepare" their children for formal schooling. Without intending to stimulate the "super home," the first goal of *America 2000* (now called *Goals 2000*), which states, "All children will enter school ready to learn," actually does risk inciting parents in this category to push even further (refer to chapter 2).

Some of the informal curriculum takes place within a community and may include children's playmates, neighborhood visits and activities, community agency activities, media involvement, and recreational areas. Haberman (1992), a specialist in urban schools, underscores the case for understanding communities before attempting school curriculum reform. He notes, "The greatest indirect [impact] of communities on both education and schooling is the influence exerted by community forces on inner city families and peer networks" (p. 31).

In addition, the larger community creates an impression on all citizens, one that children feel and internalize. Communities control children's learning by (1) providing (or disallowing) opportunities in sports facilities, recreation arenas, museums and arts areas, and clinics and other health facilities and (2) supporting or challenging particular attitudes, lifestyles, and mobility patterns. The "way of doing things here" is the community ethos and therefore part of children's informal curriculum. Minority children, for example, are still very young when they encounter the attitudes and mores, whether positive or negative, of the dominant cultural group (Lightfoot, 1978).

Components of Home Responsibility

Parents and caregivers bear great responsibility for children's early learning and for the genesis of and support for the curriculum that children will use for their entire lives. Parents also have a significant role in nurturing the academic work children experience after entering school. In chapter 7, we discuss opportunities for learning in the home.

No formal or legal demands exist that require parents to instruct their children. However, common cultural assumptions regarding child rearing imply that parents will guide and prepare children for life in a community. Also, statutes concerning neglect have emerged over the years, and parents parsimonious in nurturing and guiding their children risk citations of neglect and its consequences (Seefeldt & Barbour, 1998). It is tradition, by and large, that forces parents and homes to provide the basics or beginnings of instruction. As we noted in chapter 1, American society (considered in the abstract) has, through media, health and medical advisements, and social service agencies, tried to influence families about educating and rearing children since the 1800s.

Most societies do little to formally prepare parents for rearing children, and the United States is no exception. When extended families were more common, child raising was probably more coherent. Advice was more available, community standards were more constant, and families were far less mobile (Hoffer & Coleman, 1990; Taylor, 1997). In today's society, with its matrix of ever-increasing forces producing stress, mobility, and differing home styles, child-raising practice has become less consistent and more pressured (Elkind, 1988, 1994). Daily lives now are more frenetic, and all too often families come close to abandoning responsibilities for a home curriculum in favor of that offered by the entertainment industry—a community force that is not always appropriate.

Nonetheless, expectations exist, and persons in other social settings anticipate that families will provide beginning experiences as children grow and move into the conventional school environment and the neighborhood. Goals for *Goals 2000* will certainly not be realized without significant family and community input.

What are the responsibilities of homes and child care facilities for enculturation, habits, and social curriculum content? We describe some representative areas in the following subsections.

Early Socialization Skills.   Except in cases of severe neglect, parents and other family members automatically instill in children the basics of socialization. Children early and naturally learn to greet and respond to others, recognize acquaintances, play games with siblings, and mimic and follow one another. In addition, many parents recognize the importance of educational toys and playmates in controlled situations (Smilansky & Shefatya, 1990). As noted in chapter 5, over 60% of American preschool children are in out-of-home care, and this means that socialization skills are affected considerably by events and personnel in the center. Even though somewhat more aggression is noted in children in out-of-home care, research (Clarke-Stewart, 1993; Clarke-Stewart, Allhusen, & Clements, 1995) shows that most children mature much the same whether in or out of day care. For

some children, out-of-home care is a definite benefit—the issue is the quality of care in the day care center or family day care site.

Language.   Communication skills start before age 1 and expand rapidly because of planned and unplanned family interactions and experiences. Parents echo their infant's vocalizations, indulge in naming things, and direct attention to objects, often explaining to the baby what both the parent and the baby are doing. Later literacy development includes listening to and sharing stories, practicing reading, and modeling more elaborate speech (Dworetsky, 1990; Gadsden, 1998). Literacy expands in quality child care settings as children find it necessary to communicate with different adults and with their peers. Children need opportunities to practice their newfound language skills as well as find reinforcement in a caring environment.

Exploration.   Beginning experiments with natural phenomena are common family experiences. Children's experiments with toys and

Literacy skills expand as children find it necessary to communicate with adults and their peers.

use of materials and substances in the home or child care center are all natural and typical.

Interaction and Negotiating Skills. Imparting basic wisdom about human relationships must begin in the home. It is the family's responsibility to develop children's initial interaction and negotiating skills even though these are extended considerably in other groupings, for example, peer group, out-of-home care, and school situations. Teaching about sensitivity to others, the logic of cooperative action and taking turns, and the need to respect others and to share materials has its place in the social life of growing children (Black & Puckett, 1996).

Aesthetic Appreciation and Value Development. Early aesthetic development is normal for preschool children. Experimenting with music, graphic arts, and movement leads to pleasant associations with these art forms. Parents who validate these experiments, participate in the action, and demonstrate possibilities help young children form values and develop appreciation (Seefeldt & Barbour, 1998). Similar pleasant associations come from child care center experiences when they are quality centers. In the arena of social values, Seefeldt and Barbour state, "The democracy of an early childhood program supports and fosters the attitudes and values of equality and respect for others" (p. 570).

Health Education and Sex Education. Eating habits, such as having an interest in nutritious food, brushing teeth, and caring for bodily functions are skills normally accepted as part of the home curriculum. The same carries for child care centers where many young children spend a large part of the regular workweek. Health education is always a part of the quality child care facility, but sex education can be a controversial topic. We advocate that families can and should take responsibility for

children's sex education. At the minimum, families should focus on attention to gender differences, attention to privacy and knowledge of "good touching" and "bad touching," as well as respect and appreciation for one's own body (Calderone & Johnson 1989). Essa and Murray (1999) provide a brief but helpful background on the sexual behavior of young children and how parents and teachers can cope with their concerns over what is normal sexual play and what is deviant. Most child care centers will address the topic of sex education, but values attached to such topics may be in variance with parental values. This causes conflicts if not resolved. Children can even be placed at risk if out-of-home care is not monitored for quality.

Components of School Responsibility

A formal curriculum starts with "schooling"— no matter how young the child. Schooling, whether at nursery school, day care (including infant/toddler programs), or public or private school, will begin where some parts of the formal and informal home curriculum have paused. The word *curriculum*, used constantly in organized schools, serves as an organizer for all school programs. Different conceptions of curriculum do exist, and the philosophical orientation of a particular school's staff members will determine the how and what of children's learning. (See chapter 8 for an overview of school curriculum.) In some schools, curriculum will be an outline of content and skills to be presented, while in others it will be a constantly changing set of experiences that children and teachers decide to pursue in satisfying their interests (Doll, 1995). All gradations between these two are found in schools in the United States. As a beginning professional, you should anticipate the definition of *curriculum* as the formal and informal content and processes used by and for learners in gaining skills, knowledge, and appreciations (McNeil, 1996).

We discuss school curriculum more fully in chapter 8, but for now, think of preschool and primary-school-age children extending the skills that were started in the home—and expanded for many children in the child care center.

1. Literacy skills: reading, writing, literature, speaking, and listening competencies.

2. Math competencies: numeration skills, calculating, measuring, spatial relations, and problem solving.

3. Physical and natural science competencies: observing phenomena, drawing conclusions, experimenting with plant growth, animal care, and everyday chemical combinations.

4. Social skills: study of human relationships, increased and intensified as children grow.

5. Health education, sex education, recreation skills: extension of skills and habits begun in the home.

6. Aesthetic education: appreciation of crafts and fine arts.

7. Negotiating skills: procedures for planning activities, arranging teams, and developing assessments (mostly in the informal curriculum).

8. Attitudes and values: social, ethical, and moral judgment, respect for and cooperation with others.

By expanding and building on the curriculum started in the home, partnerships between school and home assure continuity of children's learning. Whenever one enhances the objectives of the other, the result is enriched experience for children.

Components of Community Responsibility

All communities have multiple facets, and the impact of different agencies and enterprises is pervasive in the lives of children. While it is true that the youngest children have limited contacts beyond their home or child care center, primary-school-age children will experience, at some level, almost as much community conditioning, pressure, and influence as do adults.

Responsibility accrues to the community as an institution for supporting its citizens, families, and schools and for furnishing a "curriculum" of experiences and opportunities. No laws or mandates require this involvement, and few would enumerate the particular services of a community as features of curriculum. But in formal and informal ways, each community provides a way of life, bits of knowledge, chances for skill development, values and moral education, aesthetic validations, and an array of opportunities that will affect children's perceptions and promote attitudes (Haberman, 1992; Heath, 1983).

Formal and informal learning opportunities are found in various places maintained by the typical community. In terms of Bloom's taxonomy (Bloom, Englehart, Furst, Hill, & Krathwohl, 1956), a community's impact on its children occurs primarily within the cognitive and affective domains. Three community elements with great influence on children are peer groups, entertainment facilities, and religious institutions.

Cognitive Impact. Each community supplies news and information through publishing, television, and radio outlets that provide children with specific bits of knowledge. Religious centers have definite goals for developing knowledge and practice. Sports and recreational areas promote physical skills, exercise, and knowledge about recreation. Parks, zoos, museums, and theaters all provide information and aesthetic appreciation to benefit the growing child. Community service offices all have informational outlets to promote health, safety, and good parenting practices. These social organizations, religious institutions, and educational outlets interrelate with and expand the home and school curricula to promote skills, knowledge, and attitudes on various subjects. Figure 6–1 illustrates how the three social settings interrelate to develop and reinforce one cognitive area, mathematic ability.

Affective Impact.   In the affective domain, communities and neighborhoods provide children with a sense of security, well-being, and identity. The kinds of protective services available and the attitudes and values modeled by citizens and leaders send children clear messages about community values and concerns. For example, citizens can demonstrate and support fair play in games and sports. By playing fairly and rewarding all players, as opposed to emphasizing and rewarding only winners, sports directors and spectators communicate pride in striving and participating instead of in winning at any cost.

Figure 6–1   Children's math development interrelated in three social settings.

	HOME	**SCHOOL**	**COMMUNITY**
Age 1	Exploring nearby space		
Age 2	Rote counting, comparing objects for size		Sensing larger spaces
Age 3	Contrasting sizes More counting	Nursery rhymes of counting	Rote counting experiences
Age 4	Seriation, placing objects in sequence, acquiring number sense Grasp of time	Distinguishing geometric shapes Determining more & less, basics of addition & subtraction	Applying number sense to the larger world Counting games
Age 5	Ordering objects, grasp of money Sense of measurement in cooking and home projects	Making one-to-one correspondence Grasp of rational numbers Starting to understand time	Noting sizes of larger & less; noting geometric shapes
Age 6	Using knowledge of time; using concept of number in home to calculate	Addition algorithm, subtraction algorithm Measurement study Geometric study	Applying knowledge of money for purchases
Age 7	Application of measurement to projects and hobbies Estimating quantities, distances, etc.	Continuing practice of number facts Estimation problems	Figuring how far to throw a ball Sensing how long to walk to friends' homes
Age 8		Multiplication algorithm	Using math concepts to solve problems in play, etc.

Community services and functions do not, of course, fall easily into categories of formal and informal learning, but they do in differing ways show children the range of human response—from sensitive and reasonable to greedy and malicious. Lessons emerge as children sense their community at work and at play, when celebrating, and when struggling economically and politically or with natural disasters.

Peer Groups.   As we noted in chapter 1, peer groups exert a strong influence in any community. Peer groups are social in nature and inculcate a curriculum of experience in those involved. Constructively, peer groups provide children's all-important coming-of-age experiences, where children encounter folklore and rituals, experience a sense of belonging, and begin developing competitive skills (Ladd & LeSieur, 1995). Peer groups also provide early experience in social interaction and cooperation. Destructively, peer groups may evolve into alienated gangs that commit acts of violence and hostility.

Peer groups are ubiquitous—we find them everywhere clusters of children exist. They begin to form early in children's lives and reach a high point in middle childhood when children have far less contact with adults (Berndt, 1979; Harris, 1998). A community has a responsibility regarding the formation of peer groups and their assorted actions. Some parents assume responsibility for monitoring, evaluating, and imposing codes of acceptable behavior for the peer groups they encounter (Ladd & LeSieur, 1995). This adult influence appears to have a positive effect. Consider the mother's positive monitoring in the following vignette.

🦢

Victoria and her mother walked next door to welcome to their Southern California community the new family who had just arrived from Hawaii. The two new girls, Terry and Adri-
anne, came to Victoria's yard to play. They taught Victoria a new version of hopscotch. While the girls were playing, the neighborhood "gang" appeared and told Terry and Adrianne they had to leave because "we don't play with Chinese kids." Victoria's mother, witnessing the scene, hurried out to the yard and asked the new neighbors to stay. "All children are welcome in this yard, as long as you play well together. I saw the fun you two had showing Victoria that new hopscotch. Perhaps you'll teach these other children how to play it, too?" The mother tended her shrubs and observed for a while, but as all the children got involved in play, she left them to negotiate on their own.
🦢

Victoria's mother warded off hostility toward the new children in the neighborhood by suggesting and guiding a constructive experience. Teachers in schools as well as family members have a responsibility to monitor and guide children's peer interactions.

Entertainment Facilities.   The entertainment industry is a part of the greater community and is probably the most pervasive force in children's lives today. From earliest times, societies have recognized a need for activities that lift spirits and that entertain. A thriving community sanctions and supports entertainment for its citizens; few persons would disagree with that objective.

Communities have planned occasions and established recreational facilities that provide for entertainment—sports areas, natural areas, parks, and so on—and parades, community fairs, and other celebrations are typical. In addition, an entire private industry has grown up in most communities for the purpose of entertainment on command, day or night. The following are typical entertainment formats:

- Radio, tape, and CD players
- Cable, broadcast television, and videocassette films

Peers groups provide children with a sense of belonging and experience in developing competitive skills.

- Theaters, cinemas, and arcades
- Theme parks and sports facilities
- Computer games and Internet linkages

While much of the entertainment industry's offerings are consonant with typical community endeavors, the time and expense allotted to them can intrude on families' and children's schedules, personal objectives, creativity, schoolwork, and socializing (Gunter & McAleer, 1997; Singer & Singer 1990). The challenge that parents and schools have is that entertainment may be overdone in proportion to other aspects of home and school curriculum.

What is the community responsibility for expanding or limiting its entertainment opportunities? Communities have legal responsibility to protect children from inappropriate situations but assume little responsibility for children's overexposure to sanctioned entertainment forms (Van Evra, 1998). Responsibility in guiding children's choices rests primarily with families and primary caregivers; some cannot manage this well. When schools collaborate with parents and community leaders, it is possible to provide guidance to children regarding entertainment when parents have difficulty monitoring their children's exposure.

Religious Institutions.   Another private part of community learning experiences lies with organized religious groups and occurs in mosques, synagogues, churches, and other places of worship and study. The curriculum in religious locations is directed primarily toward participants' spiritual and moral growth but includes academic, philosophical, and theological knowledge, concepts, and interpretations. While endorsed on the whole by the larger community, religious establishments are selective in membership and orientation. In the past, community traditions gave religious institutions formal responsibility for moral training, expecting the inculcation of religious faith and the development in children of moral character and appropriate attitudes and practices. The situation today is much more ambiguous.

No state has statutes requiring religious practice, but all have laws insisting on religious freedom. In spite of mandates to prevent the establishment of a state-run church, cooperative action between some churches and local schools has resulted in appreciation of different religious practices and also for addressing social issues such as serving at-risk families and stemming violence in communities (American Association of School Administrators, 1986; Benson, 1997). Too often, educators, parents, and community agents are confused about laws regarding religion in and around public schools. All professionals in social and educational practice can benefit by obtaining a copy of the concise joint statement regarding religious practices recently developed by 35 organizations spanning the ideological, religious, and political spectrum (American Civil Liberties Union, 1995).

Linking Responsibilities

All communities have established schools (indeed are legally required) within their boundaries to develop children's cognitive and affective skills. However, few laypersons recognize the heavy burdens often placed on present-day schools. When they provide two meals per day plus handle after-school care in addition to normal monitoring activity, schools are assuming a large part of the parenting role. This increased load requires good communication, more understanding, and cooperation from families if the overloads taking place in some schools are to be mitigated.

Some skills and attitudes are best enhanced through projects and activities under community sponsorship. We as educators must be alert for collaborations between community agencies and schools that promote children's education and welfare. The following vignette illustrates this point.

🦢

Life in the small coastal community was quiet, but Josh and his friends were restless after a month of summer vacation. Returning from the ball field one day, they pedaled their bikes toward home, throwing rubbish from their lunches at poles and fences. They seemed intent on marring their community's quiet roadside beauty. At one lovely spot near the ocean, they noticed an artist setting up his easel and stopped to watch. The painter paused, then asked the boys if they would help him clean up debris near the shoreline so that he could paint the scene without distractions. The boys did, and then they stayed to watch the man work. The boys became fascinated with the artist's rendering, and the artist became aware of how little experience these youngsters had in developing a sense of their surroundings.

A few days later, the artist and a colleague invited Josh, his friends, and their parents to their painting studio to talk about their art and its relationship to the world around them. This worked so well that the artists, with the help of a small group of parents, persuaded town officials to budget space and funds to open a modest gallery in the community. Classes in painting and art appreciation are now offered in the gallery, and the artists are helping teachers at the local elementary school to integrate the arts into their curriculum.

🦢

No single agency—home, school, or community—felt a need or responsibility for developing the aesthetic senses of Josh and his friends, but an interested citizen was able to establish a link with this responsibility and provide a needed aspect of curriculum for the youth in that community.

NURTURING EDUCATIONAL OPPORTUNITY

As we begin the 21st century, we find more conflict regarding education. More ambiguity occurs, and we have more to accomplish with fewer resources. At one door, critics are dissatisfied with reduced skill levels and educational outcomes. At another door, intensely involved parents challenge teachers and push for a greater voice in curriculum. And at no door, but clearly in view, we have continued social turmoil, more homeless persons, and more struggling family groups who have given up on schools.

Providing and arranging appropriate educational experiences for children require support, dedication, great interest, and commitment. All three social settings are involved in nurturing and supporting educational programs in some fashion, but less-than-uniform support exists throughout the United States.

New challenges reveal perplexing tasks for all workers in American education. Are there ways to address the issues and restore both credibility in educational objectives and a commitment for moving ahead?

One person working alone seems inadequate. Chris Zajac, as recounted in *Among Schoolchildren*, tries hard to meet challenges in her classroom and despairs when one student loses out (Kidder, 1989). In the overall picture, does one individual's effort help that much? The well-focused family is usually successful, but without a follow-up program in school and community, its work can be sabotaged. Even in affluent families, nurturing educational opportunity can be accidental at best (Metz, 1993). Quality schools can do only so much to compensate for disadvantaged children. Sustained progress requires a united front.

Do we need a child advocate to run interference for each child? Available resources, time, and human energy are not sufficient.

Child advocates (Benson, 1997; Children's Defense Fund, 1998; Leach, 1994) note there is little question: Everyone in contact with children should nurture and support children's educational experiences in society. Cooperation among institutions in children's lives is required for full nurturance and will offer far better opportunities and more continuity of educational experience for children than will any of the alternatives.

Families and Nurturance

It seems natural for families to nurture and promote education and even seek enhanced opportunity for their offspring. Generations of humans have shown a disposition for nudging youngsters up the educational ladder. Only the most callous or indifferent families deny or prevent children from profitable gains in learning; some do better than others.

Much has been written of educational opportunity and social class, which indicates that higher socioeconomic status (SES) groups provide and receive, in general, better quality education (Coleman, 1966). However, evidence exists to show that it is quality of interaction rather than socioeconomic group environment that makes the difference (Benson, 1997; Graue, Weinstein, & Walberg, 1983; Williams, 1997).

If we accept a broad definition of *nurturance*, most families show evidence of capability, at least in children's early years. It is almost natural for new parents to foster their child's growth. What parent does not express

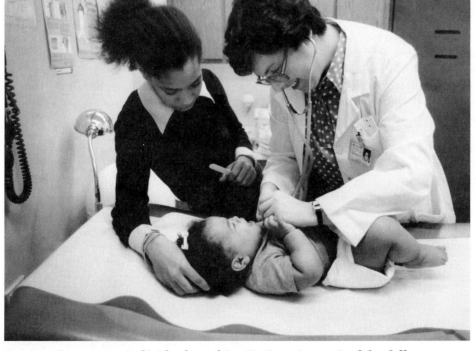

Cooperation among individuals and institutions is required for full nurturance of children.

pleasure at a baby's beginning language? Parents reinforce almost any verbalization. What parent does not take an active interest in a baby's beginning steps or ability to manipulate toys and games? The active overseeing and encouragement of these basics and their deliberate arrangement all speak to the primal and natural nurturing tendencies of family members.

This home nurturance is being assumed by out-of-home care facilities in a rapidly expanding way. Many family care and child care centers provide for children only a few months old (infants). Obviously, the expectations of parents are that other personnel will assume part of the responsibility for nurturing their small children.

Parents and other family members normally show pleasure at later educational gains. Opportunities for literary accomplishment, artistic endeavors, skill in crafts and sports, and social encounters are normally greeted with enthusiasm. Note that single parents as well as two-parent families are often successful in these endeavors (Olson & Haynes, 1993; Schwartz & Kaslow, 1997). We should point out that affluence is not a guarantee that children will be well nurtured. Metz (1983) describes the all too common cases of parental neglect and abuse in some socially prominent and affluent homes.

After children are in school, parental nurturance may be less evident. This is due to confusion about the family responsibility for directing educational experiences and to increased incursions in children's life by school, peers, and entertainment. However, an underlying principle for most families is that the objective of supporting their child's growth and education is paramount. Some families almost live for their children.

Extreme evidence of the motivation to nurture is seen when a family elects to introduce a program of home schooling for its school-age children. Of course, in this way, the parents

continue to be the dominant force in children's educational lives as they assume both parental and school prerogatives. This can be ambitious and even arrogant at times (Duffey, 1998; Van Galen & Pitman, 1991). Another example of extraordinary motivation is the willingness of modest-income parents to sacrifice in order to send children to a private school or to a specialized program in the arts.

In general, a nurturing family (or child care center) has the following characteristics:

1. Monitors and provides for children's basic needs.

2. Interacts with children in a kind and pleasant manner.

3. Provides reasonable problems and challenges for children to confront.

4. Models, extends, and enriches language.

5. Highlights successes and supports self-esteem.

6. Helps children acquire basic skills to function in home, school, and community.

7. Plans recreational activities, games, and excursions.

8. Models productive work habits and organizing strategies.

9. Provides consistent guidelines and places limits for social behavior.

10. Supports and extends aesthetic encounters.

Family nurturance and support are evidenced by accepting responsibility for "helping" children to integrate with community and school, whether preschool, day care, or regular public school. Parents support the school program, help out at school, and follow regulations (even when they are confusing) for enabling and supporting schooling endeavors.

Parents in some cases lack the background or insight to make the best choices. They become confused about priorities and fail to anticipate unhealthy outcomes of a school procedure or activity. Children are then caught in the middle. Education is impeded when parents and teachers are unable to communicate and negotiate. However, temporary confusion or perplexity does not alter these parents' basic motivation to support and enhance their children's experiences. Sometimes this type of problem precipitates school reform, and positive outcomes result (Bloom, 1992; Comer, 1997).

Other families provide minimal support for their children's education. Some provide the basics of primary care—food, shelter, clothing, and safety—but little else. These families assume "the system" will provide all other nurturance. They do not grasp the basics of educational practice or how learning comes about. Parent education can make a difference for minimally supportive families. It is possible to assist parents in rethinking their commitment for nurturance if we select the right motivation device.

Marginalized families cannot or will not provide even basic family support. This special class of family has extensive need for social intervention and rehabilitation (Wagstaff & Gallagher, 1990). Some rehabilitation has been successful. When schools are able to bring marginalized families into planning sessions and management teams, there is substantial evidence that these families' self-concept and levels of achievement, and the motivations of at-risk children, are raised (Haberman, 1992; Maeroff, 1998).

🦓

Peggy left the homeless shelter for the day with her two children, walking to the Head Start community center. She hopes the teachers there will keep her two children while she inquires about a job she'd heard about. She doesn't make it to the center, though, as the distance is far and the children start crying and are too heavy to carry. Dejectedly, she sits

on the curb, then spends the rest of the day wandering in the open-air market looking for handouts.

Peggy has no immediate family and just moved to the shelter to get away from her abusive boyfriend. She has a history of moving in and out with her boyfriend, then living for short times with a friend and then her aunt—only to lose these places because of financial problems that lead to quarrels. Peggy has a brief work history, but she lacks any sense of well-being that might give her confidence in her abilities. She does not feel connected to the larger community, and she has little understanding of how her condition might change. The social worker at the shelter got her 3-year-old son enrolled in the community Head Start program. Head Start personnel and the social worker are trying to connect Peggy with the community's educational and child care projects. But Peggy's absenteeism from the projects she starts and the periodic appearance of her belligerent boyfriend make upward progress difficult.

🦓

Peggy's situation demonstrates the crying needs of marginalized families in America. The lack of skills, the lack of options, and being locked into undesirable situations make progress difficult. Peggy has few connections to a social network for support and has difficulty keeping any commitment she makes and little knowledge of how to get help. Aspiration is lacking—only the basics appear to be a concern, and those, at times, seem difficult to manage. What will her children become? The nurturance here must be considered minimal and will not change until intensive social reconstruction is arranged.

Schools and Nurturance

All schools provide a curriculum of experience. That is, of course, the main business of schools in the 21st century, as it was in earlier

A nurturing environment provides social and emotional enhancements for children's lives.

times. But nurturance goes beyond the basic curriculum to include the social and emotional enhancements for children's lives. If the school nurtures, it demonstrates a special concern for individual children, parents, and teachers.

Teachers choose to teach because they wish to facilitate children's educational attainment and growth. Nurturing teachers move beyond academics to find ways to link experience with children's learning styles and interests. We find such teachers in many preschools and primary schools today, although we find practices in some schools that appear to serve teachers more than children. Over 30 years ago, books such as *Death at an Early Age* (Kozol, 1967) and *How Children Fail* (Holt, 1964) detailed the unproduc-

tive and nonnurturing dimensions of some schools. Regrettably, some of these situations continue.

Nurturing educational objectives means that teachers not only carefully plan, facilitate, and promote educational opportunity but also provide stimulation. In fact, some school personnel have assumed substitute parent roles in promoting the aspirations of particular children. As noted earlier, schools cannot do this alone. Haberman (1992) pleads that "special attention must be given to schools that transcend traditional distinctions between learning in and out of school, between schooling as a traditional process limited in time and place to school buildings and education as a life process occurring in a variety of community contexts" (p. 35).

A nurturing school displays the following characteristics:

1. Has a broad and up-to-date curriculum related to and guided by a philosophy that teachers and administrators support.

2. Is a welcoming place for children, parents, and others.

3. Thinks of children as individuals rather than as classes or groups.

4. Has a rich source of materials and supplies.

5. Is linked with parents, volunteers, and community agencies.

6. Works to heighten the self-esteem of all involved persons.

7. Provides a safe and healthy environment in which children develop diverse positive values and attitudes.

8. Is organized and serious about its mission.

9. Provides opportunities for children to develop concrete and abstract concepts and to use knowledge as a basis for reasoning.

10. Supports recreational and aesthetic encounters and includes them in its program.

Communities and Nurturance

Community commitment for enhancing children's educational opportunities undergirds family and school endeavors in nurturance. Children who live in an educationally nurturing community are indeed privileged.

In many communities, pride and care for schools are evident to visitors and newcomers. However, a groundswell of support for promoting education does not just happen; it means that committees, groups, and leaders have been active in establishing goals and lobbying for better conditions. We find that the electorate and the community decision makers are almost always motivated to lean over backward to support increased educational opportunities—particularly for young children.

A community that is nurturing education is doing many things, including the following:

1. Planning new schools and community recreational centers.

2. Producing scholarship money.

3. Subsidizing programs in libraries, museums, and galleries for children as well as for adults and senior citizens.

4. Supporting bond issues for educational plant and equipment.

5. Funding grants for school or community educational experiments.

6. Showing interest in participating as a partner in school activities.

7. Displaying schoolwork and highlighting children's achievements throughout the community.

8. Actively exploring new education programs.

9. Supporting all school and club activities (scouting, 4-H, sports groups).

Interestingly enough, community leaders and agencies normally consider the larger context of curriculum when analyzing programs and raising support for schools. Arts programs, as well as sports and recreation, are often heralded first by community agencies, though it may begin with a strong initiative by an individual. This was the case of the artist in the vignette in this chapter. Community members often anticipate better than teachers the outcomes of particular educational projects for promoting healthier attitudes and better opportunities for children.

Regrettably, some communities do not facilitate and nurture children's education. Some references in this text portray conditions of despair and social crisis in too many U.S.

communities (Davis, 1995; Garbarino, Kostelny, & Dubrow, 1998; Kotlowitz, 1991). Extensive social remediation is needed in all those locations. The community context affects and controls family and school settings to a huge extent. And when economic, social, and political crises arise, community problems always detract from school programs and other educational objectives. Controversy often results in minimal nurturing, and too often it prevents the community from making changes that have been initiated in schools and the community at large, e. g., afterschool activities and recreational opportunities.

GOVERNANCE OF EDUCATION

Governance for educational opportunity is, like nurturance and curriculum, a shared responsibility for the institutions involved with children's welfare. Governance involves the management, coordination, and evaluation of children's educational opportunities, and frequently the factors are summed up by the word *administration*. Legal requirements as well as traditions relate to these responsibilities. While governance in education would seem in today's world to be a basic function of schools, some features of governance devolve to homes and to the community setting.

The community at large must be the general overseer for educational practice, opportunity, and development. Direct administration and supervision are assumed by the local community school board.

Legal Requirements

Tradition, to some extent, and the large volume of local, state, and national statutes and regulations, to a major extent, are the means by which the several institutions focus on educational opportunity. All officials and administrators are aware of these requirements.

Most people believe that the United States, from the federal government to the local community, is laden with laws and requirements. In fact, the American legal system is conceptualized on the principle of "minimum restraint to be imposed on individuals to achieve an acceptable level of social orderliness" (O'Reilly & Green, 1992, p. 1). When we view this objectively, we find that U.S. citizens do make most decisions by themselves. This minimum restraint stems from centuries of precedent in Anglo-American social traditions and can be detected today in the way Americans operate businesses, schools, assemblies, and agencies. To protect citizens' rights, freedoms, and traditions to carry on life, pursue dreams, and educate children, legislatures and other authorities have, in general, enacted laws and regulations that permit people to live their lives with the least amount of interference and conflict. We are privileged, since this does not occur in many nations.

Our federal government, with the U.S. Constitution as a guide, has developed education-related laws (PL 94-142 is an example). The federal government is actually a minimal force in education; the 10th amendment to the Constitution relegates education (and many other responsibilities) to the individual states. Because of this, federal law is based on selected parts of the Constitution—those that invoke the government's role as protector of individual rights. The U.S. Supreme Court has done likewise in settling educational disputes referred to it.

Legally, then, the bulk of school law comes from state constitutions, statutes, and regulations. These statutes and regulations frequently change as a result of the changing political processes and conditions extant in the United States today (O'Reilly & Green, 1992). Examples of state responsibility are to provide free public education to all children, to compel students to attend school, and to maintain the so-called separation of church and state. Each state has established a department of education to oversee matters within that state. One appendage of each education department is the local education agency (LEA) often called the local **school board**. LEAs serve in individual communities to operate the state-required schools.

Local Level Decisions.   At the local level, the school board (LEA) operates as an agent for the state but makes its own rules, regulations, and policies, which in turn serve the community involved. LEAs develop budgets, determine policies and oversee the schools in their jurisdiction, and hire administrators and teachers to carry out the day-to-day operation of the schools.

Court Decisions.   One other agency involved is the judiciary—the courts. When adjudicating differences of opinion, courts may have much to say about education. Even though courts interpret rather than make laws, it is fair to say they became extensively involved in education matters in the late 20th century (Shoop & Dunklee, 1992). Some court decisions have pushed educational requirements in very different directions (Valente, 1998). Examples involve civil rights and free-speech issues, the so-called separation of church and state, and definitions of unreasonable search and seizure.

Home Governance

Various state laws specify parent or guardian responsibilities toward children in their care. These regulations reside in the general welfare statutes and are minimal. The laws are invoked when neglect is an issue and when local authorities or agencies find that families are not providing general safety and support for children in their care (Webb et al., 1999). In

addition, all states have laws requiring home responsibility for supervising children and making sure they attend school (Valente, 1998).

The general requirements for home support have come down through the culture and are responsibilities that most families accept without question. It is the family in trouble where negligence becomes an issue. If social welfare agencies are alerted by other parents, schools, or public safety officials, they may initiate legal proceedings to remove children. Still, negligence is the exception to the rule in most communities.

As children mature, home governance practices become more indirect, but laws and traditions still require basic support, parental guidance, and family monitoring ("Do you know where your children are tonight?") through young adulthood.

Other Family Governance.   All families informally evaluate their schools, teachers, and communities. Without objective criteria for making these highly subjective and personal assessments, families use whatever they have at hand—their own experiences in school, what they have read, seen, or heard, and their own perceptions of what is right for education. Most schools do not have a process installed whereby outsiders may evaluate personnel, programs, or other school undertakings. As a result, feedback from families regrettably is often overlooked or neglected.

While rare, there is provision in some school districts for direct family involvement in public school management and governance. We find family involvement most often in early childhood programs such as in Head Start centers, on boards for child care centers, and in parent cooperatives. One well-known foreign program that actively pursues parent involvement at the primary level is the Reggio Emilia (Italy) plan (Gandini, 1993; Hendrick,

Family involvement in school governance is found most often in early childhood programs.

1997). A number of schools in the United States are now modeling their programs on this plan in which parents and others are elected to hold advisory and even directory roles for school programs.

Families are normally disenfranchised in governance of school curriculum, except in the role of follow-up for schoolwork and minor supporting roles as helpers in the school (Henderson, Marburger, & Ooms, 1986). Actually, most families are quite willing for the school hierarchy—school board, administration, teachers, staff, and specialists—to continue with governance of the academic curriculum. The regrettable dimension here is

that the close working relations with parents that could come about do not, and a potent resource is overlooked and underused. Schools lose chances to unite community members and develop better programs when they do not seek to involve parents.

School Governance

Schools are a highly visible feature in any society's structure. Although a few citizens in the United States contest the school's viability and purpose, most accept schools as necessary for the proper development of educational opportunity for young children. The Phi Delta

Kappa/Gallup survey (Rose & Gallup, 1998) finds year after year that Americans rate their own local schools highly.

Schools are established for the management, sequencing, and coordination of that formal curriculum we noted earlier as well as to provide other educational services. In some cases, this responsibility has resulted in bureaucracies with all the trappings of large, multifaceted agencies (Figure 6–2). Because of the structure and rigidity in many urban school systems, some communities in recent years have argued for decentralization and for site-based management for individual schools. Responsive school situations often result when decentralization is done carefully and with community involvement. The charter school movement (discussed in chapter 11) is one recent example of decentralizing.

The preceding notwithstanding, we have probably no alternative to the school bureaucracy for supporting general education for the

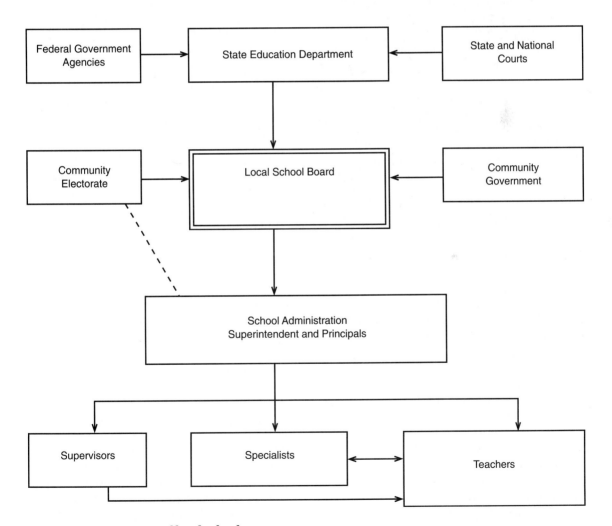

Figure 6–2   Governance of local schools.

masses of school-age children in our highly technical and work-oriented society. The demands for literacy, scientific understanding, and math and social science training, to say nothing of the socializing, recreational, and health needs of children, are immense in the United States today. To accomplish this basic formal curriculum, our society needs carefully organized schools for the majority of the population. One has only to note situations where communities experience extended school strikes to see the confusion and exasperation that come with trying to fill in the gaps left by school closings.

As agents for the community school board (LEA), administrators and teachers exert the greatest influence and authority over what happens in a community's schools regarding management and coordination of curriculum, time commitments, and assessments. This underscores the vast responsibilities that devolve to school personnel in all communities.

Community Governance

In theory, all educational governance starts with the community. All states delegate most responsibility to the local community for oversight of public safety, child welfare, and the development and operation of schools. That community may be a small municipality of a few hundred persons in Vermont or a huge metropolitan district like New York City or Dade County, Florida.

Deriving from state mandates, all initiatives in local school governance begin with the community school board (LEA) elected or appointed to oversee schools. As noted, the LEA delegates authority for administration and implementation. Monies are raised from community taxes to support school programs the LEA has proposed. The school board's central office hires personnel to carry out these programs, and the board sets general directions for curriculum and considers program evaluations.

To a large extent, board members depend on their superintendent and their principals to give counsel for board actions and to carry out the day-to-day operation of schools. This means that most of the responsibility for operating or managing schools, interpreting curriculum, and conducting assessments is in the hands of school administrators and teachers. Most citizens think of school administrators as the creators of school programs and strategies, and this image is not often diminished by the responses of school personnel.

Curriculum content for schools is also supposedly determined by the community served, but only in a general way does a community decide what is to be developed in its school programs. Community citizens most often surrender governance to the school board (whom they have elected) and its administrators, becoming involved in school matters only when a crisis surfaces in curriculum or in response to political repercussions from nonaccomplishment, such as falling SAT scores.

Considering the anxiety about school programs in the United States and the burgeoning problems in many school districts, it may well be time for more direct community involvement in school life and governance. Shared decision making, more extensive exchange of information between school and community, and alliance among community representatives would produce more thoroughly understood programs, more successful outcomes, and a more supportive constituency.

It is natural to assess those large agencies and enterprises around us—and a community's citizens do evaluate their schools in a general way by observing the outward functioning of programs. We find that most persons judge school performance by happiness of the children, by tangible outcomes such as report cards, by the later success of students, and by how school is like or unlike what they experienced in their generation. These are valuable criteria and should be held as general guides.

But it is not sensible to accept results of standardized tests that do not always connect with the aspirations of a particular community (Stiggins, 1997).

IMPLICATIONS FOR PROFESSIONALS

It is important to see the overall responsibility of who speaks for children in our society. As Penelope Leach (1994) notes, children are the most subjected minority in our society. They are the weakest, most dependent, and vulnerable persons around us. Yet, we do not have assigned advocates, and we assume the persons working with them—those folks in the three social settings—will do the best job of steering, helping, and educating them. We all know that that is sometimes far from true. As a professional, you have an obligation to find the best possible opportunities for children you encounter.

As a professional, you must be knowledgeable of the delegation of power and authority and responsibility for children's lives and futures and know how to activate action, if need be, in one venue or another.

Using the chapter's very general outline as a guide is a start for your figuring out "who is in charge here?" and, more important, "what should be happening for this child?" Once you have done that, you will have an idea of how you can be effective.

SUMMARY AND REVIEW

Many people, agencies, and organizations are responsible for and equipped to deliver education to children. Homes working with schools, which in turn work with communities, result in the best circumstances for enhancing educational opportunities for any child. The three social settings have a shared responsibility for making certain that optimal conditions and arrangements are in place and that model programs are publicized when implemented. Model programs exist today in selected areas (we discuss model programs in chapter 11).

A curriculum of experience accrues to every child, but children have very different experiences, depending on circumstances in the three social settings. The curriculum is divided into two interactive parts: formal, or academic, and informal, or hidden. Tradition and law impose requirements on homes, schools, and communities to fulfill their share in presenting the curriculum. But overlaps, disagreements, and redundancies are not unusual as children move from one setting to another. Education is most productive where strong cooperation and alliances exist among homes, schools, and communities.

The objective observer can see the unique and vital position of the school in any cooperative endeavor. Parents and communities, of course, have a vested interest in the education of their children. The school is delegated the responsibility of accepting all entrants, organizing a curriculum, executing that curriculum, and generally steering children through the educational process. Because educators are trained professionals with daily contact with children, they can best see the places where involvement from parents and the larger community will help. But if the school as an institution neglects to engender cooperative action among all social institutions, the interests and hopes of parents and communities are difficult to realize. We discuss the school as facilitator in chapter 13.

SUGGESTED ACTIVITIES AND QUESTIONS

1. Consider a new teaching situation in which you must figure out how to build support for several marginalized children. Even though all three social settings bear responsibility, how can you best enhance educational opportunity for these youngsters?

2. Find a copy of your state's legal codes regarding education and identify statutes that hold communities accountable for the education of children. Discuss with colleagues two that focus on the school's responsibility for educating children.

3. Construct a chart showing the areas of sex education that you think children normally encounter between ages 3 and 8. Indicate home, school, and community responsibilities at each age level.

4. Visit a local Head Start center and talk to the director and a teacher about the skills and understandings they feel responsible for developing with the children during the current month. Do they feel that the home and community should be involved in these learnings? What do they feel the balance should be?

RESOURCES

Books

1. Maeroff, G. I. (1998). *Altered destinies: Making life better for schoolchildren in need.* New York: St. Martin's Press.
2. Leach, P. (1994). *Children first: What our society must do-and is not doing—for our children today.* New York: Alfred Knopf.
3. Consult Appendix I for a sampling of many useful children's books dealing with family and school situations.

Films and Videos

1. *Survivor's pride: Building resilience in youth at risk.* (1994). [Video, 62 min]. Examines resiliency in children who have encountered adversity. Attainment Co., Verona, WI.

2. *Exercise with Daddy and me.* (1997). [Video, 50 min]. Presents fathers spending time with their small children, including exercise, bonding techniques, and singing. My Baby and Me Exercise, Pembroke Pines, FL.

Organizations

1. Child Welfare League (http://www.cwla.org/) 440 First Street, NW, Washington DC 20001
2. Educational Resources Information Center (ERIC) Elementary and Early Childhood Education 805 W. Pennsylvania Ave., Urbana, IL 61801
3. National PTA (http://www.pta.org/) 700 Rush Street, Chicago, IL 60611

Websites

1. http://www.cdc.gov/nchswww/default.htm National Center for Health website. Gives publications, tables, and information on health status, illness and disease, use of health care, and lifestyles.
2. http://gopher.ed.gov/ U.S. Education Department reference desk.
3. http://www.education-world.com Extensive information center for educators, parents, and students.
4. http://www.hec.ohio-state.edu/famlife/edu3.htm Subsite providing educational resources about parenting, children, divorce, urban families, and the like.
5. http://www.mainstream-mag.com *Mainstream Online.* An online magazine with news items, advocacy objectives, plus lifestyle information for people with disabilities.

Chapter 7

Curriculum of the Home

Every future leader for good or ill starts life with a mother, with a family. This primary experience leaves an imprint that sends ripples into the future of everyone who touches that life.

(Clawson, 1992, p. xix)

🦋

The home curriculum is all the experiences that children have while under the direction and influence of their families. The influences are affected by both the environmental context and the environmental process. In this chapter, we give examples of the many experiences children have at home and the resulting potential for learning. In reading this chapter, you will learn the following:

1. Parents provide an organizational structure for children that teaches them their roles and responsibilities in society. The values, attitudes, and emotional qualities that parents exhibit will reinforce this learning.

2. The amount of space and the freedom children have in using that space will dictate the extent of children's emotional, intellectual, physical, and creative development.

3. The home curriculum varies for children, depending on how the family structures the day.

4. The routines of the day, rituals and traditions, parental talents, and ways families reach out into the community create a foundation for children's learning in the home.

5. Home schooling, though not a new movement, has had a resurgence in the United States, and many families embrace this trend in assuming responsibility for the education of their children.

The educative processes of all homes are important ingredients for society in the United States, for, as Clawson (1992) indicates, how each person develops affects all who relate to that individual. Because of the diversity in U.S. families, we find not one single home curriculum but many variations. Too often, educators underestimate the power of the curriculum in the home. When this happens, teachers miscalculate and misjudge the learning that children have acquired outside of school.

Research indicates that no matter what the ethnic or socioeconomic makeup is of the family, warm and responsive parenting styles, a structured environment, and appropriate and stimulating activities support children's growth toward a productive lifestyle (Bernstein, 1972; Bronfenbrenner, 1979, 1986; Pierce, Alfonso, & Garrison, 1998; Sigel, McGillicuddy-DeLisi, & Goodnow, 1992). Regrettably, in some family situations, parental styles and habits mitigate against children's natural pursuit of knowledge and positive development.

All families have an organizational structure that defines family members and their roles. Even in homeless and migrant families, parents have some kind of organizational structure to provide physical and emotional support. Whatever their environment, children learn who they are, how to use the space, and what kind of world they live in. No matter what family structure exists, home learning will be a consequence of family interactions regarding use of time and space, routines of the day, sharing of interests and skills, family rituals and traditions, and family outreach to others.

In this chapter, we develop the thesis that parents are children's first and probably most influential teachers. Further, we illustrate that common features of parenting imply a curriculum; some families have specific goals for their children's development, while others' intentions are vague and ill-defined. It is impossible to cover all the learning opportunities that even one family provides and certainly not the range of curricula that diverse families contribute. However, we demonstrate the breadth of home activities and interactions that support children's growth. Vignettes illustrate various situations in the home crucial to education. The chapter concludes with an examination of the home schooling movement in the United States as an indication that some parents choose to take full responsibility for educating their children.

LEARNING ROLES AND RESPONSIBILITIES

In chapters 3 and 4, we discussed the diversity and functions of U.S. families and defined a family unit as any two or more persons living together, sharing common goals, resources, and a commitment to each other. Children in that household have at least one adult (referred to in this text as a **parent**) who is responsible for them. Siblings, who play an important role in any child's learning, also may be present. Many households have extended family members, who may or may not be living in the home but who give added support and nurturance. The teaching in any family situation, whether direct or indirect, intentional or accidental, will happen in a context and process where several things are occurring simultaneously. In all situations, children's learning depends on their readiness for the tasks and experiences they encounter, and this includes child/parent interactions. Figure 7–1 shows the range of children's learning at home and how particular family members are involved.

Parents Foster Roles and Responsibilities

An important part of the home curriculum is for children to learn family values and everchanging role expectations for themselves toward other members of the family. Children also learn the role expectations of family members toward each other and the extended family. All families have commitments, values, and priorities. Some of these sentiments are explicit and well-defined, but often many are only implied, and this is especially true for marginalized families (Garbarino & Abramowitz, 1992). Some family goals are more immediate and are often expressed as wishes or as "what we are trying to do." Some families have both long-range goals and those planned for a limited period of time. Other families are able only to function from one moment to the next. Whatever the organizational structure of the family, children absorb these goals and their role in accomplishing them. What they learn about themselves can be vastly different and can be quite contrary to school or societal expectations of families. The following two vignettes show two different family approaches, but both are still strongly goal oriented by societal expectations.

🐚

Every morning before her children left for school, Mrs. Martinez gathered them at the door to wish them a good day and to emphasize her view of their family. Though far from the actual words, the message was, "Remember, what you do today reflects on all of us. We are an honest and respected family, and what you do is important in maintaining such an honor." She then asked each child to make a small commitment for his or her conduct or learning for the day, frowning on a child who gave the same response each day or copied a sibling's statement. Studying hard, practicing the piano, or getting better at shooting baskets was an accepted goal. At dinner one evening when the family shared accomplishments and worries, José told his family he wasn't going to read with Louie (a Down syndrome child in his class) anymore because Louie was "just too hard to deal with." The older brothers and sisters sympathized with José, but they also re-

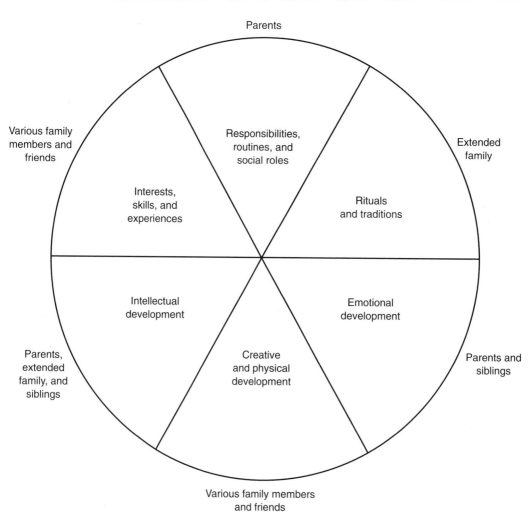

Figure 7–1   Different family members nurture the home curriculum
Note: Foundational skills, concepts, attitudes, and experiences are developed in the child's home environment. Some areas are influenced more strongly by particular family members.

minded him of the ways they had read to him when he was little. Mrs. Martinez hugged José hard a few days later when he told her, "I'm going to read with Louie. I found out yesterday he can read lots of words if you help and read along with him."

In the Martinez family, the mother was a strong and dominant influence. She believed in goal setting and certain family values and made them clear and explicit for her children.

Beth Clawson (1992), on the other hand, 1989 Michigan Mother of the Year, explains how she unconsciously set rules for her family and how important the rules were to the progress of her children.

"Long ago I put a list (titled 'A Cultured Home') on my kitchen bulletin board. It was a reminder to me of some elements that would be valuable in helping children. . . . One day I took it down. Before the day had ended, my children wanted to know why it was taken down. I had not realized that the list was a goal statement to them" (pp. Xx–xxi).

Whether goals are stated each day, written down as reminders, or merely implied, notions of having purpose and direction in one's life are modeled and communicated to children. All families, even dysfunctional ones, have house rules that members living in the home are expected to observe. Some rules may be explicit, and others implicit. In some families, the rules are fairly consistent, but in others they may be haphazard and even confusing to children. They may be communicated in dictatorial fashion, explained reasonably, or expected to be learned through observation. As children learn rules and role expectations, they also form values and attitudes that affect later learning. They learn that some rules are made to be obeyed without question and that there are good reasons for certain rules. Children's beginning lessons in how to function within their own families provide the groundwork for how to function later in school and in the community. The following vignette gives three examples of how family rules affected children's school behavior.

One of the rules in Aaron's home was that each member of the household was responsible for his or her own things. When he finished playing with a toy, Aaron was expected to put that toy away. Whenever Aaron forgot, his mother explained that his toys could get de-

All families have house rules that members are expected to observe.

stroyed or lost if he carelessly left them out. As Aaron grew older, his mother pointed out that one of his responsibilities in the house was to keep his own things picked up.

Penelope's family had different procedures. Rarely were items picked up by any one person. Things appeared to be put away randomly. Occasionally, Penelope's father would rave about the mess in the house and yell at Penelope to put her things away. Penelope usually obeyed him.

Jacob's family was homeless and lived in a temporary shelter. The family had to move out during the day and were allowed a limited time at the shelter before having to move on to a new place. Each morning, Jacob's mother communicated her expectation for Jacob's helping to pick up their meager belongings before heading out of the shelter for the day.

In kindergarten, Aaron was one of the helpful children who always picked up as his teacher announced cleanup time. Penelope attended to housekeeping duties only when the teacher told her explicitly to do so. Jacob was quite helpful but at times confused as to what was happening.

When the three children were in third grade, the orientation was that children should be creative and find ways of expressing this creativity. Penelope found that she had time now to try out all kinds of materials and to "just mess around" by herself without other children interfering. Occasionally, the teacher reminded the class there needed to be some order amid the "chaos," and Penelope usually did her share. But Aaron was often frustrated in this class. He had difficulty making sense out of the "stuff" available for creating. He wanted to work with others but had trouble when they brought more and more materials to a project without "finishing" with the materials at hand. Jacob was no longer in that school. His family had moved on and was lost to the system.

Aaron, Penelope, and Jacob learned at home about their responsibilities, and they developed attitudes about neatness. At school, Aaron's attitudes and skills were more in agreement with the kindergarten teacher's expectations, and he had an easier time adapting. Third grade at first left him in shock, and he had to learn new roles and expectations. Penelope managed in kindergarten, but with difficulty. In third grade, her teacher viewed her knack for creating "her own order" as "creative endeavors." Jacob in kindergarten was helpful, though at times bewildered, and his disjointed home life may have produced one more angry child for our classrooms today.

The attitudes and skills instilled in these families, though different, set the stage for these children as they moved beyond the family circle into school and community life. Depending on your own view of life, you can interpret one set of skills as "more desirable" than another. However, if you are to support the growth of all children in your classroom, you must recognize that children come with different skills and values, even strikes against them. It is your responsibility to help them move comfortably into their "new" environment and to seek help and supportive services when needed.

Extended Family Fosters Roles and Rituals

In most families, parents garner emotional support from the extended family and in some cases receive economic support as well. Extended family members may live close by and be seen regularly, or they may live at some distance but still have strong ties. The extended family helps to educate children in many ways. Besides teaching about role expectations and hierarchical structures, the extended family helps children absorb the traditions and rituals of the larger group. An interesting example of such learning is told by Oladele (1999) as she explains how her mother, during the daily routines of life, taught her academics and spirituality and about her African heritage. Her grandparents also influenced and reinforced this learning, beginning with a ritual of listening to her Bible verse recitations.

In some families, both sets of grandparents have equal responsibility, and customs and habits children learn from these members are of equal importance. However, since family structures differ, what children learn from the extended family depends on the influence these relatives have on the nuclear family (Berns, 1997). The extended family expands the home curriculum by interactions and through the type of gifts or other support given to the family. Because two sets of families with differing values are often joined, children can learn different interaction strategies for solving differences.

❧

Elizabeth was an active 6-year-old who had discovered the rhythms of language early. Her grandmother Dailey, a former English teacher, believed firmly that children should learn to speak correctly and not use "silly phrases" or "special invented terms." But her grandmother Denato delighted in the "discovered" terms Elizabeth used and would often repeat the terms, thus reinforcing that language can be created. At Christmas, Elizabeth received a collection of rocks from Grandmother Denato and books from Grandmother Dailey. Her thank you letters to both grandmothers consisted of a drawing of the gift plus a statement. Before sending the letter to Grandmother Dailey, Elizabeth asked her mother about Babar, one of the book characters, and with her mother's help carefully copied on her drawing the words "I liked the elephant book best." On the picture she sent to Grandmother Denato, she wrote by herself "Rnd redrks spkls lgblk rks wjshin ilvu Dne" ("Round red rocks with

sparkles long black rocks which shine. I love you, Donny"—her pet name for her grand-mother).

❧

At age 6, Elizabeth has already learned what each grandmother values. In wanting to please each grandmother, she is learning valuable things. For the grandmother who is precise, she learns about story characters, and she has learned to copy a few short words with her mother's help. With her other grandmother, she has learned the fun of playing with words and sounds and is willing to experiment and try out her knowledge of letters and sounds. Elizabeth's mother supports the values of both grandparents by supporting without judgment Elizabeth's efforts.

Siblings Aid in Role Identification

When children grow up with other children, they experience changing role patterns not dependent on age. When a new baby is born or when older siblings start school or leave home, circumstances within the family change for all members, and a different "curriculum" emerges. An older sibling who has been a playmate may suddenly become bossy after starting school, and younger children must learn new ways of interacting. Older children teach younger siblings "the ways of the world," but what is learned will depend on the younger children's interactions and emotional relationships with the older ones.

The siblings in the following vignette react differently to their older sister, and this difference could partially account for their different rate of learning certain things.

❧

Much to her mother's surprise, Caitlin learned to spell some words when she was but 3 years old. Her older sister Jennifer, returning from second grade, often made Caitlin "her pupil" and insisted she "write her letters," giving her words and letters to do. Brad, closer in age to Jennifer, didn't know letter names until he entered first grade, even though Jennifer at times tried to be his teacher as well. As a baby, Caitlin often called Jennifer her "other" mama and thus apparently was more receptive to her teaching, whereas Brad and Jennifer were closer in age, and Brad resented Jennifer's bossiness.

Academic learning is only part of the curriculum children learn from siblings. For example, children may learn physical skills faster and at an earlier age by competing with a more skilled family member. Children learn strategies for convincing others of one's point of view as siblings squabble and solve their differences within the family unit. Even learning how to unite in family loyalty against the outside world gives children important social skills—although not always desirable ones. Harris (1998) maintains that this learning from siblings and peers is even more potent than that from parents.

PHYSICAL ENVIRONMENTS OF THE HOME

Children's learning is greatly influenced by environmental factors. Amount of space, the kinds of materials found in that space, and the ways in which families allow children to use that space all affect what children learn in the home. Successful children from crowded conditions learn a great deal when the family is nurturing and supportive. If children are restricted in their movements or ignored in their environment, no matter the amount of space, learning is lessened. Before children can achieve intellectually, their basic physical and emotional needs have to be met. Clark (1983) found in his study of high and low achievers from poor families that, among other nurturing

qualities, high achievers' parents carefully supervised their children's use of time and space.

Space Influences Emotional Growth

Great differences occur in the amount and kind of space that children have in their growing years. Of course, as family situations change, so can the amount of available space. Space can be a factor in the family's ability to support children's physical and mental health. Galle, Gove, and McPherson (1972) report, from an early study on the amount of space families had per room, that the greater the density, the more the family was subjected to unhealthy conditions and stresses affecting children's development.

Children learn different things about themselves, depending on the amount and quality of space and how the adults respond to these conditions and their children. Hill (1967), in *Evan's Corner*, creates a poignant story of a child's desire for private space.

Evan lives with his family in a one-room flat. There is little sense of privacy; even the bathroom is shared with other families in the building. Evan longs for a little bit of space he can call his own. With the help of his mother, he clears a corner of the room which he barricades and furnishes with things he cherishes. Evan's sense of well-being is clearly portrayed as he has the nurturing support of his mother for his own space. However, in the crowded space, Evan also has another lesson to learn. His younger brother wants to come into his space, and it is not without a struggle that Evan learns the joy of choosing to share.

Though not stated explicitly, Evan did learn his family's value of sharing what they had with others, even though theirs was a home with limited privacy.

Space Influences Intellectual Development

When rooms have different functions, children learn categorization skills for where household items belong and where people do different jobs. When families are crowded, rooms may have more than one function, and children learn that the same space is used differently. For example, we visited a crowded one-room apartment where two people were sleeping, another was cooking, and two children were playing on the floor most of the day. There appeared to be very limited adult/child interaction. Across the hall, the same limited space had for another family distinct functions at different times of the day; the room was a living room during the daytime hours, a kitchen/dining room during early morning and evening, and a bedroom at night. With the support of the entire family, household furniture was rearranged accordingly. Lots of discussion (even perhaps argument) ensued about what belonged where. The processing skills of children in these families appeared to be affected by these situations.

In their classroom, two children, one from each of the preceding homes, were asked to put household items into categories and place them in appropriate spaces. The child whose home space was haphazard did a random assignment for the items and had no explanation of why he organized the items that way. In fact, when asked to explain his strategies, he began to rearrange the items. The other child had a definite pattern to his selection of items for each category and a clear reason for putting each item where he did.

Organization of materials within a given space can also be a means of children's developing problem-solving skills.

Curious and determined children will try out their ideas when allowed freedom to explore.

🌀

Jack discovered that the cookie jar could be reached by shoving a chair next to the cupboard and then climbing up. When his mother put the cookie jar onto the refrigerator farther from his reach, he had a new problem to solve. He began some experimentation, first with a chair and then with different sized boxes. Finally, he discovered that if he piled the boxes one on top of another, he could reach the forbidden cookies.

🌀

Such learning is usually not planned by parents. In the preceding situation, the mother was none too pleased with the child's cleverness at the moment she discovered him teetering on the piled-up boxes. Still, when homes are organized so that items for children's use are within easy grasp and other items are stored out of reach for various reasons, curious and determined children will try out their ideas if allowed enough freedom to explore safely.

Children learn concentration skills because of space available to them in the home. Children who have lots of private space and quiet time for activities often develop good study habits. Some of these skills will carry over to school, and these children may have an easy time coping with school. Others will have more difficulty sharing space or engaging in a quiet activity if there are people around them. They have learned to focus on a particular task in quiet and solitude, and a noisy classroom is confusing to them. Still other children learn to concentrate because they have learned to do so in a large family. In some ways, Richard in the following vignette profited by his large, noisy family.

🌀

Richard was raised in a family of six children. He read and studied with his older siblings

around the large family table. Often the radio or television was on, and younger children were playing nearby. The adults moved about checking on homework, tending to household tasks, and caring for younger children. As early as kindergarten, Richard displayed concentration skills. He could be found engrossed in a book right next to children playing with blocks. Often Richard didn't realize that it was time to change activities until the noise of the block play ceased. Perhaps it isn't surprising that in college, Richard was the only one of his four roommates who could study no matter how many crowded into the dorm room.

🌀

Space Influences Physical and Creative Development

Family space isn't necessarily limited to the indoor space. Outdoor space and the freedom to explore it safely will assist children in developing physical skills and creative endeavors.

🌀

Although Kenisha shared a bedroom with her sisters, and the living area seemed small when the entire family was gathered at the end of the day, outside there was a large barn and a yard where Kenisha and her siblings often played. There were trees in the yard and beams in the barn where she and her friends could climb. Cardboard boxes, old blankets, boards, nails, and hammers enabled them to create their own fantasy worlds. Kenisha and her friends tied strong ropes to the barn beams and tested their strength and developed skill in climbing hand over hand up the rope.

🌀

It isn't only in rural or suburban areas that parents find safe places for children. Parents who live in crowded cities also have managed to encourage children's imaginative use of space, though it may take more vigilance to assure children's safety. Rooftop gardens provide additional space where, with a few boxes, old boards, and blankets, children can develop physical dexterity in building as they create their own worlds.

Children thrive in whatever space they live in when adults provide consistent care, nurturing, and support while guiding their behavior and prizing their creations. Children learn important self-concepts as they are supported in their endeavors by being praised for successes and by being helped to overcome frustrations at times of failure. When children do not experience such nurturance, the home curriculum is more limited.

HOME LEARNING

In chapter 4, we defined the areas of home responsibility for children's learning as early socialization skills, language learning, beginning experiments with natural phenomena, interaction and negotiation skills, values and attitudes including aesthetic appreciation, and health and sex education. It should be clear that the home's responsibility is to develop basic skills for preparing children to function successfully in society. Fulfilling these responsibilities is accomplished to differing degrees.

Ethnographers (Clark, 1983; Heath, 1983; Stinnett & DeFrain, 1986) have found ways in which all families provide home learning experiences. Important skills are taught through daily routines. For example, significant adults transmit the rituals and traditions to the next generation as they share special interests, skills, and aspirations with their children and as they reach into the community to extend their children's learning.

In the many experiences of the home, the impact on children depends to some degree on the child-rearing practices that parents evidence (Baumrind, 1968). In chapter 4, we explicated the different styles and suggested that the authoritative parent rears children better able to cope in society. However, a simple ex-

amination of a "successful" child-rearing style does not account for the variations in children's growth toward becoming productive adults. Other qualities and the total ecological processes of family context and interaction patterns determine the competent family (Fine, 1993).

Daily Routines

A broad definition of **curriculum** includes all the experiences children have from the moment of waking to the moment of falling asleep (Doll, 1995). This implies that the home must provide a great deal of children's learning experiences.

Though modern family lifestyles may appear to be hurried or harried because of job requirements, all families establish some sort of routine, though it varies from day to day. When events happen in the home in a timed sequence, children develop a better sense of society's meaning of time. The routine events of the day are those activities that have consistent time and behavior patterns. First is the process of getting up and getting ready for school or work. When mealtimes are regular, the second routine involves preparation and a specified mealtime. A further set of routines revolves around bathing and other toileting procedures. The family reuniting at the end of the day is often another routine event. Bedtime is the final routine as family members prepare for the night. During these daily events, parents support and encourage or negate and suppress children's physical, emotional, social, and intellectual development.

Preparing for the Day.   Children who arise, dress, eat breakfast, and then brush their teeth as a routine morning activity establish a pattern whereby they learn through habit about a sequence of events. Parent-child discussions about these events reinforce parental values and attitudes toward the activities, assist in children's language development, and support children's memory and recall. Varying the routines is often necessary in any household. When parents can give explanations or answer children's questions, they often lessen the stress and help children learn to reason, to question, and to adapt to new situations. Establishing routine times and expectations for family events gives children a keener sense of time and a view of rules and role expectations. Children develop a sense of well-being and security when limits are clear and deviations to routines are dealt with in a caring and supportive environment.

Even in homeless families, the at-risk factors diminish for children when the parents are able to maintain some daily routines and rituals and are able to strengthen their positive interaction patterns by playing with their children and caring for their emotional needs (Letiecq, Anderson, & Koblinsky, 1998).

Mealtime.   Mealtime in most families offers many educational opportunities. How events are handled determines the amount and type of learning that take place. Two examples will serve to support the idea and suggest the degree of variation in family habits.

🖋

Valerie, at age 3, loved to help her mother get dinner by setting the table. She proudly told her father what a big help she'd been, and he would praise her for such endeavors. At first her mother handed her just enough silverware and plates for each member of the family. After being sure that each place had all the correct utensils was no longer a challenge, Valerie began to get the materials herself. At first she named each member of the family as she got out the materials. Later she began to count the number needed. Eventually, she was able to pick up the correct number without counting. When others joined the family, she and her mother would figure out how many more pieces they needed.

Casey, too, liked to help her mother. But since the family ate whenever they got in, setting the table meant putting a pile of utensils in the middle of the table. Plates were on the stove, as food was served from there. At first Casey would grab a few pieces of each utensil and place them in the middle of the table, as she had seen other family members do. Often there were too few, and some member would have to get up and get a needed fork or knife. Sometimes there were too many, and Casey would help put them away after the meal. At some of these occasions, her father would joke, "I see Casey helped you today." Gradually, Casey became more and more skilled at getting "the right amount" of silverware on the table.

🖋

In both instances, children were learning to share in the responsibilities of the household. Valerie learned a sense of pride, and Casey learned that she wasn't quite as accurate as she should be and needed to try harder. Both learned math skills, but Valerie's was a systematic and gradual process of learning through counting and then estimating. Casey learned how to estimate by the physical appearance of the pile.

The entire process of food preparation and mealtime provides children with many learning opportunities that are available no matter the circumstances and whenever families share in the process.

- Fine-motor skills are developed as children help in food preparation, such as when cutting up vegetables.

- Quantity measurement is learned as children help to bake cookies or a cake.

- Following along as the adult reads the recipe or the packaged directions develops sequencing skills and other prereading skills.

- Helping to make a grocery list supports writing and spelling skills and language development.

- Observing the change that takes place as liquid gelatin becomes solid in the refrigerator or as runny cake batter becomes a solid mass in the oven provides basic scientific understanding of a change process.
- Kinds and varieties of foods children eat during mealtime communicate the family's values regarding nutrition.
- Preparing or securing meals in a variety of settings extends children's knowledge of how foods are prepared (e.g., in the kitchen, cooking with the microwave, while camping, ordering in a deli and watching how the order is processed).

Different parent or sibling involvement in preparation and cleanup after meals teaches children the family attitude toward sex-role responsibilities. In some families, the mother is expected to get meals and clean up afterwards, especially if she stays at home caring for children. In other families, we find a sense of shared responsibility, particularly in homes where the mother works outside the home. A growing sense of maturity and responsibility develops as children assume some of the tasks in the mealtime process.

Bathing and Toileting.   Bathing and toileting in some families is a time when children learn attitudes about their bodies and begin sex education.

🕊

Stacey, 3 years old, was watching her mother bathing and diapering her 4-month-old brother, Jared. She watched with great fascination as her mother sang and splashed water playfully on the baby's arms and tummy, and she joined in as her mother sang, "This is the way we wash your arms . . .." The final stage of dressing and diapering Jared was a great revelation to Stacey as Jared shot urine into the air. "Whoops, there's one less diaper to wash," Mrs. B. exclaimed, then quickly began to put on a fresh diaper.

Suddenly, Stacey asked, "When will he lose that?"

Her mother replied, "Lose what, Stacey?"

"That!" emphasized Stacey, pointing.

"Oh, his penis," Mrs. B. said. "Why, he won't lose it, Stacey. He's a boy, and boys have penises, and girls have vaginas."
🕊

Even as young as 4 months, Jared is beginning to learn about his own body in a positive and enjoyable way. As his mother and sister sing about the parts of his body, he hears terms used in a sensual and pleasing manner. Stacey is beginning to gain new knowledge about basic sexual differences in positive ways as her mother encourages her to be a part of Jared's daily bath time. Stacey's mother answers Stacey's question directly using correct terminology matter of factly.

Lifelong habits and attitudes towards health are developed in the home by the ways parents emphasize cleanliness and proceed with toilet training. Children are naturally great imitators. They enjoy watching their parents do such mundane and routine actions as washing up, shaving, or powdering themselves, and they will imitate the actions. When such modeling is accompanied by occasional explanations for the action, children learn new language and begin to see relationships among actions.

Family Reuniting at the End of the Day. When the family's routine is such that each member goes off to work or to school, there is often a homecoming routine. The end of the day can be a stressful time, and both positive and negative lessons are learned.

Members of the family are usually tired and hungry and anxious at day's end, particularly when both parents are wage earners or if a single parent must do more in meal prepara-

Children enjoy observing and imitating routines of the home and learn important concepts and language in the process.

tion or if where one spends the night is uncertain. Often this will be a time when children begin to learn how to cope in difficult situations. When partners argue and disagree, children are often frightened of the anger, and their sense of security is threatened. Nurturing partners resolve their differences and provide models of negotiating behaviors. Partners who lash out, demean each other, or even strike each other are modeling ways to diminish another's self-concept. When parents or partners are able to resolve differences through discussion, apologizing, and coming to agreements, they provide lessons in how to negotiate a peaceful settlement.

Many end-of-the-day routines are pleasant experiences. In some families, children and adults at home share what happened to them during their absence from each other. Even in homeless situations, some parents are better able to cope and share their daily experiences with their children (Lindsey, 1998). In such sharing, children learn important socialization skills, such as how to listen, how to take turns talking, and how to explain so that someone else can understand, and in some instances, they learn the skills of sticking to the topic being discussed. How much understanding and skill children develop in the routine situations of the home depends on a combination of factors, such as age, sex of children, socioeconomic factors, children's interest, level of previous understanding, and adult/children interactions (Fine, 1993).

Bedtime.   As children prepare for bed, one finds many procedures that assist children's development. As in all routines, regularity and consistency help children develop a sense of time and order of events and a sense of security.

🪶

Four-year-old Kevin's parents went out for the evening, and Kevin had a new babysitter, whom he appeared to like very much. The sitter played games with him and read him his very favorite stories. At his regular bedtime, she helped him get undressed and brush his teeth. After one last story, she tucked him in, turned out the light, and went downstairs. A little later, she heard Kevin crying and went up to see what was the matter. As she calmed Kevin down, she finally heard him whimper, "I want Mommy. She says my prayers, and you didn't."

🪶

Kevin derived a great deal of security from a series of routine bedtime activities. Though he apparently forgot a part of the routine, he sensed something was wrong, and when he remembered, he became upset. Besides attending to Kevin's sense of security, the episode also demonstrates activities whereby Kevin's parents (or babysitter in their absence) fulfill their educational responsibilities. As Kevin washes and brushes his teeth before retiring, he is learning good health habits. Saying prayers at night or at mealtime can be the beginning of religious training.

Rituals and Traditions

According to Bossard and Boll (1949), **family ritual** is a formal procedure for defining patterns of behavior. Rituals and traditions are important to any society, for it is by such behaviors that individuals show respect for the value system within a family or clan (Goffman, 1967). Certainly, children learn many social, cognitive, and affective skills that are also

learned in other families. Perhaps the most important learnings children gain from rituals are the importance of family structure and the commitment that an individual makes to the solidarity of the group (Levy, 1992). In rituals and traditions, behavior patterns are neither questioned nor examined; the behavior is continued because it is important to the family. As children learn the expected behaviors of the rituals, they learn a sense of identity and self-concept.

Religious ceremonies involve many rituals from which children extend their understanding about the world and their connection to family.

🪶

At 9 years of age, Jess observed his second brother's bar mitzvah ceremony. At one point, he leaned towards his grandmother to whisper, "When will he get the shawl?"

"Soon now, just watch," replied his grandmother.

When the moment arrived, Jess's face lighted. "Oh!" he exclaimed. Afterwards he asked his mother whether he'd also receive the shawl.

"Certainly, when your turn comes."

"But I'm the only one who hasn't had it!"

"Yes, but that, too, is important, for now you have the support of your two brothers in helping you understand our faith."

For Jess, the ritual of the shawl had special meaning. Later, when he was 13, he asked the rabbi if his two brothers could place the shawl on his shoulders. At the end of the ceremony, he announced to his mother, "There are three of us now, and we are all alike!" The ritual provided Jess with a special connection with his family and religion.

🪶

Customs, chants, and folklore are often part of rituals and family traditions. Bettelheim (1976) stresses the importance of folklore to children's psychological and emotional development. He maintains that as children hear the old tales, they sense deeper meanings and thus find emotional security and comfort. Such stories serve as moral lessons as well. Oladele (1999) relates how the rituals in her family of memorizing Bible verses, singing spirituals, and reading created a sense of connection to her heritage.

In addition to providing emotional or moral support, rituals provide intellectual stimulus. Traditional rhymes, chants, and incantations have a language pattern and a story structure that support literacy development. In many families, adults chant or read the rhymes they learned as children, often in the course of playing with children. "This Is the Way the Lady Rides," "One, Two, Buckle My Shoe," or "Shoe the Old Horse" provides rhythms and language patterns that form the foundation of children's developing language. Iona and Peter Opie (1969) point out how older children teach younger ones the special games, rituals, and chants of childhood that parents do not attend to. Whether singing traditional songs, writing a letter to Santa Claus, helping count candles on the cake, or learning to read their part for the Seder, parents and older siblings are engaging children in literacy events.

Sharing Interests and Skills

The amount of knowledge that parents transmit to their children varies widely from family to family. The greatest differences in children's special knowledge occur between families who explore their interests together and those who ignore each other. For example, when computer enthusiasts involve their young children in learning rudimentary computer skills, their children often enter kindergarten more adept at using computers than their teachers. Saul and Newman (1986) point out how important parents are in interesting their children about science. When researchers asked

winners of Westinghouse's Science Talent Search how they became interested in science, most claimed it was their parents who got them interested.

A young mother on a remote island is a skilled violinist and instructs and interests her children and their friends in musical endeavors. Families may also share interest in the arts, as the following vignette shows.

🐦

When Mrs. Jacobs placed a Seurat print in her third-grade classroom, Roberto explained to the class that Seurat used a special technique called pointillism. *He and his artist father had experimented with the technique after a visit to their nearby museum. Roberto had been fascinated with the Seurat paintings, and his dad had extended that interest as the two explored the technique together through art books and in the studio.*

🐦

Children's curiosity leads them to ask many questions. Parents respond differently, depending on their own interests, knowledge, and style of interaction. Children's learning and continued interest depend greatly on the response they elicit.

Eager adults can turn off children's interest as well as expand it. For example, children may learn different things from the simple question, "Where does the wind come from?" One parent may reply, "Gee, I don't know!" Given that answer too many times, children learn that their questions are not important or that they shouldn't bother trying to find answers. Another parent may respond, "From the east" and point in the direction the wind is now blowing from. If that is the end of the conversation, children may learn where east is, that the wind's origin is east, and that adults know things and you can get information from them. Another parent may expand on this answer by pointing and then adding, "See, you can tell by how the trees are swaying." Children's knowledge is expanded to finding out something about how one determines direction of the wind. Another parent, whose own knowledge about wind and directionality is limited, may answer, "I'm not sure exactly. Let's see if we can find out." When parents and children together pursue an answer, children learn about the importance of questioning and new ways of knowing.

Besides learning the rules of the game, children learn many academic skills from children's games. For example, a game like Candyland® reinforces skills of following directions, learning color concepts, counting, reading pictures, and matching.

Watching television together provides opportunities for parents and children to develop a sense of shared enjoyment. Parents who watch programs with their children, in addition to deciding with their children what to watch and discussing the programs afterwards, enable their children to extend their knowledge. Children's appreciation of different types of programs, their ability to select an appropriate program, and even their ability to argue for their point of view are all good skills.

Reading to children and listening to children read is the strongest home factor relating to children's reading achievement in school (Adams, 1990; Hewison & Tizard, 1980; Teale, 1986). When children have favorite stories and parents respond to their requests to read and reread them, children develop an appreciation of language. The sounds and patterns for language are reinforced. When stories and pictures are discussed, children learn much about the framework of stories and how words and text go together (Applebee, 1989.)

Gardner (1983, 1999) discusses various intelligences that result because of children's different learning styles. These styles may be innate, but parents also support, reinforce, or even squelch their children's natural learning style by their ways of responding. Linguistically oriented parents tend to teach their children through explanations and expressive use of language. Parents with strong logical-mathematical orientations enjoy math and strategy games and encourage orderly and logical thinking in arriving at solutions. Spatially and kinesthetically oriented parents help their children move through space and use their bodies as they figure out how the world functions. Artistic parents expand their children's knowledge through imagining and creating. Naturalist-oriented parents discriminate among living things and are very sensitive to features of the natural world such as cloud, rock, and land formations and configurations. These responses not only reflect the parents' orientations but also communicate different ways of knowing.

Children whose parents reinforce their ways of knowing succeed better in school. But when learning styles of home and school are too disparate, children are at a disadvantage. However, teachers who try to understand what and how children have learned at home can create classroom opportunities for supporting and expanding children's skills and knowledge.

As a teacher-researcher, Voss (1993) points out how she discovered a student's learning style by visiting his home and watching as his father taught him how to build. Eric could never explain in class how he did something other than by using his hands and saying, "I first did this and then this and then this." No amount of questioning and attempts at expanding his language worked. Expressing himself orally and reading were painful for Eric. Eric enjoyed school only when the class worked on projects, and he spent hours figuring out how something went together. Upon visiting the home and getting to know the parents, Voss discovered that Eric had a special relationship with his father and was allowed to work on the projects his father did as a business or around the house. Eric's father rarely explained what he was doing, but when asked by the child how he was doing something, he would slow down his activity to demonstrate. Realizing how kinesthetically oriented the child was, the teacher was able to adjust the classroom learning to accommodate Eric's way of knowing and to expand his ability in other areas.

Family Outreach

The home curriculum is enriched or limited in the ways families engage in various activities in and out of the home. The amount of learning varies as a result of many factors, including economics and personal preferences. Even though parents living on a limited income can provide their children with many and varied learning opportunities, poverty does have a debilitating effect and reduces family choices and energies for learning opportunities (Clark, 1983).

Affluent parents have the means to provide a rich array of toys and reading materials in the home. Children may have their own televisions and computers. These parents arrange trips for their children as well as a variety of entertainment events, cultural activities, and recreational opportunities.

On the other hand, poverty limits children's experiences with travel and equipment as well as opportunities for scheduled outside activities, such as music or dance lessons, horseback riding, Little League, scouting, and club experiences. Although poverty is limiting, it does not mean that poor families are not committed to their children's education. We find many do make wise choices, enriching their children's experiences with appropriate toys, books, family outings, and even scheduled home lessons.

Parental opinions of the importance of different activities and the time they have to commit to their children vary considerably, and commitments change depending on children's ages. For example, in one study (National Center for Educational Statistics, 1992) regarding parents' involvement with children's reading, art activities, sports, and educational television viewing, the percentage of parents involved with their children decreased as children entered school and continued to decline as children progressed through third grade. This is understandable as children become more involved with peers. However, in spite of this decline, at the end of third grade, a larger percentage of parents were still involved with their children in sports and games than in any other activity. In all families, parents who find time in their lives to enjoy and engage their children in activities together, whether it be in the home, out for a walk, or on the drive home from work, provide a rich context for their children upon which further learning is built (Newman, 1998).

Learning opportunities for children vary not only with parental involvement but also with the way that parents interact with their children during these activities. The vignette in chapter 1 about Steven's riding lessons demonstrates that curriculum provided by structured lessons is not limited to the skills being taught. In that example, Steven, encouraged by suggestions from his mother, was also learning important social interaction skills with adults.

Two other examples of the family outreach curriculum are toys and games and travel.

Toys and Games.   The types of toys parents buy reflect the parents' value structure and extend development in different ways.

🐦

On the birth of her daughter Suzanna, Mrs. Williams bought a complete set of unit blocks. When Suzanna was old enough to sit and stack things, Mrs. Williams would take out a few blocks for Suzanna to play with. The blocks were always stored on shelves according to their unit size, and gradually Suzanna became involved in restoring them to their correct place on the shelf as she expanded her use of the blocks. Over time, other materials

Parents involved in their children's games provide a rich context for learning.

were added, such as play animals, toy trucks and cars, pieces of cloth, and paper and crayons for signs. At times, Suzanna's father would join her in playing blocks and building towers or complicated structures.

Ashley's father, delighting in his new daughter, bought her a huge toy panda. He would sit on the floor beside the panda holding his infant as he fed her or played with her. As Ashley grew older, the panda became an important source of comfort and a wonderful companion to sit with while hearing a story or watching television. Ashley had many small toys that entertained her, and she punched them, turned them over, and examined them when playing.

Both children experience a curriculum provided through the toys they receive. And both sets of parents play with their children as they use the various types of materials. In selecting blocks as the most important toy for her daughter, Mrs. Williams established a highly cognitive curriculum that expanded with Suzanna's growth and development. Ashley's father's first gift reflected his wish to provide a warm, cozy support system to be supplemented with random selections of fun toys. Both children are prized and cherished, and their parents are teaching important self-concept and academic skills that will help them as they enter school. But each parent provides a different curriculum. How these two children progress in school will depend on many factors, among which are the stability and continued support of adults in their lives and how well teachers are able to support and extend each child's home learning.

Travel. Most families take trips together, some to the grocery store or to visit local relatives, others on lengthy vacations traveling throughout the United States or abroad. Local trips provide rich learning experiences when parents extend the experience with observations about the scenery and what has changed in the familiar environment or with discussions about what is to be bought, why, and where to find it. Such involvement helps children learn about their natural environment and become keen observers of change. Among other things, they learn the give-and-take of discussion, reasons for doing things, and classification skills. Parents provide valuable emotional support and express values as they demonstrate pleasure in sharing these times with their children.

For extended travel, parents usually make plans, buy travel guides and maps, and make reservations. If travel is to a foreign country, passports are procured and currency is exchanged. The curriculum of such trips is extensive, and the learning depends on how much children are interested in and involved with the plans. Social studies, science, math, language, literature, the arts, cultural differences, social relationships, and problem-solving skills are integrated into such trips. In the following vignette, we find parents without specific cognitive goals in mind for their trip, but through their interactions and involvement, the children had many opportunities to gain new skills and knowledge.

🦅

Camping across the country, the Hi family discovered that temperatures varied considerably when they awoke in the morning. Mai Lin never seemed to dress right for the day. She was either too hot or too cold as they hiked or drove. Without saying anything to anyone, she began to solve her problem by sticking her hand out of the tent each morning to "test" the weather. As the trip progressed, she began to get better at sensing what the day's weather would be like and became a much happier traveler. She also learned how to dress by observing her parents and hearing their discussions on what they were going to wear that day. She discovered how to adapt to abrupt changes in temperatures that sometimes occurred within a few hours as the family traveled through snow in the mountains to the hot desert valleys below. In addition to learning about geography and its effect on changes in climate, Mai Lin learned during the trip to figure out how to make herself more comfortable.

The Hi family never traveled without their children's favorite books and puzzles, plus lots of paper, crayons, and pencils. When the children got restless, everyone took turns reading favorite stories or poems aloud to each other. Both children and adults introduced various games they had learned. Some games were counting games about the things they were seeing out the window; others were guessing games that required remembering what they

had done on the trip or stories they had read together. Rules were made and remade so that all could "win" at something. Paper and pencils were used to write down things they wanted to remember. Crayons helped in drawing scenes they'd seen. Besides learning literary, math, and memory skills, the children were learning about rule making, how to adapt activities so that the youngest could have fun, and how to compromise.

🦅

When school programs build on children's travel experiences and teachers encourage experimentation in class projects, all children benefit. The following vignette portrays a productive outcome in a multiage group of children.

🦅

Eight-year-old Manny and his classmates were creating a story that included a volcano eruption. The children interrupted their story to build a pretend volcano in their classroom sandbox. As Manny watched the simulated lava roll down the sides of the "volcano," he shared his experiences of visiting a live volcano in Hawaii. Struggling to explain what he had seen, he remembered a book his teacher had added to the classroom collection that contained pictures of an erupting volcano. Manny's limited explanations of the hot lava, the students' experiments in building a volcano, and the pictures in the book helped the other students give a more vivid description of an erupting volcano when they continued their story.

🦅

When classroom teachers provide an environment whereby children can share family experiences, usually all children in the classroom benefit.

All families educate their children to some level of functioning in society. Although we have dysfunctional families where children's learning is hampered or even distorted, most families provide varied educational opportunities for their children through daily routines and ongoing family activities. The best outcomes occur when families assume their share of responsibility for the education of their children and work with schools and communities to assist in the process. In chapter 13, we discuss more aspects of family functioning and delineate the characteristics of competent families where positive learning takes place.

HOME SCHOOLING

Families that assume total responsibility for their children's education often opt to educate their children at home, at least for part of their schooling years. Home schooling is not a new concept but has gained popularity in recent years. The term is used to define academic learning that occurs as a result of activities provided in the home (or extensions of the home), with the parents acting as teachers/facilitators. Home schooled children are engaged, often with other siblings, in different activities that are geared to children's interests and abilities (Van Galen & Pitman, 1991). The definition is made more clear by Kerman's (1990) description of a typical day of home schooling, summarized here:

🌿

Their day starts with the family's eating breakfast. Then the 9-year-old daughter leaves with her father for the library, where she will engage in some preplanned library study, and then will carry out some errands for the family. At home, the mother provides unscheduled activities for the two preschoolers that relate to the children's interests, to household needs, and to events that happen in the neighborhood. They read several stories, wash dishes, make play dough, do "dress-up" and dramatic play,

and then walk down the road to watch when they notice a fire truck putting out a fire.

🌿

History of Home Schooling

Home schooling was the norm for most families during the early years of the United States' development. In chapter 2, we described the role of the home in U.S. education during those years. In the late 19th and early 20th centuries, with the advent of compulsory education, home schooling diminished and was confined mostly to children in remote areas, to children whose parents traveled abroad, or to children in homes with strong religious beliefs (Van Galen & Pitman, 1991). Since the 1980s, interest in home schooling has increased, and some of the reasons seem associated with the failure of the alternative school movement of the 1960s (Guterson, 1992). In the late 1970s, John Holt became a strong advocate of home schooling, and parents, disenchanted with their local schools, found support for their efforts in his writings and especially from his newsletter *Growing Without Schooling* (Gorder, 1996).

Mayberry, Knowles, Ray, and Marlow (1995) contend that in the past three decades we can identify four chronological phases for home schooling. The first phase of renewed interest in home schooling in the late 1960s was marked with a period of contention, fueled by school reformers such as Kozol, Holt, Kohl, and Illich. Some parents decided that "the public school experience would harm their children in some way, or that the parents could provide a superior learning environment" (Knowles, 1989, p. 400).

The second phase, peaking in the 1970s, was marked by confrontations with the courts (Guterson, 1992; Knowles, 1989). School officials, concerned about the quality of education that homes could provide and alarmed by the loss of state funds when children were home

Home schooled children are often engaged with siblings and neighbors in different activities.

schooled, began litigation over parent rights to home school their children. Although confrontations with public officials continue, landmark cases have provided parents with precedents for educating their children at home. Wisconsin v. Yoder (1972) established the right of parents to home school their children because of their religious beliefs. And through rights to privacy, parents gained the right to choose alternative forms of education, according to Perchemlides v. Frizzle (1978) (Bumstead, 1979). In addition, parents won the right to home school their children based on the free exercise clause of the First Amendment (Richardson & Zirkel, 1991). For exam-

ple, Michigan officials were adamant that children be taught by certified teachers, but in People v. DeJonge (1993), the Michigan supreme court ruled that school officials had not shown that certified teachers provided a better education for students than noncertified ones (Mayberry et al., 1995). In many states, as litigation costs have risen, educators have become more reluctant to prosecute home schoolers.

Cooperation, which defines phase three for home schoolers, is a result of changes in attitudes. Some state officials have begun to change regulations regarding education policies, especially as home school parents become more open and vocal in seeking cooperation with local schools. Kerman (1990) relates how she armed herself with knowledge of local and state laws in Michigan as she prepared for home schooling her children. By dealing in an open and friendly way with local schools, she was able to get support so that her daughter could attend school part-time when her needs and interests were best suited to the school setting.

As more parents select home schooling and schools become more receptive in giving additional support, the fourth phase is becoming apparent. Increased networking among home schoolers has provided such benefits as organizational support, publications, workshops for parents, and improvement of materials and curriculum programs (Knowles, 1989; Lines, 1995). This consolidation of gains in influence and support systems is marked by a greater public acceptance of home schooling as a viable alternative to public education. In some school districts, educators are joining parents in a team effort and allowing children dual enrollment—attending some classes, participating in extracurricular activities, and using schools' special services (Terpstra, 1994). In other areas, there are organized education centers, and school districts share their special resources and allow students to take what special classes they desire (Deckard, 1996; Duffey, 1998). Schools can also support home schoolers by being sure that notices, announcements of school events, and newsletters are mailed to their homes. Teachers can also keep in touch with home schoolers through telephone calls and home visits.

Motives for Home Schooling

Reasons parents home school their children are probably as varied as the number of parents who have decided on this option. Presently, two distinct groups—the ideologues and the pedagogues—appear in home schooling decisions, and both groups disagree with

what is happening in schools today (Gorder, 1996; Van Galen & Pitman, 1991). Ideologues disagree with the values and belief systems presented by teachers or by children's peers. Since schools do not permit religious education to be taught, these parents choose to home school so that the family's religious values are what their children learn.

The growing group of pedagogues, troubled by their perceptions of school curricula, feel their children can receive a more personalized and better education if taught at home. Some parents choose to home school because they fear their children's being exposed to problems such as violence, drugs, teenage pregnancy, and disruptive behavior. Others disagree with the instructional and managerial styles of teachers and school administrators. Some are concerned with the inability of teachers to meet all the individual needs, interests, and learning styles of their children and are concerned that school will turn their children off to the excitement of learning. Some had unpleasant experiences in their own schooling and wish to prevent that for their children. Still other parents decide to home school because their children experience difficulty in school, and they find school personnel unresponsive and or even punitive when addressing problems (Gorder, 1996; Jeub, 1994; Nelson, 1986; Van Galen, 1988).

Who Does Home Schooling?

Getting accurate statistics on parents who home school is difficult, partially because some parents fear litigation if their practices are revealed. However, Lines (1991) estimated that 250,000 to 350,000 children in the United States were home schooled at the beginning of the 1990s. Since then, numbers quoted for home schoolers has risen drastically. Estimates as high as 1 million have been quoted, with some suggesting that by 2010, there will be 5 million home schooled children (Gorder,

1996; Ray, 1997). These estimates are based on information from state departments of education, home school leaders, and curriculum suppliers for home schoolers.

If the reasons for home schooling are varied, the largest number of home schoolers is amazingly alike demographically. The typical home schooling family has two parents, has an income near the U.S. median, and is Caucasian and Protestant. Parents tend to have some college education, are professional or skilled workers, and come mostly from rural areas, although some are suburban. Home schoolers appear to be conservative and law-abiding but also individualistic and very child centered (Gorder, 1996; Lines, 1991; Van Galen & Pitman, 1991).

Teaching Methods in Home Schooling

Curriculum and methods for home schooling depend on the home, but most methods fall into three categories: fixed curriculum, units of study, and unstructured learning events (Farenga, 1990). The fixed curriculum consists of guides with specific lessons, suggestions on how to teach, and evaluation techniques. This satisfies parents who are unsure of what to teach and who find comfort in a fixed schedule and prescribed curriculum. Some parents, especially those parents who view home schooling as a temporary solution to their children's educational needs, use the same texts used in the local schools. Correspondence schools, in which some parents enroll their children, meet this need and provide a structure and routine for home schooling. More and more home schooling parents are using the various resources of the Internet to provide learning opportunities for their children.

Home school organizations, as well as regular publishing companies, have curriculum guides and suggestions for units of study. In these, the teaching/learning is more flexible, and children move through specific

units at their own pace and as their interests dictate.

The instructional learning events consist of the things children are interested in, and development of skills takes place as children experience various aspects of adult life. Each child's curriculum will be very different when parents follow this outlook. Parents using the "unschooled method" often write about the many ways they enable their children to be successfully schooled. Some read to their children a great deal and provide a range of quality materials. For these families, books of all sorts, including reference materials, are always available. Computers provide these families with many more learning opportunities for their children. Access to the Internet for searches on current events or other topics, use of E-mail for communicating with friends or relatives in distant places, and the multitude of computer games are but examples that knowledgeable families use.

Children schooled at home are normally included in all family work activities, such as washing dishes, doing laundry, fixing plumbing, or building the extra room on the house, as well as family recreational/educational activities, such as visiting libraries and museums. Some families write plays and poems together, and some share their musical talents. Math skills are developed as parents involve children in building, using money, and figuring out family finances. Many children and parents explore their natural environment together, learning science concepts as they follow their interests.

As children grow older and their interests expand beyond their parents' expertise, some parents apprentice their children to artists, naturalists, and even sheepherders. One parent said that she had made a list of people she met who had special interests or hobbies so that when her child showed an interest, she found she had resources to draw on (Barker, 1990). Parents also see it as their responsibility

Home schooled children and their parents explore their natural environment together.

to extend their children's interest and enthusiasm, especially at moments when boredom seems to be setting in.

Even within a single family, the routine and methods followed by home schoolers will vary from year to year as children develop skills, new interests, and the ability to pursue their own learning. The common element is that children's interests are always paramount, and drill or practice is done at the pace the children set. In most home schooled families, projects become a major motivating factor, and parents encourage their children's pursuit of such activities (Wallace, 1990).

As children grow older, some parents allow them to select whether to continue home schooling or to go to a public school. In some states, home schoolers are permitted to take part in certain school activities and even attend school for specific courses or for a part of the day (Priesnitz, 1990). Some families even alternate between sending their children to school one year and keeping them home the next, depending upon which avenue they feel provides the best education (Nelson, 1986).

Legal Aspects of Home Schooling

The laws concerning home schooling vary among the states, and as home schooling has gained momentum, some states are changing statutes. All 50 states have compulsory attendance laws, and home schoolers encounter legal problems depending on how states interpret these laws. Court and state offices use the following four issues in deciding the legality of home schooling:

1. Parental rights of choice regarding their children's welfare
2. Equivalency of education
3. Home schools defined as private schools
4. Need for certified teachers

Some states mandate that home schooling must provide an equivalent education to what the public school provides, and many states define these terms conservatively. Determined home schoolers in these states must provide required curriculum outlines and have their children take required state tests to show that children's education is not being neglected. Incidentally, parents normally win the legal battles rising from equivalency cases.

Other states are more supportive of home schoolers and even cooperate with parents in their efforts to provide what they consider the best possible education for their children. For example, Wisconsin, Missouri, and Wyoming are favorable toward home schooling requests. They do require submission of a curriculum plan, but testing, certification, and proof of equivalency are not required. Other states are much stricter in their regulations (Figure 7–2).

Figure 7–2   State support for home schooling.
Source: From *Home Schools: An Alternative* (p. 119), by C. Gorder, 1996, Mesa, AZ: Blue Bird Publishing. Reprinted by permission.

Legal climate for
home schools

☐ Ideal states for home schooling

▨ States where home schoolers have generally
    been treated well

■ States that have numerous and/or some strict
    regulations regarding home schooling

▨ States that are very very strict regarding
    home school regulations

The three most rigorously regulated states are Michigan, Iowa, and North Dakota. All three require a curriculum plan that has proof of equivalency filed with the local superintendent, and home teachers must either be certified or be supervised by a certified teacher. In addition, North Dakota requires a list of courses taken and annual tests, and children who fall below the 13th percentile must be professionally evaluated. The remaining states fall between these extremes in terms of their openness to home schooling (Deckard, 1998; Gorder, 1996; Lines, 1991).

Criticisms and Successes of Home Schools

As the home schooling movement has grown, some states have registered concern. Some observers maintain that the alarm means that officials are concerned over loss of tax monies to districts because of lower enrollment figures and because they view home schooling as strong criticism of public school systems (Van Galen & Pitman, 1991). Publicized successes of some home schoolers can, of course, be taken as a refutation of public efforts. The following criticisms are often leveled at home schoolers:

1. Children will not develop important socialization skills or be able to function in the real world.

2. Parents do not have the knowledge and skills to teach a broad curriculum.

3. Parents are unable to provide sufficient equipment to study different subjects, especially science.

4. Parents often ignore drill and practice necessary to acquire basic skills.

Few data have been collected to support or to refute these criticisms of home schooling, but in those states requiring standardized tests, home schoolers score academically as well as, if not better than, their counterparts in public schools (Calvery, Bell, & Vaupal, 1992;

Lines, 1995). Studies also indicate that no significant relationship exists between home schoolers' achievements and parental education level (Ray, 1997; Van Galen & Pitman, 1991). This appears to counter the argument that parents lack the skills to teach a variety of subjects.

The criticism that home schoolers are not being as well socialized to society is harder to support or refute because we lack studies examining the differences. However, home school parents maintain that their children are being socialized by a greater diversity of people than are children in schools. Home schoolers often interact rather regularly with children and adults ranging in age from very young children to the elderly, whereas children in schools are limited to a classroom of their peers. The limited testing that has been done on the social and psychological development indicates that home schoolers are above average in this area (Lines, 1995; Ray, 1997).

Examining the individual success stories of home schooled children, we find evidence that some home schoolers do well academically and socially when they return to public school, find jobs in the community, or gain acceptance to college (Colfax & Colfax, 1992; Farenga, 1990). But communities and authorities do have an obligation to all children under their jurisdiction, and educators recognize that home schooling is not for all parents or for all children. The reported successes are probably due to parents who wish to be an integral part of their children's learning and are willing to devote the hard work and commitment it requires. Certainly not all parents have the time, inclination, patience, or ability to sustain such nourishment on a long-term basis. We must keep in mind that teachers are key personnel in many phases of children's education, including those children being home schooled. Therefore, communication with homes where children are home schooled is vital. As a teacher, you need to give support and keep communication lines open. The situation must be analogous to the home-school-community partnership.

IMPLICATIONS FOR PROFESSIONALS

Understanding how rich a curriculum is available in the home, whether through regular routines, family events, or the total home schooling process, will help you assess your own curriculum for children. If you follow this advice, you will be better equipped to extend all children's learning rather than be limited to teaching a narrow curriculum.

As you think of your students, you need to consider how you and your students' families reinforce each other's teaching strategies. For example, consider the vignettes in this chapter:

- The Martinez family reinforced with their own child the school's policy of inclusion of the Down syndrome child by encouraging him to tutor the child with special needs.

- Manny's teacher was aware of Manny's trip to Hawaii and provided an environment that was supportive of his sharing his experiences.

- A teacher aware of the types of trips children take reinforces children's memories of what they had seen, drawn, and written down on such trips.

- All children can participate when such trips as visiting a relative, going to the grocery store, or walking in the woods are valued by the teacher as important learning opportunities.

Careful observation, interested listening, and learning about children's home environments provide you with a base upon which to build children's learning and enrich your own curriculum.

SUMMARY AND REVIEW

Children receive a great deal of education outside the classroom walls. Whether intentionally or accidentally, parents provide a rich and varied curriculum in the home. Although great differences appear in quantity and quality of home curricula, all parents, as well as other family members, provide emotional, social, physical, and intellectual stimuli for children's development. Children learn role expectations and responsibilities as the family carries out routines and rituals. Parental interaction styles as well as the physical environment in which children are raised affect children's learning.

Children's home curriculum is an accumulation of all the experiences the children have in their home environment. Thus, each child's curriculum is different, but similarities occur as a result of the daily routines that exist in most families. Both skills and knowledge about the world are acquired as children participate in preparing for the day, in meal preparation, and in bathing and bedtime rituals. From family traditions and rituals, children gain an understanding of their ethnic and cultural identity and of their place in the world. As parents share their own special interests and talents, children expand their concepts of the world around them.

Parents committed to assuming total responsibility for their children's learning may choose to educate their children at home. Although a small group has always believed in education at home, the home schooling movement has grown rapidly since the 1960s. While numerous reasons are given, most parents choose this route for religious reasons or because of philosophical differences with schools regarding education. Home schooling parents, though rather conservative, are individualistic, and most are middle-class, Caucasian, and Protestant. Home schooling is not for everybody, and all agree that this process requires lots of hard work and a strong commitment to sustain positive outcomes.

SUGGESTED ACTIVITIES AND QUESTIONS

1. Visit a suburban house and a city apartment and compare the amount of living space. What are some of the things you think children living in each space would learn about themselves? What opportunities for physical development exist in the two homes?

2. Interview two parents and ask about their routines of the day. What learning do you think their children might gain from what they indicated?

3. List the kinds of trips that you took with your family when you were growing up. Include items such as shopping, visiting relatives, and recreation outings, as well as vacation trips. From your memory of the experiences, what do you think you learned (physically, emotionally, socially, and intellectually) from these trips?

4. Check with your state's department of education to find out about the legal aspects for home schooling in your state. Discuss with classmates your feelings about parents who choose this route for their children.

RESOURCES

Books

1. Applebee, A. N. (1996). *Curriculum as conversation.* Chicago: University of Chicago Press.
2. Thomas, A. (1998). *Educating children at home.* Herndon, VA: Cassell Academic.

Films/Videos

1. *Infant curriculum: Great explorations; Toddler curriculum: Making connections.* (1997). [Videos, 20 min each]. South Carolina Educational Television with National Association for the Education of Young Children.
2. *Nourishing language development in early childhood.* (1998). [Video, 31 min]. Davidson Films, Inc., with National Association for the Education of Young Children.

Organizations

National Association for the Education of Young Children (http://www.naeyc.org/)
1509 16th Street, NW, Washington, DC 20036-1426

National Homeschool Association (http://www.jayi.com/sbi/aagc/homesch.htm)
P. O. Box 157290, Cincinnati, OH 45215

Family Service Association of America (no web address)
44 East Twenty-third Street, New York, NY 10010

Websites

1. http://www.concentric.net/-skiplac/ Website provides information on home schooling, links to educational sites, and information on multimedia's impact on education.
2. http://www.nauticom.net/www/cokids/index.html Website is designed for educators but contains a family pages category providing useful material for parents of young children and links to other sites.
3. http://www.ehow.com A new website called "eHow" with thousands of files offering step-by-step instructions for all sorts of home tasks and projects.
4. http://www.edexcellence.net Education Excellence Network site for promotion of educational reforms: vouchers, charter schools, and privatization.

Chapter 8

Curriculum of the School

After the family, schools represent the most important developmental unit in modern social systems.

(Comer, 1980, p. 268)

❧

Following the first several years of family life, young children enter school, another major institution in their young lives. At this point, a different world emerges for children as well as for parents. This chapter discusses curriculum experiences in typical schools and how they relate to children's other experiences. In reading this chapter you will learn the following:

1. School programs, including many child care facilities, enhance the cognitive and socialization processes that begin in the home.

2. Staffing, administration, and the location of school facilities all affect the atmosphere and the quality of school programs.

3. Some school environments support children's learning and development better than others.

4. Formal public and private schools as well as out-of-home care facilities differ in program because educators have differing philosophical orientations and differing work styles.

5. All school programs are enhanced when homes, schools, and communities cooperate and collaborate.

Since schooling extends the cognitive and socialization processes children have begun with their families, naturally, the relationships between home and school are of major importance for children's growth. In addition to providing skills and content, the school affects children's self-concept, molds aspirations, starts the foundation for community participation and future employment, and affects a good deal of preteen socialization. Schools are particularly important for at-risk children, for as Werner and Smith (1992) conclude, "Re-

silient children are able to use the school experience profitably as a refuge from a troubled home environment" (p. 109).

The success of children in school is heavily dependent on the relations that exist between home and school. Conflicts over skills and values, differing views about content, or confusion about roles erodes the effectiveness of schoolwork, confuses the objectives that both homes and schools subscribe to, and detracts from children's functioning (Hess & Holloway, 1984). Cooperation and compatibility between home and school enable both institutions to provide stability for children and engender progress toward healthy development.

Since schools are more impersonal than homes, children in school function in a different way. Most schools have a distinct chain of command. Rules and regulations abound, and authority figures are seen everywhere. A prescribed order for the day is established in the vast majority of U.S. schools, and freedom for the typical student is lessened considerably. The following vignette dramatizes the situation of a 7-year-old entering a conventional school after being home schooled.

❧

"Jessica, please return to your seat. You shouldn't be wandering out to the hall."

The second grader turned and blurted, "I . . . saw my brother, and he needed some help."

"I understand Jessica, but there is a school rule—no leaving the classroom without permission," Ms. Strong said firmly.

When Jessica was 7, she entered school for the first time. Her mother had rejoined the family lumber business after home schooling

Jessica and her 5-year-old brother. Now in second grade, Jessica was just getting used to things that her neighborhood friends had been doing for the past 2 years. "We get lots of books," Margo had said, and that was true, but they were a lot different from the library books and magazines Jessica's mom had used in teaching Jessica. "I really liked the number blocks we used last year," Cicely had mentioned. "I hope we get 'em again." Jessica enjoyed most school activities, but she yearned for the casual pace with her mother. She was reprimanded twice in one day for chatting with two boys in her cluster. Ms. Strong didn't like to have social conversations going on, and visiting anyone else in class was forbidden. "Mom, she gives us directions all the time. I can't keep track of the things she says. It's a good thing Harry showed me where to put the date on my spelling paper."

Curriculum for any child involves what happens to the child each day from the time he or she wakes until he or she goes to sleep. For children 5 years old and older, the school will have a significant impact on that total life curriculum. For an increasing number of preschool children (over 60% now), the nursery school and day care combinations affect that life curriculum.

Schooling involves a formal curriculum of skills and content, an informal curriculum (which starts at home) of habits, practices, and attitudes that all school personnel seek to implement, and a hidden curriculum that unfolds in an unintended way but nonetheless permeates children's consciousness. Each curriculum will be affected by educators' philosophical orientations, which in turn influence the organizational arrangements and patterns we find in individual school buildings and classrooms. The following sections discuss the typical school curriculum and its impact on children.

OVERALL PROGRAM OF THE SCHOOL

In general, schools are seen as places where kids "grow up," learn to interact more skillfully with other children and adults, and assume new responsibilities. While still nurturers, early childhood educators play a role different from that of parents; their attitudes, goals, and procedures also are usually quite different. Everyone knows that a teacher's association with a group of students will be short-lived (usually less than a year), and most parents and teachers thus feel that more formality in relationships is normal. Children, of course, must adjust as they move between home and school.

In most schools, children find themselves in a rule- and ritual-bound environment. Teachers frequently compare children to one another and regularly evaluate their performance. Jessica in the preceding vignette was used to more independence, and it was hard for her to learn the school culture and to operate in a manner where rules did not always make sense to her.

Consideration or allowances for what happened prior to this grade are no longer relevant in most school situations. It is what you know now, what you look like now, and what is going on now that are important for the agenda of most schools. Children in school are expected to be more conforming and less assertive, to accept responsibility for behaviors and achievement, and to be part of a group that they know little about. For most young children, school is a very different place, and life is starting over.

During the 20th century, school represented one major link to adulthood, and in recent years, school experiences seem even more necessary for children to adjust to a postmodern society. And though success is sometimes limited, school aims and objectives are focused on preparing children for later roles in a bureaucratic, industrialized, high-tech society. The advantages or disadvantages that children bring to school will naturally influence their progress in the formal learning environment. Experiences in preschool programs and in community agencies such as church, summer camp, or libraries may help children to make adjustments and transitions more easily.

But what of children in the danger zone? It is especially imperative for at-risk children to have healthy school experiences. School is frequently the only safe, stable, or consistent environment in an at-risk child's life. Numerous accounts show that endangered children linger at their schools as long as possible to avoid neighborhood conflicts and abuse (Garbarino, Dubrow, Kostelny, & Pardo, 1998; Kotlowitz, 1991; Osofsky, 1997) The rise in numbers of at-risk children in the United States is sobering—one fourth of our young are in danger (Children's Defense Fund, 1998; Comer, 1997; Garbarino, Kostelny & Dubrow 1998).

The case is clear for dramatically increased collaboration by all human service institutions to produce better environments and better transitions between home and school. To emphasize the need, a Carnegie Corporation report (Cohen, 1994) calls for educators, communities, and health care providers to incorporate services for even the youngest children (birth to age 3) in plans for 21st-century schools.

PRESCHOOL AND CHILD CARE PROGRAMS

Before moving to components of formal school programs, we should point out how various programs for 3- and 4-year-olds fit into the curriculum picture. As noted in chapters 4 and 5, 60% of American preschool-age children are in some type of care facility for some part of each week. Situations vary from mother's day out programs to goal-oriented Montessori preschools.

Is there a curriculum in these preschool and child care facilities? Most assuredly there is. Some will have a fairly structured scope and sequence chart of particular objectives, and teaching personnel will have philosophical orientations not unlike those noted in the discussion of curriculum orientations in the following section. Others will consider their free-flowing activities as learning experiences and participation. Many out-of-home care programs will resemble in form and substance the experience of the home where, we have maintained, a curriculum of some sort exists. There will also be that informal and incidental curriculum that undergirds so much of children's later learning.

In many programs for 3- and 4-year-olds (Head Start centers, nursery schools, and the 4-year-old rooms of large child care centers), you can find definite planned activities with expectations identified for children attending those classrooms. In many ways, they resemble the kindergarten curriculum in regular public schools. One would hope that preschool teaching personnel are considerate of young children's developmental levels and have means for adjusting expectations to the learning styles and backgrounds of individual children (Bredekamp & Rosegrant, 1995).

CURRICULUM ORIENTATIONS

As an educator, you will develop expectations for children's conduct and accomplishments, and these expectations will reflect your philosophical orientation. Since one character or disposition normally dominates in a particular school building, we usually find the educators there similar in orientation and outlook. Of course, teachers and administrators attempt to accomplish school expectations using different teaching styles and with varying degrees of success.

Volumes are written about different curriculum orientations, and writers use various

Many preschool programs emphasize participation in free-flowing activities to support learning.

ways of labeling and explaining the different perspectives. For this text, the continuum discussed ranges from a traditionalist, teacher-dominated stance at one end to a progressive, child-centered stance at the other (see Table 8–1). All curriculum orientations focus on developing children's potential, but how to best do that and with what tools define the different perspectives. As shown in Table 8–1, we can section the continuum into several parts and ascribe to each a philosophical base, authorities, features, and teacher roles.

Five categories or positions that appear consistently in the literature and are supported by curriculum authorities (Doll, 1995; Eisner, 1994; McNeil, 1996) are academic,

technologist, cognitive process, social reconstructionist, and personal relevance. Table 8–1 provides a summary of these orientations. You will note that borderlines are ambiguous, categories overlap, and authorities use different terms to describe each perspective.

We describe here a 3-section continuum of curriculum orientations condensed from the perspectives in Table 8–1. These three areas represent situations observed in many early childhood classes today:

1. Traditional—combining aspects of academic rationalism and the technologist.

2. Constructivist—combining aspects of cognitive process and social reconstructionist.

Table 8–1   Typical Curriculum Orientations

Labels	Academic Rationalism; Humanism	Technologist	Cognitive Process; Constructivist	Social Meliorist; Reconstructionist	Personal Relevance; Individual Fulfillment
Philosophical Bases	Idealism	Realism	Pragmatism, Experimentalism	Experimentalism	Existentialism
Proponents	Adler, Hirsch, Hutchins, Bennett	Bobbitt, Tyler, Hunter, Bloom	Bloom, Bruner, Piaget, Vygotsky, Dewey	Counts, Apple, Freire	Rousseau, Neill, Holt
Features	Classic studies. Wisdom of the ages. Focus on arts.	High order and discipline. Back to basics. Mastery of here and now.	Learning to learn. Experiencing world and accepting change. Problem solving.	Study of world and improving one's surroundings. Social experiences.	Freedom to choose. Student assisted in exploring personal learning journey.
Teacher Role	Teacher mastery and enthusiasm required. Models the ideal. Lectures and discusses.	Well-planned and detailed objectives. Lectures and demonstrates. Interprets and informs.	Develops projects, stimulates study. Directs attention to levels of analysis and progress.	Suggests explorations supporting learners. Resource person.	Assists learners in explorations. Minimal teacher agenda.

3. Personal relevance—follows the personal relevance orientation for individual exploration.

The first two orientations are found in most U.S. schools. Though aspects of the third orientation may occur within the first two, curricula based solely on this perspective are found only in a few private or experimental schools.

Traditional

Traditional academic and teacher-dominated programs expect children to be conforming, respectful of authority, and anxious to learn and to look to their teachers for guidance and stimulation. Intellectual growth in "worthy subjects" is the agenda, and programs of this kind will be as structured and efficiently organized as the teacher is capable. Classrooms are replete with behavioral objectives, and standardized tests are most often used for assessing because the goal is to develop a particular core of knowledge.

This orientation is known as **traditional schooling**, and it has held sway for generations. Given the right circumstances—well-focused and humane teachers working with interested and organized children—it is extremely successful in promoting basic skills and cultural literacy. The following vignette illustrates a well-functioning traditional classroom.

❦

Ms. Washington is noticeable and vibrant in her second-grade classroom. The room purrs with efficiency, and Ms. Washington covers every part of the room dozens of times each day in maintaining control and helping the children. The class has won the PTA banner for 5 months running now, and the 7-year-olds eagerly inform visitors that theirs is the best room.

The class is arranged as three reading and two math groups, using textbooks that Ms. Washington occasionally supplements with her own material. Assignments are neatly and clearly presented on a side chalkboard, which children consult periodically. Every student is busy at 9:15—two groups work quietly on skill sheets while Ms. W. conducts a directed reading activity with the third group. While working with the group, she beckons two children from the seated groups to check their progress. She gives frequent signals to class members in response to their raised hands; her eyes sweep across the class like a lighthouse beam on a recurring pattern.

A change in groups is handled like clockwork. In less than 2 minutes, groups have rotated and are at work once more. Ms. W.'s pleasant voice distributes accolades: "Wonderful work in Jawon's group!" "All papers are completed here, too. Super!"

Ms. W. carefully plans all activities and is ready to go at 9:00 every morning. Even such activities as science projects, which the curriculum guide called for children to do at home, Ms. W. has decided to have at school where she can monitor and supervise. Her movements are quick and energetic, and the class emulates her.

Ms. Washington is the classic traditional teacher; she has everything down pat. She does all the planning, demonstrating, and guided practice and anticipates almost every problem. "I work hard at what I do, and I get good results," she notes, and this is demonstrated in her students' yearly achievement test scores.

Teachers in traditionally oriented schools think of themselves as in a means-to-an-end situation, as Ms. Washington does. They see themselves working diligently to overcome obstacles—whether ignorance, missing skills, or lack of interest—and devise strategies that will entice learners and build skills to support later education. The curriculum is didactic and teacher centered in nature, focused on structure; such teachers are businesslike, and their can-do aura permeates the traditional classroom.

In keeping with the industrial model, contract learning, programmed learning, and mastery learning all fit with this design. Time-on-task studies, goal-analysis plans, scope and sequence charts, critical paths for learning, and management by objectives all fit here very well, too. Since accountability is foremost, norm-referenced testing is appropriate. The expectation is development of literacy, computational, scientific, and social skills. The traditional orientation makes for a socially efficient, skills-outcome-based educational system, which is easy to rationalize. A clear goal is in sight, and teachers pursue ways to get there.

Traditionalists accept new objectives as they become relevant for contemporary living. Personal living skills, health education, and computer literacy all make sense for primary-school-age children in today's world, so schools with the traditionalist orientation assume responsibility for these areas to produce students tuned to today's needs.

The traditional program is by far the most dominant orientation in the United States today, and its advocates form a long line. Franklin Bobbitt was an early proponent when, in the early 20th century, he made the case for a curriculum responsive to the time. Since then, advocates such as Benjamin Bloom, Hilda Taba, Ralph Tyler, and Madeline Hunter have propounded the idea. William Bennett, a recent secretary of education, supports the bases of traditional education, as does John Silber (1989) in his book *Straight Shooting.*

A school with traditional outlook and academic goals does not always have a successful program. Some schools have evolved this way because that is the heritage for the community. Even when a program has questionable objectives for the population served and garners unenthusiastic response, school boards often perpetuate it. Many low-achieving schools are of this type; they cling to inappropriate goals and teaching methods while seen by their communities as irrelevant.

The ongoing popularity of the traditional curriculum assures its continued existence, but the lockstep approach seems deadly for some learners. In addition, teacher-centered programs in preschools seem to hold some risk for increasing the later antisocial behavior of disadvantaged children (Schweinhart & Weikart, 1997; Weikart & Schweinhart, 1991).

Certainly the traditionalist plan does not flexibly accommodate different learning levels in the way that constructivist and personal relevance orientations do. However, traditional education appeals to many educators working with marginalized learners. Because programs are carefully structured and are developed in steps, dedicated teachers can provide consistency, predictability, and stability for children who would otherwise not find this pattern in their lives.

Constructivist

Constructivist curricula have social efficiency goals similar to the traditional orientation but employ quite different strategies, permitting individualized instruction and varied content.

Instead of employing the traditionalist emphasis on skill sequence, the constructivist works to develop children's thinking skills. Valuing the process rather than the product, the constructivist objective is for children to learn how to learn so that they may adapt knowledge and skill to new situations. Teacher behaviors differ from those of the manager/director stance of the traditionalist, but constructivists maintain a strong teacher presence in their classrooms to direct projects and anticipate next steps.

Rather than use carefully designed skill ladders, scope and sequence charts, and behavioral objectives, constructivists favor problem-centered work. Theme-focused programs, units of study, and other similar programs belong in this camp. Since content is often serendipitous and subject to change, teachers with a constructivist orientation must be very secure in knowledge of content and perspectives on child development. They must keep programs relevant to the age levels of students and move the students in the direction of social and cognitive competence.

The constructivist orientation stems from educational theorist John Dewey's (1913, 1975) writing, and the progressive education movement of the 1930s and 1940s was based here. It is supported by Piagetian theory of development, and today we find a resurgence that includes team teaching, cooperative learning, and whole language programs.

Constructivist teacher styles encourage free pupil participation. The school program will be heavily project centered, and teachers think of themselves not as founts of knowledge but as helpers and guides. We do not find a predetermined knowledge base or a set of learnings such as is found in traditional schools; teachers and students enter into investigations and develop or refine skills as they proceed. Curriculum content often focuses on what is interesting and important to children. For example, since social consciousness begins in the primary grades, a focus on environment and care for the earth may be appealing for second- or third-grade children. Constructivist teachers would move in that direction.

Some teachers will retreat to specific tasks at times, and some do have drills and lectures, but group work dominates, and teachers easily

In constructivist classrooms, the program is heavily project oriented.

move from whole-class to small-group to individual instruction. As in traditional rooms, children in constructivist classrooms are expected to be cooperative, good helpers, willing to share, and anxious to learn. In the following vignette, Mr. Perez conducts his primary program quite differently than what we would find in a traditional classroom.

Mr. Perez's third grade is relaxed. Two large rugs cover most of the floor, and well-worn sofas occupy the center of the room. Mr. P. has no desk at all and uses almost the entire day in conferences with small groups and individuals. Children are at different stages in their writings about people living in their neighborhoods. Mr. P. suggested the activity more than a week ago, and students approached it in different ways—interviewing people, observing folks at home, and just recalling recent events. Youngsters are working this morning all over the room trying to get their final drafts ready for presenting to one of the response groups.

Two children are sitting with Mr. P. on one sofa discussing their impressions of the custodian. They read each other's papers and nod. One asks about the word, codruy.

"Maybe it's corduroy?" Mr. P. wonders. "That right, Jason?"

"Yup," comes the answer.

"Do you want the dictionary spelling, Tyrone?" Mr. P. smiles. Both say, "Yeah, O.K.," and Mr. P. spells it for them. "These papers both make good sense to me," he states several minutes later. "Where do you want to go from here?"

Mr. Perez teaches from a constructivist philosophy. He is casual and relaxed and corrects indirectly. All children seem happy with the slightly noisy room, and students seldom interfere with each other's projects. One of Mr. P.'s few rules is that everyone sit on the rug near the end of the day to listen to those who have decided to share their projects. Today, Andrea does not wish any reactions to or comments on the model neighborhood street she is building; she just wants to talk about it. The other presenter, Shana, does ask for comments on her description of the school principal.

Mr. Perez says, "It's easy to get this group to plow ahead on things like this. I think we're keeping up with reading skills, and I know we're way ahead on writing skills. We'll do fine at the end of the year."

Evaluation in constructivist programs is more likely to be criterion referenced and to involve teacher-developed instruments. In that a common core of knowledge is not the issue, standardized tests are less relevant. Teachers will favor holistic evaluation to determine group progress, and assessment is frequently based on presentations or portfolios (for a thorough discussion of this type of assessment, see Stiggins, 1997).

Programs following a cognitive process orientation can be mishandled, of course, by persons with a limited grasp of curriculum. Generally, constructivist teaching is not undertaken unless personnel are confident about their background, committed to flexibility, and earnest in developing an experimental design. In its true form, it exists in less than 10% of all classrooms in the United States.

Personal Relevance

In the personal relevance, or completely child-centered, program, teachers assume a counseling or resource role. Some would say that the child-centered orientation is rooted firmly in Rousseauistic philosophy, but it is more than that. The orientation's basic premise is that children possess natural motivations for learning and adults help best by making things available, interacting to guide and stimulate, and being supportive. The Summerhill program (Neill, 1960) is the prototype for the totally child-centered program. Presently this orientation is found in a few laboratory schools, in some alternative schools (the Path-

finder Learning Center in Amherst, Massachusetts, is an example), and in a number of preschool programs. Many home schooling situations also are very much of this order.

Responsibility for all educational progress and work is shifted to the student in these liberal programs, and learners must be proactive to make progress. Children must be interested in exploring, setting their own agendas, and working individually. Students are likely to challenge authority and abandon their projects on occasion, and often they come up with very different results. These behaviors can be disconcerting for parents and teachers who have firm ideas about what children should learn.

Since motivation and incentive are expected to rise from within, students in personal relevance programs determine where, when, and how to go. These learners are often aggressive and highly individualistic, often going on "work binges." Since no published curriculum exists, teachers are responsible for displaying a smorgasbord of materials, ideas, and projects to encourage interests. Children make choices and follow their interests with all that they can muster. Typically, children work by themselves for several weeks exclusively on one study, perhaps of insects, airplanes, or computers.

Some stunning examples of success for the personal relevance orientation are evident when we view programs such as the Sudbury (Vermont) School (Gray & Chanoff, 1984) and those at some alternative schools. At the same time, we can find situations that are disastrous because students were not oriented to the programs or because teachers lacked commitment for this pattern.

Completely child-centered programs represent a tiny proportion of all school plans because they depend on highly committed staff members with dispositions for guiding and nurturing and require a community favoring this type of education. These conditions are quite foreign to the general American public.

We find combinations and variations for these three curriculum orientations. Different degrees of "purity" exist for all types. How do these orientations relate to marginalized children, to inner-city programs, and to multiethnic situations? The traditional schooling orientation is based on Euro-American values, which do not always make sense to poor and disadvantaged populations. Yet many would argue that the most structured plan allows marginalized children to learn basic skills, which some maintain, must be attained before further learning can occur (Doll, 1995).

On the other hand, the project focus of the constructivist orientation, especially when its programs include social investigation and social relevance aspects, seems logical for improving understandings among culturally and ethnically diverse groups. However, we find such plans are rare in schools for disadvantaged children. The constructivist orientation requires children to acquire patterns of self-control and to assume responsibility for classroom learning. When children are raised with little or no structure or security in their lives, many teachers find their classroom exploration difficult to manage.

Programs with minimal structure, such as the personal relevance program, which depend on individual incentive, also may be difficult to manage with some disadvantaged populations. If children lack experiences in work and study habits and if their world is a confusing one, programs based on personal relevance will likely render minimal value even though they are based on the premise that children's needs are foremost.

ORGANIZING SCHOOLS

All schools have their own culture and circumstances. The orientations discussed in this chapter, the student body, the adults who staff programs, the school's physical arrangement, neighborhood priorities and politics, and funding all contribute significantly to school culture and its characteristics.

Staffing Plans

Staffing involves administrators, teaching personnel of all types (regular teachers, specialists, aides, and volunteers), and the service personnel (secretaries, nurses, custodians, food service personnel, bus drivers, and others) who come to school each day. All individuals affect the school program, and the character a school possesses comes largely from the personalities, attitudes, and styles of the people who work there.

Administration.   Principals and, to a lesser extent, supervisors set the programmatic, social, and emotional tone for schools with which they are associated. We find several administrative styles commonly observed in U.S. schools.

Businesslike administrators who place a premium on efficiency, organization, and discipline inject those qualities into a school building's life. This style fits well for the school with a technologist or academic orientation. Managed with skill and tenacity, these schools show a no-nonsense air of business and urgency. While not always the most friendly or open communities, they are predictable, clean, and usually efficient. Rules and regulations are in evidence, things happen on time, all people know what is expected, and most feel secure. There are no surprises. It is the industrial model brought to school. Opinions vary on the appropriateness of the business or bureaucratic model. Many teachers, parents, and students enjoy the comfort of the organization, the discipline, and the high expectations. Others do not enjoy it, labeling the program as paternalistic, stifling of creativity, and not conducive for teachers exercising professional judgment or for students learning decision-making skills.

Inner-city schools with the right mix of personnel have often followed the businesslike style profitably. The combination of rigorous discipline and personal power has produced highly touted success stories, such as those of Joe Clark at Eastside High in Patterson, New Jersey, in the late 1980s and Deborah Meier's (1995) work at Central Park East School in Harlem.

Other schools are run on a more democratic, less stringent, basis. Democracy is the objective in many schools, and one finds a partnership tone and an agenda for cooperative action. Principals in these buildings are normally exuberant and accepting, and people thrive in their own way. Naturally, characteristics of these schools are considerable movement, activities that are encouraged (and that can bring about a high noise level), lots of experimentation, and even friction. The school is the playground energy and spirit brought indoors.

Many people find the less directive stance and the accepting tone of the democratic ad-

A democratic administrator takes time to nurture and interact with school-children.

ministrative position to be conducive to working at one's pace and own agenda. Teachers with charisma, dramatic flair, and outgoing personalities find this climate suitable; they can do what they enjoy doing, and incursions on their turf are not demands but collaborations. On the other hand, low-key persons often will not respond to this type of school atmosphere. They feel lost in the busy shuffle and cannot tolerate the high energy levels, the noise, or the distractions. However, a democratic principal, who should be a quiet consensus builder, will take time to nurture, listen, and build support for programs and policies. Many of these consensus-seeking persons are highly valued in many American communities. For example, Mr. Rider made all persons entering School #6 in Baltimore feel welcomed and valued. He arrived early in the morning and spent the hour before classes complimenting custodians, welcoming faculty, and asking children how the day was starting. This value produced an emotional environment that supported the esteem of all persons associated with the school.

We find other variations on these two administrative styles. Mamie Johnson has made a success story of P.S. 146 in East Harlem by her combination of structure, enthusiasm, and family involvement (Clinchy, 1993). Quite a few schools begin an administrative era with one style in place and then evolve to a comfort level tolerable for most teachers and community representatives.

Children always sense the administrative tenor in buildings and adapt to it. They know what they can expect of principals and how far they can go in approaching them. This is all part of the informal curriculum discussed later in this chapter.

In the final analysis, it is the public served that determines the patterns and style for a school. A community gradually asserts its wishes for an organizational plan and a climate that fit it best. Administrators must accommodate the community served if programs are to go forward.

Teachers.   In keeping with administrative styles, teachers bring a presence to schools. Much of the teacher's style is a function of philosophical orientation or belief about how children learn and how schools should work. Just as there are parenting styles (refer to chapter 4), we find comparable teaching styles, which are merged with personal outlooks and ways of presenting. In general, these form a 4-part grid on 2 axes (Table 8–2): warmth (responsive vs. nonresponsive) and control (demanding vs. undemanding). Note that Table 8–2's categories are similar to Baumrind's (1968) categories for parenting. In the following vignette, the teacher's style works well in her school where teachers collaborate in a team spirit to ensure inclusion of students with disabilities.

🖎

Mrs. Larkin is seated in her multiage primary classroom with children who are sharing their morning work before heading for the day's

Table 8–2   **Matrix of Different Teaching Styles**

	Responsive	**Nonresponsive**
Demanding	Businesslike teacher: demanding but responsive	Autocratic teacher: demanding & nonresponsive
Undemanding	Permissive teacher: undemanding but responsive	Indifferent teacher: undemanding, nonresponsive

gym activity. Eric, a special-needs child with an abusive family background enters the room accompanied by Mrs. Stanford, his counselor, who nods to Mrs. Larkin and leaves. "Good morning, Eric. We're preparing for gym. You're just in time," says Mrs. Larkin. Eric doesn't respond but walks behind the circle to the class folders and picks up his folder, but then he bops the child nearest him on the head. Mrs. Larkin says quietly but firmly, "Eric, that is not acceptable. Sit at your table there and work on your folder. I'm sorry, but you'll need to miss 5 minutes of gym class." Eric responds by sitting and opening his folder. From time to time he looks at Mrs. Larkin, who sort of smiles but gently shakes her head.

After 5 minutes, the class lines up to wait for the gym instructor. As the instructor appears at the door, he looks questioningly at Mrs. Larkin and at a seated Eric. "Yes, Eric will be a bit late for class. I'll bring him shortly." As the class leaves, Eric's counselor returns and says she'll take Eric to gym. ". . .He did so well with me this morning." Yesterday had been a difficult day, and the two had struck a deal about Eric's behavior and rewards for the next day. As Mrs. Larkin explains the new situation to Mrs. Stanford, she says to Eric, "I was so pleased to see you come in and go right to your folder, but I'm sorry you weren't able to do the next step. But since your day has been so good otherwise and since you have worked well for these past 5 minutes, I think Mrs. Stanford will agree that you may go to gym." Eric's face lights up, and he hurries to put his folder back.

Eric is an ADHD child, and his individualized education plan provides for an increasing length of time in the regular classroom. Though his teachers dislike keeping children from the needed physical activity, it is the one thing they have found that Eric considers worth "behaving" for. Though other strategies are used and though Eric's teachers all have somewhat different styles, they all agree on certain rules and procedures that Eric is expected to follow. With warmth but firmness they consistently maintain this emotional environment. The other children in the classroom are friendly with one another and with Eric.

Though Eric has some difficult days, improvement is growing in how he manages his behavior. At the beginning of the year, Eric spent most of his time with the counselor and a special-needs instructor. He now receives over half of his instruction in the regular classroom setting with other students and participates in special activities with his classmates.

The demanding but responsive teacher, similar to the authoritative parent, is normally popular because this person pursues plans aggressively but in a humane and friendly fashion. Mrs. Larkin in the preceding vignette exemplifies this style. The style coordinates well with all curriculum orientations except personal relevance, where an undemanding but responsive teacher is more likely valued. The demanding and nonresponsive, or authoritarian, style can exist in traditional programs but seems out of place in constructivist programs, where human dynamics play such an important part. The undemanding and nonresponsive profile produces an indifferent demeanor, which has little chance of succeeding in any program.

Teaching styles relate to all levels of teaching, since volunteers, aides, and specialists all project a teaching style. Various styles can be successful in different venues, and teachers are aware of this; however, all must be able to match children's learning modalities with different circumstances and different materials (Dunn, 1999; Dunn & Frazier, 1990; Hunt, 1961). Good and Brophy (1996) state that "different situations and goals call for different methods [and] a given method may have different effects on different students" (p. 375).

Service Personnel.   While teaching and administrative staff dominate the adult interaction time with schoolchildren, other members of the school community can project social and emotional qualities. Custodians, nurses, lunchroom workers, and secretaries all play a part in a school atmosphere. While teaching style is not an issue, the responsiveness that these adults show toward children and the manner in which they cooperate with teachers add to or detract from the overall school environment. Schools that are happy places have personnel who are responsive and genuinely interested in helping children to grow and develop.

Physical Organization

The physical aspects and space associated with schools differ with age and location, but these elements always suggest what can happen in particular educational environments. A large majority of U.S. children of primary school age attend schools in classrooms containing 20 to 25 students and one teacher per group. The physical plant for most school programs is still the "egg box" type of construction with a central hallway and branching individual classrooms. Variations exist for the basic plan and also may exist within the egg box, including learning stations and highly flexible constructions and equipment.

One can see that physical organization of schools and classrooms relates to program (Figure 8–1). A traditionally organized room is likely to have a traditional orientation. This message communicates itself quickly to children and others who enter a school. Some older schools built for traditional programs have been reorganized into settings containing open spaces, workstations, and resource areas. Space, including hallways and out-of-doors areas, can be used in an entirely different way to support a program where teachers want experiments and freedom in movement. Teachers

who have reorganized their space have given new life to the adage Form follows function.

Open-space schools were developed in the 1970s in many U.S. communities. In general, they were large buildings planned around pods, or divisions that housed various grade levels or "families." The large spaces, or pods, were generally allotted to specific grade levels, and the teachers for each space developed the area as they saw fit. This often meant that one group of 25 second graders was within sight and hearing of two or more other groups.

With this plan, many activities in open-space schools are total group events, and subgroups move between the designated sections in the pod. Noise levels tend to be higher in open-space schools, but with carefully scheduled activities, study, and transition time, the interruptions are minimized. The open space permits the flexibility to move to other groups within or outside the pod for specific activities or for partnerships, and then to move back when the home group is called to session. The plan fits well with the cognitive process (constructivist) orientation and other, more individualized orientations. It does not jibe with academic or traditionalist patterns and has for this reason lost popularity in many school districts.

CURRICULUM

Schools were established originally to teach areas of skill and knowledge more efficiently and with better results than could be achieved at home. Even though the nature of this task has changed and expanded over the years, the need for skills and knowledge is still the basis for school curricula.

In the 19th century, the overarching objectives were to ensure reasonable competence in the ability to read, compose written work, and master computation skills and general problem solving. Schools were arranged exclusively on the traditional or teacher-dominated

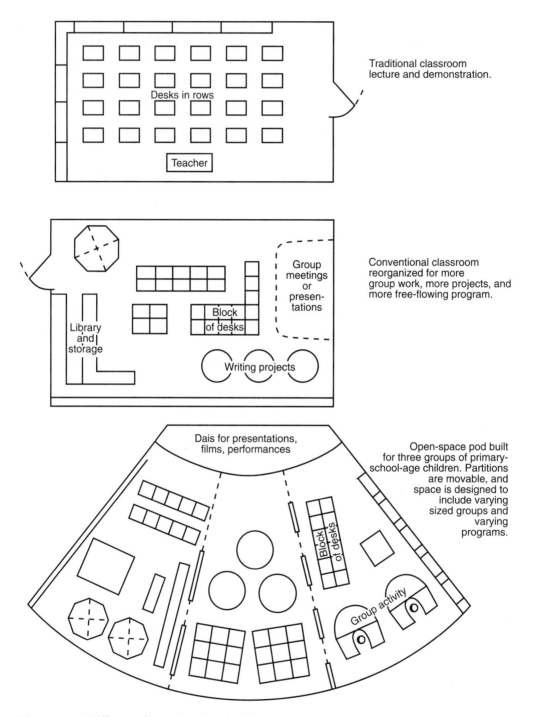

Figure 8–1   Different classroom organization patterns.

plan. Schools assumed an extensive role in providing more and new content for children as time went by. At present, U.S. schools have curricula that include not only language arts and mathematics but also social studies, science, health and recreation, and fine arts. As noted at the beginning of this chapter, the school curriculum has three distinct forms— formal, informal, and hidden. All are evident each day that children attend school.

The formal, or explicit, curriculum includes the established content, concepts, and skills found in curriculum guides and teacher plan books. It is the material included in textbooks or in the projects that teachers and students decide to pursue.

The informal curriculum includes the social learnings, the work and study habits, and the protocols that learners must master to fit into school life. Students learn these through modeling by school adults, by persuasion and advisement, and sometimes simply by having a buddy to associate with and thereby to "learn the rules" from. This process compares to the etiquette practices of homes and with the social organization rules found in any subculture.

The hidden, or covert, curriculum consists of unintentional learnings accruing to children from their school experiences. Informants in this case are frequently peers; children also absorb messages from adults by observation. Through the hidden curriculum, children learn such things as whether it is a good time to make a request, which teachers get the things they want from the school office, or that third-grade boys "do not play" with girls. They also learn how school personnel and peers view their habits, dress, and home life experiences.

Formal Curriculum

The formal, explicit, or intended curriculum of a school is the plan of action or experiences delivered to attending children. Curricula are promoted in different ways and, as noted, can differ considerably from one school to another, depending on staff, district philosophy, materials and equipment involved, type of community, and acceptance level of teachers.

Often the curriculum is a detailed, written document produced through the work of teacher study groups and disseminated from a central office. The content fits neatly into a scope and sequence chart, and material often correlates closely with published textbooks. Many state offices of education publish curriculum guides for particular grade levels or subject matter guides for all grade levels, developing them in a manner similar to that of local school districts.

In each of the curriculum orientations discussed in this chapter, educators have different ways to organize and schedule curriculum content. The following sections present examples of how formal curriculum is developed for each orientation in contemporary schools.

Formal Curriculum in Traditional Schools. Predetermined curricula fit academic or traditionally oriented schools because the philosophy of such schools holds that a common core of knowledge exists and that the facts, concepts, and skills of that core can be written down, turned into objectives, and then developed with children.

Schedule and Structure. Grade levels for elementary schools established in the early 19th century have remained much the same to the present day. While somewhat arbitrary, and contributing to many lockstep curriculum designs, the practice arranges a considerable amount of content into grade-specific levels. Teachers in traditionally oriented classrooms organize a day primarily through various routines, then schedule lessons and practice, followed by evaluation of some type. A typical day in a traditional school is shown in Table 8–3. This is a minimal plan, showing only the highlights, but it suggests the extent of

Table 8–3   Traditional Classroom Day for Grade 2

9:00	Opening activities
9:15	Reading and other language arts
10:15	Recess
10:30	Mathematics
11:30	Physical education
12:00	Lunch
12:45	Social and physical sciences
1:30	Arts and music
2:00	Recess
2:30	Language arts review
3:15	Closing

schoolwork for 6- to 8-year-olds in a traditional program.

Organization. An exception to the self-contained classroom with children of specific ages is the departmentalized program, where children move from room to room for instruction in particular subjects. Departmentalized plans, normally associated with upper elementary grades, also have been developed in primary areas. Teachers specialize in one or more areas; for example, one teacher develops reading, writing, and spelling (language arts) and handles those areas for two or more classrooms. Team teaching is another model that combines departmentalized features with group planning, support, and evaluation.

Cooperative learning models replace many individual assignments with a small-group focus and responsibility. Teachers may combine this strategy with most staffing arrangements and classroom organization patterns. However, the strategy blends most successfully with constructivist classrooms.

Formal Curriculum in Constructivist Classrooms.   A constructivist curriculum is carefully thought out. The teacher's plans are developed in conjunction with school and community expectations; children's developmental stages and individual patterns of growth are accounted for. A constructivist

teacher may use a curriculum guide but will freely interpret it as needed. Content covers all disciplines—reading, writing, math, social studies, science, fine arts, and physical education. Rather than following a sequenced listing of content and concepts, classes pursue investigations of differing topics, projects, or themes. The curriculum is integrated and involves children in active learning. Through involvement with different issues in the units studied, children develop the same set of basic skills encountered in a traditional school plan. Teachers are responsible for content and for providing continuity of experience and opportunities for learners. Classroom social interactions, which are important to curriculum development, are provided through shared experiences, flexible groupings, interactions with the teacher, and opportunities for children to reflect on their learning.

A constructivist at work is presented in the following vignette, as one teacher tells visitors about her grade 3 unit on trees (adapted from Barbour & Seefeldt, 1993).

🖋

I operate my third grade by establishing a flexible schedule so that I can reorganize if interests and projects require more time. I have a framework of the subject area skills that children should acquire that I pulled, along with themes and unit suggestions, from the curriculum guides. Beyond that, I try to be flexible enough to respond to children's interests and needs.

Planning for our tree unit went something like this: Children were just finishing explorations on different birds when one child brought in an apple tree branch about to blossom. Children had all sorts of questions, so I suggested that our next unit could be on trees. I encouraged children to bring some books about trees, and I gathered several as well. The next day I read Parnall's Apple Tree, *and we discussed some of the things in the book that interested the students. Some of the concepts were that trees provide food for us and for other animals, trees change during the seasons, trees provide joy and delight, and trees provide shelter for some creatures.*

Then I thought of some activities we could do that connected to our reading, social studies, and science curricula. In reading, we're looking at settings for stories; in social studies, we're doing mapping skills; and in science, we're studying the environment. I began to devise some projects that would engage the class in learning more about trees and their importance to the environment but that would still be linked to subject area skills.

In reading, children are studying story settings; and from reading Apple Tree and other books, they'll examine settings and thus learn about the environments that trees need.

In social studies, children are studying mapping skills. On global maps, children will locate places where our "tree stories" take place. Children will then make topographical maps and place models of their trees appropriately. In art, they'll portray different houses that animals develop in trees.

In writing, children will reflect in journals what they're learning about trees and what is of particular interest to them. Since children are always encouraged to list new and interesting words, as they attempt creative writing, they'll have a list of new words to use.

In science, we'll examine the different foods that trees provide. We will collect some of these foods for snacks on different days.

Some of the presentations or projects will be total class, and others will require children to work in groups or individually. As a total group, we'll discuss the findings and plan out the different projects: topography, reading discussion groups, snack preparations, creative stories or reports, house-building projects. Four basic work areas will be prepared: maps area, house-building area, food-preparation

area, and arts and creative writing area. Depending on children's discoveries and their interests, they can elect to be part of two, three, or all four activities. There'll be a formal independent reading time when children read from their selected books, and then the children will meet in a discussion group to share information from the stories. Discussions during snack time and after reading time, children's journals, their creative stories, and their art projects will provide me with information on what students have learned. At the end of all our units, I will ask children to reflect on what new information or skills they've acquired. You see, I'm trying to get them to become aware of their own learning.

The typical day in a constructivist class is organized through various routines, projects, meetings, and skill sessions. Activities are usually followed by evaluations, sharing, and exhibiting. A typical schedule for a constructivist school day is shown in Table 8–4.

The advantage of doing projects in the cognitive process and constructivist programs is that such work is more informal and lends itself to experimentation and collaboration. Assignments tend to hold children's interest longer, especially when they get to help

Table 8–4 Constructivist Classroom Day—Grade 2

9:00	Meeting time, greeting friends, checking and discussing day's schedule
9:30	Reading & writing workshop
10:30	Class meeting
10:45	Recess
11:00	Skill session on subtraction
12:00	Lunch
12:45	Class meeting
1:00	Independent work time for projects
2:00	Art and music sessions
2:30	Presentations, publishing, and wrap-up
3:15	Closing time

choose the topics and how to extend their study. Some sessions will seem disorganized, with children searching for materials or collaborating with others, but the advantage is that the approach to mastering material is self-selected. In these programs, children feel empowered for much of their own learning and grasp concepts and skills far beyond traditional grade expectations.

A major disadvantage to constructivist plans is that projects can become trivial or repetitive. In addition, some teachers have difficulty incorporating or inserting reasonable skill development sessions in the investigations that classes propose.

Formal Curriculum in Personal Relevance Programs.   A truly child-centered program is difficult to describe, since all content emerges from the interests of the children involved. As an illustration, however, imagine that a small group of children has elected to consider frogs for a week while other groups or individuals are focused on different topics. The classroom teacher and aides would provide as much help, guidance, and support as possible for their study, and a scenario such as the following might develop:

- Teachers accompany children on a visit to a nearby wetland after they decide to observe frog habitats.

- Discussions about materials collected follow the visit, and children ponder ways they wish to continue.

- Teachers assemble resources—books, magazines, films, and the like—while students explore what they wish to concentrate on.

- The group shares with the entire class, and children brainstorm, or at least discuss, how they could learn more. They consider books, museum exhibits, presentations by persons in ecology departments, and interactions with local specialists and with other class-

rooms or schools nearby. New members join the group.

- Students incorporate writing and mathematics into their study by keeping journals on experiences and planning experiments, such as hatching frog eggs in different media. Teachers help and provide information or instruction when needed.

- The project evolves into a larger study of swamp ecology as it serves the interests of students and continues to be a stimulating topic.

Certain home schooling programs are conducted along this line, and evidence shows that children's interest blooms when they are given chances to investigate their surroundings. One fascinating example is the plan the Colfax family used with their four sons (Colfax & Colfax, 1992).

The content examples presented here are all explicit or intended curriculum activities of a school program. This means that teachers feel a responsibility to plan for and to steer children toward some substance or experience. As we have stated, other forms of curricula also are associated with all schools. The informal curriculum is acknowledged by most educators and parents as part of what we come to school for. The hidden curriculum is rarely apparent to teachers and parents, but its effects often outlast those of the explicit curriculum. These curricula are discussed in the following sections.

Informal Curriculum

Much of the informal curriculum is implied and unplanned; it consists of those learnings teachers and parents expect to come about but rarely bother to state, plan for, or present to children. The informal curriculum has to do with socialization into school life, and it is similar to the etiquette of other institutions in children's lives.

The implied curriculum includes events such as teachers' expecting their new students to discover procedures for lining up, passing in papers, getting recognition in class, or responding. No one plans the activities, but all are expected to follow the rules. Recall the vignette in chapter 4, where Greg helped Philip understand their teacher's request. Informal curriculum was at work when Greg instructed the younger child. The teacher expected Philip to know the practices, but since he did not, the older child interpreted.

Teachers expect children to internalize a number of general school procedures and protocols. Some teachers, particularly primary school teachers, are more cognizant of this area of informal curriculum than others. For instance, they are aware of a need to remind children of appropriate responses and helpful communications. They often discuss possibilities for team efforts and list things to consider. We find the following items of informal curriculum in typical U.S. schools:

- School activities are organized and differ from spontaneous situations at home. Children are expected to differentiate, adapt, and fit in without any focused instruction.

- Competition is a fact of life in U.S. schools. Teachers employ notions of being first, being best, and achieving more in all areas of classwork and sports. Children are expected to absorb this value.

- Time and schedules are paramount in school life. Children are expected to work on command, change quickly to new ventures, and meet deadlines many times per day.

- Group activities are common in all schools. Children are expected to learn group roles and participate in groups cooperatively and smoothly.

The home curriculum is basically an informal curriculum (refer to chapter 7), and learning accrues in a haphazard but reasonable way. Few formal or organized experiences are associated with the home—exceptions are music lessons, homework, and the like—unless parents have developed a home schooling program. Language skill is a good example of the informal home curriculum. Families have no planned times for language instruction. However, by the time children enter kindergarten, they have almost complete control of their native language, and this has all come through interaction with family, caregivers, and peers.

Hidden Curriculum

We have defined *curriculum* as those experiences that make up children's waking hours, and when you consider carefully, you can see that the thousands of impressions, interactions, and experiences children have each day do amount to a curriculum. Children constantly receive stimuli that contribute to learning. Some stimuli are intentional; adults plan things that children are "supposed" to learn through school, home, or community instruction. But some learning is unintended; it comes about in accidental ways as children observe phenomena, experience situations, and associate with others. This is often called the "hidden, or covert, curriculum" and makes a considerable impression, although its extent and effects are frequently ignored. Recall Jana's drawings from the vignette in chapter 4 about her family configurations at different periods in her life. These drawings indicate Jana's evolving hidden curriculum.

Children continue to encounter the hidden curriculum after entering school. When we examine it closely, we find that the hidden curriculum occupies a large part of the school day. For example, first-grade teachers plan about 5 hours of in-class time per day, but when we calculate the time actually spent on planned activities, we often find that less than one half is spent on task work. In fact, some

Some learning is unintended or accidental, coming about informally as children observe phenomena.

time-on-task studies reveal that primary classrooms in some cases were on task less than 1 hour of the total day (Stallings, 1980). This leaves a large amount of in-class and out-of-class time, in addition to time spent going to and from school, given over to the hidden curriculum. Whether beneficial or negative, the hidden curriculum is a potent force in any child's learning.

🕊

Ryan only shrugged when, during dinner, his father asked him about his school day, but later when they were reading the comics in the newspaper, some things came up about a new child in Ryan's class.

"I think Charlie takes money," Ryan said.

"Oh, really," said his dad.

"Yeah, he had three quarters that he spent on candy at Ed's Variety today . . . said he found 'em."

"Maybe he did," his dad replied.

"Yeah, but he didn't know where. . . . I think he stole 'em."

"Has Charlie been here visiting?" Ryan's father asked.

"Nope. I asked him over last week, but his dad don't let him go places. It's funny, 'cause he knows a lot."

"Oh, that so?"

Ryan nodded and volunteered, "He told me all those dirty words on the fence back of the variety store."

"Hmmm, well . . . when . . .," his dad began.

But Ryan continued as he picked up the comics again. "There's those funny red marks on Charlie's arms. I'm gonna ask him tomorrow if we walk home from school."

🕊

Ryan is a 7-year-old doing well in his traditional second-grade class, but you will note a host of items he is learning that are unrelated to school objectives. In his walk home with the new boy, Ryan is encountering a hidden curriculum. Its features are unrelated to his formal school curriculum, but the stimuli— scatological language, questions about theft, and hints of abuse—all have an impact on Ryan.

The covert or hidden curriculum for at-risk children can, of course, have a negative impact and may have heartrending consequences. Aspects of these experiences surface in media reports describing particularly poignant family situations. The distressing accounts of children's lives given in chapter 4 present all too graphically a savage curriculum that cries out for redress.

Special Education and Curriculum

As we noted earlier, 12% of American school-children have special needs, and you will encounter some children in almost all schools who do require special services or some adaptation of instruction. The range of special needs is great, ranging from special learning disabilities (about one half of the total) through mental retardation to specific physical impairments (a small proportion). If you work in urban areas where poverty and minority representation is considerable, you will find even larger proportions of special-needs children. As we have noted before, poverty is always linked to more problems in health, social situation, and learning difficulties.

In chapter 2 we alerted the reader to the beginnings of federal legislation that ushered in a new era for recognizing and ensuring educational opportunities for children with disabilities. In the succeeding 25 years, America has undergone considerable adjustment (not without difficulty certainly) in providing special education facilities, restructuring buildings, reorganizing staffs, and modifying curriculum. Perhaps most of all, more educators have a new outlook, appreciation, and interest for accommodating special-needs children in regular classrooms.

As Table 2.1 in chapter 2 indicates, the several legislative endeavors since 1975 have expanded and clarified the provisions for special education. In 1986, legislation expanded school programs to cover preschoolers (ages 3–5) with disabilities. The notion driving this move was that early identification of disabilities meant that additional time and instruction would enhance the child's later schooling. It was only a matter of time until the first 3 years of a child's life were also considered for special services when needed. Therefore, in 1992, legislation brought services (though not through schools) to infants and toddlers. In this cohort, specialists meet with parents to help establish a better foundation for their children's later schooling.

Text limitations preclude our discussing the details for implementing good special education programs, but we refer you to the considerable number of texts published in this area. Examples are Turnbull, Turnbull, Shank, and Leal (1999), *Exceptional Lives: Special Education in Today's Schools*; and Culatta and Tompkins (1999), *Fundamentals of Special Education*.

Readers anticipating a career in early childhood education or related human services professions must be cognizant of the following provisions in the IDEA statutes that reflect the heart and intention of the legislation. The following seven principles undergirding special education reform (summarized from Culatta and Tompkins, 1999, and Turnbull et al., 1999) have become the specialized language of special education.

1. Zero rejection. Rule against excluding any student.

2. Nondiscrimatory evaluations. Rule requiring schools to evaluate children in their own language to determine disability and how extensive.

3. Appropriate education. Rule requiring educators to plan individually tailored education for each student with disabilities.

4. Least restrictive environment. Rule requiring schools to merge exceptional children with regular classrooms to the maximum extent appropriate for the child.

5. Due process. Rule to safeguard all students' rights for privacy and rights for legal redress.

6. Parent and student participation. Rules requiring schools to collaborate with parents in designing and carrying out programs.

7. Preschool programs. Rule requiring school districts to develop early intervention programs for children with disabilities from birth through primary grades.

You will hear and read about several other fundamental terms identified with special educational practice: *mainstreaming, inclusion*, and *individualized education program*. We refer you again to the specialized texts already mentioned for in-depth discussions of how these terms undergird a lot about the field of special education, but the following descriptions will aid you in considering other content.

Mainstreaming has been used since 1975 legislation was enacted. Though the concept brought special-needs children into regular schools and classrooms, it provided for only limited connections in most schools. Special education students were included in art, music, and other areas with their nondisabled peers but frequently were relocated for instruction in academic areas.

Inclusion emerged in the 1990s as a concept meaning that special-needs students are part of a regular class and participate fully in that class for almost the complete day. Inclusion practice has generated more controversy among regular and special education teachers, but in its true sense, it calls for teachers (regular or special) to modify content, adjust material, secure more

IEP means that an individualized program is worked out to serve the particular needs of a student.

support services, and the like, to enable the special-needs learner to enjoy the full life of a classroom. The most practical way to accommodate these children in the regular classroom is by using a team approach in planning for all children in the classroom. Such an approach would require more small group and individualized instruction. This requires a huge leap for the typical traditional educator and would move instruction toward a constructivist approach.

Almost all educators subscribe to the principle of including a large majority of special-needs children in regular schools and regular classrooms. Over a period of a generation (and numerous defining court cases) this adjustment has come to pass. A debate continues on how best to accommodate students with severe disabilities. Full inclusion for this last group involves restructuring classrooms, adding extra services, and adding more personnel as well as seriously modifying curriculum content and delivery of that content. You will meet educators and specialists with differing opinions about whether full inclusion is workable.

Individualized education program (IEP) is a contract for carrying out instruction for a special-needs child between ages 3 and 21. The term has been in education practice for the past 25 years, and it means basically what the phrase implies, that is, a program worked out by regular teachers, specialists, parents, and sometimes the learner as well to serve the learner's needs. A modified form of this is the *individualized family services plan* (IFSP), which came with the 1992 legislation expanding services to infants and toddlers. The IFSP concept is similar, except that services are usually at the child's home or in a child care facility.

RESULTS OF SCHOOL EDUCATIVE PROCESSES

Millions of children attend schools in the United States each year. Also each year, between 3 million and 4 million young Americans (many of whom are dropouts) move beyond school to the workforce, to college, to homemaking, or to unemployment (U.S. Bureau of the Census, 1998b). It is common knowledge that a vast difference exists in outcomes for differing educational environments, ranging from the sublime to the pathetic.

Some schools have an easy time. Schools accepting highly motivated, advantaged students with few deficits in background and experience frequently produce quality results. With skilled administrators and energetic and focused staff members, students from these schools measure up against all expectations that communities could have. Selective private schools and well-endowed suburban schools in affluent areas show these results.

Other schools are far different and need extraordinary energy from all sources to produce even modest gains. This problem escapes the attention of much of America's middle-class community agencies. Schools in disadvantaged areas frequently enroll children with problems in nutrition, health, and socialization and even in emotional stability. The background of deprivation has taken a toll on interest and outlook and all things of an educational nature, for day-to-day survival is the paramount consideration in the American underclass (Bradley, 1995; Kotlowitz, 1991; Schorr, 1988). The comprehensive nurturing from community families needed to engender children's self-esteem and a positive self-concept or readiness is often lacking. These schools need outstanding teachers and skilled administrators, but they often get neither, as staff assignments are often determined by length of tenure. How can schools like this compete? The answer is that they cannot. Most will continue to struggle unless or until receiving massive investments of support and supplements from outside and well-organized cooperative action with the community served. (In chapter 11, we identify productive models for school-community partnerships.)

IMPLICATIONS
FOR PROFESSIONALS

Schools differ in structure, in view of curriculum, in equipment, and in space. School leadership varies, as does the skill of staff members in charge of day-to-day activities. The background, support, and preparation that enrolled children possess will differ. All these factors will produce different educational outcomes and will affect your professional involvement when you are affiliated.

Of course, changes are possible in all educational situations; the poor can be made better, the good can become outstanding. You can make a difference if you affiliate with schools that have a vision for improvement.

Differing curriculum orientations and various teaching strategies and techniques will all fit into the teaching equation. Keep in mind that all can be successful. The traditional teacher who demonstrates, explains, and then pursues application may be rewarded with inquisitive, enthusiastic students. The indirect teacher, with goals firmly in mind, also can stimulate and guide students toward achievement using the same basic equipment.

As you approach work with schools, give thought to the informal and hidden curricula engulfing the children you will work with. These curricula are a fact of life for all and come with all environments. You will be powerless as an individual to change much, but you must consider them as you incorporate activities into your school day. For instance, you can take time to model modes of greeting, general rules of etiquette, or particular social language skills that will help young children's maturity.

In the final analysis, teachers must know who they are, where they are going, and the best ways to get there. If you plan to teach, this means that you must have a clear grasp of your skills and your preferred work style and then be able to see how that style matches children's interests and work habits. Teachers who are not self-aware in this way must depend on circumstances to place them in comfortable situations with eager students.

SUMMARY AND REVIEW

In this chapter, we have discussed the dimensions of school curricula, the philosophical orientations associated with curricula, and the variation in practices and structure found in U.S. schools. Philosophical orientations differ from school to school and from teacher to teacher, and orientation makes a great difference about what content teachers consider for classrooms as well as how teachers approach instruction. The physical organization of a school also reflects the school's philosophical orientation.

Formal, informal, and hidden curricula exist in all types of schools. The results of school educative processes can be positive or negative, and all results have implications for the school program, the surrounding community, and the families involved.

Schools are taken for granted in U.S. society, and parents send their children to schools expecting them to partake in productive activities. The public expects schools to provide care and safety for children, stimulation of minds and bodies, and skills and knowledge for participation in adult life. Most parents feel that home cannot provide the requisite skills even young children require today, and they do not trust themselves to guide children's interests or monitor their progress.

In productive schools, irrespective of curriculum orientation, children will master basic literacy skills, interactive and social skills, general study habits, computational skills, social and natural science concepts, and the ability to experiment and to learn through investigation. All schools have a duty to meet these basic features of curriculum, although each may approach this duty differently. Schools showing minimal or incomplete results for these basic expectations cannot survive in the 21st century.

SUGGESTED ACTIVITIES AND QUESTIONS

1. Observe the classroom behaviors of the teacher in your field assignment and determine from things said, assignments given, and general demeanor which of the philosophical orientations that teacher holds.

2. Take the matrix presented in Table 8–2 and use it to assess teaching styles of your college instructors, high school teachers, other teachers you recall, and classroom teachers you are in contact with now. Which quadrant contains the most?

3. Develop a profile of interests, habits, and skills on one child you are working with now or one you know well. Determine which curriculum orientation would suit the child best. Defend your choice.

4. Interview several children to identify the informal curriculum they experience at school. You will have to start them off with suggestions about lining up or taking breaks, and so on. Try to determine yourself, or get them to tell you, where the expectations originated. Were these rules stated, picked up through others, inferred, or carried over from other years?

RESOURCES

Books

1. Bennett, K. P., & LeCompte, M. D. (1990). *How schools work: A sociological analysis of education*. New York: Longman.
2. MacNeill, J. D. (1996). *Curriculum: A comprehensive introduction* (5th ed.). Reading, MA: Addison-Wesley.

Films/Videos

1. Kids Express Field Trip videos. Examples for primary-school ages are *Happy campers* (on exploring nature) and *Kids can cook*. [45 min each]. Kids Express, Springfield, MO.
2. School Works videos to supplement field trips. Examples for primary-school ages: *To the zoo* and *To the glassmaking studio*. [30 min each]. School Works, Alameda, CA.
3. *All aboard the elementary Internet*. (1998). CD-ROM for Grades 1–6. Introduces teachers and students to the Internet through CD-based lessons that incorporate links to monitored websites. BonusPoint, Saratoga, CA.

Organizations

1. Association for Supervision and Curriculum Development (ASCD) (http://www.ascd.org/) 1250 N. Pitt Street, Alexandria, VA 22314
2. Association for Childhood Education International (ACEI) (http://www.udel.edu/bateman/acei) 17904 Georgia Avenue, Olney, MD 20832
3. National Education Association (http://www.nea.org) 1201 Sixteenth Street, NW, Washington DC 20036

Websites

1. http://www.wri.org World Resources Institute. Focus is on environment, with sites on items such as health, marine resources, and global trends.
2. http://www.techlab.com/k12.html Contains a listing of online resources pertaining to education and technology.
3. http://www.onlineclass.com An example of Internet and curriculum integration where students join a global classroom studying topics from dinosaurs to watersheds.
4. http://www.techlearning.com Website for the periodical *Technology and Learning*. A good multi-purpose site for identifying software reviews, teaching tools, and professional resources.

Chapter 9

===== ❦❦❦❦❦ =====

Curriculum of the Community

❦❦❦❦❦

The child is an ever-attentive witness of grown-up morality—or lack thereof; the child looks for cues as to how one ought to behave, and finds them galore as we parents and teachers go about our lives, making choices, addressing people, showing in action our rock-bottom assumptions, desires, values, and thereby telling those young observers much more than we may realize.

(Coles, 1997, p. 5)

🐚

The purpose of this chapter is to examine the rich but often overlooked features of the community for children's learning. Just as we have a curriculum of the school and of the home, we also have a curriculum of the community. In reading this chapter, you will learn the following:

1. Organizations and agencies within a community provide many and varied learning opportunities for children.

2. Some community education is purposeful and planned by members of community organizations and agencies.

3. Much of children's learning within the community results from their observations of how things work and how people function and from their interaction with materials and people.

4. The physical and emotional attributes of a community will either support and extend or hinder children's opportunities.

5. Social networks, involving both adults and peers, will affect the amount and quality of learning children derive from their community.

Whether or not educators recognize other curricula, children's knowledge and understanding come from various sources. The community, an amorphous mass surrounding us all, is one of these sources. As in the family and school curricula examined in chapters 7 and 8, community curriculum is affected by the type, location, and physical makeup of the region and the social networks established by its inhabitants.

Chapter 1 discussed the many influences on children's learning. All curricula are affected by these influences. The community curriculum determines many learning experiences affecting children. Some are deliberately planned, and some exist by the very nature of the community's organization. Although we find great differences in communities, we also find many commonalities that suggest similar educational experiences.

Various organizations within the community offer different aspects of curriculum, and children learn just by being exposed to these organizations. In addition, the physical and emotional environments children encounter in their immediate neighborhoods enhance or hinder intellectual development. Each community is composed of interconnected social systems, and how the people of these systems relate to one another greatly affects children's learning and development (Bronfenbrenner, 1979; Lightfoot, 1978).

In this chapter, we examine the context of the wider community and its potential for helping children grow. We examine community organizational structure and suggest how some of the diverse agencies "educate" children. The physical and social-emotional environments in a community together constitute a basic support system for all families, one that enables parents and child care workers to stimulate children in different ways. There are, however, communities where the physical and social-emotional environment is so destructive that children are placed at great developmental and educational risk (Randolph,

Koblinsky, & Roberts, 1998). The supportive interaction of community agencies with families and with schools is the key. The level of children's positive participation in community and the social networks that children establish depend on that interaction.

COMMUNITY STRUCTURE AFFECTS CURRICULUM

Although every community varies in structure and in the kinds of services available to its citizens, we find similar human, natural, and material resources. Table 9–1 presents a partial listing of these resources. A child's neighborhood may be in a city, a small town, a suburb, or a rural area. The resources available in each setting will vary, but all form the bases for a community curriculum. Whether in a rural area or in a city, children observe different aspects of nature. Trees, birds, animals, and stars at night are more available to rural children, but city children witness the warmth of the sun, wetness of rain, scrubby grass and small plants pushing up between concrete slabs, and ants or other creatures carrying away crumbs

Table 9–1   Community Resources That Educate Children

Natural Resources

Plants, animals, insects, fish, seashells, minerals, woods, ponds, streams, beaches, parks, nature preserves, farmland

Services

Education: zoos, museums, libraries, schools, parks

Communcation: telephones, radio and television stations, post offices, newspaper offices, computer networks

Entertainment: theaters, music halls, movies, fairs, festivals, circuses, restaurants, television and radio stations

Recreation: playgrounds, church or community clubs with athletic facilities, ballparks, public tennis courts, golf courses, parks

Transportation: airports, train stations, bus terminals, taxis, gas stations, rental agencies

Commerical: department stores, grocery stores, pharmacies, different types of farms (orchards, fish farms, dairy farms), special shops (toy stores, ice cream parlors, beauticians, pet stores, craft shops, and so on), factories, business enterprises

Professional: offices of doctors, dentists, lawyers, and other professionals, fire and police departments, funeral parlors, courts, clinics, hospitals, political offices, state or local departments of education, universities

Service agencies: employment offices, social services and public assistance offices, counseling services, food co-ops

Living environments: children's and teachers' homes, houses, apartment complexes, mobile homes, new homesites, real estate offices, retirement communities, nursing homes

Materials (available from most listed services)

Printed: books, pamphlets, brochures, magazines, newspapers, advertisements

Audiovisual: films, television, radio, audio- and videotapes, slide-tape shows, computer programs, exhibits, models

Collections of recyclables: scraps of fabric, carpet samples, wood scraps, buttons, ribbon, wallpaper samples, bottles, cans, boxes, wire, spools, paper scraps, large cartons

Social Networks

Adult: friends, neighbors, colleagues and coworkers, social clubs, religious groups, sports groups, community theater

Peer: young relatives, school and neighborhood friends, club and team partners from garbage. Southern children know palm trees; northern children, deciduous or fir trees; and southwestern children, juniper and cacti.

Children constantly learn from persons in their neighborhoods. How much learning children gain from others besides kin in the home depends on how much association they have, how safe the neighborhood is, and how many community services and agencies parents use. In safe neighborhoods, children have more freedom to move beyond their homes and to observe and interact with people involved in the various activities and occupations. How different people dress, what distinguishes young people from old, what people do to cross the street, how adults treat each other and children in passing, and many other qualities and interactions teach children about life. In violent neighborhoods, children also learn important lessons from observation of community activities, but too often parents must confine their children to their apartments or closely supervise them. This limits children's opportunities for physical exploration and experimentation in favor of simple survival skills.

Children learn from various materials generated by people in society. Some materials, such as a brochure about good eating habits for primary-school-age children, are prepared with educational intentions. Toy companies attempt to attract adults to buy various items for their children, and often advertisements will suggest a device's educational value. Children also learn from many other materials, including those adults consider junk. From observing, touching, smelling, and manipulating wood scraps, earth and sand, Styrofoam, bottles, shells, cans, and the like, children learn variations in texture, size, shape, and smell. Without adult support, the learning may be minimal, or the result could put children in harm's way. Even so, children left on their own do gain considerable knowledge about materials around them.

Every community has service agencies, political establishments, social-cultural agencies, and business enterprises. Just as schools and homes provide their curricula, so do community establishments and agencies. The efforts, products, and resources of each agency all provide formal, informal, and hidden curricula, similar to the school environment.

Children acquire knowledge, values, and social skills (positive as well as negative) from their experiences within their communities. We will find, of course, no single established curriculum for a community, any more than we find a common curriculum for all families. Resources vary, and how these resources are made available, plus the family's and children's ability to make use of them, determine learning potential.

Service Agencies

Service agencies provide families with health, transportation, protection, communication, and professional services. These agencies provide experiences from which children gain knowledge, both through the formal presentation of materials and in informal ways. Formal educational experiences from some agencies have been carefully thought through. Some prepared materials are directed towards parents or teachers to assist children in their instruction. Other materials or experiences are directed toward children. A child's first experience with the family dentist is one example of a community professional's "educating" young clients.

🌱

Since Rodriquo was 3 years old, he accompanied his mother to the dentist for her semiannual checkup. While his mother was in the chair, he would sit in a nearby chair with a book and a toy. One day Dr. Garcelon asked him if he wouldn't like to sit up in the big chair where his mother had sat. As Rodriquo climbed up, the dentist allowed him to touch the instruments and told him what they were for. He encouraged him to press the water tap and to rinse out his mouth from the paper cup nearby. Gradually, over two or three visits, he introduced all the "cleaning" instruments and even turned on the polishing brush so Rodriquo could see how it vibrated. At first, Rodriquo refused to have the brush in his mouth, but gradually he became so intrigued with the instruments that he wanted to see what would happen. One day a small squirrel came to the dentist's window and chattered away. Dr. Garcelon and the young child took a moment to feed the squirrel before the dentist gave Rodriquo a toothbrush and tube of toothpaste with verbal and written "picture" instructions on how to use the brush at home.

🍂

This dentist had a planned program for introducing dental hygiene to young patients. At first children observed parents' experiences—a rather informal learning experience. Parental comfort and the dentist's reassuring ways provided a safe and secure environment for the next phase. The formal instruction of what happens in a dentist's chair was designed to build children's trust as well as to start children on the road to good dental hygiene. The pamphlet Rodriquo received had simple instructions with pictures so that even at age 4 he could see how to brush his teeth. The squirrel's appearance was an accidental event, during which Rodriquo observed an animal close-up, discovered something about feeding animals, and experienced an adult's gentle treatment of a particular animal.

Just as teachers and homes vary in how they instruct children, so do people in various agencies and professions. Some dentists are not as thorough as Dr. Garcelon in giving information to parents whom they expect to in-

struct children. Many medical professionals work with schools, day care centers, and health fairs to provide free initial health check-ups. In some communities, free health clinics are regularly available for needy families. It is through these avenues that materials and curricula on health care are provided. The curricula in these settings vary and depend upon the interactions of the medical professionals with their young clients, parents, and teachers.

Most community agencies provide materials that schools and parents can use to help children understand the purposes and functions of the agencies. Police and fire departments, for example, normally provide speakers for schools or encourage field trips to their stations. Some police officers and firefighters get special training in how to work with young children, and children who visit are allowed to climb, under supervision, onto fire trucks or into police cars. Department representatives wear their uniforms and explain the equipment they carry and use. They also explain what children are to do when a police officer or firefighter is trying to assist them.

Transportation Services

Transportation agencies provide learning experiences for children, and it is not uncommon to witness a group of children trooping through a bus terminal, an airport, or a train station, where the companies are collaborating with schools to provide a formal learning experience. Usually a company employee accompanies the class and informs children about the various services within the terminals. In addition to formal lessons, many unexpected events happen in transportation terminals that convey important messages to children. Teachers and agency personnel may capitalize on these events because of children's interest, as did Dr. Garcelon with the squirrel. The hidden or covert curriculum emerges as children witness events around

Police officers will provide speakers for school affairs, wear their uniforms, and describe their equipment.

them and absorb different messages, depending on their prior experiences. A guard running a metal detector over a passenger at the airport security checkpoint affects children differently. An astute guide might stop and explain what is happening, perhaps reassuring a child who has witnessed a neighbor being frisked by police. Without an explanation, the same child may have a fear of uniformed authorities reaffirmed.

Political Agencies

All communities have government agencies, school boards, and task forces or committees empaneled by the community government to provide different types of community curricula. The management decisions these agencies make will affect—directly and indirectly—the social, intellectual, and physical development of children in that community. As with social agencies, political agencies often provide written materials, films, or audiotapes designed to educate the public about their functions or about the community. Such agencies make use of newspapers, magazines, radio, and television to carry their messages to the public, and the assumption is that families and schools will then "educate" children.

In some communities, the formal curriculum is more apparent, especially during election years, and is usually handled through the schools. Mock elections are held in some schools, using locally collected political campaign materials. Students sometimes visit local and state political offices, where teachers and political workers attempt to explain the functions and responsibilities of the resident officials. Children whose parents are active politically may begin to comprehend how the system works. However, the political implications of messages are usually beyond the comprehension of primary-school-age children. Children whose parents use social services managed by political officials can acquire confusing notions of how the system works, especially when their parents have difficulty obtaining services. The political knowledge that children gain from such experiences tends to be serendipitous.

In the United States, we have no national policy that supports children and families. Thus, families benefit from such community resources only in relationship to the personal networks they establish within the community (Pardeck, 1990). Social policies established by community leaders affect the options and determine the resources that any family has for establishing networks and making use of available resources (Cochran & Niegro, 1995; Cochran & Riley, 1990). For instance, people living in wealthier communities often are able to negotiate with political figures for funding well-equipped and well-maintained parks or recreational areas. They see that libraries and museums have appropriate materials and outreach programs. Citizens in affluent areas have better access to child care support services, community-based activities, and protective and health services. They tend to be better educated and so have developed better networking skills, which enable them to access these services (Cochran & Niegro, 1995). Children reared in poor communities are often discriminated against and have fewer opportunities for learning. Parents in these neighborhoods appear to have less clout with governmental

and management agencies, and with less education have fewer skills enabling them to access fully the benefits of community learning. The following vignette illustrates different potentials for social, intellectual, and physical learning as a result of two different policies for park maintenance.

❧

In Wexton, the recreation department has provided a park with grassy areas and paths. There are a few swings, one piece of climbing equipment, and a basketball court. Maintenance of the park is poor. Swings are always in disrepair; garbage and debris litter the ground. Parents bringing children to the area will briefly exchange a smile or a word with the ever present "bag man" and occasionally with adults rushing through on their way to work or with those bringing dogs for an outing. Parents appear to use the park for children to play in, but they display little sense of coming here to meet other people. Parents are likely to discourage their children from interacting with others in the park.

In Overton, situated near a small shopping area, the community has provided a small park with lots of climbing equipment, paths for tricycles, a basketball court, bicycle paths leading off into an open grove area, and benches where parents sit and supervise their children's play. The park is well maintained, with little debris. Paths are well cared for, as is all equipment. Park maintenance people are seen frequently cleaning up the area and have been known to remind the older, often unsupervised, children to watch out for others as they play. In this park, parents chat with each other, watch their children interact with one another, and often begin to develop friendships. There is a sense of bringing children for outings, but one that expands parental contacts with others in the neighborhood. ❧

Children in these situations will learn many things in both parks, but the park in Overton, where more people, materials, and natural resources exist, has greater potential for positive learning opportunities. In both parks, one observes children gaining physical skills as they climb on equipment or play ball. Children use various strategies to engage other children in their play, and some appear to be skilled in interacting with other adults, such as when they crouch to pet a visitor's dog. However, there are differences.

In Wexton, there are fewer chances for personal interactions, since most parents discourage such interchanges, especially with "disreputable-looking characters." Since maintenance is poor, children receive different messages about the value of a clean environment. Some adults passing through the park are seen picking up trash and throwing it in available receptacles, but children witness other adults carelessly dropping litter. More potentially dangerous spots exist in Wexton, and children learn to be chary of their environment and aware of the danger signals.

In Overton, a different learning potential exists. Safe paths for children riding bicycles and tricycles from their homes to the park provide more opportunities for expanded physical development. Adults feel more comfortable with each other. The ambiance is welcoming, and the sense of trust among adults provides a stronger sense of trust in children. The park is kept free of debris, and maintenance personnel do not hesitate to remind children about respect for their environment and for each other. On the other hand, opportunities for learning danger signals may be more limited.

The community policy of providing and maintaining a park varies in these two communities. These policies are management choices, which in turn are influenced by the residents' pressure (or lack of such pressure) for maintaining a safe environment for their

children's learning opportunities. Certainly adults' abilities to use the resources available in the parks either enhance or limit what is learned in both situations.

It is not just with parks that communities provide options for adults to develop the social networks that enable them to use their community more advantageously. Governmental policy is inextricably interwoven with a community's social fabric. In some communities, policies regarding social service agencies make it much easier for adults to get the services they need.

Darlene, a shy person, had moved to a new community with her new baby and 4-year-old son. She needed help but dreaded applying for food stamps at the Women, Infants, and Children (WIC) program because of unpleasant experiences she had had when seeking welfare in her previous community. However, when in desperation she finally went, she was pleasantly surprised at the quality of support. A community health organization had pressured the mayor's office into allowing food stamps to be distributed at their well-baby clinic. Also, a group of volunteers had begun a program of reading and playing with the babies and older children at the clinic while the parents waited for their appointments or discussed with the nurses their children's health and nutritional needs. Darlene and the nurse discussed ways to entice children into good eating habits, and during her first visit, one of the volunteers invited Darlene to attend a parent support group for mothers with new babies. At these meetings, Darlene gained new confidence in herself and new skills in raising her children.

Political decisions can affect the community curriculum presented to children. Not only is Darlene gaining help in feeding her children, but also she is learning to educate them about good eating habits. As a more subtle message, parents at the WIC office are exposed to models of adults reading to and interacting with children and thus may in turn provide expanded language experiences and positive social interactions for their own offspring.

Social and Cultural Agencies

The more skilled parents become at securing community services, the more opportunities they have to use other community resources, as illustrated in the following vignette.

🦢

Louisa's husband abandoned her and their two small children after they moved to a new state. Louisa had little money and no extended family support. She swallowed her pride and went to a church soup kitchen so that she and her children could have one nutritious meal a day. A series of contacts with people at the center led her to the social agencies in her community where she learned how to use resources for the welfare of herself and her children. It wasn't always easy, for some of the policies seemed to hinder Louisa's progress. The support systems she began to establish for herself, however, enabled her to continue. Louisa eventually was able to finish high school and find a part-time job. She presently has a federally funded scholarship to college. In the process, she expanded her network of friends in the service areas so that she could use community programs to enrich her children's experiences, of which library and museum programs and a 2-week summer recreational program were recent highlights. 🦢

Churches, libraries, theaters, and sports and recreational facilities are community

agencies that supplement children's education. As with all situations, some children experience a richer curriculum than others. How well families are able to use available resources and how well agencies are able to reach all families in the community account for some of the disparity. These social and cultural agencies do not exist apart from one another, as the vignette illustrates. A church agency providing physical and social nurturance helped Louisa work through the governmental policies, which in turn helped her find other community resources for her children.

Governmental policies, concerned with so-called separation of church and state, can limit the resources that a church provides a community. Church leaders, concerned with developing memberships, often wish to provide religious activities for young people within schools, but community policies normally exclude such events.

Librarians, theater personnel, and museum directors often try to develop programs with schools whereby children are invited to cultural offerings in their centers. But too often communities will not financially support such programs, or they will believe that children are missing "schoolwork" so must not be permitted to go. Those children whose parents have financial and social capital are able to profit by such community curriculum offerings while other children are left out. Some cultural agencies locate financial resources other than political agencies to help community programs expand their curriculum to include more children and families. In one community, when schools eliminated art programs because of cutbacks in funding, the local artists' association extended art lessons to all children in the community with help from a local community foundation.

Many social and cultural agencies provide a rich formal curriculum to children. Such settings have a strong impact on children's information-processing skills as well as on physi-

Parks offer educational programs relating to conservation and land protection.

cal, emotional, and moral development (Grumbine, 1988; Koran, Longino, & Shafer, 1983; Miles, 1986/1987).

Art museums offer both art instruction and art appreciation. Science museums and zoos often have formal presentations for young children. National and state parks have various educational programs that emphasize education relating both to the park theme and to conservation and environmental protection (Jacobson & Padua, 1992). Often theaters have acting lessons, summer camp experiences, children's performances, and lectures about plays and playwrights. Most libraries have educational lectures, storytelling events, and book talks. Hurst (1993) describes a library program in which she uses poetry to enhance knowledge and feelings about the weather. She

extends the language of poems by having children use computer graphics to create the effects of storms. The theme expands as children use reference books to find facts about storms and storybooks for descriptions of storms. Children who participate in these literacy events expand their language, reading, writing, and computer skills as well as personal interaction skills and knowledge about where to find information.

Churches offer religious education classes, and many of these classes integrate art, drama, and music as a part of the instruction. Recreational facilities offer instruction in different sports, such as gymnastics, basketball, golf, or archery, as well as health-related classes, such as aerobics, nutrition, and physical fitness.

As with curriculum in any context, children acquire a great deal of knowledge through the informal and hidden curricula of these social and cultural agencies. For example, several church leaders provided a curriculum that went well beyond teaching the group's religious beliefs—to involve areas of the informal curriculum.

🌀

The instructors of a Sunday school class decided to make the biblical story of Joshua and Jericho come alive for their 8-year-olds. As in a school curriculum, their activity focused on writing, creating, memorizing, and cooperating as the children wrote a play, designed costumes and props, learned their parts, and supported each other in a final production. At the end of the performance, children passed a collection plate, imitating the adults in church. This included keeping an eye on their partners and nodding to each other before moving to the next row. It was apparent that children were learning the rituals of that congregation in following the collection procedures.

As in any curriculum, some learning is unintended and may even be considered undesirable by the teachers. For example, at the reception after the performance, special bonbons were placed on a dish, and one portly gentleman took five pieces. Travis, following suit, took five as well, but his mother reprimanded him, saying, "Think of others and take only one." Travis got mixed messages, perhaps one he resents: Both he and the portly gentleman were rude, but only children are expected to be thoughtful.

🌀

Other social-cultural agencies also present formal and informal curricula through classes they offer and by the materials and facilities available to children. For example, posters announcing coming events and programs inform adults, but in indirect ways, they inform children as well.

🌀

In a local theater while awaiting a performance, a 5-year-old observed an adult commenting and pointing to an announcement of the next play. "Oh, look, Bill Braunhof will be playing in Cats! *I wonder what the dates are?" Running her finger under the date, she exclaimed, "Oh, too bad. It's Wednesday the 22nd, and we won't be here."*

🌀

With no intent of teaching young children, theater personnel have provided materials that can and do instruct. The adult, in seeking information for herself, unwittingly demonstrated to the child that such a poster offers information and that pieces of that information are found in different places on the poster. The child may even have discovered that "C-a-t-s" spells *cats* and recognized it when seeing it again, or that "22" can mean 22nd.

Sometimes such informal teaching is intentional. In Overton, the community librarian discovered that children would pick up, look at, and often take home those books that were displayed attractively. He began to more carefully select for display outstanding books that had heretofore sat unused on the shelves. The quality of books selected by young readers took a quantum leap. The librarian then began to coordinate his efforts with units of study done by local teachers. The teachers were pleased to find children bringing into class these extra resources from the local library for current topics.

Community clubs are another means of educating children. Scout organizations, trail clubs, outing clubs, ski and skimobile clubs, and so on, often have projects in which students participate. Some take trips into the community and surrounding areas where children cook outdoors, practice trail maintenance, observe different natural phenomena, and learn lessons in getting along with others. Some lessons are intentional, and some are unexpected. On one such trip, three 8-year-old boys came upon a family of skunks in a meadow. Wondering what the skunks would do if startled, the children gently tossed some pebbles toward the nest. To their and the other campers' dismay, the boys learned how startled skunks respond.

Business and Commercial Enterprises

All communities have business and commercial enterprises, many of which are located in large malls or along highways, though some communities still have main streets and neighborhood shops. Wherever they are, these establishments have identifying marks to advertise what they sell or what service they perform. Intentionally and unintentionally, adults and older children help younger ones sort out information regarding such businesses. Drive or walk through any of these commercial areas and observe carefully what the buildings or shops look like, the signs in and about the community, the types of vehicles in the parking areas, and the displays in the windows to get a feeling for what children learning about their world must sort out.

Children hear comments from adults, note certain identifying characteristics of buildings, and learn without specific instruction where to buy ice cream, get stamps, find interesting books, or buy a desired toy. Children begin to recognize similar and different shapes. The stop sign is always red and octagonal. Children may question why their parents are stopping or may even figure out from adult conversations what *stop* means. They learn to recognize their own car and eventually may be able to help find it in a large parking area.

Business enterprises distribute advertising circulars as well as put signs in shop windows. Such materials provide information about prices and kinds of items a store sells. Window signs, especially in smaller communities, may also present information about events in the community. Children who become adept at using such resources acquire many skills about how to get information. They may also become skilled in using adults as resources for achieving certain purposes. As with other curricula, how and what children learn depend on many factors, including the kind of community in which they live, their developmental stage, and how significant adults share such information with them.

Parents, of course, are major influences, and how much parents talk and interact with their children as they are involved in the community also influences children's learning. Sometimes an important community person compensates for parental neglect or disinterest. Comer (1988) tells about a shopkeeper in his community who taught a child, whom everyone believed couldn't speak, to talk. The shop was a candy store, and the child would only point to candy when he entered the shop. By refusing to acknowledge the child pointing out candy, the owner gradually got the child to tell her what he wanted and then eventually to talk to her. In the large and impersonal malls, the lessons taught may not always be so positive, but many clerks will take the time to answer children's questions and assist parents as they support children's learning. Many business enterprises have special programs or relationships that support children's learning. Chapter 11 discusses examples of these.

Media

Extensive learning opportunities for children are offered through various forms of media. Some children's learning takes place serendipitously, but adults extend and enhance it. We have a number of educational television and radio programs as well as Internet sites for young children. The Public Broadcasting System (PBS) has for years provided educational programs, such as *Sesame Street, Mr. Rogers' Neighborhood*, the ever popular *Barney*, and *Teletubbies*, which in spirited ways introduce children to the alphabet, to new words and concepts, and to interesting stories and facts about everyday events. Early research on *Sesame Street* indicated that children watching such programs were learning the alphabet, numbers, and vocabulary faster than children not exposed (Ball & Bogatz, 1970; Rice, Huston, Truglio, & Wright, 1990). Subsequent analysis of *Sesame Street* indicated, however, that rather than being a boon to disadvantaged children, the show was more likely to be watched by middle-class children, and the gains children maintained were dependent on adult reinforcement of concepts (Cook et al., 1975). Some learning from these programs may have an unintentional and perhaps undesirable effect. Children become accustomed to fast-paced materials and do not develop longer attention spans or ability to sustain interest in events that aren't moving rapidly.

On both educational and commercial radio and television stations, science and social studies programs, story reading, and reenactments of children's literature offer rich educational opportunities. In addition, network educational offices often provide teacher or parent guides for assisting children in gaining more from these programs.

Printed materials in the form of books, pamphlets, magazines, and newspapers also educate children through pictures and printed words. Printed language is different from oral language. Oral language and life experiences assist children in learning to read, but printed materials to which they are exposed also facilitate intellectual growth. In nearly all families we find some form of printed materials. Children learn early that pictures relate to real objects and have names. As stories are shared, children learn more about their world. For ex-

ample, when children read Parnall's *Apple Tree*, their knowledge and concepts expand as they view an artist's interpretation and hear language describing the different ways the familiar features of apple trees are used. Children have experienced apples, if not apple trees, but may never have realized that ants and other insects feed from the trees, as do birds, who feed on the insects.

Children grow emotionally and intellectually when they can find, through books, security in loving and being loved, even while learning academic content. In Bang's *Ten, Nine, Eight*, a loving father hugs and tucks in his child as the two count objects in the room. Such a book conveys, besides the knowledge of rational counting, many and different messages to children. One child may have his understanding of a caring parent reaffirmed while another child may realize that males as well as females can be nurturing. An Anglo child sees that African American children do things just like she does.

Feelings of security come as children see that book characters like themselves can be angry, frightened, frustrated, hateful, sad, or lonely. Models for resolving conflict, as well as lessons, can be learned. In Zolotow's *The Hating Book*, children learn how misunderstandings come about when one listens to gossip and doesn't trust a friend.

Most newspapers have a special children's section, and some offer guidance on how to use the newspaper with children. Comics have always been a source for nudging children towards reading. Comer (1988) tells how his mother always read the comics from three different newspapers to him and his siblings each Sunday. This undereducated mother instinctively realized the importance of rereading the parts that especially interested each child and how this would assist her children in learning to read.

Not all influence from printed materials is necessarily positive from an adult point of view. The excitement of Max chasing his dog with a fork in Sendak's *Where the Wild Things Are* may be so attractive that a mother of a 4-year-old finds her child imitating the action with another child. Stories and other printed materials, as with television programs, also can reinforce prejudice and bias when characters of different ethnic origin are interpreted as having the characteristics of a certain cultural group. Fairy tales have been cited as reinforcing male and female stereotypes. It is possible to interpret such female characters as Cinderella, Snow White, and Rapunzel as passive women in need of rescue by active and handsome Prince Charmings. Many comic strips portray stereotyped characters and advocate violence for solving problems. Television and computer games have also been criticized for their violence.

When stories, other printed materials, television, and computer programs are not comprehensible or not within children's range of experience, then, without support from an adult, the influence may be harmful to a child's self-concept and to the child's emotional, social, or intellectual development. Cornell (1993) maintains that this may be especially true for children coming from particular cultural heritages. For example, many European tales present witches as old, ugly, mean, and to be feared, but in Asian cultures, the old are wise, kind, and to be revered. The clash of cultures may be confusing, especially to new immigrants, whose understanding of and adaptation to their new country can be deterred.

Not all books and printed materials are well written, and the language in some is stilted and uninteresting. Well-written materials have integrity, whereas poorly written books have "flagrant repetitiveness, stiff dialogue, a gross exaggeration of humor or fantasy, conflict between realism and fantasy, didacticism, superciliousness, or a use of language that is poorly chosen for the genre of the book or for the characters in it" (Sutherland & Arbuthnot, 1991, pp. 49–50). Children acquire language and richness of expression from books. Hackneyed, mundane expressions do nothing to enrich a child's vocabulary or imagination.

A rich curriculum provided through printed materials requires adults (1) to be sensitive to children's acceptance or confusion about these materials and (2) to help children interpret printed matter in light of their own experiences.

The Internet, with its expanding websites, is now a part of many young children's learning environment. No longer is the computer a part of children's lives only through programs and games. With access to the Internet, a child's world expands tremendously. Children have access to chat groups, computer conferences, bulletin boards, and connections to individuals through E-mail. In some ways, this larger networking is very positive, but as with all media, it has risks. Not all material is appropriate for the children using it; adult-oriented entertainment, plus vicious hate-group materials and video images, is easily obtained by young children. In addition, some children become so involved with their cyber journeys that they become addicted and have difficulty reconnecting to their regular peers. Many professionals argue that computers will change, for the better, the way we educate young children. Some investigators see teachers moving into a constructivist model of learning with their computers, with project learning and more individualized instruction tailored to children's learning styles and preferences (Papert, 1996; Tapscott, 1999).

With all their benefits, the media also have an intentional curriculum that seeks to educate children through advertising. Some altruistic advertisements are aimed at drug or sex education, but most are directed at enticing children to be consumers. The media also have their informal and hidden curricula. Much of

Some teachers use computers to enhance project learning and promote individualized instruction.

television, radio, and Internet programming is for adult consumption, but many children are exposed to programs that confuse, frighten, or misinform them when there is little or no adult guidance. Certainly judicious use of V-Chip, compulsory in new television sets in January 2000, and Internet web filtering systems is logical now in homes and should be mandatory in schools. Chapter 1 contains a more detailed discussion of media influence on children and illustrates the importance of adult intervention.

PHYSICAL, SOCIAL, AND EMOTIONAL ENVIRONMENTS IN A COMMUNITY

The physical and social-emotional environments in a community where children live provide a curriculum that both positively and negatively affects children's development. Children's chances of becoming confident and competent adults are greater when they have both a safe home environment and a safe neighborhood where they are able to play, explore, and form relationships (Garbarino, Dubrow, Kostelny, & Pardo, 1998). Regrettably, today many children are exposed to dangers both within family situations and in their communities. When too many risk factors exist, children's total development is affected. Emergent intellectual capacity, motor development, coping strategies, social-emotional development of trust, autonomy, a sense of self-worth, and the ability to benefit from the environmental curriculum can be hampered (Gouvis, 1995; Randolph, Koblinsky, & Roberts, 1998).

Social Networks

Children's ability to benefit from their neighborhood is influenced extensively by the social networks their parents have established. As children mature, they develop additional social networks within their peer groups. In earlier generations, families tended to be stable, and community members formed bonds that enabled them to look after each other's children and to some degree control children's peer groups. Today, communities tend to step in only when parents truly fail to support their children, and most parents have less control over their children's friendships. Yet nowadays, children and their families need community support more than ever as a result of larger numbers of dual-income families and single parents, plus greater mobility (Kagan, 1994).

Adults.   In today's society, adults are likely to move often during children's growing years, and children's development is affected by adults' ability to adapt to change (O'Hare, 1996). Some parents establish new relationships easily, thus helping their children to profit by participating in neighborhood activities.

The ambiance of a particular neighborhood may be welcoming or threatening, making it easier or riskier to initiate social contact. For example, in one part of Eastern City, homes, streets, and sidewalks are well maintained. One residential street is a dead-end street with little traffic, so residents sit outside on doorsteps and watch their children play close to the street. Families moving into this community feel secure in reaching out to others. Children come to know the adults in the neighborhood easily and are able to interact with them.

In another part of Eastern City, broken bottles litter sidewalks, poorly maintained buildings restrict families from venturing out, and illicit activities are common. Adults and neighborhood gangs are in such conflict with each other that children are unsafe, even in their own homes. The street violence causes such trauma for families that children have difficulty learning anything positive from any community source.

Rural and suburban neighborhoods also vary in providing physical and mental safety for inhabitants, thus influencing learning. Poverty is perhaps the greatest deficit, as it limits families in making the diverse social ties that enable children to participate in a neighborhood's growth opportunities (Cochran, 1990). When children are able to move comfortably throughout their neighborhoods, socialization becomes more available, and children benefit.

✍

Janice and Peter lived on the same street in look-alike houses in a large suburban neighborhood. Although the yards were all fenced, children felt free to visit from one house to the other, stopping to watch and ask endless questions of kindly neighbors. One day, Janice and Peter roamed and stopped to watch while one neighbor trimmed roses in her front yard and another washed his car. They even got to spray some water on the soapy car, getting a bit wet themselves. After a while they wandered onto a nice muddy area in another neighbor's backyard. Making a few mud balls, they proceeded to toss the balls at the neighbor's garage. When Janice's mother caught up with them, she obtained buckets and water from the neighbors and insisted that the children clean up the mess they had made. With help from some of the older neighbor children, Janice and Peter managed to get the garage quite clean.

✍

That day, among other lessons, Janice and Peter learned a bit about the why and how of gardening, how cars are cleaned, and what makes water spray. They may also have increased their throwing skills while discovering that they would be held accountable for any mess they created. They learned about helping others when they received help from the older children. Of course, children's every-

day lessons from the neighborhood are not always the ones adults might wish. Still, Cochran and Riley (1990) point out that when children have more adults and older children with whom they do a variety of activities, they tend to do better in school. Children who have caring adults beyond family members to assist them in mastering skills and attitudes in a gradual way have greater metacognitive and problem-solving strategies.

Children learn how to cope with their environment differently depending on their circumstances, as the following vignette demonstrates.

✍

By November, 4-year-old Tobias was able to go without his parents to the Head Start center down the street from his apartment. He had been to that building many times and knew just how to maneuver through the street. One day he noticed a folded dollar bill lying in the gutter. He picked it up and then proceeded down the street to the mom-and-pop store on the corner. He went directly to the aisle for cookies and found some of his favorite, which he took to the counter. Handing Mrs. Jameson the dollar, he asked, "Is this enough money?"

"Yes, and you'll get some change," she replied, then added, "Is this what your mom wanted you to buy?"

"She don't care. I found this dollar in the street." And with his cookies and change, Tobias hurried off to Head Start.

In Vermont, 4-year-old Clara also went to Head Start, but her mother took her every day, for they lived in the country and her mother didn't want her to walk the road to the church alone, although they had been there many times. One day Clara's mother was ill, and Clara decided to go to Head Start by herself. She started down the road but soon got lost. A neighbor driving by noticed Clara alone and stopped to pick her up. When she explained what she was doing, the neighbor said, "But Clara, you are going in the wrong direction. I'll take you home and then to Head Start if your mother would like."

✿

Both children have been exposed to their community environment, and both children have other supportive community adults who assist them. But Tobias is much more street-wise and able to maneuver than is Clara. Clara has always had the support of an adult and has never ventured down the road alone. Not all children have such extended support, and many could have regrettable experiences in either of the preceding situations. Tobias might be able to negotiate problems more success-fully than Clara, depending on the circum-stances, and he is probably more alert than she to danger signs. In some ways, Tobias has had more opportunities to learn from his commu-nity and has become more independent. Ku-move (1966) found that when children under age 7 were able to move more freely in their immediate environment, they became more in-dependent than children whose parents found it necessary to keep them homebound. Chil-dren unable to move about in their community because of pervasive community violence often are unable to develop coping skills and thus are more likely to become aggressive or violent themselves (Slaby, Roedell, Arezzo, & Hendrix, 1995).

Peer Groups.   Tobias in the preceding vi-gnette moves freely about his neighborhood. Even at his young age, he demonstrates knowl-edge of the social mores of his society. He knows where to find cookies and that he must pay for them, and he feels comfortable inter-acting with the adults in the shop. Some of this learning is through observation, and some through the impact of adult teaching. Tobias already shows considerable independence, and friends in the neighborhood will affect his

learning more and more. Peers become strong socializing agents, and it is from them that children learn more about who they are and how they fit into society. Parents teach chil-dren moral and ethical values, but the peer group is powerful in setting the social tone and imposing behavioral patterns.

Even as young as 18 months, children learn how their actions affect others and thus begin the process of learning behavioral codes (Hartup, 1983). A toddler who tries to take a desired toy away from another child soon learns the consequences of the behavior. It may be an indignant yell; it may be a slap; it may be acquiescence and subsequent loss of a playmate. As children begin to form peer groups and play with each other, they begin to form rules of conduct so that they can con-tinue to operate as a group. It is in peer groups that children learn to negotiate, problem solve, and compromise in order to continue to play and work together. Some children will be more dominant than others and will learn the rules for domination and acquiescence. Chil-dren are often rewarded by significant others in the group for conforming, or they are ostra-cized (Elkin & Handel, 1989).

Children experiment with various roles (leader, compromiser, follower, negotiator, etc.) and discover from their peers how to act to fulfill roles as well as how their peers re-spond to them. Children also learn about their own abilities from their peers. They learn that they can run faster, jump higher, or read better as they compare their skills with others. But the group also dictates what skills are prized.

Although parents teach children about gender roles, by preschool, peers begin to seg-regate into boy and girl groups that dictate what roles each group is permitted to play. A physician's daughter, after beginning pre-school, insisted that her doctor mother was re-ally a nurse. At school, she had learned in her play group that doctors are boys and nurses are girls, even though her teacher and parents insisted differently. In addition, children learn cultural and social differences as they interact with their peers. They compare notes about their own family's customs, values, and ways of doing things. Peer group acceptance or rejection can influence how individual children change their own behaviors.

Sexual understandings and misunderstandings are learned from peers. Many young children learn the physical difference between boys and girls by examining each other. They often learn about birth when some "wiser" child informs them of their knowledge or misunderstanding. It is through such discussions, along with other teachings, that children figure out for themselves the confusing information they receive.

Cognitive information and development of numerous skills come from children's interactions with peers. Children have rituals and routines, just as adults do. Older peers teach to younger ones the chants and rhymes of childhood. Memory skills and counting as well as physical endurance are enhanced as children jump rope to such rhymes as "One Potato, Two Potato" or "First Comes Love, Then Comes Marriage." As they play together, children learn from more skilled peers how to climb higher, catch a ball, read a story, or add up their money for ice cream. Learning may result from a desire to compete with a peer or because the peer has more information and passes it on. Learning may also come because a new idea has been introduced and children need to test out the new concept.

🖋

Billy was watching Ahmed copy words from a book he was reading. "Whatcha doing?" asked Billy.

"I'm making an 'r' for 'red'," replied Ahmed.

"Nunh, nunh, that's not an 'R'. I'll show you how to make an 'R'." Billy wrote a capital R.

Ahmed retorted, "Oh! That's a big 'R', and I'm making a little 'r'!" After much discussion, Ahmed in disgust turned to his book. "Look," he pointed, "that says 'Red' and that says 'red.' See, that's a big 'R' and that's a little 'r'."

🖋

Ahmed has challenged Billy's thinking about r's, so now Billy will examine writing in a new way. New learning has been opened up to him by a friend. Ahmed's scorn for his not knowing seemed to spur Billy on, for later he got a book and paper and came to sit beside Ahmed and tried to make the "little 'r'," asking his friend for help.

Not all learning from peer groups is positive. Gangs can be a destructive force in any society as children seek approval and find that they must develop antisocial codes of behavior to be accepted. Some children can be targets for peer victimization. But when these at-risk children have a "best friend," this friendship acts as a strong buffer against such attacks (Hodges, Boivin, Vitaro, & Bukowski, 1999). When a community provides opportunities for children to develop social networks among different adult and peer groups, children have more options. When this happens, the lure of destructive peer groups is lessened, and children are helped to find more positive peer associations.

Natural Environments

As children move about their neighborhood, the outdoor environment offers a rich curriculum from which they gain understanding about their world. This curriculum is, of course, all of nature. Learning differs depending on the combination of children's ability, social interactions regarding the environment, and children's freedom of movement to explore. Louv (1990) discovered that many U.S. children spend very little time outdoors. Although they do learn about nature in various

Outdoor environments offer a rich curriculum by which children gain an understanding of their world.

ways, their understanding and appreciation of nature are limited.

Studies on children's play activity indicate that the quality of children's outdoor and indoor play differs, and thus different learning opportunities emerge. Children engage in more dramatic and constructive play outdoors (Moore, 1985) and in more exploratory play (Anderson, 1972; N. J. Wagner, 1995), when they feel, touch, examine, crunch, and test materials, such as when learning the sounds different rocks make when dropped into the water. Balancing while walking on uneven rocks in a dry riverbed develops different skills than balancing on the smooth surface of a gymnasium balance beam. Children may climb indoors, but viewing the world from a tree branch gives them broader perspectives. "Twigs, soil, mud, stones, leaves, and grass are materials of sensory pleasure, play, and learning" (Dighe, 1993, p. 58).

Good children's books capture the many wonders of nature and can extend children's appreciation of what they experience, but without experiencing the reality of the world, their knowledge is limited. In the following vignette, Davon has book knowledge about snow, but it is the real experience that enriches his understanding.

❦

Davon lived all his 5 years in Florida. He had read lots about snow and was especially fond of Ezra Jack Keat's The Snowy Day, *but he had never seen real snow. While visiting his cousin in Boston that winter, he awoke to white flakes outside his window. He had never imagined snow to look like that. As the week wore on and more snow fell, Davon learned much more about the feel of snow on his face and the taste of snow as he and his cousin held out their tongues to catch it. He learned how snow could limit and enhance activity and how it felt to walk through drifts.*

❦

Not all of nature's lessons are pleasant. The first snow can be an exciting and beautiful time, but a blizzard followed by power outages and snarled traffic teaches a different lesson. Learning to observe the outdoor environment enhances children's cognitive learning as well as their social and emotional understandings. Joshua learned many things about his surroundings one late-winter day while watching the waterfront.

❦

Joshua lived near the St. Lawrence River and with his mother loved to watch the seals bob up and down in the harbor. One winter day, a small, and undoubtedly ill, seal crawled out on the ice floe and collapsed. While watching and wondering about the seal, Joshua noted two eagles swoop down on the seal and begin tearing at the carcass. Alarmed, Joshua ran to get his mother, who tried to explain about the natural process of creatures in the wild. Then

she remembered Cherie Mason's book, Everybody's Somebody's Lunch. *Together they read how a young girl whose cat was devoured by a fox discovers that there are predators and prey in our world and that all are part of nature's food chain. Joshua then became quite fascinated with the eagles and their 3-day venture of cleaning up the dead seal. He watched as several crows tried to claim their share but were chased away. A neighbor farther along the shore telephoned and asked Joshua's mother whether she knew what was agitating the crows. An excited Joshua took the phone to explain to the neighbor about the eagles.*

❦

Joshua's nature lessons didn't all happen in one day, but he gradually became a more interested and astute student of the world around him, discovering other fascinating avenues for learning.

INTERACTIONS AMONG COMMUNITY AGENCIES, FAMILIES, AND SCHOOLS

The learning that took place in the vignettes in this chapter did not happen in isolation within these communities, for the community curriculum was affected by how the families and schools linked children to community resources and agencies (see Figure 9–1). Stronger links heighten the potential for children's learning.

Many community agencies welcome children's visits, either with their families or with schools. Some agencies actively attempt to reach families of differing cultural and economic backgrounds. Other agencies limit their support to those families who can afford their services, or to those families who reach out. Louisa in the earlier vignette was able to use more community resources because church members aggressively presented programs to

Figure 9–1   Community impact on children through the environment and from interactions among agencies.

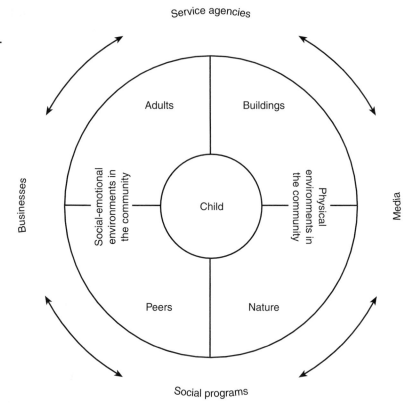

assist her in her dilemma. As she became more confident of her ability to help her children, she more actively sought those recreational programs that provided richer learning experiences.

All families at some time use the business enterprises of a community. In today's society, many families patronize large, impersonal organizations for purchases, banking, and communicating, and the education that children receive is more limited than what happens in a small neighborhood. The mom-and-pop store in Tobias's neighborhood was used by his parents, and Tobias felt comfortable entering the store and asking for information. "Mom" knew the child well enough to check on him and inquire about his purchase. Clara, on the other hand, had more limited neighborhood re-

sources, but her parents had developed connections with some neighbors. Clara was lucky that someone found her and helped her. Joshua, too, has supportive parents and neighbors who are interested in his observations and explanations, thus enriching his learning.

Many community agencies that offer programs to children depend on family or Big Brother/Sister types of support. A Scout-sponsored camping trip, for example, may include one or both parents or another adult accompanying children. Trail-blazing and fire-building lessons may be a planned part of the trip, but how the learning is extended depends on parental involvement with the organization. Some churches have family nights where leaders invite entire families to be involved in extended learning situations.

Communities and schools can collaborate to provide concrete experiences to extend children's learning, but this is not done as much as is possible. Trips into the community are enriched when the agencies have materials, people, and specific events appropriate for the learning level of the children visiting. When teachers make visits and discuss the trip with community agencies beforehand, learning is more likely to be enhanced. Some school trips within a community are not done collaboratively, however, and children's learning is thus limited and may even be negative.

🐎

One child care center decided to make a trip to McDonald's without checking first with the establishment. It was noon, and McDonald's was crowded. Children, when let off the bus, ran to the play area and began to play noisily. Teachers' attempts to find a place for children to eat together and to give them experience in selecting and ordering food were disastrous. The bus driver had left, and the harassed teachers had to corral the children in the play area until he returned. The children finally received their food, but the bus arrived, and the teachers hurried everyone onto the bus carrying uneaten food with them. The children, the teachers, and McDonald's personnel were all unhappy with the experience.

🐎

Many restaurants welcome children's visits and provide opportunities for children to visit the kitchen and to experience ordering and eating food in a relaxed manner. Lack of planning with the establishment in the preceding episode resulted in an unpleasant experience for both adults and children. It would be wrong to assume that no learning took place from this trip; however, with more care, the trip could have been more valuable and pleasant for everyone.

In community programs, where children interact with materials, observe events, or see animals acting in a natural situation, youngsters usually learn more than in those programs where adults lecture, expecting children to be enraptured with what they say. The community, through natural phenomena and by the nature of the community's organization, offers a rich curriculum for all children. Children learn from this curriculum in direct relationship to the social networks available to them.

🐎

Eve was on her way to Africa to visit her son and his family. In the local airport, Mrs. Thomas, a third-grade teacher, and an airline representative approached Eve and introduced themselves and Wrinkle. Mrs. Thomas, in collaboration with the airline, had devised a plan to enrich her students' knowledge of the world through Wrinkle, a stuffed dog. Wrinkle has a notebook in which his experiences can be noted. Mrs. Thomas wondered whether Eve would be willing to take Wrinkle with her to Africa and keep Wrinkle's diary. Once Eve had returned from her travels, the airline had agreed to assist her in finding someone traveling to another continent and request that Wrinkle accompany that traveler. Wrinkle was to have an "Around the World in 80 Days" experience.

Eve was delighted, and in the process of traveling with Wrinkle, she, in collaboration with the airline personnel, Mrs. Thomas, and other friendly adults along the way, provided a rich curriculum for children in that third-grade class, for children traveling in the same planes and trains as Eve, and for the children in Eve's own community.

Eve dutifully wrote down Wrinkle's experiences, but she also had Wrinkle send postcards to the children in Mrs. Thomas's class, telling them what he was seeing. On one or two occasions, Wrinkle met people who added

**Community areas where children observe and experience life promote more
learning than do adults explaining.**

*something to the notebook or sent a postcard
to the class saying they had met Wrinkle. The
flight attendants knew about Wrinkle and during the trip to Africa used him to help other
traveling children gain some insights. For example, one young child was traveling alone to
Africa and was quite apprehensive. The airline hostess asked Eve to introduce Wrinkle to
the child, and together they visited the cockpit
where the pilot explained the many instruments. On returning to the cabin, the lad drew
a picture in Wrinkle's notebook of the cockpit
and the pilot so that "Wrinkle's children would
see better what a cockpit was like." Periodi-*

*cally, the boy, Wrinkle, and Eve would look out
the window to see "where they were," how the
sun looked coming up over the horizon, and
the size of the ships in a harbor. The boy even
dictated a few sentences about his discoveries
for Eve to put in the notebook. Eve returned to
her home community before taking a trip to
Hong Kong. In the school in her community,
Eve took Wrinkle to class and, using a map,
described Wrinkle's trips. Some of the children
communicated with Mrs. Thomas's class also,
explaining how they had met Wrinkle.*

*Eve then took Wrinkle for new adventures
to Hong Kong. Before boarding the plane for*

her return trip to America, and with the assis-
tance of the airline personnel, Eve found a
family with young children returning to Eng-
land, and so Wrinkle took off on another leg of
his journey (Hamblett, 1994, personal commu-
nication).

A teacher collaborated with an agency in an imaginative way to provide an extended school curriculum involving community agents and an interested citizen. The community in this situation transcends the local one; people plus natural and material resources from around the world provided an extended curriculum for children of Mrs. Thomas's class and, incidentally, for other children along the way. The amount of learning for children in Mrs. Thomas's class will depend on the children's interest and developmental level and on their families' ability to network and to make connections.

IMPLICATIONS FOR PROFESSIONALS

The curriculum of the community is a vast resource for teachers. Information from this chapter can be used to start your resource file (or a computer file) that will assist you in classroom instruction, in working with families, and in making use of community resources. There are many ways to organize and build such a file. The following steps are suggestions for proceeding.

- List the four major categories from Table 9–1.
- Under each category, select one subcategory that is likely to be part of your professional assignment (e.g., you think you will teach in the inner city, so you select animals).
- Be specific on items: What animals are children in a city environment likely to observe? As you choose items, keep in mind

what children may be familiar with but could learn more about.

- Expand by selecting one animal and begin a list of resources (e.g., places animals can be found; persons who might bring animals to classroom; books, fiction and nonfiction about animals; films about animals and their owners or trainers; Internet sources appropriate for age group).
- Examine the other categories to ascertain if at this time you might wish to cross list (e.g., pet shops for kinds of free materials available regarding animals).
- Move on to another category. Consider what general information at this point you think will be helpful in your teaching (e.g., select Services, then the subcategory Recreation, then Parks).
- Expand the above by listing different types of parks and what learning opportunities would be available to children. Include any materials or resources that you could bring into the classroom.
- At a later point, consider what resources would be helpful for working with children and which are better for parents.
- An important category in your file will be the service agencies. List them separately with addresses and the services they render for parents. Collect brochures from these agencies.

Beginning a resource file before teaching helps you to organize so that you are able to add specific addresses and resources later as you discover what works for your classroom.

SUMMARY AND REVIEW

Most community curriculum is not expanded to such a worldwide view as Mrs. Thomas was able to create. It can, however, be made equally rich and varied, depending on how adults in society structure the environment and how they develop supportive educational policies in various service agencies. Political, social, cultural, and business agencies offer, both intentionally and unintentionally, a learning environment for children in a community. Political agencies, for the most part, focus formal education about political endeavors toward adults or older children, expecting the teaching to be done by significant adults. However, political decisions in different communities regarding management of a community and its social agencies can result in children learning from totally different curricula.

Service agencies, transportation services, social and cultural agencies, and business and commercial enterprises usually produce materials aimed at educating the public about their services. What children learn from these formal materials depends largely on the use parents and teachers make of them.

Like schools, all agencies provide informal and hidden curricula whereby children learn about their world. The natural and manufactured resources found within communities provide learning experiences even when there is little adult intervention. Children see signs, notice buildings, observe nature, note adult actions, and learn something from all their encounters. The ways that important adults use the resources, explain things to children, and interact with each other all enhance children's learning.

Children who live in communities providing safe physical and emotional environments have more educational opportunities, for in these communities families are better able to establish social networks that enable them to tap community resources. For children outside such safe environments, schools and other agencies must work especially hard to compensate and must strive to build a solid curriculum so that these children, too, will thrive in tomorrow's world.

SUGGESTED ACTIVITIES AND QUESTIONS

1. Take a 2- to 3-mile hike around your neighborhood. List all the natural resources, human resources, and materials that you observe. Rate the learning potential linked to them for children living here and start a resource file from information gathered.

2. Visit a business establishment in your community. Interview the owner or manager to learn whether they have materials aimed at educating children and how they distribute such materials. While there, ask yourself what children might learn just from being in the building.

3. From the list of community resources in this chapter, identify those your family was connected with as you grew up. List three things you think you learned from involvement with these resources.

4. Observe two or more children playing together. What learning do you think is taking place in this interaction? What community resources could support or hinder what these children are learning?

RESOURCES

Books

1. Cornell, J. B. (1998). *Sharing nature with children* (2nd ed.). Nevada City, CA: Dawn Publications.
2. Moore, R. C., & Wong, H. H. (1997). *Creating environments for rediscovering nature's way of teaching.* Berkeley, CA: MIG Publications.
3. Prasuraman, S., & Greenhaus, J. H. (1997). *Integrating work and family: Challenges and choices for a changing world.* Westport, CT: Quorum.

Films/Videos

1. *The adventure begins: Preschool and technology.* (1997). [Video, 10 min]. Demonstrates how computers enhance learning. Produced by National Association for the Education of Young Children with Apple Computer, Inc.
2. *Early intervention: Natural environments for children.* (1998). [Video, 28 min]. All children grow in special ways when learning environments such as schools, homes, parks, and restaurants provide for the special-needs child. National Association for the Education of Young Children.
3. *Exploring science and nature.* (1995). [Video, 28 min]. National Association for the Education of Young Children.

Organizations

1. Smithsonian Institution (http://www.si.edu/) Washington, DC 20560
2. Community Relations Service (http://www.usdoj.gov/office/crs.html)
   U.S. Department of Justice
   5550 Friendship Boulevard, Suite 330, Chevy Chase, MD 20815
3. National Legal Resource Center for Child Advocacy and Protection. 1800 M Street, NW, Washington, DC 20036

Websites

1. http://www2.childrensoftware.com/childrensoftware/ Website for Children's Software Revue, a publication helping teachers and parents examine software programs for children.
2. http://artsedge,kennedy-center.org/artsedge.html Website focuses on increasing art resources for education and provides links to other arts-related information.
3. http://www.nceet.snre.umich.edu/ Enables teachers, parents, and students to explore the environment by providing facts, statistics, and links to projects and activities.
4. http://lcweb.loc.gov/ Library of Congress home page with links to all congressional sites. Useful for accessing library services.
5. http://www.c-zone.net/fisher/wn An online source for nutritional news and up-to-date articles on health and nutrition.

Chapter 10

Traditional and Innovative Strategies for Working Together

Programs designed with strong parent involvement produce students who perform dramatically better than students in otherwise identical programs that do not involve parents at all, or as well.

(Henderson, 1987, p. 1)

🦋

Someone must start collaborations, and the beginning steps may be small ones. If partnerships are to flourish, teachers will need a wide range of techniques for involving parents and community agencies in children's learning. This chapter examines traditional and innovative practices for collaborative action and discusses items to consider when using these strategies. In reading the chapter, you will learn the following:

1. Teachers have long used traditional practices that involve parents in children's learning.

2. Creative teachers develop a variety of strategies to involve parents and community members in children's schooling.

3. Teachers have different effective strategies for communicating with parents.

4. Teachers must establish parameters for parent and volunteer roles in classroom operations.

5. Successful home visits and parent-teacher conferences require careful consideration and well-planned strategies.

6. Many strategies for working with parents of children with special needs or with different family lifestyles are similar to those for working with all parents, but you must consider particular factors as you work with different parent groups.

Our changing society, even with the advantages of mass communication systems, has evolved to a point where at the beginning of the 21st century, school programs alone are not sufficient for the task of formally educating children. The collaboration of parents and community agencies is essential if schools are to succeed in educating young children for a different society. A quarter of a century ago, Evans (1975) pointed out that the ultimate goal of active parent involvement is "enhancing the family's ability to respond to its children" (p. 11). This goal is as vital today as it was then.

Parental and community involvement have always been a part of U.S. education. As we have discussed, most parents historically were totally responsible for their children's education, but beginning in the 1800s, schools accepted more responsibility for academic learning. Later, professional educators began to assume the responsibility for communicating with parents, instructing them on ways of preparing their children for school, and even educating parents about children's growth and development.

By and large, parental cooperation in educational matters during the 20th century meant parental acquiescence to school suggestions, but now in many ways this has begun to change. Parental and community involvement in some districts has moved gradually from teacher-dominated procedures to collaborations with parents and community agencies. The authors contend that successful schools need to become embedded partners with parents and community members to cope with increasing challenges in the educative process. In this chapter, we discuss traditional but still useful strategies that teachers continue to use for involving parents and note helpful variations and innovative practices.

Most teachers' established ways of communicating with parents and community members have proven to work well, but many parents are not reached by these methods. Teachers must be open to new means of establishing communication. Parents and teachers, like children, have different communication and work styles. If children are to benefit, teachers must provide the impetus to break down barriers of communication resulting from different cultural expectations and habits of interacting. Of course, to be successful, both teachers and parents need to adapt and respond to each other's interests, concerns, and needs. But keep in mind that, it is the school's responsibility to lead in this endeavor.

As schools develop more welcoming strategies towards all parents, parents and community members feel more comfortable in visiting classrooms, becoming aides or volunteers in schools, and contributing special expertise to children's learning. These individuals learn about the schools and about school culture, which enables them to help their children and to communicate to the larger community their sense of the importance of school programs.

The community is also an important educating force. Schools and families have always made excursions into their community for educational purposes or have invited community members into the classroom. This involvement becomes more important as schools include community and environmental issues as part of the curriculum and as community agencies become partners. Some businesses are also devising ways to meet some of the needs of single parents and dual-career families.

COMMUNICATION WITH PARENTS

Almost all parents are keenly interested in their children and what happens to them at school. Teachers, knowing of this concern, have developed various ways to communicate to parents about their children's school experiences. Parent-teacher conferences, newsletters, telephone contacts, E-mail, websites, and written communiques inform parents about children's progress, school programs and curricula, and ways parents can help their children. Most techniques have proved very successful, and many innovative ideas are variations on these basic strategies.

Parent-Teacher Conferences

Teachers have traditionally used conferences for telling parents about children's progress, informing them of the school's way of doing things, and soliciting their support and involvement. As schools begin to develop a sense of partnership, conferences, although not different on the surface, become forums for mutual exchange. **Partnership conferences** mean that both partners share examples of children's development, show respect for each other's responsibility, and propose ideas for continuing a program or changing direction. In successful conferences, both parents and teachers feel that they (1) gain new insights about children's learning, (2) have an opportunity to pose questions about school and home behavior, and (3) exchange ideas relating to children's needs (Rotter, 1987).

Establishing Collaboration Through Conferences. Teachers work from a sound traditional base when creating an environment for successful collaboration. Current strategies reflect changes in attitudes of teachers and parents. Figure 10–1 presents a general scheme that you as a teacher may use to ensure that your parent-teacher conferences result in effective collaboration (adapted from Coleman, 1991; Seefeldt & Barbour, 1998).

Innovative Practices for Conferences. Although initiating conferences has traditionally been the teacher's responsibility, innovative schools encourage parents or other involved adults to suggest meetings and to come to conferences prepared. Student involvement in

PREPARATION FOR THE CONFERENCE

1. Develop mutual respect by scheduling conferences at convenient times for both teachers and parents.
2. Establish a sense of equality with seating arrangements. Avoid physical barriers by sitting beside parents at a table where everyone can view all materials.
3. Prepare an agenda and send it to the parents. Include a statement of purpose and allow times for parent input, your input, and questions from both you and parents.
4. Assemble materials from areas of the curriculum that demonstrate children's classroom work over time.
5. To demonstrate the value you place on parental teaching, invite parents to bring items their children have produced at home, such as charts of children's home responsibilities, craft projects children have made, food they have prepared, letters they have written, any collections, or sets of favorite books.

THE CONFERENCE

1. Begin the conference on a positive note by sharing with parents children's accomplishments at school.
2. Invite parents to share their children's meaningful achievements at home.
3. Share your mutual academic and personal concerns.
4. Discuss ideas for resolving these concerns.
5. Allow time for parental questions. If parents appear reluctant to ask questions, assist them by suggesting what other parents often ask: codes of behavior for the classroom, academic questions not attended to in this particular conference, parent involvement in schools or in children's learning.
6. Keep conference to allotted time. If you need more time, schedule a new conference.

ENDING THE CONFERENCE

1. End the conference on a positive note, be complimentary to the children involved.
2. Review conference highlights.
3. Restate your understanding of any decisions mutually made.
4. Indicate how information or material parents have shared has helped you understand their children better.
5. Thank the parents for coming and inform them of the next conference period, next school event for parents, or next PTA meeting.
6. Indicate your anticipation at seeing the parents again.

CONFERENCE FOLLOWUP

1. Write a brief summary for your records. Include any and all parental suggestions or questions.
2. Follow through on your promises and inform the parents of your efforts.

Figure 10–1   Making parent-teacher conferences work.

conferences also has proven to be successful for all concerned.

Parental Involvement.   To enhance parent involvement, some teachers have been successful in recommending ways parents can prepare for the conference. Innovative schools will make sure that parents know about the following strategies and will clarify that teachers recognize different family lifestyles:

- If children have more than one adult responsible for them, both adults should plan to attend, if possible. A single parent may bring a grandparent or another significant adult.

- Since the conference is an important part of the child's education and evaluation, adults should make the appointment a priority and get it on the calendar early.
- Children's understanding of the purpose of the conference is important, and parents or surrogates should talk with children about the conference and ask for their input about school and how they view their progress.
- Any materials that parents and children want to share with the teacher should be organized and brought to the conference.
- Adults attending the conference should make note of any questions or concerns that either they or their children wish to share with the teachers.
- Because of busy schedules, teachers and parents may need to work out special arrangements so that all can attend the conference.
- Parents need to talk about the conference afterwards as positively as possible to help the children see the relationship of the home environment to school life.
- A follow-up letter or E-mail to the school clarifies for the teacher the parents' or surrogate's view of the conference.

Parents and teachers all develop a sense of partnership in children's learning when they recognize the significant impact these meetings have on that learning.

Student Involvement. Traditionally, students have had little say or involvement in parent-teacher conferences. As parents assume some responsibilities for conferences, both teachers and parents seek input from children regarding questions they would like the adults to discuss. Another facet of innovative conferences is including students themselves.

When students are included in the conferences, steps need to be taken to prepare them:

- Determine the reason for including the children in this particular conference; for example, students have been working on a special project and evaluation of the project, will be enhanced with student input; or students at this point need to be involved in the decision for next steps.
- Review with the class the purpose of the conference, and help the children as a class to develop some possible questions and ideas to discuss in upcoming conferences. Students may want to consider their strengths as learners, how they have changed during this time period, any difficulties they may be having, and how they might improve (Weldin & Tumarkin, 1999).
- Help students gather materials they wish to bring to the conference to demonstrate the ideas brought up and questions asked.
- During the conference, have students describe their materials and how they see their progress. Have them ask questions of both teachers and parents.
- Have parents discuss their observations, and then discuss yours, being sure that children are addressed.
- Review the conference highlights and any recommendations made.
- Understand the importance for all parties to follow up conferences with notes to one another. You might initiate such action with a handout for each party such as Teacher Reflections, Student Reaction, Parent Feedback, listing such things as pride I take in my student/myself/my child; what I learned about my student/myself/my child's progress; what I hope my student/I/my child will focus on next.

In nearly all classrooms, teachers and children often have individual conferences without the parents. It is important that children understand that parents and teachers will also have some conferences without the children.

Home Visits

Visiting the homes of preschool-age children has been common practice for many years. Such programs have been and continue to be sponsored by school systems, and earlier programs were sponsored by health departments and mental health agencies (Miller, 1987). Whereas early programs focused on health needs of young children, in recent years, home visiting has become a means of enhancing cognitive and social development (Powell, 1990).

Head Start is a federally funded program that requires home visitation. In the 1970s, the U.S. government funded **Home Start**, a component of Head Start, to create early intervention models that required home visits from specially trained persons. Three exemplars from this period were the Mother-Child Home Program (Levenstein, 1977), the Florida Parent Education Infant and Toddler Program (Gordon, Guinagh, & Jester, 1977), and the Early Training Project (Larner & Halpern, 1987). Today, Head Start continues to have a home visiting component, and many public preschool programs, day care programs, and private nursery schools also require teachers to visit children in their homes. Some programs are well-defined, modeled after the early Home Start program and requiring specially trained home visitors. Most are aimed at assisting parents in providing better health care and obtaining needed social services as well as in becoming better teachers of their children.

Other home visiting programs are designed to establish home-school relationships early by helping children become acquainted with the teacher and helping the teacher to understand the home situation. The responsibility for such visits always rests with the classroom teacher.

Traditional Practices.   Traditional practices for making the home visit comfortable for both teachers and parents abound in early childhood literature. Recommendations include the following:

1. Clarify the purpose of the visit with an initial telephone call.

2. Arrange a convenient time so that children will be part of the process.

3. Set a specific time for the visit. Arrive and depart on time and leave earlier if events warrant it.

4. As a guest in the home, respect the cultural and ethnic values the family exhibits.

5. If other family members are present, include them in your conversation.

6. Be an attentive listener, but don't oversocialize or get drawn into family controversies.

7. Be prepared to suggest agencies and types of services that parents might pursue in getting help if the family asks.

8. Invite the parents to become active participants in the school program, suggesting several levels of involvement.

9. Follow up the visit with a thank you note and indicate action on what was agreed on during the visit.

Innovative Practices.   In the traditional home visiting arrangement, the teacher was the resource person assisting parents in some way, especially by helping parents understand how they could support their children's education. Innovative programs change this relationship, making home visits collaborative efforts. This means that parents can and should initiate visits, plan an agenda, and discuss educational aspirations for their children.

Some home-visiting programs include learning kits where child and adults interact to reinforce concepts.

Parents and teachers may then become equal partners in developing good educational programs for children (Powell, 1990).

One school in New Mexico, in an effort to help parents support their children's learning at home, developed a Home Kit, Home Visit Program. Teachers prepared home learning kits that included activities requiring different learning styles. The activities taught or rein-

forced different concepts, such as shapes, colors, and numbers, using common, everyday materials. Tapes for music, idea cards for making simple toys, activity cards, and recipes were included. The idea was introduced at parent-teacher conferences at the start of the school year and was further explored in follow-up home visits where teachers modeled use of some of the materials, answered parents' concerns and questions, and responded to parents' suggestions for improvement of the kits. At the end of 3 years, children's basic skills improved, but the greatest success was the improved rapport between school and homes. Parents became more involved in the schools, and teachers became more verbally and emotionally involved with children from culturally different homes (Gorter-Reu & Anderson, 1998).

No matter how home visiting is seen, it is apparent that successful programs depend on a teacher's ability to develop a trusting relationship with parents. Home visits can provide teachers with new insights into the social, cultural, and cognitive functioning of children and their parents. By working cooperatively, parents and teachers can more easily find solutions to children's problems.

Telephone Contact

In the past, parents and teachers telephoned each other only when they were concerned about a child's progress. Today, the telephone is a tool for collaborating on all aspects of a child's education. As in all contacts, the communication should be a positive experience for both teacher and parent, even if the call is to discuss a concern.

Establishing good relationships early in the school year is important. You can do this with a brief telephone conversation. In this first call, introduce yourself to the family and express pleasure in having their child in your class (Gelfer, 1991). Inform parents that unless they wish otherwise, you'd like to call them on a regular (once a week/month) basis just to keep in contact, inform them of their child's progress and school events, and answer any questions or concerns they might have (Gustafson, 1998). Establishing communication early in the school year enables parents and teachers to be comfortable about contacting each other when later confusion or

misunderstanding arises, as the following vignette demonstrates.

Melissa Jacobs was entering a new school during the third grade. She knew no one and was terrified, especially since she "didn't read so good." Mrs. Jacobs was relieved when Ms. Thomas called to welcome Melissa to school and to invite the mother to visit. As the year wore on, Mrs. Jacobs was delighted in Melissa's successful adaptation to school. She called Ms. Thomas one morning to check to see how Melissa's reading was going.

The next day, Melissa came home very angry, not wanting to go to school. "I don't see why I have to go to that dumb teacher and do phonics. I hate phonics!"

Distressed, Mrs. Jacobs immediately called Ms. Thomas to ask what was happening. Before Mrs. Jacobs could say much more than hello, Ms. Thomas said, "I am so glad you called. I was about to call you. I really don't think it is a good idea for Melissa to go to the special teacher. I know you are concerned about her reading, but she was just miserable today. Her reading is coming along well, and she doesn't need this extra pressure."

In the course of the conversation, it became clear that there had been a misunderstanding during the last telephone conversation. Mrs. Jacobs had intended to just maintain contact, and Ms. Thomas had interpreted it as concern. Since good communication had been established early, both teacher and parent could resolve the misunderstanding in good faith and do what was best for Melissa.

Innovative Practices. Technology expands possibilities for communicating with parents. Electronic mail and telephone answering machines are two ways that teachers provide more information to parents. Bauch (1989) designed a program called the TransParent

School Model that allows teachers to communicate daily with parents. Teachers have individual answering machines or electronic mailboxes. At the end of the day, they prepare a 1- to 3-minute message, noting homework assignments, events of the day, things children have been asked to bring to school, and upcoming meetings. Parents can call in at their leisure and have easy access to information (Bauch, 1989). Parents may also leave messages for the teacher. Some schools now have websites that parents use to find out class assignments and school events. Since not all homes have computers, answering machines may reach more parents.

Informal Contacts

Parents with children in preschool normally accompany their children to school, and this gives both parents and teachers a chance to talk informally. Teachers can allow time at the beginning and end of the day for brief conversations with parents. Parents like to hear what their children have been doing, and a brief statement, such as "Phil climbed to the top of the jungle gym for the first time today; he'll be excited to tell you about it," communicates to parents that you are aware of what is happening with each child. Parents also must share in the communication process. Parents who comment about how their child is at home or note their child's enjoyment of a school activity communicate their involvement in their child's learning. By asking questions and being attentive, you can help parents who are unsure of how to establish communication.

Lengthy conversations are a problem at the end of the day. Busy parents are anxious to get home, and busy teachers need to welcome other parents, get children organized, and clean up after a long day. Brief statements at this time are important, and if a parent needs more time, you should suggest either a scheduled conference or telephone call. When par-

ents linger in the classroom, skilled teachers suggest they observe something special or help their children in some constructive way.

Parents do not accompany their older children to school but are often present in open schools where partnerships have been formed with parents and communities. These parents still anticipate brief words of welcome or an exchange about what is going on with their children. These contacts with parents are helpful if conversations are positive and demonstrate an interest in how children are learning in different settings. Such exchanges communicate to all parties, including children, that responsibility for educating the young is shared by the entire community. All school personnel can assist or hinder parents' reactions to schools. When principals, school custodians, school secretaries, aides, or other teachers look up from their work and smile at, greet, or offer assistance to persons entering, parents get the feeling that the school community cares about them. A pleasant remark about their child or a comment about a new exhibit goes a long way to encourage parents.

Written Communication

Teachers have traditionally given assignments with the hope that parents would oversee the homework and help their children as needed. Such homework provides children with practice on skills and concepts taught at school, and parents who review the work with their children get information about what they are expected to learn. In addition to assigning homework, some schools have devised other interesting ways for communicating with parents about their children's school involvement, including bulletin boards, newsletters, and informal notes.

Bulletin Boards.   All classrooms have bulletin boards, and most schools have boards in the halls. Traditionally, teachers place on these boards children's work, information about special events, and material for a particular unit. Parents visiting the school gain information about the school through reading the boards. They see their children's artwork, their written or retold stories, reports on books they have read, and information on units they have studied. Many teachers also use photos with captions to show children's involvement in classroom activities.

Innovative schools have special bulletin boards just for parents, and the interests of parents dictate what is posted. If teachers regularly change postings, parents will learn to look to the board for information. Teachers may post special articles regarding children's growth and development, information regarding meetings and availability of social services, and health and nutritional information. Parent volunteers often arrange the board or assist teachers in highlighting information, such as bibliographies of children's books, educational toy suggestions for birthdays or holidays, and recipes for nutritional snacks. Sometimes teachers photocopy materials and put them in a wall pocket for parents to take home.

Newsletters.   Classroom and school newsletters, while varying in purpose, are traditional methods for schools to communicate with parents. Most newsletters communicate school news, including notices of school events, parent-teacher conferences, and other important meetings. Traditionally, most newsletters have included tips for helping children at home and for parents seeking resources. All information can go on a school website, too, with paper copies sent home to those families without a computer.

Innovative teachers find extended purposes for newsletters or websites. One teacher includes in her newsletters artwork by children, photos of classroom activities, thank you notes for parental and community support, examples of how children use materials parents

contribute, and extracts of classroom discussions children had because of parental support. Such a complete newsletter provides parents with many examples of what and how children learn from various resources.

Informal Notes and E-mail.   Traditionally, teachers have used informal notes to inform parents of their concerns regarding their students' work. Now, more teachers recognize the value of notes that reflect students' special accomplishments in developing social, cognitive, or physical skills, thus giving both parents and children a sense of well-being. Of course, all notes can go to parents via E-mail for homes so equipped. Most notes don't require a response, but you may occasionally wish to query how parents see their child's skill development at home. You might also use notes to express concerns about a child's changed behavior.

When notes are positive in tone, even if you have some concern, parents come to understand the importance of working cooperatively to provide the best for their children. Most teachers believe it is wise to let children know about communications with their parents and, in general, what the note contains. Children's involvement is important, for children need to know that parents and teachers are working together to help them learn. In classrooms where children's parents speak a language other than English at home, teachers have elicited the aid of bilingual parents in translating notes sent home. Students who are fluent in both languages can translate messages themselves.

Keys To Effective Communication

Whether communication is verbal, written, or electronic, there are certain key elements to consider for effective communication and for avoiding pitfalls:

- Work at understanding the other's point of view. It is important to listen and to read

In effective parent-teacher conferences, it is important for teacher to listen to parents and consider their viewpoint.

messages considering parents' points of view. In discussing differences in perspective with parents, it is important to deflect blame—speak from your own experiences and listen to parents' experiences.

- Language differences can cause misunderstandings when care is not taken. Avoid seeming to model or correct another's speech pattern. When terms are used that either party is unfamiliar with, ask for or give an explanation in a nonjudgmental way.

- Status of teacher and parent and how one clings to that status can cause poor communication. Traditionally, the teacher has been seen as the expert. Good collaboration means that you shift from the focus of teacher as expert to focus on concern for the child and on how each of you contributes to the child's development.

- Body language can communicate different messages from the verbal message, and different interpretations can be made of a gesture or a movement. Try to learn by observing how parents and their children communicate with each other using gestures and space. Inviting nonthreatening conversations around specific topics will open up better channels of communication.

- Voice pitch and tonal qualities are used to convey different meanings. Cultural and family differences exist, and they can cause misunderstandings. Learning about these differences in a reciprocal exchange can ease potential conflicts. In chapter 4, Greg helps Philip learn "the school way." In the same way, it is incumbent on the teacher to lessen the gap by recognizing that parents may not have "the school way." Being honest in how you have been affected by differences will open communication and will help parents recognize and even accept differences.

Thoughtful, ongoing communication with parents is an important component of parent-teacher cooperation. It involves parents at a basic level in their children's education. Table 10–1 summarizes the traditional and innovative communication strategies discussed in this section of the chapter.

Table 10–1   Parent and Teacher Communication Strategies: Traditional and Innovative

Conferences	
Traditional	**Innovative**
Teacher schedules and directs conference.	Parents as well as teachers prepare for conferences.
Teacher prepares materials, provides input, and strives for cordial and productive exchanges.	Parents schedule appointment.
	Child contributes ideas to conference and/or attends.

Home Visits	
Traditional	**Innovative**
Teacher attempts to understand home and establish positve relations.	Collaboration is sought.
	Parents become partners in planning visits and sharing ideas.
	Parent empowerment is sought.

Telephone Contact	
Traditional	**Innovative**
Teacher initiates calls when concerned.	E-mail allows either parent or teacher to initiate calls or leave messages.
Teacher uses phone as substitute for conference.	Answering machines with messages on schedules, homework, etc. permit exchange of information.

Informal Contact	
Traditional	**Innovative**
Beginning and ending of school day are times for brief exchanges between parent and teacher.	Parents can accept more responsibility for communication.
Demonstrating interest is goal.	

Written Communication	
Traditional	**Innovative**
Teachers develop bulletin boards.	Parents can help arrange bulletin boards or collaborate with school personnel in developing one.
Newsletters include school news, dates to remember, and tips for helping children at home.	New items are included: photos of schoolwork, artwork, notes on parents' contributions, and how kids learn. Websites highlight school news.
Informal notes are ways to keep in contact with and inform parents.	Notes reflect children's special accomplishments.
	Notes and E-mail are designed to give both parents and children and a sense of well-being.

PARENTS IN THE SCHOOLS

When parents are in classrooms, they see firsthand how their children respond to the school learning environment. Though we find exceptions, involved parents usually become strong supporters of their children's schools. They come to appreciate what schools are doing and what is involved in educating their children.

Parents can be observers, paid aides, or volunteers or may serve as classroom resources. Whatever their role, it is important that parents have orientation or training for participation. Teachers are legally responsible for the children in their classroom, and if parents don't understand classroom rules or procedures, conflicts can arise. Misunderstandings can result, and neither children, parents, nor teachers are well served. Parents need to know there are many levels of parent participation and to be encouraged to contribute where and how they can on the continuum.

School Visitations

Traditionally, parents are invited into children's classrooms on special occasions, such as during National Education Week, or as audiences for special events. Innovative schools are establishing an open-door policy, welcoming parents whenever they wish to visit. This can be a distraction for some teachers, although visits and observations may be productive and informative for parents and not distracting for teachers if guidelines are developed. The following paragraphs describe methods that creative teachers have discovered work for their classrooms.

Early childhood classrooms are active places, and children are not always sitting at desks involved in paperwork or listening to the teacher. In such classrooms, teachers find it helpful to explain to parents what the routines of the day are and how children are involved. So as not to disrupt the flow of activity, the teacher suggests where the parents should sit to get the most out of their observation. If there is activity that parents can observe better moving about the room, the teacher suggests the best time to do so. If the class and teacher prefer that parents not interact with children, the teacher explains why this is important.

In some classrooms, children are accustomed to adults and are comfortable asking them for help. In such cases, parents are advised that children will approach them. If parents are visiting to observe general classroom activities and how children interact with one another, the teacher provides a list of things parents can watch for. If a parent is visiting for a particular reason, the parent and the teacher confer regarding what to look for and how. Parents are encouraged to visit their children on the playground and during special activities. Teachers who use these visiting strategies believe that parents who understand about the total school program will be more supportive of it.

In some families, grandparents, uncles, and aunts are closely involved in a child's life. Teachers should make it clear that these other important people are welcome in the school. At the David A. Ellis School in Roxbury, Massachusetts, one grandfather explained how he was the one who brought his granddaughter to school and picked her up every day. He expressed his pleasure in the openness of the school by saying, "Boy, I'm telling you, what an education we are getting together" (Johnson, 1990).

Some day care programs encourage parents to drop in to observe or even to be with their children whenever they can. If a day care center is near a parent's workplace, the parent can come during breaks or lunch hour to have a snack, eat with his or her child, or even play with the child for a few minutes. Some parents are able to come before naptime to read to their children and tuck them in.

1. *Stone Soup Day.* As part of their folktale study, a third-grade class invited their parents to celebrate the end of the unit. Children performed their version of "Stone Soup" and then had parents join them in eating a nutritious meal of "stone" soup and corn muffins, which they had prepared the day before.

2. *Celebrating Mrs. Jones.* Once a month, the second-grade class celebrated a special person in the school and invited her or him in for snack time. Besides preparing the snack, children always made a special gift reflecting some aspect of their current study unit. Different parents joined to help with preparations and to express their appreciation for the person's services.

3. *Circus Day.* A kindergarten class invited parents to the culminating session of their circus unit. Their circus had only one ring, but all contributed special skills as acrobats, lions and dogs or trainers, clowns, and a ringmaster. One parent, a skilled pianist, accompanied the acts with appropriate music.

4. *Father's Day Breakfast.* A first-grade class invited their fathers, grandfathers, or special adult males to join them monthly for a special breakfast they helped prepare. As a variation, the class had unrelated adults from the school and community join parents and students for breakfast. The price for breakfast was $1.00; however, if a student found an unrelated adult to join her or him, the student saved the $1.00 charge. At first teachers helped engage students and adults in conversations regarding school events. As the idea caught on, students began to seek out volunteers other than their parents to join them. Not only did community volunteers get a better understanding of what happens in schools, but also students began to appreciate the diversity of interests within their community.

5. *Coffee Hour.* At one school, the principal, staff members, and teachers, on a rotating basis, were freed from responsibilities each Friday morning. Parents were invited in to have coffee and chat with them about school in general and to get to know one another. As the year progressed, sharing "things that were working well" and "things that could work better" became part of the agenda. Gradually, the evolving good fellowship and trust led to both parents' and school personnel's taking responsibility for seeking solutions for expressed concerns.

Figure 10–2   Special events for classrooms.

Most classrooms have special events to which teachers invite parents. Such occasions give children experiences in writing invitations, planning for the event, demonstrating some skill or talent, and even preparing special snacks. The list of events for such visits is almost endless. Some interesting examples are noted in Figure 10–2.

Child's Role in Visitations.   Children need to be prepared for adults visiting their classroom. Teachers usually have explained to their classes that parents and other adults enjoy coming in to see what things they are doing. Traditionally, teachers introduce visitors, explaining to children the purpose of the visit. Innovative teachers make such explanations a part of the child's responsibility.

Mrs. Horton has many visitors to her class at school near Atlanta, and she established the role of greeter to be filled as one of the weekly classroom duties. Children practice the role so they will feel comfortable with adults. When adults come into the room, the greeter quietly welcomes them, takes their coat, and suggests where to sit. The child points out the daily schedule, which is always posted, and tells the visitors what is currently happening.

Parents as Aides or Volunteers

Recently, teachers have come to realize that having a paid aide or having parents volunteer to regularly assist children in the classroom pays off in a richer curriculum for students. Since most parents now work, these volunteers often fill the role of other important adults in children's lives.

Skillful teachers make good, creative use of volunteers. Although methods vary for training volunteers, the following procedures have proven successful for many teachers.

Teachers solicit reliable, regular parent volunteers at the beginning of the year and have a brief meeting to explain the classroom regulations and how parents can assist. Sometimes volunteers help individual children with projects or in practicing certain skills. They also may read to individual children and, when it is comfortable, may read to small groups or to the class. Volunteers also may help the teacher prepare materials or set up activities.

Volunteer schedules work more smoothly if teachers make a monthly calendar and send home reminders for parents of the volunteer days. Each morning before the children arrive, the teacher and volunteers spend a few minutes discussing the events of the day. At the end of the day, they meet again briefly to discuss how the day went. For the experience to be successful, both teachers and volunteers need to recognize that the teacher is the major decision maker and authority figure in the classroom. Teachers must respect the skills volunteers bring, but they must establish and communicate the classroom rules to volunteers so that children do not receive mixed messages.

One creative teacher has an open policy on volunteers, inviting working parents to observe and help whenever they have time off. He keeps a list of special activities that need extra classroom help. When parent volunteers arrive, the teacher is then ready to use them productively to assist children. This policy has been especially helpful in securing more male volunteers.

Parents as Classroom Resources

Teachers and schools are finding other ways that parents and community members can assist them. Some programs use volunteers as tutors or mentors. Some tutors work with students having particular difficulties, while others work with gifted children who need enrichment programs. Other mentors work with children who have a special interest in their area of expertise.

Traditional Practices.   Many programs use parents to help children with reading. Volunteers come regularly, take children to a quiet area, and read with and to them. Some programs even have special work sessions for volunteers, helping them to develop skills for involving children in the reading (Lancy & Nattiv, 1992).

Volunteers with computer or clerical skills help office staff by typing newsletters, preparing reports, addressing letters, and even designing an attendance program. The custodial staff tends to school maintenance, but volunteers have assisted this staff when special projects required setting up different areas of the school or when special carpentry work was required. In more than one preschool classroom, parents have joined the custodian in building a classroom loft, building extra cubbies, preparing outdoor tables for a playground, or setting up playground equipment. When the staff and volunteers work together for children, all have a better sense of ownership in the school program.

When parents do not have time for regular classroom volunteer work, they can help on special occasions in ways that parents have been traditionally involved. When children go on field trips, parents often accompany children or help in organizing the trip. All schools have nonclass functions in which parents can render support services, such as helping organize for National Education Week, helping with fundraising activities, or supporting the "Read a Book Club."

Innovative Programs.   Some educators have devised plans whereby volunteers offer an enriched program for children in their school. In one Maryland program, on Wednesday afternoons, community members present a variety of programs that reflect particular volunteers' skills and interests. An expert quilter provided quilting lessons for 6 weeks. A bird carver introduced the beginning steps of carving. A computer programmer taught children how to create simple programs. A chef offered lessons in Italian cooking. A dancer gave 10 weeks of ballet lessons. There were flower-growing and -arranging classes, bird and rock identification classes, and discussions on topics from Caldecott and Newberry Award-winning children's books. At the beginning, volunteers wrote a brief description of their "course," indicating the number of lessons and appropriate age range. Children then signed up, but as the program developed, some adults began to join their children in taking the classes. Both children and adults found they enjoyed learning in such multiage groupings.

Assisting With Homework.   Homework assignments are often seen by teachers as a parent's obligation and by parents as a great nuisance. Changing the emphasis of homework can help parents see that they are indeed a contributing member of their child's classroom success. Assignments can be given that develop certain skills but are also a part of the family's life. Children and parents might cook something together to share in the classroom. One teacher had children and parents look at the moon each night and mark the time of observation and the spot on the horizon where it was seen. Another teacher devised a Love Note Project whereby children selected a book to read with a parent or special person each evening. The parent wrote a simple love note about the interaction, and the child (or teacher) read it to the class next morning. In all the preceding examples, the teacher created a follow-up system that informed parents of the success of their work with their children.

Expressions of Appreciation.   Volunteers receive rewards for their efforts in different ways. Seeing children's progress is very satisfying, and children have their unique ways of showing delight in having someone read to them or help them with a project. Reaching to take the adult's hand, offering a hug, expressing, "I read this entire book to my mom after you helped me yesterday," or making a special drawing of "us reading together" expresses better than anything how much children benefit. Letters of appreciation can come from children, teachers, the parent coordinator, or the school principal. Many schools have special dinners or events to formally thank volunteers.

Parents and community members involved in classrooms or school events find themselves at a participatory level of involvement from which they gain knowledge about their schools. Children's education is further enhanced when the entire community arrives at this level of cooperation and participation.

Parents as Advocates

In general, teachers and staff feel comfortable when parents are involved with children's education at the basic or the participatory level. Many teachers are willing to take responsibility for trying to get more parents involved, and they find it produces better results for their students (Bloom, 1992). However, there is a third level of involvement that teachers and school administrators are not always comfortable with—that of advocacy.

When parents or community members become advocates for children, they become decision makers, serving as equal partners on school policy boards, curriculum committees, steering committees, and school councils. Some parents in this role work within the framework of committees and the administrative structure. Parents who feel that the school policy is adversely affecting their children may initiate action. In such cases, they meet with teachers, principals, school board members, and even local and state legislators to advocate a change in policy. Recall that it was a single parent, and then a group of parents on a grassroots level, who eventually succeeded in securing appropriate education for children with disabilities through PL 94-142, the Individuals with Disabilities Education Act (IDEA).

Other parents become strong advocates for change within an entire school system. Parents may seek election to school board positions because they wish to see change and feel that this is a way for their voices to be heard. Federal legislation also has resulted in some parents having a policy-making role. Head Start programs, Chapter I programs, and programs under IDEA are required to have parents on their policy level councils. These parents then have a voice in program development, in hiring teachers, in the kinds of training offered to teachers, and in other policies that affect the programs.

Not all school systems or teachers embrace parent advocacy enthusiastically, nor can all parents operate at an oversight level of involvement. Such advocacy and involvement work well only when both parties—parents and teachers—have a voice in the decisions and work cooperatively together. Some parents have served on curriculum committees, steering committees, or school councils and have advocated or demanded change, only to find nothing changes. This means frustration. Only when parents, teachers, and school administrators are able to recognize each other's expertise and are willing to assume responsibility for pulling together can changes occur. Building coalitions of parents and teachers working for the best interests of their children is the most powerful advocacy role any person can undertake (Bloom, 1992).

PARENT EDUCATION

For over a century, parent education has been viewed as an important component for parental involvement in schools. Chapter 2 discussed the trends of parent education during the past century. As noted, in the early history of the United States, parents learned about educating their children from their own parents or relatives. Then, as psychology moved to the fore, professionals became the experts, and parent education regarding child development and wise parenting practices became a part of the school's responsibility.

Presently, we again find recognition of parents' skills and expertise. In some innovative programs, **parent education** means that teachers are learning new skills for interacting with parents. Teachers value parents' ideas, help parents understand their own skills, and more effectively integrate home and community knowledge with classroom learning. Parent education and parent involvement thus go hand in hand.

Education Through Meetings and Classes

Programs of parent education range from meetings conducted by parents themselves to formal classes on parenting skills conducted by professionals. Traditional parent-teacher association groups still provide support for schools and sponsor special parent programs or workshops. Professionals today are especially anxious to include those parents who have traditionally been excluded from such groups.

Innovative practices in parent education tend to reflect efforts to include parents from all economic and ethnic groups within a community. Some schools attempt to involve their parent group in those education programs that parents themselves see as particularly needed. Seefeldt and Barbour (1998) describe a program of outreach in which a principal succeeded in getting parents involved by allowing parents to choose and plan their own topics. Many hard-to-reach parents became intrigued and began coming to these informal but educational sessions.

Some schools find that developing a parent center within the school gives parents a sense of belonging, and such parents feel more comfortable attending classes geared towards their needs. Sessions in parent centers run the gamut from good child-rearing practices to dealing with behavioral problems and drugs in the community to language instruction for non-English speakers. The meetings often are unstructured, are led by laypersons, and involve a great deal of discussion and idea exchange among the participants.

Several specially designed programs exist for training parents to develop skills in working with their children. When implementing the programs, leaders typically follow the format described by the programs' creators. Parent Effectiveness Training (PET) (Gordon, 1975), Systemic Training for Effective Parenting (STEP) (Dinkmeyer & McKay, 1983), and Active Parenting Discussion Group (Popin, 1990) are three popular program models used during the past 25 years.

The Parenting Center at Marquette University developed a series of introductory parenting classes aimed especially at parents of young children (Fox, Anderson, Fox, & Rodriguez, 1991). The objectives are to teach parents the STAR (*Stop*, *Think*, *Ask*, *Respond*) approach to parenting, specific strategies for dealing with behavioral problems, and reasonable behavioral and developmental expectations for their children. Strategies used in parental instruction include lecture/discussion, practice sessions using parenting techniques, responses to particular problems parents are currently having, and homework assignments.

Education Through Materials

With research indicating the importance of parents' involvement in their children's education, schools are increasingly looking for ways to reach parents at home. Homework has traditionally been the device teachers have used to increase children's skills, and teachers assumed parents would supervise the work and thus come to know what school expectations were. All too often that homework consisted of worksheets or ditto sheets to complete or drill work on specific skills. Recently, different types of materials are sent home that serve to involve parents with their children's education and at the same time educate parents on helping their children learn. Learning Packets (Spewock, 1991) and Family Theme Bags (Helm, 1994) are two innovative practices that teachers have devised for helping parents of at-risk children.

In both programs, parents receive a packet of information and ideas for how to interact in a way that increases children's early literacy development. Learning Packets are sent to parents of newborns and each succeeding year until at age 5 the child receives a birthday card plus a new packet. The packet contains information about child development, ideas for fostering growth, and tips on good parenting. Ideas include such things as ways to use books, simple games to play at each age level, and arts or crafts to create with inexpensive materials (Spewock, 1991). In a similar program, parents and teachers prepare some of the packets together. In this way, parents learn more about teaching important skills at home, and teachers learn about parents' different approaches to teaching their children (Babbitt, 1999, personal communication).

Family Theme Bags are cloth bags sent home with preschoolers that contain a stuffed animal, a journal, a file-folder game, "What if . . . ?" cards, songs/fingerplays, a storybook, and art supplies. An introductory letter outlines the purpose of the bag and the value of the activities suggested. The stuffed animal or puppet provides a theme, and games, songs, and activities relate to that theme. For example, the Zoo Bag contains ideas for making zoo sandwiches, a song about an elephant, and a simple board game with a zoo pattern. The journal is provided so that parents can write how children respond to the materials and games. When children return the bags, the teacher reads the journals to the class (Helm, 1994).

Parent education programs differ in how they are structured and delivered, but all are designed to help parents become more involved in their children's education. When parents are active participants and decision makers in the developing programs, new understandings are likely to be long lasting.

COMMUNITY INVOLVEMENT

Although much is accomplished when parents and teachers form a strong partnership, children receive even richer educational experience when the larger community is included. As discussed in chapter 9, the community is a strong educational force in children's lives. Places exist in all communities that children should know about and visit, and all communities have material resources that teachers and parents can use. Businesses and social service agencies can often provide support systems enabling children to develop the traits that make them productive citizens. Teachers have traditionally tapped many of these resources, but we are finding new ways for teachers and parents to engage community services for children's education.

Trips Into the Community

All children have experience with their community and have learned many different concepts from these encounters. Traditionally, preschool and primary schools take field trips that focus on specific aspects of community life and provide children with new and extended insights.

Carefully planned field trips enhance and make more meaningful the objectives of a unit of study. Students studying economics, for example, can set up a bank and a store in their classroom and practice using the bank and store in ways they learned from their parents or from books they have read. A trip to an actual bank and store, where they can ask specific questions, allows them to view how adults behave in such places. It gives students behind-the-scenes experience. When children have particular questions to ask or things to see or do, they gain skills in observing, collecting information, making inferences, comparing information with others, and drawing conclusions. Also, trips produce new ideas, which children transfer to their dramatic play, their reading, their writing, and other classroom instruction. A trip provides motivation for further interests and learning, as it did for the first graders in the following vignette.

🐾

Nigel's class, accompanied by several parents, took a walking trip to the pet store to get food for the lizard they had found in the play yard and were now studying in class. While at the store, they were fascinated by a hermit crab and convinced their teacher to buy one for further study. Nigel became so interested that with his parents he visited the local aquarium. A naturalist at the aquarium told him more about hermit crabs and where they lived. With this information, the family took a trip to the seashore, and all were able to observe hermit crabs in their natural habitat. Nigel's stepfather videotaped the family's excursion, and Nigel showed the tape to the class and described his experience to his classmates. 🐾

Community members, family, and teachers can all become involved in children's learning when schools plan and carry out field trips. Nigel's teacher needed parents to go on the trip. She also needed the support of the pet store owners to have the trip become

Field trips focusing on specific aspects of community life provide children with new and extended insights.

meaningful. Then Nigel's family extended the learning for the whole class by arranging a family trip, using as a resource aquarium personnel, and bringing back results. Teachers organize and plan children's formal education, but when a community and parents are interested and involved, enhanced exposure and greater learning emerge.

Innovative Trips.   Trips into the community are not restricted to gaining understanding of the neighborhood. Children can make trips intended to contribute in some way to the community, such as enhancing the local environment. Trips around the school can focus on

cleaning up the area or planting flowers, trees, or shrubs. Some organizations "adopt" a highway, assuming the responsibility to clean up litter along a specific section of the road. Classrooms can adopt a neighborhood park, a playground, or a street and keep it attractive. Besides picking up trash, children often find ways to make the area more attractive, such as by planting and caring for flowers. Extending the idea, children could notify a sanitation department to ensure proper trash pickup and present posters to local newspapers and shopkeepers urging people to keep the area clean.

A visit to a nursing home or hospital presents opportunities for children to show older or ill people their artwork, sing or play some special songs, or present a dramatic presentation. When child care centers are located in health facilities, older persons often regularly read to children or engage in activities, such as cooking or making collages, with the children.

A related idea became a project for older children, who followed the Foxfire concept of visiting and interviewing older residents to hear their stories of yesteryear. The class collected and published the stories in book form and sold them at school functions. In this case, the intent was not to help other people but was to help children interact, appreciate, and be involved with an older generation. Also, when children became responsible for the sale of the books, they learned something about economics.

The following year, a new drama coach, after reading the book, planned with the third-, fourth-, and fifth-grade teachers a special production using the stories to create a play about local history. Local writers, artists, and musicians collaborated with the teachers and drama coach to help the children write a play text, design the scenery, and create words and music for the play and then work with the children in perfecting their performance. Parents worked with children not involved with the production in advertising, selling tickets, and arranging for the performances at different community events.

Good ideas for collaboration aren't always between school and community agencies. The Chicago Public Library and the Chicago Police Department teamed up to provide a number of interactive programs. One program was a Mystery Beat Book Club, where students read mysteries and met various police officers who explained how mysteries are solved in real life. Another was a Get Hooked on Fishing, Not on Drugs program. Police personnel spent time with youngsters, both in the library and at special fishing spots, examining the art of fishing. All agreed the programs helped the police

reach youngsters in positive ways, the library maximized its resources, and children had fun, associated with good role models, and became involved in interactive activities that enhanced their reading skills (Burnette, 1998). Schools become a part of such enterprises when they inform, encourage, and support children's involvement.

Community as a Resource for Materials

Children can travel in their community for educational purposes, but it is also possible to provide community resources within the classroom. Community members with special expertise may be willing to present their craft, knowledge, or skills for children's enlightenment. Traditionally, teachers have invited doctors, dentists, firefighters, or police officers to share their services with children, but imaginative teachers have found others to extend or enhance a unit. One biology professor enjoyed taking part of his collection of rare butterflies to a second-grade classroom each year during their "butterfly unit." In the spring, he walked in nearby fields with children hunting out cocoons or newly hatched butterflies. In one kindergarten classroom, an ornithologist shared her knowledge of birds, using stuffed exhibits and special bird books to point out the birds' characteristics. She left the books and birds on display, and for days, children could be seen examining the materials and then drawing their favorite birds in sometimes remarkable detail.

As in planning for field trips, teachers need to plan for special guests. They tell children about the guest, encourage them to think of things they want to know, and help them understand how they are expected to act during the visit. It is important that teachers remind visitors of children's interest level, attention span, and need for hands-on experience. Follow-up activities are similar to those for field trips. Relating the visit to classroom events through discussions, reading, writing, and projects enables children to integrate their learning.

Some resources from the environment can be brought into the classroom for closer examination, but teachers must carefully choose these resources. Endangered plants must not be disturbed, and certain animals are unsafe to bring into classrooms. But colorful leaves, nuts, and fruit, or twigs fallen from trees, rocks and seashells, minerals embedded in bits of rock, insects in aerated jars, and pond creatures for classroom aquariums are specimens that children can examine and study in the classroom. Some teachers have been successful hatching baby chicks or watching a cocoon develop into a moth or butterfly. Often, classroom volunteers have an interest in or particular knowledge about certain materials and will be able to supervise children's involvement.

Community service agencies and businesses often have materials that classrooms can recycle, such as scraps of fabric, boxes, bottles, juice and coffee cans, buttons, wire, and different types of spools. Some offices have old uniforms and business supplies representing their occupation. These materials can be placed in prop boxes for dramatic play or for presentations.

Often agencies have printed materials, models, or audiovisual materials that are appropriate for classroom use. Some local television studios have tapes of educational programs that teachers may borrow and show. Community volunteers are often willing to assume responsibility for obtaining such materials.

Involving the Business Community

Businesses have provided support for schools in various ways for many years, most often in the form of funds for some particular project or materials. Band uniforms or costumes for a school production are items that local businesspeople take pride in providing for community junior and senior high schools.

Lately, primary schools have also profited from business support. One kindergarten teacher doing a panda project convinced a local toy store manager to subsidize part of the unit. In addition to finding and donating toy pandas in different sizes, the manager agreed to donate money for children's books and other appropriate classroom materials. Although she didn't pay for the zoo trip the class took, the manager did subsidize the venture so that all children were able to go. Other businesses have contributed classroom equipment including typewriters, calculators, and computers. Some businesses will sponsor special programs like "Read to a Parent and Get a Pizza." A school-supplies store agreed to provide one enterprising kindergarten teacher with a year's supply of fingerpaints when her classroom budget was reduced. In return, children's work, demonstrating the creative potential of fingerpaint, was exhibited in the store.

Businesses have also provided programs for helping children understand the different jobs in their businesses. For example, in one community, the businesses established an Accompany-a-Parent-to-Work-Day, where children accompany a parent or other adult to his or her job and have lunch before returning to school. One child accompanied her aunt, who was a recreation director. She attended a meeting at which the committee was discussing ways to raise money for a new swimming pool. The second grader got so excited that she went back to class and convinced the class to have a bake sale to raise money.

Businesses also cooperate with schools by providing release time for employees to volunteer in the schools. In some instances, it is parent/employees who wish to be a part of their children's classroom, but in other instances, time is allowed for unrelated employees to become volunteer readers or mentors or to relate their special expertise with children.

Collaborating with business for better schools requires a spirit of mutual respect and

When children visit parents' workplaces, they gain new understandings about the world of work.

reciprocity of benefit. For partnerships to be effective, teachers must visit the business establishment to determine its educational possibilities, and business personnel should visit schools to become acquainted with their function, goals, and daily operation. Each partner needs to know the other's resources, ideas, and commitments. Committees for each organization need to make decisions affecting the support and purpose of the collaboration. Teachers must be represented on the appropriate business committee, and involved business personnel should be a part of the school planning committee. Through such collaborations, teachers, parents, and community members gain new understandings of the importance of good schools to a community and of how the

community can contribute to the school's excellence.

Another way businesses become more responsive to children's needs is by being more responsive to the family/work relationship and complying with the 1993 Family Medical Act. Some businesses provide more family leave time to both men and women, more part-time work options, and flexible schedules. Some companies provide emergency child care in employees' homes when children are ill or the regular child care providers call in sick. With less stress in the home, families find more time for their children, and businesses profit from a less stressed worker (Rissi, 1993). In their role as advocates, some teachers have worked with parents in forming strategies to present to the CEO of the parents' workplace.

WORKING WITH SELECTED FAMILIES

The strategies used for collaborating with parents of all children in your classroom can be effective, no matter what the circumstances are. However, some groups need special consideration, especially when traditional methods are not working.

Parents of children with disabilities, members of ethnic minorities, homeless families, and gay and lesbian parents often find that schools do not reach out to them as easily as they do to other parents. It is imperative that schools reach all parents, and some teachers and administrators have found ways to be sensitive to special-needs children. The first step is for teachers to examine their own feelings toward parents who are outside the mainstream and who may be more difficult to reach. It is natural for teachers to feel angry, guilty, frustrated, exhausted, and even disapproving when no communication seems to work or when others exhibit different priorities or a different lifestyle. Being honest about your feelings and discussing them with others will help you to avoid using terms or making statements that hurt or anger parents who may have been rejected in other situations (Ramsey, 1998).

Children With Disabilities

All professionals must know the legal rights and the responsibilities parents have with regard to their children's education. Public Law 94-142 requires that parents of children with disabilities participate in planning and implementing educational programs for their children. Parents also have the right, if they deem it necessary, to challenge an educational plan. Regulations regarding educational planning include the following requirements, intended to establish positive communication between home and school (Gearheart, Weishahn, & Gearheart, 1996):

1. In discussions, the parents' native language must be used, with an interpreter if needed, so that good communication can be established.

2. Parents must give permission for assessments to be done on their children and must be informed about conferences whenever results are being considered.

3. Parents should attend the meeting when the child's individualized educational plan (IEP) is confirmed. The law requires the time and place to be convenient for the parents.

4. Parents have a right to review their children's school records and ask for amendments if they feel records are inaccurate. If they disagree with the records or the evaluation, they have the right to an independent evaluation.

Parents of children with disabilities often feel alone and as if they were walking on a tightrope (Griffel, 1991). Many need to be treated more sensitively than do parents of able-bodied children. Educators must make a special effort to be knowledgeable about disabilities and their implications for families. It is all too easy to use specialized language and educational jargon when discussing learning principles and teaching techniques, and most parents do not understand the terms. With the increased amounts of communication between teachers and parents of children with disabilities, we must be especially clear and precise about procedures and objectives. It is important that parents understand the continuum of services available within the school system and what the 1997 mandate regarding "inclusion" means. Parents and teachers, in selecting options, should define the goal in terms of students' outcomes and with intent in moving toward full inclusion as quickly as possible in the regular classroom (Fuchs & Fuchs, 1998).

Special workshops may be held to help teachers learn how to communicate without offending. Also, workshops in which parents of children with disabilities and teachers participate together are particularly valuable in facilitating cooperation. Parents and teachers need these workshops to share information, deal with everyday situations, help all parties cope with stress, and cement bonds with others.

Ethnic Diversity

When working with ethnically diverse families, teachers must understand the differences that exist between the language of the school and that of the home. Keep in mind that over 13 million residents of the United States do not speak English well. If parents speak limited English, it is essential to find someone who can translate. When teachers work with different linguistic groups, learning some words and expressions in the other language communicates to parents that the teacher values their language and accepts the two-way responsibility for communicating.

Educational activities designed to respect all cultures in the classroom enhance communication between home and school. But teachers must make special efforts to involve minority parents in classrooms. Most parents have special knowledge of their heritage and culture that they will share with a class when approached in a positive way.

In one California school, parents of different ethnic backgrounds contributed in several ways. A Mexican American parent helped children prepare tacos for snacktime, and a Japanese American mother showed children how to make origami birds. A Native American father invited a second-grade class to his workshop and demonstrated basic skills in silver work. A recent German immigrant brought her collection of dolls to the school and explained the regional costumes the dolls wore.

Parents become much more involved in their children's learning when they help gather materials that children share in the classroom. This is especially beneficial for ethnically diverse families. One teacher developed a "Me-Museum," where each child displayed items and pictures that reflected favorite objects from family life. The students' parents had helped their children collect and label the items, at times using native expressions as well as English translations. Parents and grandparents were encouraged to come with children to explain in more detail about the objects (Anderson & Suntken, 1989).

Prop boxes have been used in many early childhood classrooms as a means of providing enrichment for children's dramatic play, and this idea can be extended to include the home. The teacher can send theme prop boxes home with children to be used as stimuli for reading, writing, and play. For example, a grocery prop box would contain empty food boxes, play money in a box, signs for the items, and a pad for writing a grocery list. Inviting parents to add special items to the prop boxes from their family's cultural experience gives a multicultural aspect to the play and also connects children's home experiences to the school (Neuman & Roskos, 1994).

Homeless Families

Working with homeless families is one of the most challenging tasks a teacher faces. In spite of the McKinney Homeless Assistance Act of 1987 (PL 100-77) and amendments of 1990 and 1994, which require states to guarantee access to education for homeless children, many homeless children are not in school. The requirements for registration, such as proof of residency, age, immunizations, and health records, are too much for many homeless families to cope with, and these families find it easier to keep their children out of school

Teachers may need to be released from classes or compensated for evening meetings. Businesses need to examine the possibility of flexible hours of operation or flexible working hours for their parent employees. Having options for parent and community member involvement establishes a good basis for collaborative efforts, allowing all who are or wish to be involved to select a comfortable participation level.

A welcoming physical environment always helps to establish good relationships. Schools must place a priority on image. Sometimes a simple change in what parents see when entering a building makes a great difference. A welcome sign directing visitors to the principal's office helps. Student artwork and other projects brighten up an entrance. Space where parents can comfortably wait, perhaps with a coffee pot and some interesting literature about schools, gives visitors a sense of being welcome.

The process of collaboration is one of identifying, establishing, and cultivating positive factors to support interactions. Many ideas make sense for cooperative arrangements—the strategies of most any helping profession can be adapted appropriately. If

To develop strong partnerships, parents, teachers, and community members need to meet to examine educational needs and objectives.

schools are to become engaged in true partnerships, all concerned must expand and refine their communication, negotiation, and cooperation skills.

Barriers to Good Relations

No matter how well intentioned people are, some barriers surface that will result in breakdowns of communication and good relationships. One basic hurdle revolves around the different philosophical positions and perspectives people have regarding how children learn and what they should be taught. For example, if a school attempts a constructivist approach to learning and parents do not understand how their children are being taught to read, write, and learn number facts, a barrier can develop. Parents could well become angry and accuse the school of ignoring discipline and not teaching the basics.

Different beliefs about how and who should teach sex education can create misunderstandings among schools, parents, and community. Parents may consider discipline measures as either too harsh or too lenient, and these different perceptions will cause friction between home, school, and community. Issues such as these can spark problems, and they will fester and add to existing subsurface distrust if no mechanism is present to address them. Parents and teachers must openly examine their philosophical viewpoints so that they can establish better relationships.

Attitudes can also present barriers to good relationships. Parents and community members have feelings and attitudes about school that date back to their own childhoods. Parents who had unpleasant school experiences are often reluctant to become involved with their children's schools. A diminished self-concept is often present in such cases, and the isolation breeds more fear. Such parents resist contact with schools out of fear of criticism of themselves and their children. This circum-

stance helps no one, least of all the children. Schools need to work gently but with determination to overcome negativism and encourage positive contact.

Nonverbal interactions often cause barriers to good relationships. Teachers or parents may state one thing while their nonverbal stance communicates another. For example, during a conference, one parent crossed her arms, saying, in what seemed an annoyed tone, "I thought Janey did well on that project." The teacher interpreted this to mean, "I don't agree with what you said." The teacher then paused, moved slightly away, and murmured, "Well, it was an interesting project." When both moved on to another topic, the real significance of Janey's effort was lost. Both left the situation feeling defensive because the nonverbal behavior of both parties cut off further communication.

Fear affects teachers as well as parents, and teachers may do little to encourage parental or community involvement. When teachers are uncertain or insecure about their own teaching skills, they fear criticism of how they do their job and discourage parent participation in their classrooms. When we have local criticism of schools, teachers become tired of being scapegoats for all the wrongs of society, and they often express a desire to be left alone to teach. When such attitudes permeate the school, parents are made to feel unwelcome in many different ways.

When wide socioeconomic and cultural differences exist between school personnel and local families, misunderstandings can cause friction and often anger. Barriers are created when value systems differ and neither party is willing or able to examine differences and find common ground.

External features may also become barriers. Entering a school for the first time can be daunting even for the experienced. In some instances, doors are locked for safety reasons, and one must ring to enter. Sometimes the first thing one sees on entering a school is the notice, "All Visitors Must Report to the Principal's Office." Parents who were sent often to the principal's office during their school years will not feel very welcome. When the office is difficult to find and no one is around to assist, schools again communicate that visitors are unwelcome. Office personnel are sometimes too busy to assist or may appear annoyed at the interruption, or they may ask in an intimidating way, "Do you have an appointment?" Unwelcoming signals are easily discerned and too often found.

Teachers and administrators are busy people struggling to maintain a productive environment for student learning. That is their most important task, and many think the time and energy needed to add parental and community involvement to their workloads just isn't available. Such school personnel communicate the unimportance of parental involvement.

Parents also find external barriers as they try to maintain a commitment to schools (Swap, 1993). Many have busy schedules, and families who live a distance from the school may have a problem with transportation. When involvement means going to the school in the evenings, child care may be difficult to arrange. Few businesses have flexible hours that allow parents to meet teachers during daytime hours. Hot lines and help lines can resolve some time and schedule conflicts when schools have a priority for maintaining communication.

IMPLICATIONS FOR PROFESSIONALS

We have described some strategies that schools around the country have found helpful. The important concept to draw from this information is that you have a number of ways to involve families and communities in children's education. Not all families or agencies can participate fully, nor is it even desirable to do so. But it is incumbent on you to help parents and others understand the continuum of involvement that will assist their children:

- *Basic level.* Assisting children at home is an important basic level of involvement and doesn't require any time off from work. It requires such involvement as reading to/with children, supervising TV viewing, playing games that require special cognitive skills, assisting with homework and projects.

- *Participatory level.* Visiting in the classrooms and attending parent-teacher conferences and special school events require parents to participate in the educational process. These visits are more doable for working parents than classroom volunteer work. Parents may also be resources for working on occasional projects.

- *Commitment level.* Volunteering regularly as an aide or helping with special projects or tutoring requires a fair commitment of time during the day.

- *Advocacy level.* The advocacy or decision-making level requires the most involvement from parents and other citizens. This means serving on boards and committees and rallying others to support schools.

SUMMARY AND REVIEW

Forming special relationships with parents and communities to enhance the education of children is not a new concept in the United States. As educators have gained more responsibility and authority over children's education, they have realized that parental education and parent involvement become part of the equation. Although educators have normally considered themselves experts in teaching children, they acknowledge that without parental and community support their job is more difficult.

Teachers over the years have developed many effective strategies for involving parents in their children's education. Many traditional strategies still work very well, but when these strategies are not sufficient or are outmoded, creative teachers and administrators test innovative means for reaching parents.

Frequent communication between home and school is important. Parent-teacher conferences, newsletters, phone calls, home visits, E-mail, and websites as well as parents participating in classroom and school activities are more effective when teachers experiment with different strategies so that each family is reached at some level.

Teachers have developed many effective traditional and innovative strategies for parent education, for involving the community, and for working with parents of children with special needs. Most traditional strategies can be extended in innovative ways.

Many educators now recognize that when teachers, parents, and community members form a relationship of equality and shared responsibility, schools become strong and children acquire greater cognitive and social skills.

SUGGESTED ACTIVITIES AND QUESTIONS

1. Ask your parents (or someone you know well) about parent-teacher conferences or home visits in which they were involved. Determine how useful they felt such activity was. If you know a parent of a primary-school-age child, ask the same questions and compare strategies and parental reactions then and now.

2. Interview parents who volunteer in their children's classroom. Solicit their opinion of this involvement, asking how often they volunteer, how they became involved, why they think it is important, and what they are learning from the experience.

3. Locate a commercial establishment that displays children's work and ask how the school became involved. Compare notes with classmates who have interviewed other establishments to determine what kinds of involvement your community appears to have with schools.

4. Obtain from a school administrator (or parents of a school-age child) copies of newsletters sent home to parents. In your class, organize the collected newsletters by type and compare the kinds of information they contain. Discuss whether some are more "parent friendly" than others, and why.

RESOURCES

Books

1. Fuller, M. L. (1998). *Home-school relations: Working successfully with parents and families.* Boston: Allyn and Bacon.
2. U.S. Department of Education. (1996). *Putting the pieces together: Comprehensive school-linked strategies for children and families.* Washington, DC: U.S. Government Printing Office.

Films/Videos

1. *Partnerships with parents.* (1996). [Video, 28 min]. South Carolina Educational Television with National Association for Education of Young Children.
2. *Windows on learning: A framework for making decisions.* (1996). [Video, 20 min]. Documents children's learning in the classroom. Macomb Projects, Western Illinois University with National Association for the Education of Young Children.

Organizations

1. Center for Media Education (http://www.epn.org/) 1511 K Street, NW, Suite 518, Washington, DC 20008
2. Association for Childhood Education International (ACEI) (http://www.udel.edu/bateman/acei) 17904 Georgia Avenue, Olney, MD 20832

3. High/Scope Perry Preschool Program (http://www.sharingsuccess.org/) 600 North River Street, Ypsilanti, MI 48198

Websites

1. http://www.access.GPO.GOV Lists different government bureaus through which one accesses specific government documents related to children and families.

2. http://www.familyeducation.com Provides comprehensive resources to assist parents, students, and schools as they collaborate.

3. http://www.futureofchildren.org/ Disseminates information on issues related to children's well-being. Also emphasizes promoting constructive institutional change.

Chapter 11

═══════════ 🖋🖋🖋🖋🖋 ═══════════

Models for Parent-School-Community Partnerships

🖋🖋🖋🖋🖋

The nation's schools must do more to improve the education of all children, but schools can't do it alone. More will be accomplished if families and communities work with children, with each other, and with schools to promote successful students.

(Davies, Palanki, & Burch, 1993, p. 22)

🦋

In this chapter, we detail four particular program models that have had success in improving schools through school-based collaborations. We examine various components that led to success of these models and remark on some of the changes made as a result of implementing them on a larger scale. We also give examples of other school/community partnerships that have been tried. In reading this chapter, you will learn the following:

1. Home-school-community partnerships work because of thoughtful planning, careful implementation, straightforward accountability, and honest communication.

2. Four major partnership projects have provided a framework for operation and have designed activities that now serve as models for other programs.

3. Parents and community members become involved in partnerships at different levels—from occasional volunteer work to advocating for children.

4. Partnership models vary considerably, but quality programs have many common features.

Parent-school-community collaboration is not a recent phenomenon in the United States, but currently there is a new emphasis on drawing these three social settings together for educating the whole child. Schools not only provide cognitive stimulation but also nurture the physical, social, and emotional aspects of the child. Schools alone cannot do that job. Community support systems must work together to strengthen the family as special services are provided young children. At the be-

ginning of the 20th century, the cooperative nursery school movement required parents and teachers to cooperatively plan education and work with children. Community schools in the 1960s integrated many community services into school programs so that families could receive needed services in one central place. A hallmark of collaborative efforts for U.S. schools began in 1965 with Head Start.

The Head Start and later Even Start programs were established to provide comprehensive services for poor families. Parental and community involvement was mandated for these federally funded plans, and the programs were required to support parents as they learned new roles for educating their children. These early programs provided patterns and models for later ventures in forming partnerships. As concern for continued poverty and poor student performances in this country continues, there have been legislative and private foundations monies supplementing programs for children in poverty and for special-needs children. Welfare reforms, national goals for education, and family literacy programs all emphasize the responsibility of and collaboration among all elements of society: schools, homes, community agencies, and businesses.

In 1988, when federal legislation established the Educational Partnerships Program, the concept of partnerships was extended to include alliances between different community organizations and public schools. As a result, a small number of programs began in the early 1990s. Some were initiated to unite social services, public schools, and business organizations while others focused on educational improvements through gradual changes within school systems (Danzberger & Gruskin, 1993).

In 1994, the Department of Education under Secretary Riley established the Partnership for Families in Education. The result is a network of support for the various partners committed to increasing family participation in children's learning by offering resources, ideas, funding, and conferences (PFIE, 1999).

In this chapter, we describe program models and note research studies that confirm the importance of such programs for children. Though these programs differ in content from one another, all validate the notion of drawing efforts and resources from all major social settings in children's experience. We also find in these models certain planning procedures and strategies that seem to ensure successful programs that result in meaningful change.

Following our discussion of these model programs, we highlight other programs to give a flavor of different collaborations across America. Presently there are more than 5,000 schools and communities that are experimenting with collaboration. We can present only a few of the many excellent programs. The ones we selected have a particular feature that is easy to generalize.

COMPONENTS OF SUCCESSFUL CHANGE

Research shows that children improve academically when schools work for better school and community involvement (Epstein, 1999; Thompson, 1993; U. S. Department of Education, 1994). Because of this conclusion, and because of extensive federal interest in partnerships, a number of school districts are now caught up in the rhetoric of "collaboration." Some have taken serious steps to establish links with social service agencies, arranging for more parental involvement, providing integrated services for their total school plan, and

becoming full-service schools. Some have struggled and had little success. Others have gotten only to goal statements and committee assignments (O'Neil, 1997; Tushnet, 1993).

As more businesses and community agencies become involved with schools, there always exists a danger that leaders in these agencies start to usurp the rights and responsibilities that classroom teachers owe to their students. In any collaboration, parents and teachers must assume the ethical responsibility for ensuring that everyone involved understands children's developmental levels and vulnerability. Most school personnel want parents and community members to share in the responsibility of educating children, and they seek outside support for school events and for resolving nonacademic problems. In academic matters, however, educators are more hesitant to involve parents and community members. Nonetheless, successful partnerships mean shared responsibilities, and successful schools mean that parents, school personnel, and community groups share responsibilities for educational decision making.

The programs that have been successful have different strategies for achieving collaboration, but all have certain elements in common, which Gardner (1993) calls "the hooks, glue, and joint ventures" (p. 15). All good programs have a planning process, an implementation process, and an accountability process (Carter, 1993). Equally important is that in each process, all involved pay constant attention to establishing good communication and developing trust, familiarity, and understanding (Smrekar, 1993).

Planning

Collaboration requires a communitywide team. Members of social agencies, businesses, and government agencies and teachers, administrators, and parents come together in some fashion, and all make a commitment to work for the benefit of the community's children. The community team needs a strong leader, and all participants must be willing to work out differences when necessary. Key people in the community are crucial for the project. Trust and respect for other viewpoints are even more vital.

During planning, the team determines the needs of children in the community, develops goals, and designs procedures for accomplishing these goals. The team identifies children's particular needs within the various community contexts, then assesses the community to identify resources to meet these needs. Communication, collaboration, and cooperation among the various team members mean that all agencies will surrender some autonomy in seeking solutions, but in so doing, all recognize their mutual benefits.

Implementation

As the collaboration team develops procedures for implementing strategies, members ascertain which agencies can provide personnel and financial resources. Implementation is guaranteed greater success when a team provides orienting and training sessions, ensuring that parents, teachers, and community people have collaborative skills.

A major step in beginning collaboration is providing workshops that help reduce the social distance among participants and that also improve relationships among parents, school staff, and students. Another involves understanding the interests and expertise of teachers, parents, and other volunteers so that all can contribute their best. All contributions must be respected, and ideally, all gain an understanding of how their service contributes to the goals and objectives.

After the team sets the priorities for the community's needs, it begins to plan and collaborate on such activities as providing families with needed services, improving school

and home discipline, adapting curriculum to particular community needs, establishing appropriate social activities, and developing program evaluation strategies.

Assessment

People working with collaborative programs must have ways to determine how well their goals are being met. Most projects will review students' classroom work, and many programs develop questionnaires to get feedback from the community about the success of their activities. Data are collected and interpreted regularly, and then strategies are altered or continued accordingly. Parents, school staff, and community members are kept informed about progress and the changes being made to improve conditions. Project members normally summarize progress once a year for the community at large.

Communication

The success of all collaborative programs depends on good communication and careful monitoring of activities. Parents must feel welcome to visit schools and to participate, and teachers must feel they are able to visit homes as needs arise. Community persons must also be part of the communication loop. All must feel welcome in schools and free to offer suggestions.

Many avenues provide parents and community members with information about school activities and what is happening with the collaboration. Routine notices, telephone messages, personal notes, newsletters, articles in local papers, a website, and the direct approach, which volunteers employ in contacting hard-to-reach parents, are all used. Parents are encouraged to write notes or call teachers when concerns arise and are encouraged to express appreciation.

Features of Successful Collaboration

New partnerships are rapidly emerging across the United States, and though the stimulus varies, often projects start in response to educational problems at the local and state levels. Irrespective of the motivation, we find that collaborative efforts do result in greater opportunities for students when the "whole child, whole community" concept is adopted (Davies, 1993). Each successful partnership will be unique, but all seem to include the following features (Comer, Haynes, & Joyner, 1996; Davies, Burch, & Palanki, 1993):

- Programs (comprehensively and intensively) integrate educational and social services for all children, but especially for needy families.
- Parents, school personnel, and community members are empowered to make decisions about, plan for, and implement changes for their community's children.
- School bureaucracy reduces, and involvement of community and home in school management increases.
- Schools become family centers to promote better interactions among teachers, parents, and community members.
- Programs include strong volunteer programs, with parents, grandparents, and community members contributing expertise to support children's learning and to assist in school operations.
- Community and home are viewed as important children's learning environments and are integrated into school learning.
- University programs provide training for the establishment of successful partnerships.
- Faculty and staff have time for training and develop skills needed to build and maintain relationships of trust and respect with children and families.

- Researchers, teachers, and parents work together in assessing the successes of school programs.

PROGRAM MODELS

In this section we examine the beginning steps that four program models undertook. Though changes have been made in each, the basic underlying concepts tend to remain. As you read about and compare these models you should get a feeling for how the process unfolds.

Head Start

When Project Head Start was conceived in 1965, authorities acknowledged that children were not only family members but also community members. Thus, if Head Start was to succeed in changing the lives of children, parental involvement and community commitment to the program's goals were paramount. Through this involvement and commitment, Head Start began to provide, in holistic rather than fragmented ways, comprehensive services in health, economics, and nutrition, as well as school readiness, for children and their families. Today Project Head Start is referred to as an integrated service program for low-income families. A caseworker is assigned each child, and that person monitors the health, education, and social services provided for the child and his or her family (Hurd, Lerner, & Barton, 1999).

Purpose.   The purpose for involving communities in Head Start was to make the community aware of the importance of providing adequate health, educational, and nutritional services for children's development. If skills developed in the Head Start programs were to be sustained, parents and community had to reinforce the learning. Parent involvement reached even further, since the programs created avenues for parents to gain skills for participating in different social contexts and thereby gain greater confidence and sense of self-esteem.

Types of Parental Involvement.   Parents assist in a variety of ways at Head Start centers or in classrooms. The Head Start Manual of Policies and Instruction, still in force today, outlines the types of parental involvement available.

Parents as Partners. Parents are partners with professionals in the decision-making process, and we find two levels open to parents of Head Start children. At the informal level, parents work with center staff in determining program content and how their children will participate. At a more formal level, parents serve on a parent policy committee or council. Fifty percent of council membership must be parents of current Head Start children and be elected by other parents. Council parents are involved in program improvements, parent activities, recruiting volunteers, and planning and developing a budget for the parent activity fund. They are also involved in decisions about program goals, criteria for selection of children, hiring of Head Start staff, and major changes in budget and work programs.

Parents as Observers. Parents participate in Head Start classrooms as observers, volunteers, and paid aides to observe different ways of working with their children. They gain a better understanding of what their children are learning and what they can do to assist them at home. Children seeing their parents in the classroom know that their parents are interested in their learning and witness the cooperation and support between parents and teachers. When parents become more involved as volunteers or as paid aides, they gain skills and confidence, which in turn help them qualify for employment elsewhere.

Parents as Learners. Head Start parents become involved in their own learning by planning and identifying opportunities that correspond to their own interests and aspirations. Workshops and other learning experiences for a center are often requested and designed by parents, who in this fashion increase their own education. Career ladders have been developed where parents are able to progress through workshops to obtain their GED. Some parents in Head Start programs have continued their education at technical schools, community colleges, and 4-year colleges, increasing their opportunities for employment.

Supporting Children's Learning. Parents work at home with their children to support and reinforce children's Head Start experiences. Center personnel create and distribute ideas and suggestions for home activities and often visit homes to observe and suggest ways family members can support children's education. As parents become aware of their impact on children's learning, they become confident about helping their children grow and develop (Greenberg, 1990; Head Start Bureau, 1980).

Research.   Since Project Head Start's inception, the effects of early intervention on children's development have been a subject of much research and public concern. Initial research by Westinghouse Learning Corporation—Ohio University (1969) indicated cognitive gains for Head Start children after the first year, but by the third year, these gains had nearly disappeared.

The study had many critics who pointed to several limitations of the study, including viewing all Head Start programs as if they were of equal quality, examining only one aspect of potential benefits, not recognizing the importance of medical and nutritional benefits, and ignoring the questionable validity of some evaluation instruments (Evans, 1975). The study did alert the public that a basic as-

Parents of Head Start children serve on a parent policy committee.

sumption of the War on Poverty was unrealistic: A single summer or 1-year program could not produce rapid academic results for economically disadvantaged children.

Long-term studies of the initial Head Start programs, reveal that the programs have been both cost-effective and beneficial to society. Both the Consortium for Longitudinal Studies and the Perry School Project indicated that children of poverty had indeed profited from Head Start experiences. Though initial achievement gains tended to disappear and Head Start children never "caught up" cognitively with their middle-class peers, by high school, these children demonstrated signifi-

cant differences from those disadvantaged children who had not attended Head Start. Head Start children did better in school, repeated fewer grades, had fewer emotional problems, and were less often placed in remedial classes. As adults, they were less likely to end up in jail, more likely to attend college, more active volunteers in their communities, and more likely to marry than their peers who had not attended Head Start (Schweinhart & Weikart, 1997).

Studies revealed also that Head Start children's social development improved to equal their middle-class peers. Children became more task oriented, sustained attention to task longer, and developed curiosity about learning. Children with disabilities appeared to benefit the most after involvement in Head Start programs. Collins's (1984) synthesis of over 1,500 Head Start studies confirmed the positive impacts on children's cognitive, social, and health development, as well as improvements in parenting.

Many Head Start programs successfully coordinated health and social services for children, and a large percentage of participants thus maintained their immunizations as well as medical and dental exam schedules. As a result of this medical attention and the sound nutritional school programs, Head Start participants are found healthier today than other disadvantaged children. This feature has been emulated by other programs as they attempt to include medical and social services within the school program.

As noted, parental involvement is a requirement of Head Start programs and was really the first large-scale involvement of parents in children's formal education. Parents have served as policy makers, teachers, aides, and volunteers, and two of every three students in Head Start have parents involved in one of these capacities. An additional payoff exists for that connection: Studies indicate that children of involved Head Start parents had higher academic achievement, were more likely to graduate from high school or college, and were more apt to have full-time employment. A further benefit for a small percentage of Head Start parents was assistance in finding jobs and in continuing their education (Collins, 1984).

Communities that established and maintained Head Start programs have benefited as well. A number of poor and minority parents in these communities have moved into the workforce, and area public schools have changed because of the models that Head Start provided. Advantages include providing strategies for parental participation, implementing developmentally appropriate curriculum, mainstreaming children with special needs, modifying health services, and implementing practices accommodating the needs of poor children and minorities.

Certainly, Head Start has not succeeded in fulfilling the dream of diminishing poverty in the United States or in eliminating all learning gaps, but its impact has been positive, and its benefits for helping poor and minority families become partners in their children's education outweigh the costs. All collaborative efforts have profited from the procedures and experiences of this model program.

Home-Based Programs

With the lessons of Head Start came the realization that children—even before the age of 4—need help if they are to overcome the debilitating effects of poverty. The realization of the importance of parents as children's first teachers led to ideas for developing home-based programs. Several such programs were funded by the U.S. Office of Education in the late 1960s and 1970s. Ira Gordon, David Weikart, Phyllis Levenstein, and Susan Gray were among the first educator/researchers who developed model home-based programs serving families in poverty. Many communities adapted one or another of these model programs as extensions of their Head Start programs. Other home-based programs have been developed and funded by private foundation monies and because of local and state initiatives.

Purpose.   The intent of all home-based programs is to use the home as a beginning point in children's education. The concept recognizes that parents are children's first teachers and that it is important to help and train parents to become more effective teachers. The emphasis since the early 1990s for many home-based programs has been family literacy.

Recognizing that "the family is the primary system for transmission of values from adults to children" (Smith, 1994, p. 2), the focus of home visits in these programs is to make parents aware of the power of their influence on the development of their children's prereading skills. In the late 1980s, Even Start, a family literacy program, was initiated under Title I, Part B, of the Elementary and Secondary School Act. The funding for this program, administered through the states, was to provide all-encompassing support to enlist parents as full partners in their children's education with the hope that they could then help their children reach their full potential as learners. Because each state is allowed freedom in administering the funds, a variety of family literacy programs serves poor families with young children. In addition, all centers are required to coordinate all relevant programs serving families in poverty (Even Start, 1999).

Types of Involvement.   The focus of individual programs depends on the needs of families in particular communities. Gordon's (1969) Parent Education/Involvement Model was replicated throughout the United States and still serves as a model for communities reaching out to families. The program had direct links to Head Start programs, because the Head Start teacher and the parent educator worked together and planned appropriate activities to be carried out in the home. In many programs today, the parent educator, often a sort of educational social worker, is associated with a center-based program and collaborates with a teacher or supervisor in that program.

In Gordon's original model, the parent educator, a person from the community served, was the key component of home visiting. These parent educators spent half of their time in homes demonstrating prepared lessons and the other half in classrooms working with teachers and children. In homes, they engaged parents in role-playing lesson activities as well

as in discussions of the intent and purpose of the teaching. In the classroom, they became better acquainted with the children and learned techniques for the school curriculum. Changing school curriculum to meet the needs of parents served was not a goal; instead, the activities for home-based programs were intended to extend and build on the cognitive and affective development of children to get them ready for a school environment (Gordon, 1969).

Many activities were language related, and the home teaching encouraged parents to follow closely the demonstrated strategies so as to understand effective teaching. Considerable emphasis was on extending parents' ability to use an elaborated language code, which would in turn extend children's language development. The model emphasized both positive reinforcement strategies and techniques for explaining and eliciting explanations and questions from children.

Today, programs of this type are often referred to as family literacy programs, and directors continue to seek involvement with other agencies serving these children: professional social workers, early childhood specialists, psychologists, and nurses. Ideally, some team members have specialized training in the development of infants and toddlers and in the specific needs of parents with very young children. Many programs are adapted from these early models, but currently, educators focus more on collaboration as they seek to build on skills parents already possess. Programs differ, but for many, the home curriculum emphasizes the role of play in children's development, the importance of reading to young children from infancy, and the value of quality interaction between parent and child. Nutritional, health, and safety information continues to be a feature of most programs (An Ounce of Prevention Fund, 1994).

Many home-based or family literacy programs have special features that are developed

Family literacy programs emphasize the importance of reading to children from infancy.

outside the home but establish a continuum of services for children birth to 8 years of age. Well-equipped parent resource centers in a community center or in a school provide materials for families and children. Planned neighborhood gatherings enable infants and toddlers (and their siblings) to have opportunities to play together and give parents the chance to socialize and discuss their children's learning. Opportunities to hear experts in early development are available, as is participation in more formal discussion groups. Summer-long programs, including recreational events, are featured, as are many after-school care programs. As the child care community stresses the need and importance of quality child care, many of the Head Start programs are increasing to full-day care.

Research.   Although research on home-based programs encounters many of the same difficulties associated with Head Start, evaluation results indicate that participants showed increased self-confidence in parenting ability, quality of mother-child interactions, and skill development of the children involved (Florida State Department of Education, 1992; Gordon, 1969).

    Research on Even Start programs, often encouraging on a single program basis, is also difficult to assess because of variations in programs and the difficulty in maintaining consistency for participation. Still we have some very encouraging results. For example, the amount of participation in the Even Start programs is directly related to intensity of services provided. When participation is high, children gain significantly in tests of school readiness and language development. In these programs, children and their families were involved together in more literacy-related activities, and parents provided more appropriate discipline techniques.

One aspect of Even Start programs is to provide adult education for participating families. Results of these programs for increasing math and reading proficiency of participants are more modest, but we find that more teenage parents are being served and there has been a 10% increase in involved parents attaining their GED. One of the greatest challenges of Even Start programs is keeping parents of infants and toddlers involved over a long enough period so that children can benefit from parents' improved skills (Tao, Khan, Gamse, St. Pierre, & Tarr, 1996).

Comer's School Development Program

In 1968, James Comer and his colleagues at the Yale Child Study Center began the School Development Program, a collaboration with two New Haven elementary schools to increase parental involvement in children's education. Both schools were located in low-income areas, all children were African American, and parent participation in school activities was very low. When examining parent interest and involvement, the team discovered three levels or patterns that revealed home-school connections: (1) most parents expressed interest in the activities their children participated in at school, (2) some parents were also interested in volunteering for particular activities in the school, and (3) a few parents were interested in curriculum and how teachers instructed their children (Comer & Haynes, 1991). With this knowledge, Comer and his team began a series of experiments and adjustments that used parents' interests to bring about collaboration. Now, over 2 decades after the conclusion of the project, the experiment has become a highly touted model for involving parents.

Major Goals. The initial School Development Program evolved over a 5-year period, and participants gradually adjusted the structure as programs evolved and needs changed. A steering committee, formed of administrators, teachers, parents, aides, professional and nonprofessional support staff, and the Yale Child Center mental health team, established the following major goals for the project (Comer, 1980):

- Modify the social and psychological climate of the school to facilitate greater student learning.
- Improve students' basic skills.
- Raise students' motivation for learning and their academic and occupational aspiration level.
- Create a sense of shared responsibility and decision making among parents and staff.
- Connect child development and clinical services to the educational program of the schools.

Structure of the Program. The program consisted of three teams: the school planning and management team (SPMT) (originally called the steering committee), a Yale Child Study Center mental health team, and the pupil personnel team, plus four major features: a parent program, a focus program, workshops, and an extended-day program.

School Planning and Management Team. This committee, composed of "stakeholders" in the school, developed and implemented academic and social programs, designed staff development, evaluated the program, and made necessary adjustments. After various experiments, three important guidelines evolved for the SPMT: (1) solving problems with a no-fault approach, (2) using principles of child development for decision making, and (3) ensuring that collaborative management did not paralyze the school principal (Comer & Haynes, 1991).

Mental Health Team. The mental health team consisted of a child psychiatrist, two social workers, an educator with early childhood education training, an educator involved in teacher training, and a psychologist/program evaluator. Its main purpose was to assist school staff in understanding and applying principles of social and behavioral science to school problems and opportunities. The mental health team at first helped parents and school staff develop skills of cooperation and assisted teachers in managing behavior problems and in changing or creating school rules. After behavior problems decreased at the school, the team began to help with curriculum planning and facilitating communication between school personnel and families, between teachers and students, and among teachers, administrators, and nonprofessional staff.

Pupil Personnel Team. A pupil personnel team initially cooperated with the principal, community social service personnel, and special teachers by giving services directly to students who needed such support. As conditions in the school changed and behavioral problems lessened, this service then became more educational in nature and less behavioral.

Parent Program. A parent program started with a small group of parents receiving a stipend for assisting teachers. This core group formed the nucleus of the parent group and served on governance bodies and subcommittees that helped plan social and educational programs. Their function was to "bring attitudes, values, ways, and needs of the community to these committees and activities" (Comer, 1980, p. 65). As the program changed

to meet school and community needs, the parent program evolved to include parent involvement at three different levels.

At the first level, five or six parents were elected to serve on the school planning and management team, where decisions about programs and operations were made. These parents enlisted other community residents for other levels of participation and helped overcome the barriers inhibiting hard-to-reach parents. They also brought a community perspective to the planning process, assisting teachers in planning culturally appropriate programs.

At the second level, parents were involved in helping in classrooms or in sponsoring and supporting school programs. The strength of this involvement was that parents and teachers worked together to motivate students to achieve academically and socially.

At the most modest third level, parents became involved in activities in which their children were engaged. They attended student performances and other teacher-parent activities, where "good news" was shared, and generally supported the program from a distance.

Focus Program. At the start of the project, a focus program was established to help children one or more years behind in reading and math skills. Three times a week, these children were taught in small groups to supplement classroom teaching of reading and mathematics. The focus groups changed as children's learning needs were identified.

Workshops. At the beginning, 2-week summer workshops allowed parents and teachers to get to know each other and share their perspective on the academic and social experiences they felt children needed. Workshops became ongoing and were offered when teachers or parents indicated a need.

Extended-Day Programs. Initially, teachers were required but were paid to attend after-school programs. This program included workshops for teachers to learn more about child development and behavior, teaching and curriculum development, and the use of arts in promoting academic skills. In addition, teachers developed skills in meeting with parents and planning parent participation projects. These extended-day programs ceased after a while, and groups processed any new concerns by participating in the workshops described above.

Social Skills Curriculum.   In establishing community involvement, Comer's team found that many distinctions between low-income and middle-income children involved differences in social skills that middle-income children acquired in their homes. As a result, the team devised a social skills curriculum for inner-city children consisting of four units: politics and government, business and economics, health and nutrition, and spiritual and leisure time. Field trips, visits by community members, and lots of hands-on activities enabled low-income children to enhance their interpersonal skills, writing skills, and interactive skills with adults. A banking unit provided experiences in receiving a "bank check" for work done and then spending the check or learning to save it for a specific purpose. A gospel choir helped students learn group responsibility on how to plan, organize, and select programs, as well as learn rehearsal procedures and performance demeanor. In the government unit, students learned to write and give speeches, then hold a miniconvention and election.

School Development Program.   Many aspects of the original implementation serve as guidance for schools associated with Comer's School Development Program. Figure 11–1 illustrates the current Comer model. To implement a model that offers respect to all and sustains learning, Comer et al. (1996) maintain that there are three guiding principles, three teams, and three operations:

- Three principles—consensus (planning requires that all parties come to agreement on the plans), collaboration (all work in tandem with each other), and no-fault (no one party is at fault for any lack of success, but all share in the responsibility to improve).

- Three teams—School Planning and Management Team (SPMT), which plans and coordinates all school activities; Student and Staff Support Team (SSST), which addresses student and staff problems and manages individual situations; and Parent Team (PT), which involves parents at all levels.

- Three operations—comprehensive school plan, developed to meet academic and social goals; assessment and modification, for periodic assessments and provision for change when necessary; and staff development, as needed to achieve goals.

Comer, Haynes, and Joyner (1996) believe this model permits communities to transform and change their programs by involving school personnel and families in a participatory approach. To sustain change, they emphasize that all adults must feel respected and all children must feel valued and be motivated to learn and achieve.

Research on Comer's Model.   After 5 years of working through problems and modifying procedures, rules, teaching strategies, and programs, the School Development Program showed remarkable success. The two participating schools progressed from having the worst attendance records in New Haven to having the best. Overall academic achievement went from third from the bottom to among the top schools in the city. Behavior problems were greatly reduced, and parent-teacher misunderstandings lessened as parental participation in school activities increased. When the program started, only 30 parents participated at a major Christmas program; 4 years later, 400 parents attended.

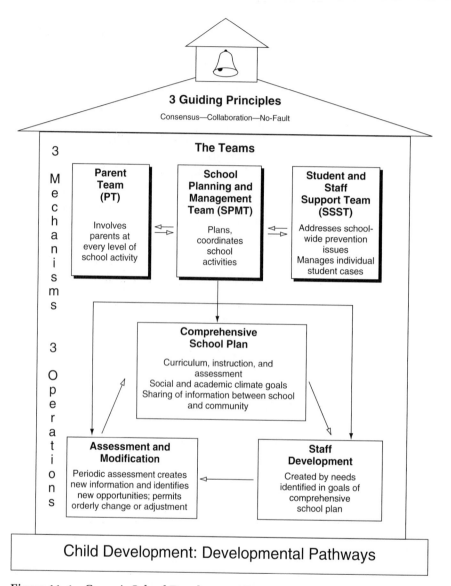

Figure 11–1   Comer's School Development Program.
Source: Comer, J.P., Haynes, N.M., Joyner, E. T., & Ben-Avie, M. (Eds.). 1996. *Rallying the Whole Village: The Comer Process for reforming education,* p. 10. New York: Teacher's College Press. Reprinted with permission.

Major activities attracted an average attendance of 250 for a school population of 300 (Comer & Haynes, 1991). The consensus is that home, school, and community links growing from the School Development Program in New Haven have provided essential ingredients for children's healthy development.

The Comer model has been replicated in over 650 schools across the nation. In Washington D.C., several neighborhoods have successfully changed their schools from places where violence, drugs, and crime were paramount to schools with "high expectations and where everyone working together . . . has become an attitude, a way of learning and an education for life" (Ramirez-Smith, 1995, p. 19). Further success of the Comer model is explicated in the new publication by Comer, Ben-Avie, Haynes, and Joyner (1999), in which readers find firsthand accounts of communities working through the Comer process.

Schools Reaching Out Project

In collaboration with the Institute for Responsive Education, the Schools Reaching Out project began in Boston and New York City during 1988, with two laboratory schools trying new strategies to build closer relationships among families, communities, and schools (Heleen, 1990).

Basic Assumptions. The project started with the premise that attitudes toward family involvement in learning could be altered by changing the structure and manner in which teachers and parents interacted. All workers were convinced that if the project schools were to succeed, family involvement was a necessity, and that all parents, even those hard to reach, could be involved (Heleen, 1990). A guiding principle was that children achieved better in school when home and school maintained a continuity of values, expectations, and attitudes. A second principle was that it was imperative for school personnel to help parents understand what and how schools taught their children so that parents could reinforce those efforts at home (Swap, 1993).

Structure of the Program. Each school formed a school-community council that made decisions regarding objectives, policies, and strategies for involving parents. Both schools were required by the institute to have a parent center, a key teacher, a home visitor program, and a teacher-action research team.

The parent center was a room especially for parents, where individuals could meet with other parents, relax, and hold special meetings. The room was to make parents feel comfortable and welcome in the school and give them a place within the school they could "own."

The key teacher, released from classroom teaching, became the coordinator of most project activities. In both schools, surveys dictated some of the activities that the key teacher supervised, such as English as a second language classes (Heleen, 1990).

The home visitor program stressed the importance of family empowerment, building on family strengths, and building family involvement in neighborhood networks. Four paid parent support workers, trained in counseling and work in community settings, provided three types of service in the home. They distributed information about school programs, homework requirements, and special events. They assisted children in their homes and demonstrated to parents various ways to help children develop academic and social skills. They met with teachers to exchange information about children in their classes and to make suggestions on how teachers could help parents.

Teacher researcher teams studied home-school relationships and devised strategies to include more parents in working with schools. After conducting surveys and interviews, one small teacher-action research team designed several programs that helped parents enrich their children's learning activities, including a toy lending library (Davies, 1990).

Selected Activities. Activities in these programs included GED courses for parents and English as a second language classes to assist parents in increasing language proficiency. To develop more idea exchanges, grade-level breakfasts were held. When one school launched a "whole language" initiative, a parent and community volunteer group as-

Home visitor programs
stress the importance of
building on family
strengths and family
involvement in the
neighborhood.

sisted teachers in teaching reading and writing. Special projects were established, such as the toy lending library, a clothing exchange, and a school store. Trips, social events, and workshops where parents, teachers, and community members could work and play together were held (Davies, 1990; Heleen, 1990).

Extensions of the Project. In 1990, the Schools Reaching Out project became the League of Schools Reaching Out and has since become a network of over 90 schools nationwide involving homes, schools, and communities in collaborative efforts. The major goal for all programs now is to provide academic and social success for all children, although different schools provide various activities for children and their families. Two key elements we see in all programs are that collaboration is a requirement for delivering comprehensive services to a community and that multiple ways exist for families, communities, and schools to share responsibility for making good partnerships work (Davies, Burch, & Palanki, 1993).

Epstein's Levels of Partnership.   The league has adopted Epstein's (1992) typology of six

family and community involvement activities to keep track of and to ensure progress for programs for the League of Schools Reaching Out. We describe this typology in the following subsections and give examples of how league schools adapted activities (examples adapted from Davies, Burch, & Johnson, 1992; Davies, Burch, & Palanki, 1993; Epstein, 1999).

Basic Obligations of Families.   Families are responsible for providing children with the basic health, emotional, social, and educational support to enable them to develop in increasingly complex ways. Schools help families develop child-rearing practices with strategies such as the following:

- Parent education workshops.
- Family resource centers.
- Home visitor programs involving trained parent outreach workers.
- Grade-level meetings with parents to discuss curriculum, learning goals, and how parents and teachers can work together to help children to achieve goals.

- Trips for parents and teachers to cultural events.
- Before- and after-school care in cooperation with other agencies.

Basic Obligations of Schools.   Schools are responsible for communicating with parents regarding their children's progress and the school programs. Partnerships are strengthened when there is effective two-way communication, including the following:

- Teachers visiting homes
- Parent—teacher conferences and report cards
- School handbook, fliers, newsletters, and activities calendar
- Dial-a-Teacher program, web pages, and student homework club
- Phone conferences

Involvement at School.   Parents are involved in league schools in two ways: (1) they attend school events to show support for their children and for schools; and (2) they are volunteers, helping in classrooms, offices, the library, or special areas. Schools vary schedules so that more parents can become involved, and recruitment and training events help volunteers understand the routines and objectives of the teachers. Parents assume some of the following activities:

- Recruiting other volunteers
- Organizing and assisting in field trips
- Organizing summer enrichment programs
- Volunteering as classroom aides, librarians, and clerical assistants or as lunchroom and playground aides
- Organizing special programs and fairs
- Tutoring other children

Involvement in Learning Activities at Home.
Teachers collaborate with parents in supporting children's learning at home. They coordi-

nate home and classroom learning and provide enrichment activities. Teachers help parents understand the academic skills children need at each grade level. Activities include the following:

- Toy and book lending libraries.
- Specially designed materials for parents to use with children at home.
- Workshops on how to use materials and exchange of ideas for making low-cost materials at home.
- Home visitors who work with parents on use of materials.
- Special reading and math projects for parents to work on with their children.

Involvement in Decision Making, Governance, and Advocacy.   Parents become part of the policy-making team for the school. Parents are trained in decision-making skills, ways to communicate with all parents they represent, and ways to use community advocacy groups to address issues of school improvement through the following methods:

- Workshops to train parents for advocacy.
- Participation with selected school councils and committees (school management teams, Chapter I and Head Start councils, curriculum committees, budget committees, and social committees).
- Participation in community decision-making councils.

Collaboration with Community Organizations.
Schools collaborate with social service agencies, business organizations, and cultural organizations to extend children's learning experiences in communities. They share responsibility with these other organizations to assist families in obtaining support services and information about community resources that strengthen their children's learning. League

schools and communities have collaborated in the following ways:

- Partnerships with specific businesses in a community.
- Full-time community service personnel service on school staff.
- Civic leaders meeting regularly with parent-teacher groups regarding neighborhood and school issues.
- Partnerships with local police, fire, drug abuse, and child abuse officers to provide families with information, prevention, and tutoring services.
- Partnerships with radio and TV educational networks to develop programs and activities that involve families in educational and community endeavors.

Research on Schools Reaching Out.   The Institute for Responsive Education studied 42 urban schools in the national network of League of Schools Reaching Out (Davies et al., 1992). The intent of the investigation was to examine the practices of urban schools for involving parents in collaborative efforts and to determine how the policies affected these practices. The study drew the following conclusions.

Many of the schools are becoming "community institutions" by serving families and exchanging resources with other community agencies. The level of activity proved high in all the schools, and partnership activities increased.

Although researchers found that traditional strategies for communicating with families were predominant, all schools showed they used multiple means for linking up with families. Parent volunteering was high, and the range of volunteer activities had expanded to accommodate needs of working parents. Multiple advisory and policy councils existed in all schools studied.

Support from the school principal was essential for League of Schools Reaching Out member schools to achieve their goals.

Other Promising Initiatives

In the past decade, a number of collaborative ventures have emerged in different U.S. communities to improve education of children in their areas. Many communities have adopted comprehensive models like the Comer model, and these follow-up models have proven successful. Successful national and state programs have emerged that have also established collaborative model programs. Other communities are trying small projects, expanding their focus as they meet important goals. In some projects, schools work with a single organization; others involve alliances with several organizations. Since federal, state, and private funding sources now either strongly advise or require collaboration, most projects are joining other local community agencies for achieving greater school success.

We have selected only a few of the programs as examples of what is happening on a national scale. The Aliza Brandwine Center started as a single project in collaboration with a university, but by forming collaborations with school and community agencies, it has been able to service many at-risk families. Communities in Schools is another model program that encourages multiple partnerships while encouraging independent designs. Project FAST is based on the principles of the early model programs but stresses a multifaceted program with multiyear assignments for children enrolled in school programs. Coordinated School Health Programs emphasize the importance of health to students' success in academic achievement. The judicial system in New York City has collaborated with service agencies to serve children whose parents are in court. The charter school movement, expanding rapidly now in many states, is the final program initiative that we describe. Charter schools conform to local school districts' standards, but the charter frees personnel from most bureaucratic measures.

Aliza Brandwine Center for Parent-Infant Development.

The Aliza Brandwine Center was established in 1970 at Towson State University in Baltimore as a parent education program for new parents while their young children participated in a play group. At the center, trained early childhood specialists provided a play-rich environment for infants and toddlers. Parents learned to observe their children at play with other children, and college students joined them for experience working with the infants and toddlers.

The parent education program consisted of (a) parents meeting with an early childhood specialist to discuss observations of their children, (b) parents identifying concerns related to other parenting skills, and (c) parents attending workshops or lectures presented by experts in child development. This program started as a lab school model at a university and has since formed collaborations with public schools, Maryland Department of Social Services, agencies for special-needs children, local libraries, private businesses, and even apartment complexes. With these other agencies, the center has opened more classes, extended services to a larger metropolitan population, and developed connections with other family services, thus servicing more at-risk families.

With this outreach and collaboration, families from all socio-economic and cultural groups, including families of children with special needs, are learning about and respecting cultural differences in parenting styles. They are understanding the importance of developing strong social networks that function as support systems (Moyer, Pate, & Simons, 1998). Other universities are finding that their preservice college students benefit by being involved at a grassroots level in maintaining collaborative efforts. Preservice teachers receive training in interdisciplinary collaboration for curriculum study that spans all aspects of a child's development (Lerner & Simon, 1998).

Communities in Schools.

Communities in Schools (CIS) founded in 1977, today reaches more than 300,000 children in more than 1,000 schools. Its purpose is to unite community resources such as health care and mental health professionals with teachers, parents, principals, and volunteers in a partnership relationship so that all children have:

- a healthy start in life and continued health services

- a one-to-one relationship with a caring adult

- a physically and emotionally safe place to learn during and after school hours

- skills that enable them to find work after graduation

- recognition of volunteerism as responsibility to a community.

CIS programs are independent, but each develops partnerships that span communities, cities, or counties to meet local demands. The Communities in Schools Program of Charlotte-Mecklenburg in North Carolina has multiple partnerships and programs to support children, among which are the following:

- Area corporations, religious groups, and civic organizations offer financial support as well as volunteers to serve as career counselors, tutors, lunch buddies, mentors, and pen pals for children.

- Health care providers offer their services once a week for basic health exams and dental cleaning.

- Community service groups work together with young people in community-service projects, modeling volunteerism in the children's neighborhoods.

The Communities in Schools program emphasizes the importance of physically and emotionally safe places for children to learn after school hours.

- After-school programs open all year offer many projects, including art, dance, recreation, and parenting classes.

- School social workers visit the homes of expectant mothers or mothers with small children to offer help and services.

- Special social events for parents, students, teachers, and staff offer chances for families to form social networks within the community.

- Staff act as community brokers who find necessary resources for families in need.

Each CIS program has its own special organizational paradigm but focuses on the goals of keeping children in school and teaching children to make good life choices. A team of workers connects families and children with social services and schools. For example, the school social worker visits families with infants and small children to establish an early school connection and invites them to social events. The program locates resources in the community, such as clothing, eyeglasses, and educational toys, for families in need. Collaboration on projects avoids unnecessary duplication of programs and helps families to develop a sense of belonging to a caring community (Lewis & Morris, 1998).

Project FAST.   East Cleveland, Ohio, and Cleveland State University began the Families Are Students and Teachers (FAST) project, based on the principles of the Comer and Schools Reaching Out projects. Research indicated that to enhance low-income children's achievement, a program based on success for all children and significant parent involvement was necessary.

Project FAST is a multifaceted program for school improvement directed at parent involvement, multiyear assignments for children, improved teaching strategies for all children, and a summer skills enrichment program. Many activities in the program are similar to those of other models in this chapter, but the multiyear assignments and the summer enrichment program allow teachers and parents to build a 3-year plan, offering a sense of stability and structure. The benefits of the multiage placements help parents recognize that involvement can occur at different levels. Over a 4-year period, teachers, students, and families get to know each other better and spend less time at the beginning of each year settling children into classroom routines. Children have a chance to move at their own pace, and grade retention, a major predictor of school failure, is reduced.

The summer skills enrichment program is for parents as well as children. The program keeps children's skills honed and provides children with a variety of projects and out-of-class learning. Parents learn that attending even a 1- to 2-hour workshop each month gives them the tools to spend even more productive time with their children at home. The workshops are designed to (a) help parents reinforce instruction at home; (b) create an environment that facilitates learning, such as developing a schedule, finding appropriate space, reading together, visiting libraries or museums, limiting television viewing and using encouragement and praise; (c) emphasize the techniques that promote children's positive self-concept, such as listening, praising, engaging in enjoyable activities together, and rewarding accomplishments; and (d) provide parents and teachers with opportunities to discuss basic parenting skills and ways to overcome some of the obstacles of inner-city locations.

Early results of the project indicated that children's achievement in math, reading, and language greatly improved. Parent involvement affected children's learning when what the children did was meaningful to the parents. It became meaningful when parents realized how committed teachers and administrators were to their children's learning and that what the parents did at home clearly made a difference in their children's school success (Hampton, Mumford, & Bond, 1998).

Coordinated School Health Programs. A large part of federal school reform efforts in recent decades have focused on improving academic standards without first recognizing that many academic problems are a result of poor physical and mental health. Recognizing the problem, the federal government, through the Improving America's Education Act of 1994, allowed states to redirect some appropriations to provide a comprehensive approach to meet the educational, health, social services, and other needs of families and children (Bush, 1997). Coordinated School Health Programs have developed partnerships to address this concern. Most efforts have originated at the school level, but teams have also been successful in other locations.

A school health coordinator trained in negotiating skills helps a school form a school team. Like any collaboration, the team assesses the needs of the community and then plans with teachers and community members a program that suits the community and engages all in developing programs that improve learning conditions. The model Coordinated School Health Program has eight components:

1. Health promotion for staff so that they become better role models for children and parents.

2. A planned sequential K-12 curriculum that addresses all dimensions of health.

3. Collaboration with community health services that focuses on prevention and early intervention.

4. Dependable school-based mental health services that provide for both individual and group services and are linked to public and private services in the community.

5. A K-12 sequential physical education program that promotes lifelong physical activity.

6. Provision for a safe physical and an emotionally supportive school environment for all children's development.

7. Programs that involve the entire family and community members in healthy activities.

8. Nutrition services offer a variety of nutritious meals, promote healthful food choices, and support nutritional instruction (Marx, Wooley, & Northup, 1998).

The Dallas, Texas, Independent School District operates the largest school based health center in the nation, although there are over 900 such centers in the United States. Based on the eight components of the model Coordinated School Health Program, the Dallas health center provides an array of health services right within the school to meet children's basic health needs. For children who need special services, a child study team evaluates the child and with the parents contacts a special clinic. Clinic staff members observe the child in the classroom, meet with the child and parents, and develop a treatment plan that encompasses the child's total health and academic experiences. The Coordinated School Health Programs have been successful in building strong partnerships, so that children's health has improved and school attendance has risen. Parents have become more involved in the schools, teachers have found their energies more focused on classroom teaching and less on discipline, and children's test scores

are up. Like all partnerships, the Coordinated School Health Programs require time and commitment to sustain school improvement (Tyson, 1999).

Children's Centers in New York Courts. Children whose parents are involved in litigation often accompany their parents to the courthouse, where they must sit and wait for long hours. In such situations, children are missing educational, social, and physical opportunities. To provide relief from such situations, the New York State Department of Social Services has collaborated with the judicial system and the private sector to provide Children's Centers in or near the courts. The Children's Centers were established to provide care and a safe environment for children who had to accompany their caregivers to courthouses while their caregivers were engaged in legal proceedings.

The Children's Centers provide a well-equipped and inviting environment for the children on a drop-in care basis. The room has areas for educational activities and for eating, sleeping, listening to music, working on art projects, reading books, and role playing. Teachers trained in child care and sensitive to the needs of families in crisis work with the children to stimulate educational, physical, and emotional development.

Since many families finding themselves in legal difficulty often do not obtain the services that they need or are entitled to, thus exacerbating their problems, the Children's Centers also establish collaborative links to other vital services that parents and children need when the court visit is over. Programs such as WIC, Head Start, local child care services, food stamp programs, and child health programs maintain a presence at the centers, where specialized workers provide information and make referrals for the families needing help from social service agencies. By linking families with needed services, the New York Judicial

Commission hopes to break the cycle of repeated visits to court and to return children to school (Permanent Judicial Commission on Justice for Children, n.d.)

Charter School Movement. The charter school movement began in the early 1990s, when the Minnesota legislature passed the first charter school statute. The movement grew rapidly, and by the end of the 20th century, 34 states had enacted legislation to permit formation of a variety of charter schools. Over 166,000 students were enrolled as of 1998 (Wells, 1998). The basic concept of the movement was to free public schools from big-city bureaucracy and grant them autonomy to make decisions regarding structure, curriculum, and educational emphasis while holding them accountable for academic achievement.

As with regulations on home schooling, laws vary from state to state on the definition of a charter school. In some states, the local school authority grants the charter; in other states, it is the state education department, and a few states allow the boards of colleges and universities to grant charters. But all charter schools are publicly supported schools and must be nonsectarian, cannot violate federal and state regulations or violate students' civil rights, may not charge tuition, and in most cases are not allowed to use admissions requirements. In addition, they must conform to either a district or a state's learning outcomes and have clearly defined goals, a solid administrative structure, a comprehensive curriculum plan, and an assessment and evaluation plan. To promote accountability, most states plan not to renew the charters of those schools that fail to meet their required standards (Raywid, 1995).

Charter schools vary widely in their concept of "good schooling" and in establishing partnerships with parents or the community. One chartered school in the southwest United States adheres to an academic curriculum that uses Hirsch's cultural literacy outline and has a principal making all decisions. Another school in that same district has a very permissive program. Instead of the school's having a designated administrator, a group of parents, teachers, and community members have formed a partnership to provide for the learning needs of the students (Raywid, 1995).

A common belief in granting charters is that without the encumbrances of regulations, these schools will be able to work more closely with parents, respond better to children's needs, and reflect the aspirations of families served (Harrington-Lueker, 1994). This reform means that schools will be more accountable, have greater autonomy, be more efficient, present greater choices to families, infuse competition, and be models for innovation (Wells, 1998). Research on charter schools does show that some charter schools show promise of fulfilling some of these goals, in spite of overwhelming odds. Many parents, teachers, and community persons who work in or send their children to charter schools are committed to and pleased with their schools. Students feel challenged and respected in a school community that prizes learning and innovation (Weiss, 1997).

With the many differences in state regulations, results from the different state studies are likely to reflect differences. For example, research thus far indicates that in many of the states, accountability, greater choices for all students (not just the more vocal or wealthier), models for innovations, and even greater efficiency are not happening (Garn, 1998; Wells, 1998). Nevertheless, we believe that some of these programs are likely to fulfill the notions of this text, that is, harnessing more and greater family and community resources than has been the case historically. The experiments bear watching, for some will become exemplars, showing what happens when we ask more of the adults involved in a school endeavor.

All of the above-described programs have provided needed services to our neediest families, but long-term commitment and dedication to the idea that collaboration can make a difference in children's education is required. Maintaining that commitment is hard work and often difficult, Comer estimates that one third of the projects maintain change, one third achieve limited change until the initiators depart, and one third do not have any success (O'Neil, 1997).

Critical Features of Partnerships

Partnership models and collaborative arrangements are all different, but we find most of the following features appearing in quality programs. These ideas may be helpful as evaluation tools when you have an opportunity to become involved in a partnership program.

1. Collaboration requires strong leadership, committed coordinators, and partners able to gain the support of the power brokers in their social setting.

2. Each participant knows that he or she must surrender some decision-making power so as to find common ground for collaborating. To keep communication channels open, each partner must express feelings and reactions while respecting skills, knowledge, ideas, culture, and values of other partnership members.

3. Partners know that it is imperative to establish with the group some long-range goals at the beginning yet be able to redirect their objectives when necessary to overcome barriers.

4. Leaders realize that all program steps require careful planning, that these steps must

Partnerships require strong leadership, committed coordinators, and members able to gain group support.

include learning experiences from all social settings, and that all partners are to participate in educational decision making.

5. Continuous assessment is needed to determine progress or to determine change so that participants can recognize and reward each other's efforts.

7. Because change in educational structures is slow, partners recognize that alterations cannot be rushed.

6. The entire community must be kept informed of progress.

IMPLICATIONS FOR PROFESSIONALS

As you reflect on this chapter, you should beome cognizant of the extended role of the classroom teacher in the new world of partnerships. No longer will a classroom teacher be responsible only for events in the classroom, but he or she will also need to understand how to work in partnership with many others, even if a formal partnership doesn't exist. The information on successful model programs will give you some ideas that could work in your own setting. Think about how parents can be enlisted to support their children's learning and how such support can work for you, even if a formal partnership isn't in place in your school. Consider the myriad of support systems a community provides. You will not find all community services available or supportive, but incorporating just one or two ideas can change the dynamics of your classroom for the better.

Trying to tap all those resources described in this chapter to meet the needs of one classroom would be a lonely and arduous task. Studying ways in which others have become partners will give you an understanding of some tasks you can do and some of the support systems you are likely to find in any school.

SUMMARY AND REVIEW

The factorylike and bureaucratic school developed in the early 1900s is not viable for the 21st century, but the task of changing schools so that families and communities work in partnership is not easy, either. Model interinstitution collaborations have succeeded in changing and improving some schools to enhance the social, intellectual, moral, and physical potential of children. All professionals must work vigorously to extend these models.

Although its main goal was to make war on poverty, Project Head Start initiated an era of collaborative work for schools, homes, and communities that continues as an exemplar of uniting social settings. Even Start extends Head Start's beginnings and increases the amount of experimentation with partnerships while extending services to the entire family. Another boost to partnerships came with the Educational Partnerships Act of 1988 and the development of Partnership for Families in Education in 1994, which stress collaboration among all federal, state, and local agencies that service children.

Comer's School Development Program and the League of Schools Reaching Out demonstrate clearly that families, schools, and communities can work together in strengthening educational progress. Not only have numerous schools throughout the United States adopted one of these models, but also their communities are developing successful programs to provide better education for their children.

Many communities recognize that children's educational progress begins long before they enter school at age 5, and is dependent on many other social factors outside the realm of the school. A program started at Towson State University in Baltimore found that the staff can extend programs for infants and toddlers to reach more at-risk families by collaborating with the public schools and social agencies. Communities in Schools of Charlotte-

Mecklenburg, North Carolina, brings to the school setting the resources of the entire community to enable children to stay in school developing life-long skills. Cleveland State University joined with East Cleveland, Ohio, schools and designed a model following the Comer and Schools Reaching Out principles. Project FAST has discovered that multiyear assignments for both children and teachers with summer enrichment programs for children and parents results in much improvement in children's academic achievement. Coordinated Health School Programs originating in school or local health services support children's health so that children are better able to function academically.

Recognizing that children whose parents were in court were being badly served, New York City developed Children's Centers with New York courts. Not only do the centers provide a safe and educationally rich environment for children, but also staff collaborate with other social services to direct these families in locating other needed services for their children.

If schools are to succeed, children must be provided with more support than a school can accomplish alone. It is incumbent upon the entire community along with the educational establishment to provide both teachers and parents with additional support. Developing collaborations and extending programs to involve these many agencies has made a difference in many communities, even in programs where total involvement hasn't been achieved. Schools and communities have many different model programs to guide them as they work toward partnerships. Many strategies work, and several elements are common to most projects. The strongest components for success appear to be the motivation in a community for solving some of its problems and the commitment of key people involved.

SUGGESTED ACTIVITIES AND QUESTIONS

1. Interview the project coordinator of a partnership program. Ask how the program got started and what is the program's structure. How does the coordinator view the results of the collaboration?

2. Compare this program to one of the model programs discussed in this chapter. What activities, if any, do they have in common? How do the program's successes compare to the research on the model program?

3. Read James Comer's *Maggie's American Dream* and discuss with classmates the impact the book has on you. From your reading, what home and community influences do you think might have affected the way Comer engineered his School Development Program?

4. With a group of classmates, design a hypothetical collaborative project that would benefit an imaginary class. Each member should select one social setting (home, school, or community) to represent. Then plan the steps of the process, assigning roles and responsibilities for implementation. What problems did you encounter in coming to an agreement on collaboration?

RESOURCES

Books

1. Dryfoos, J. G. (1994). *Full service schools: A revolution in health and social service for children, youth, and families.* San Francisco: Jossey Bass.

2. Epstein, J. L. (1996). *School and family partnerships.* New York: Basic Books.

Films/Videos

1. *A reason to care: Corporate support of community child care.* (1996). [Video, 28 min.] Indiana's

Public Broadcasting Stations with National Association for the Education of Young Children.

2. *Cultivating Roots—Home/school partnerships.* (1997). [Video, 30 min.] National Association for the Education of Young Children.

Organizations

1. Home and School Institute (http://www.megaskillshsi.org/) 1500 Massachusetts Avenue NW Washington, DC 20005
2. National Committee for Citizens and Education (NCCE) 900 Second Street, NE, Washington DC 20002

Websites

1. http://www.pfie.ed.gov Features a database for members of Partnership for Family Involvement in Education and gives examples of successful collaborative programs.
2. http://info.med.yale.edu/comer Gives information about Comer's School Development Program and examples of successful applications in the United States.

Chapter 12

Effective Social Settings for Learning

Public education has been a light in our changing society—uniting, educating, and caring for children, to help ensure a better future. We must support positive structural changes in which children, teachers, parents, and society benefit from a "shared vision."

(Stone, 1999, p.304.)

❦

After looking at the various curricula found in homes, schools, and communities, we turn now to identify those settings that will provide the best possible educational experiences. The model programs described in chapter 11 will thrive in settings that include the features associated with effective homes, schools, and communities. In reading this chapter, you will learn the following:

1. Particular characteristics and traits identify effective homes, schools, and communities.

2. Educators have a number of tools to use for evaluating the different social settings.

3. For the best educational environments for children, connections are needed among the three social settings where children spend their lives.

4. The school is the logical and most capable force, both to begin and then to nurture partnerships, for uniting the three social settings.

Well-functioning homes, effective schools, and dynamic and prosperous neighborhoods and communities are goals to which all cultural groups and political units aspire. These goals are being reached in some areas across the United States, and those areas are heralded in media reports under such banners as "most desirable location in America." Investigators inform us, however, that many towns and cities in the United States are suffering, have damaged parts, and show stress (Garbarino, Dubrow, Kostelny, & Pardo, 1998; Kotlowitz, 1991; Quint, 1994). Consider the following descriptions of two very different U.S. communities.

1. The southwestern city has the most sought-after climate in the United States. Days are sunny, atmosphere is clear, and the demeanor on city streets is uplifting. Careful development from the area's small-town origins produced wide streets, inviting parks, and pleasantly designed neighborhoods. The multiethnic population flows in harmonious ways and appears truly integrated. Electronics production provides a strong economic base, and poverty seems completely absent. Crime statistics are the lowest in the United States for small cities, and a pleasant ambience in the city is felt by even short-term visitors. All schools are new, spacious, and well-equipped. The curriculum for students is conservative but apparently in keeping with community wishes. It seems an almost utopian setting (adapted from A. B. Prescott, 1994, personal communication).

2. The public housing project is an impoverished community with rat-infested apartments, where plumbing often does not work and there is almost no maintenance. Buildings and grounds are in constant disrepair—windows are boarded up, and the effects of vandalism are seen everywhere. The project is also dangerous. Crime has increased 400% in recent years, and death is so frequent that young children play funeral in the after-school program. Gangs and drug lords dominate the community, instilling fear in all residents. Conditions have made families into internal refugees, and rules that parents give their children reflect the sobering conditions: "Don't go out in the hallway. Stay away from windows. Stay together all the time. When you hear shots, hit the floor" (adapted from Garbarino Kostelny & Dubrow, 1998, pp. 130–142).

The two settings described result from the overarching social, political, and economic forces at work in their respective communities. Certain favorable circumstances produced one venue; a series of misfortunes and miscalculations produced the other. It is beyond the scope of our text to define or explain even part of the dynamics producing quality and distressed areas in any city. However, we can identify characteristics of effective social settings and recommend ways to make our own workplaces effective examples.

All three social settings in children's lives naturally affect children's learning and experience. Also, for good or ill, one setting will affect the other two. Problems in one setting can make functioning in the others more difficult, although the positive effects of two settings often counterbalance an inferior third. For instance, effective homes can and do offset negative community influences (Clark, 1983; Comer, 1988, 1997), and effective school programs can make a difference for struggling families and peer groups (Meier, 1995; Quint, 1994; Thompson, 1993). From the model programs discussed in chapter 11, we take assurance that better things are possible for children's experiences in the United States if more cohesion develops among the major social settings. So, how do we get there?

We must first assess what exists in children's lives. Then, establishing goals for improvement and creating plans for action become relevant. One underlying thesis of this text is that schools are best situated to assess the social settings of an area, make plans for remediation, and begin the process of drawing institutions together for the betterment of children.

Collaborative efforts are easily instituted in vigorous and healthy social settings; when deficits and problems exist in the settings, the challenge is, of course, far greater. In problem settings, agents of change must be more engaged, work harder, and experiment aggressively to bring about improvements.

In this chapter, we examine the features of competent families, effective schools, and effective communities. We also include the converse of some features when they illuminate explanations. We conclude by examining the role of the school as broker for linking social settings.

COMPETENT FAMILIES

As noted in chapter 4, U.S. families have different organizations, values, and socioeconomic bases, plus different approaches to health care, nutrition, and experiences. No family is perfect, yet most families have their particular strengths. Families function in the context of a community and in association with a school, and the quality of this interaction determines to a large extent the success or failure of children attending a school.

Areas of home and family competence that we explore in this section are organization and management, beliefs and value structures, intellectual stimuli, parental knowledge of child development, health and nutrition practices, social and emotional environments, and social networking. Since all these areas have a serious impact on children's growth and learning, what if problems exist in one or more? As stated, all families have deficits, but the issue is the number and extent of those deficits. Recall the Sameroff et al. (1987) research and the Werner and Smith (1992) studies, which inform us that at-risk children with one or two risk factors seem to manage well when compensating help is available from other social settings (refer to Chapter 4).

Organization and Management

As discussed in chapter 3, the United States contains numerous cultures, each of which represents a somewhat different pattern of child rearing. Also, across cultures, we find strands undergirding the competent home and differentiating it from less effective ones.

We discussed family management styles in chapter 4, and these styles bear repeating here. Since the Bernstein and Baumrind studies in the 1960s, social scientists continue to recognize these several management styles in U.S. homes. The styles overlap and combinations exist, but most families tend toward one style or another. Baumrind (1966, 1968, 1971) labeled three basic parenting styles: authoritarian, authoritative, and permissive. Others refined Baumrind's terms somewhat and added different labels, but in essence all authorities focus on similar major categories. The authoritative, democratic, or sponsored-independence style is the one we associate with the effective family. Family members managing according to the authoritative style are democratic and controlling but warm and receptive. These attributes contrast with the authoritarian's detached control and the noncontrolling and nondemanding approach of the permissive style.

Maccoby and Martin (1983) and Dornbusch, Ritter, Leiderman, Roberts, and Fraleigh (1987) failed to find all the relationships that Baumrind's Anglo population revealed between style and schoolwork in selected ethnic families. However, Clark's (1983) teams looked at Caucasian, Mexican-American, and African American homes to identify the effective families in difficult living conditions. He found that particular attitudes and behaviors—generally the authoritative style—that parents displayed made the difference between success and failure in school and life for children in his studies. The Baumrind and Clark findings are reinforced by more recent research (e.g., Brophy, 1989; Hart, DeWolf & Burts, 1993; Hbrabowski et al., 1998).

A significant finding in Clark's work is that "these [effective] families believe they can make a difference in a child's life, and they are not overwhelmed by circumstances" (1983, p. 198). Clark identified 10 characteristics of effective families, irrespective of socioeconomic condition:

1. A feeling of control over their lives
2. Frequent communication of high expectations to children
3. A family dream of success for the future
4. Hard work as a key to success
5. An active rather than sedentary lifestyle
6. Twenty-five to 30 home-centered learning hours per week
7. View of family as a mutual support system and problem-solving unit
8. Clearly understood and consistently enforced household rules
9. Frequent contact with teachers
10. Emphasis on spiritual growth

Frequently we associate the preceding as characteristics of the Protestant ethic—a hallmark of prospering U.S. families—although Clark found these characteristics in poor homes having many economic and social disadvantages.

So what can we do about the families that lack many of these features? It is useless to wring our hands and write off 20% or more of U.S. homes as unsalvageable. Changed circumstances for families with children are key. Governmental policies (federal, state, and municipal) must aim to improve health conditions, stimulate economic opportunities, and attempt to redirect living conditions of those in poverty. The welfare reform efforts by federal and state agencies have indicated these as goals, but results are mixed. Some reporters note that the successes are largely due to overall economic gains in the United States in the several years since reform was instituted (Children's Defense Fund, 1998). Even without government intervention, school and community groups working together can bring about changes in the perceptions families have of themselves. Good schools and humane communities do make a difference in the pressures affecting families and can provide incentives for families to grow in effectiveness. Model programs show this! (See particularly the Comer plan in chapter 11.)

In some instances, parents are so remote and out of touch that the best teachers can do is to give constant support, believe in children, and hope that some success unfolds in the classroom. Some hard-to-reach parents can be included through persistent communication and emphasis on their strengths and their successes with their children. Parent education can no longer mean simply telling parents what they must do. It means seeking ways to support parents to gradually accept responsibility for their children's education—and at the parents' level of ability. It means trying out different approaches, such as listening to parent responses, and building on what works. As in teaching children, teachers must be ready to listen, to observe, and to support parents' efforts before offering new challenges.

Beliefs and Value Structures

A number of writers point out that children's attitudes, beliefs, and values resemble those of their parents (Coles, 1997; Goleman, 1995; Scarf, 1995), but all allow that schools and communities extend these considerably. Parenting practices and parent values do become critical in children's lives.

Educating about stealing, lying, and disorderly conduct is normal for most families, although the instruction can take different forms. Some parents teach morals and values through intimidation and punishment while others approach the challenge by explaining children's problems and the impact of one's actions on others. The latter approach, called **induction,** results in stronger development of conscience and internal control (Sadker, Lerner & Sadker, 1999). The effective family will focus on values, morals, and attitudes by modeling behaviors and discussing them with their children, reasoning through solutions,

and labeling the behavior when seen in public (see Table 12.1). Children very much need a sense of purpose and direction in their lives, and this begins with values established by the home.

Literary and Intellectual Stimuli

Competent families provide children with lifelong learning interests as they go about their daily lives. Families that provide intellectual challenges stimulate children's interest in natural phenomena and sharpen skills used in acquiring knowledge from different media (Bruer, 1998). Parents encourage these practices by conversing, questioning, demonstrating, and

Table 12.1   Helping Children Develop Internal Locus of Control

1. Be aware that when caregivers are responsive, affectionate, and comforting, children know that their actions count.
2. Allow children to accept consequences for their actions (such as cleaning up after some water play).
3. Avoid performing tasks children can do for themselves. When caregivers encourage effort and experiments, children learn to do for themselves.
4. Give children responsibilities that fit their age levels.
5. Let children know when they perform well.
6. Model behaviors and attitudes that show you are proactive. Communicate to children that people can make things happen.
7. Encourage and support children's particular interests and show respect for their accomplishments.
8. Explain the reasons for needed rules and limits, but establish reasonable standards for behavior.
9. Allow children to make age-appropriate decisions as often as possible. Start with minor choices and graduate to consequence-bearing actions.

Adapted from Berns, 1997; Lefcourt, 1984; Sadker & Sadker, 1995.

modeling use of literary, problem-solving, and investigative skills.

Language Patterns. Children's vocabulary and grammatical abilities are patterned almost totally after caregiver modeling (Heath, 1983; Sigel et al., 1984) in the course of family interactions. Competent homes provide a rich language environment where conversations, active listening, and interactions with all members are valued and demonstrated. Bernstein (1972) noted the elaborate codes that middle-class families use that prepare children for interaction and communication within schools and the greater community. In homes where multiple languages or dialects are used, competent parents through their demonstrations ensure that children learn "code-switching" to deal with different social venues.

Published Materials. Competent families read, have books, and refer to other publications in the home. Numerous studies confirm that the amount of reading in homes is directly related to children's success in reading as well as other school subjects (U.S. Department of Education, 1986). Quality day care arrangements and Head Start programs contribute to literacy, and their efforts can compensate somewhat for deprived circumstances, but the major influence still comes from the family (Edelsky, 1996; Hart & Risley, 1995). Some school-community collaborations, as in the following vignette, are intended to increase the amount of reading in homes.

𝓐

The Growing Up Reading program in a small New England community is a community-school-home collaboration directed at improving literacy. Books are delivered to homes of new babies born in the community, and then each preschool birthday is celebrated with another good, age-appropriate book. "Grandparent" volunteers deliver the books to homes and interact with parents and children. Parents and their children meet once a week with childhood specialists and grandparent volunteers. At these meetings, parents, teachers, and volunteers exchange stories, demonstrate techniques of book sharing, and discuss how to use other materials while children engage in play activities.

𝓐

Studies confirm that the amount of reading in homes is directly related to children's success in reading at school.

Illiteracy is a lingering problem afflicting many marginal homes. The United States has a surprising number of functionally illiterate young parents who have few printed materials in their homes and therefore meager ways of stimulating the prereading skills and interests of their children. Collaborations and networks, as in the preceding vignette, to involve these parents are critical. School early-intervention plans are backup strategies when collaborations are not available.

Use of Television and the Internet.   As is *not* the case with published materials, almost every home in the United States has one or more television sets. How each family uses television is, of course, the salient factor. Sitcoms, game shows, and soap operas, while providing some stimulation, give children few readiness skills for reading. Children's shows are aired in all areas of the country, but unless parents and children both watch and discuss them, the shows appear to have little cognitive benefit (Van Evra, 1998).

Positive links to achievement have been found when children viewed television programs such as *Sesame Street* and *Mr, Rogers' Neighborhood.* In addition, some researchers have found benefits when parents watched television with their children and then discussed the programs (Gunter & McAleer, 1997; Singer & Singer, 1990). Here again, it is the effective family that pursues the objective of tapping the educational dimensions of television or Internet sources. To ensure that disadvantaged children can maximize learning from television, community and school programs must be instituted whereby advocates can influence home behaviors through parent education.

Parental Knowledge of Child Development

In effective family situations, caregivers are aware that children move through developmental stages and that instruction and expectations depend on where children are in their growth.

Some young parents have extended families and other social networks of neighbors to inform them about normal and reasonable stages of children's growth. Others have books, such as the guides published by Dr. Spock, Dr. Berry Brazelton, and others, from which to view their children's progress. Others will depend on services gained through clinics, such as WIC programs, well-baby clinics, and family health centers. Still others remain quite ignorant of the basics of child development and depend on intuition and even on folklore.

When communities address child development needs, results are haphazard at best. Adult education programs on child care and community outreach programs are available in some areas, but historically they attract few parents. Some high schools provide a basic course on home management and child development for students. Such opportunities (e.g., the Dunbar [Baltimore] High School program for pregnant teens and young mothers) provide some knowledge and experience about developmental concepts and nurturing. However, information is constantly challenged by the ever-present television, which promises much and implies that young mothers must shower their children with material things.

Health and Nutrition

Health implies attention to complete personal well-being, not just the absence of disease or infirmities. Competent parents provide safe and healthy environments in which children develop and prosper. Most health and safety concepts derive from parents and caregivers and grow out of situations associated with everyday living. As a result of poverty and depressed living conditions, marginalized families frequently suffer from chronic health problems, accidents, and inadequate nutrition.

A surprising 33% of Americans have little or no health care plans, and children are often in that group (Children's Defense Fund, 1997). Illness and health problems become all too often a function of income.

Health problems affect all poor families. Inadequate housing, high population densities, poor sanitation, poor diets, smoke, and poor habits in managing resources engender unhealthy homes. Some problems stem from ignorance about basic home maintenance, some come from poor habits and substance abuse, and many come from the inability of persons to secure and follow through on available care and help from social agencies. Clearly, one way to address these problems is through parent education.

Competent families, on the other hand, know about health practices, the basics of nutrition, and how to secure medical attention. When health and nutrition standards are preserved, we observe the following in competent homes:

Nutrition

- Meals with food from major food groups
- Reduced use of prepackaged, treated foods containing fat, salt, and additives
- Reduced use of sweets, soft drinks, and fatty products
- Regular eating habits and sensible snacks

Hygiene and physical health

- Immunizations
- Annual checkups and evaluations
- Adequate lighting, ventilation, and heat in homes

Sanitation

- Avoidance of toxic substances
- Washing before meals and food preparation

- Regular bathing
- Keeping rubbish cleared away
- Sensible, maintained home space

Most of these practices can be extended to all homes when collaborations, networks, and parent education practices emerge.

Consistent Social and Emotional Environments

Effective homes develop environments that nurture children's social and emotional well-being. The overriding dimension is one of care and interest. Too often children state that they are not watched over, that no one cares. This situation worsens when we encounter families in stress—7% of our poor children state that no one cares about them (Noddings, 1992). Children's range of perceptions about self, from confidence to spiritual growth, will be affected by this feeling.

Parents' workplaces affect their perceptions of life and the way they interact with children and other family members (Bronfenbrenner & Crouter, 1982; Wohl, 1997). In turn, these perceptions foster parenting styles that conform to parents' experiences and how they see themselves in the world. On the positive side, we have the effective-family investigations (Clark, 1983; Rich, 1987; Scarf, 1997) showing that the functioning family views itself as a problem-solving unit with a mutual support system and that valuing spiritual life is important.

How can we encourage parents in guiding and nurturing their children and in establishing contacts outside the home? Workshops, modeling, and discussions are only part of the answer. Supporting families through family-school-community collaborations and involving parents in extended networks will enhance social and emotional health in homes (Benson, 1997).

Child-rearing patterns certainly affect children's level of moral development. Children's attitudes are formed early, and parents and peers have a significant impact through instruction, modeling, rewards, and punishments. Children's values tend to reflect those of their family. Other experiences also affect this development; individuals exposed to many socializing agents are more likely to achieve a higher level of moral reasoning than those exposed to only a few (Bronfenbrenner et al., 1984; Damon, 1988).

Locus of control is directly related to parenting (refer to Table 12.1). Whether children see themselves or others in control determines the way they look toward the future.

Developing Interactive Skills.
Competent families engender interactive skills that permit children to interact with the world with their values and moral notions in place. Modeling, discussions in the home, and being a part of the larger community, that is, extending children's social contacts so that they use more than one interactive style (Salzstein, 1976; Walker & Taylor, 1991), all help children develop these skills. Children's growth will reflect their participation and experience.

Developing Problem-Solving Skills.
Homes foster problem-solving skills through participation and experimentation. By modeling problem-solving skills and exploring problems and solutions with children, parents steer their children toward competence (Leach, 1994). Homes where highly directive and punitive behaviors are the norm actually discourage interest and skill for analyzing tasks, and some even produce a sense of helplessness (Bronfenbrenner et al., 1984).

Teaching Coping Skills.
Children able to confront adversity and seek ways to approach difficulties usually have had guided experiences in approaching tasks. Competent families entertain questions about solving problems. This means that caregivers verbally or kinesthetically lead children through a series of tasks and also frame questions leading to a reasonable conclusion (Dyson, 1986). Children with experiences in considering alternatives and choices have a background for confronting challenges and even adversity. Domineering, prejudiced, or autocratic adults engender thinking for one "correct" set of rules or format. This does little to help children develop coping skills.

Recreational Pursuits.
Competent homes value recreation, gaming sessions, and play. Children normally select their own levels of participation in play, sports, and creative work, but parents and other family members may encourage and support their interest. Children require time, space, and equipment to pursue recreation, and effective parents will plan for this, support it, and even participate. Few things solidify families better than recreational pursuits. Benefits children derive include the following (Seefeldt & Barbour, 1998):

- Working with others
- Small and large muscle exercise
- Establishing fitness
- Lifelong interests and attitudes
- Guided exploration of challenges and new ventures
- Sensible and accurate use of equipment
- Release from tension

Figure 12–1 provides questions that professionals may wish to use when evaluating whether a family is effective. An effective family will display a high percentage, though not necessarily all, of the features.

In evaluating effective families, assessors will answer yes for most of the following questions:

1. Is an authoritative parenting style evident?
2. Is there consistency in home management, family routines (bedtime, meals, and relaxation), and household regulations?
3. Are rules and codes of conduct understood and consistently enforced?
4. Are discussions, conversations, and interactions noticeable and frequent?
5. Do children have responsibilities in the home?
6. Are expectations of children in keeping with the children's stages of development?
7. Do parents have high hopes for their children's success?
8. Do family members evince a sense of success and pride?
9. Are good nutrition practices observed?
10. Are sanitary practices in evidence?
11. Do family members know where others work, play, and socialize?
12. Is there warmth in the home—do members accept others?
13. Do family members encourage and praise each other?
14. Does the family have a social network of friends?
15. Are values and moral codes apparent in the family?
16. Are literary and other intellectual stimuli present in the home?
17. Do members read to each other?
18. Does the family show skill in using the social and welfare services available to them?
19. Are health checkups done regularly and immunizations scheduled?
20. Can parents verbally and kinesthetically lead children through tasks and problems with appropriate questions, comments, and demonstrations?

Figure 12–1   Evaluating Family Effectiveness.
Source: Adapted from Berger, 2000; Berns, 1997; Curran, 1983; Galinsky, 1987; Rich, 1992.

EFFECTIVE SCHOOLS

Numerous publications discuss the programs and character of "effective schools", and we frequently see such items as student achievement, values and beliefs, and individual differences highlighted. Of course, these areas are important, but other school features also are factors in school success. On the other hand, some other traits have a defeating effect when we carefully analyze situations.

Student Achievement

Often we think that standardized achievement test results are proof of what happens in schools. When related to aptitude scores, pro-gram resources, or support, these tests may indicate statistically whether particular school programs have realized expected gains. But the results of norm-referenced tests cannot be used in guiding individual children.

If overall success rates are high when comparing achievements among schools, educators and citizens alike often assume that all is right at their school and that programs must be appropriate. However, group tests often hide areas of deficiency and often fail to assess specific children's skills. Frequently a test may be inappropriate for a particular sub-group in the school. For example, gifted children, while performing adequately in school, sometimes receive lower than anticipated scores on tests.

When problems appear in effective schools—for example, if scores are well below an area norm—educators, parents, and other community citizens demand explanations. Are community problems or area demographics confounding parts of the program and school curriculum? Are scores lower because schools are reserving time for nonacademic areas, such as developing esteem and readiness or expanding cultural background, before returning to achievement-tested basic skills? Again, standardized tests measure particular academic skill levels and do not assess achievements in all the curriculum areas schools work with today (refer to chapter 8). Schools can determine children's achievement using tools other than batteries of norm-referenced tests. In effective schools, teachers incorporate other assessment forms to diagnose needs for remediation or program changes. (For a thorough discussion of the relative strengths and weaknesses of the different types of assessment available to teachers, see Stiggins, 1997.)

Values and Beliefs

Anna Freud once observed that the early elementary years are "times when a child's character and conscience is built—or isn't!" With school comes the beginning of a child's community participation, and of course there is much to wonder about and to learn about the rights and wrongs of life.

Just as parents model values and beliefs, so do teachers and other school personnel (Coles, 1997). Getting along with others, sharing with others, and helping others are areas that successful schools expand on after these basics are started at home or child care centers. It is one thing to post rules for courtesies or sharing, but another to inculcate these valuable features in an effective school. First, teachers, like parents, must model these behaviors. For instance, recall Victoria's story in chapter 6 where the mother shows that she believes in accepting all children who come to her yard. In effective schools, primary teachers develop units on social communications and ways of getting along with others. A variety of successful techniques have been used. Challenges can be taken from everyday life or even from newspapers, and the students have an opportunity to analyze and discuss ways to work through the problems.

Many teachers find that some of the best ways to address values is to use a story narrative. (The children's book section in Appendix I includes many suitable titles.) Others have used film or video clips focusing on a social situation.

Effective schools also promote the values relating to appreciating diverse cultures in their community and interacting with persons with special needs.

Provision for Individual Differences and Inclusion

Many American schools here at the beginning of the 21st century are administered under the principles **mainstreaming** or **inclusion**. We have used a generation to move to this place, but at present, all schools are obligated to provide educational experiences for children at all learning levels and in the "least restrictive environment." We discussed inclusion from a historical perspective in chapter 2 and from a curriculum viewpoint in chapter 8. Effective schools have an inclusion model that provides services for children with special needs from birth through high school.

Though you may find some schools in America with more traditional orientations and techniques, in large part you will find that effective schools will be working toward the concept of inclusion. Full inclusion indicates that *every* child belongs in a regular classroom and that support services are used so that appropriate instruction is carried out by the

Successful schools model values and beliefs of homes and child care centers—such as getting along with others, sharing, and helping as part of the curriculum.

classroom teacher and others. Inclusion means that instruction for each child will be provided by whichever personnel or setting is most appropriate for that part of the child's curriculum. In this manner, special-needs children are in contact and associating with regular (able-bodied) children for a large part of their school day. Of course, as schools, and child care facilities, too, have moved to incorporate the legislation, schools have needed to alter some parts of their programs.

More than restructured buildings and more specialized personnel, the thing you will notice most in a school practicing inclusion is the attitude and demeanor toward abilities of all children. Remember that able-bodied children of a generation back rarely encountered diversity in their classrooms. Most schools up through the 1960s were monolingual and monoracial and showed little evidence of special needs. In effective schools today, the mix is truly comprehensive, and most educators agree that living and learning with diversity makes all individuals more tolerant, more accepting, and more eager to use the skills and talents of persons they heretofore did not come to know or value.

Education in an inclusive school situation means that teachers work and interact with different personnel, for example, specialists for different disabilities, diagnosticians, and aides trained to work with particular needs. They adjust content and mode of instruction to fit the needs of particular individuals—not just those individuals identified with "special needs" but also able-bodied children who have different learning modalities or even gaps in experience (Culatta & Tompkins, 1999). Teachers involve parents and other specialists in planning the educational program. Effective schools are thus already involved in supporting one main thrust of this text.

In effective schools, teachers have particular knowledge and skills regarding children of varying abilities and from diverse cultures. The following undergird the effective teacher's work.

1. An open mind and a humane disposition.
2. Ability to recognize disabling conditions, knowledge about the general characteristics and general needs of children with frequently observed disabilities, and an openness for seeking diagnostic services to help merge the needs of particular children into the classroom.
3. Knowledge regarding the homes from which special-needs children come and willingness to work with the parents for the benefit of the child.
4. Knowledge regarding the support services in the school and how the services support teachers and ability to present anecdotal information, hunches, and other experiences to persons making evaluations.
5. Ability to adapt the classroom environment to address any special needs that particular children have.
6. Familiarity with the child's and the child's family's rights.
7. Knowledge regarding responsibilities as a part of an IEP team.
8. Ability to enlist help from aides and volunteers and ability to work with those persons for children's benefit.
9. Ability to merge students with disabilities into the classroom in a productive, healthy, and forward-moving fashion.
10. Sensitivity to one's own feelings about working with students with disabilities.

Positive School Features

School effectiveness researchers have identified several characteristics that are observed consistently in schools demonstrating good achievement gains (Cruickshank, 1990; Good & Brophy, 1986, 1996). In addition to the above-listed qualities, the following items appear consistently on most lists:

1. Strong academic leadership that produces consensus
2. A safe, orderly school climate
3. Positive teacher attitudes toward students
4. High expectations regarding children's abilities
5. Efficient use of instructional time
6. Careful monitoring of progress
7. Strong parental involvement programs
8. Emphasis on importance of skills and achievement

9. Frequent use of praise and encouragement

10. Support for different learning modalities

The preceding are general school practices and will fit with almost any program, goal, or strategy. The curriculum content, teaching strategies, equipment used, and level of instruction to develop a program can, of course, vary greatly among classrooms and schools. For example, two effective teachers can develop a topic in very different ways and still have successful outcomes. One may use direct instruction (showing and telling) to establish ideas of growing plants or writing poems while the other uses inductive thinking (discovery) with several experiments so that children arrive at the same understandings. Successful classrooms use a variety of models, and successful teachers understand how to apply different models, techniques, and strategies when appropriate.

Children attending our schools today will work in a different world tomorrow, and that world means increased diversity of interests, abilities, cultures, and ways of working. Effective schools will prepare children to live productively and contentedly in that new world.

Barriers for Effective Schools

Some schools do less well than others in supporting educational opportunity. Problems may exist only in certain areas, or they may range throughout the curriculum, administration, and school life. Impediments to learning come from such things as inappropriate curriculum, negative teacher attributes, bias, problems in physical facilities, and community forces such as special interest groups, defensive attitudes, and dangerous streets.

Inappropriate Curriculum. Educators occasionally miscalculate when selecting and implementing curricula. For example, when content doesn't relate to the developmental stages of children served or when material is redundant or too simplistic, a program falters. Some material may also be inappropriate because of social or cultural mores in a community.

Some teachers lack motivation and a sense of urgency about education. They excessively repeat material or resurrect old material and keep students "busy" with worksheets unrelated to the day's activities. Large segments of time can be absorbed in mindless tasks that go nowhere. Children quickly tire of repetition and make excuses for avoiding work. The myth of "boring" school thus becomes reality.

Negative Teacher Attributes. While it is difficult to accept the notion that teachers can be less than helpful, from time to time it is true. Some individuals come to teaching for the wrong reasons, perhaps because they wish to dominate situations, have children look up to them, or enjoy expounding. Such individuals rarely fulfill the requirements of guide, director, or supporter of learning and may overlook children's needs or misunderstand children's perceptions of concepts being addressed.

At times, a teacher's personality does not support learning situations. Brittle and demanding personalities logically do not serve children, nor do indifferent, sarcastic, or introverted temperaments. It is paradoxical that persons with these characteristics wish to be in a helping profession, but we do meet them once in a while.

Bias and Prejudice. Our society still struggles to shed the problems associated with racism, ethnocentrism, elitism, and sexism, and these qualities regrettably still affect some schools. Perpetuating stereotypes in monocultural schools is a problem; stereotyping restricts everyone's social competence. The situation becomes worse in ethnically integrated schools if hints of bias and careless use of ethnocentric language appear. The same can be said of coed schools when sexist language is used. When demeaning language surfaces, minority persons are affronted, their aspirations suffer, and children's growth in social competence is diminished (Comer, 1988; Sadker, Lerner, & Sadker, 1999). For all persons involved, bias is costly.

Problems With Physical Facilities. Limited physical facilities, while sometimes adaptable by creative people, become burdensome for inexperienced teachers. Poorly lighted buildings, poorly ventilated areas, and a badly maintained school become difficult to work in and are dangerous and depressing. Rooms too large or too small for instructional activity are a problem; poorly arranged materials contribute to confusion.

Poor and inappropriate equipment does not serve a facility well, since maintenance is always high and use is unpredictable. In addi-tion, sometimes machines and supplies are stored at a distance from classrooms, requiring unneeded traffic and additional time spent in securing equipment and moving materials about a building. For example, one Chicago principal secured a grant to buy 12 computers for an early literacy program at her inner-city school. The machines were fitted with programs for young children to use in creating stories.

The objective was excellent, and first and second graders enjoyed using the new equipment, but the logistics of scheduling became a burden. The computers were housed in one secured room to prevent theft. This meant that eight groups of children had to be scheduled to travel en masse to and from the room once each day. Time with each group was spent leaving the classroom, traveling to the computer lab, waiting for the previous group to finish, and moving in for the 22-minute period.

Minority children's social competence is diminished when unwelcome messages are given to minority parents.

The problem of trooping about the building and everyone's sensing insufficient time to actually work on the computers depressed enthusiasm for the literacy program. A better plan would have maintained the computers on mobile carts, assigned one or more to each primary classroom for individual use during the regular school day, and secured the equipment at the end of the day.

Special Interest Groups.   Special interest groups can be advocates and sources of support for schools. Groups formed to lobby for school funding or to increase interest in a new building are positive in impact. However, some special interest groups are formed, as in the following vignette, to counteract school projects or to prevent curricula from being implemented.

🍃

A group of parents and other interested persons in one Texas community organized themselves as a self-appointed school review committee. When they reviewed the reproduction-of-creatures unit for the second-grade classrooms, the books and charts used became a highly charged topic. The group's complaints about the material became intense, and the committee visits to the school caused confrontations and wild charges. One teacher resigned because of accusations, and emotions dragged on for weeks before the administration abandoned the unit. Even though the unit had been developed in previous years and had been accepted by the health education committee, a militant anti-sex-education group spread dissension. Community and school working relations were set back considerably for more than a year.   🍃

Censorship of books is a common occurrence in school districts throughout the United States (Sutherland & Arbuthnot, 1991). Too often schools acquiesce to pressure from spe-cial interest groups to abandon certain resources; then programs can suffer in scope and purpose.

Other   Challenges.   Community   violence can spill over into schools. Weapons are carried to school by too many children who seek to protect themselves, prey on others, or maintain status in a peer group (Jenkins & Bell, 1997). Whereas some schools have been considered safe havens from distressful conditions in a neighborhood, too often this haven is savaged by intrusions, bullets, and intimidations from gang activities. Weapons have an unsettling effect on any school climate, but in the hands of secure teachers, the trauma resulting from witnessing violence can become a part of the school curriculum. One teacher, trying to resolve fears in a Baltimore neighborhood experiencing periodic violence, used story writing and sharing to deal with children's anxieties and to help the children understand about precautions and safety measures (Notar, 1992).

Changes in Schools

Schools in the United States are always evolving. New building plans, new procedures, new equipment, curriculum innovations, and new strategies appear on a regular basis. Adjustments appear that seem serious or far-reaching at times, but in fact schools change very slowly (Bennett & LeCompte, 1990; Webb et al., 1999).

It takes time for a school staff to adopt a new method of teaching: New materials are needed, inservice must be arranged, and teachers need to be convinced of the method's efficacy. Even though some teachers implement a new plan, the school as a whole often lags behind. Consider the phased-in "writing to read" program in the following vignette.

🖉

In fall 1991, a New Jersey school system set up a "writing to read" workshop. Two second-grade teachers from Elwood Elementary (in the school district) were interested in trying the new plan immediately, and their experiment encouraged them. The two gave glowing reports at faculty meetings the following spring, but only one third-grade and one first-grade teacher agreed to try the next year. Halfway through the year, the first-grade teacher supplemented her program with basal readers, and her evaluation of the experiment was iffy. With heavy urging, two more teachers agreed to experiment later that year. At the end of 3 years, only half of the primary teachers in the building were involved. Although most evaluations were positive, the principal still wondered how she could increase participation. It took 5 years and repeated reports of success before most of Elwood's primary teachers adopted the program.

🖉

Schools change faster socially than they do academically. Neighborhoods can change quickly in urban and suburban areas, and the cultural and socioeconomic mix can alter demographics in a school within a few years. Many U.S. schools have experienced this phenomenon in recent years (refer to the demographic changes discussed in chapter 3). For many reasons, a large number of schools are less successful today than in previous decades. Achievement results, SAT scores, school attendance, the rising amount of school-identified disabilities, and crime and other social problems have alarmed many. The result has been a host of studies and evaluations to assess what is happening in U.S. education.

National Reports and Assessments

A number of task forces representing various interests have conducted national studies to identify problems in U.S. education. Some offer recommendations to correct the problems they find. Some results have to do with school practices and curriculum, but many have implications for huge changes in society at large regarding health care, prevention of substance abuse, correcting violence, changing U.S. attitudes, and so on. Some studies also include new plans for teacher preparation.

A Nation at Risk.   In 1983, the National Commission on Excellence in Education (NCEE) produced the warning *A Nation At Risk* (NCEE, 1983). The study identified the following indicators of risk: (1) higher illiteracy in the United States, (2) decreasing achievement in school, and (3) lack of preparation for military and business careers. The commission found four aspects warranting concern: content, expectations, time, and teaching. These findings, while considered "a thunderclap across the landscape" (Bell, 1993, p. 593), were hardly revolutionary—educational leaders had known of them for years. The report did succeed, however, in energizing discussion of the issues. Regrettably, attracting public attention to education concerns has been the only significant outcome (Fordham Foundation, 1998; Lund & Wild, 1993). Little improvement in achievement, teacher preparation, or time in school had been documented 10 years later (Bell, 1993; Lund & Wild, 1993). And in the late 1990s, criticisms were still appearing (Bennett, 1998; Crump, 1999; Rodriguez, 1997).

A Nation Prepared.   The influential Carnegie Forum on Education and the Economy (CFEE) (1986) followed the Commission on Excellence with a report focused on changing the preparation of teachers. The report, *A Nation Prepared: Teachers for the 21st Century,* quickly affected programs in the United States and inspired the American Association of Colleges for Teacher Education (AACTE) and individual state certification offices to recast accreditation standards. Using a purely economic rationale, the Carnegie Forum concluded that a constructivist curriculum directed by more intellectually skilled and empowered teachers was the only way the United States could retain its competitive edge in a global economy.

The objective was to ensure that schools produce students "who have the tools they need to think for themselves, people who can act independently and with others, who can render critical judgment and contribute constructively to many enterprises, whose knowledge is wide ranging and whose understanding runs deep" (CFEE, 1986, p. 20). The forum recommended the following to accomplish this objective (CFEE, 1986):

- Create a National Board for Teaching Standards.
- Restructure schools to provide a professional environment for teaching, allowing teachers to decide programs and holding them accountable.
- Set up a new plan for lead teachers to provide leadership in schools.
- Require a bachelor's degree in arts and sciences before study for teaching.
- Develop an education curriculum for a master of arts in teaching.
- Bring more minorities into teaching careers.
- Relate incentives for teachers to student performance and provide technology, services, and staff needed for teacher productivity.
- Make salaries competitive with other professions.

Government Action. The accumulation of education reports prompted both the Bush and Clinton administrations to address the problems perceived in U.S. schools. Their initiatives grew out of several annual conferences of governors.

The Bush administration in 1990 advanced *America 2000: An Education Strategy*

(U.S. Department of Education, 1991), a formula for addressing the large problems in the country's education. The objectives were very sound and desirable (refer to the listing in chapter 2), but the means for implementation were not clear. Authorities generally applauded the plan and asked for the time, money, and training to bring about the goals. At the end of the Bush administration, the plan remained as it had started—a desirable goal statement.

The Clinton administration followed in the footsteps of the previous plan, and the Goals 2000: Educate America Act in 1993 extended the *America 2000* plan to add family involvement (U.S. Department of Education, 1993). Even though the administration has steadily emphasized social reconstruction, implementation of the principles to achieve Goals 2000, except in a few states, remains in the beginning stages.

The awareness of difficulties and needs in the United States has reached high levels. Problems with schools and student achievement continue to worry many, but movement is slow (Bennett, 1998). Colleges and universities have only started to redefine programs, and federal action is still at the report level. In fact, federal financing for educational programs actually decreased for the decade ending in the mid-1990s (Lund & Wild, 1993). On a positive note, some communities have started experimental programs, which do provide models for use (U.S. Department of Education, 1994). As this text goes to press, significant bipartisan support for major federal support of education appears imminent. Renewed focus and funding for enhancing education seems near.

Evaluating Schools

Nationwide, the present state of U.S. schools appears fairly stable (Lund & Wild, 1993; Rose & Gallup, 1998). Phi Delta Kappa's annual sur-

For effective schools, assessors will answer yes for most of the following questions:

1. Is consonance of philosophy found among board of education members, administrators, and teaching staff members, as well as aides and volunteers?
2. Are school facilities adequate?
3. Is the school facility maintained and serviced well?
4. Is space used appropriately and efficiently?
5. Does continuity of content and concepts exist between grade levels and from home experiences?
6. Are collaborations between home and school evident?
7. Do children evidence achievement in social and academic skills through their practices and activities?
8. Do teachers show a command of various teaching strategies and techniques?
9. Are teaching techniques varied for different children?
10. Are children constructively engaged in projects, in follow-up activities, or in application of ideas? Or are they nonfocused, disruptive, glancing about, wandering from place to place?
11. Is time off task kept to a minimum?
12. Do children evince various levels of thinking as they work and investigate?
13. Is a pleasant climate for learning and enthusiasm noticeable?
14. Are children allowed opportunities to interact with others and grow in social relationships?
15. Do teachers display command of several teaching models (direct instruction, discovery learning, roundtable discussion)?
16. Are teaching approaches sensible and realistic for the particular classrooms?
17. Do teachers praise and encourage learners and value different contributions to classwork?
18. Do all children succeed from time to time?

Figure 12–2   Assessing Schools for Effectiveness.
Source: Adapted from Doll, 1995; Good & Brophy, 1996; Joyce & Weil, 1996; Rich, 1992.

vey even shows some gains in public attitudes about America's schools. In regard to particular areas and projects, we find amazing success stories (Thompson, 1993). In others, such as in most inner cities, polls show conditions, services, and outlooks deteriorating badly (Garbarino, Kostelny, & Dubrow, 1998; Kotlowitz, 1991).

Figure 12–2 presents questions that professionals may wish to use when evaluating the effectiveness of a particular school. The items will reveal much about a school's effectiveness, adequacy, and chances for success. An effective school will display positives for most features indicated.

The quality future school will emerge from the connections among homes, schools, and communities as they become complementary and supplement all school objectives. But educational change and enhancement affect more than academic achievement. Also linked to school success are changes in health care, improved living conditions, improved interethnic relations, and diminished crime in neighborhoods.

EFFECTIVE COMMUNITIES

Because communities are made up of sets of subsystems, research on competent communities is problematic. It is difficult to determine cause-and-effect relationships within a community, especially those that affect children. Also, such terms as *community* and *neighbor-*

hood are not yet perceived as important refer-
ents by authorities in child development
(Bronfenbrenner et al., 1984; Garbarino &
Abramowitz, 1992), and this means less attention to this third social setting.

Substantial research is available on the effects of community on family health and prosperity and school attainment (Bronfenbrenner,
1995; Bronfenbrenner et al., 1984; Quint,
1994). For instance, communities with consolidated health services support prenatal and
perinatal situations better than those without
such consolidation. Researchers identify a
number of features of more promising communities, irrespective of economic base, that can
be linked with children's educational achievements.

Community Organization

Formal community organizations that we find
almost everywhere are health services, welfare
and social services, religious institutions, civic
services, businesses, and media. Informal organizations that develop but are far less obvi-
ous are (1) special interest groups and (2) the
social networks that individuals and families
form.

Health Services. Children must remain
healthy to develop properly, yet access to a
health care system depends on the community
children live in and on the economic status of
the family. It is well documented that poor
families have greater health problems, including chronic health problems, more infectious
diseases, higher incidence of low-birth-weight
babies, and higher infant mortality rates (Children's Defense Fund, 1998).

The effective community will have comprehensive care systems striving to serve citizens impartially. Many communities have
both neighborhood health centers (such as
those funded through the Office of Economic
Opportunity) and a private health care system.

By uniting family care offices in one setting,
officials diminish the expense, frustration, and
transportation problems that poor families experience when seeking services.

In addition to offering health care, all medical facilities have an educating function. Important features of health services include distributing materials about disease prevention
and counseling by personnel who are positively oriented to their clients.

Welfare and Social Services. While directed primarily at those in poverty, welfare
and social services are relevant to the larger
community. Employment offices, legal aid offices, and counseling centers cut across socioeconomic levels and are needed in addressing
concerns for most U.S. communities. Regrettably, welfare services in the United States
have always carried a stigma, and only in recent years have programs such as Head Start
led to changed attitudes and the welcome involvement of middle-class citizens.

As with health care, accessibility of social services is a key to their use. Media,
local directories, and interagency referrals are
the normal channels for distributing information on services, and word of mouth is of
considerable importance. One Florida community established a family services office in
its new elementary school. An active director
and proximity of services led to teachers'
reevaluating the types of services available
for families and children. Increased accessibility brought more parent visitors to school,
and all persons involved showed a greater
acceptance of the need for and benefits of the
programs.

Religious   Institutions. Churches, synagogues, and mosques are central facets of
many communities. While less so in recent
decades, religious associations have dominated large portions of community life in the
United States. In fact, they represented the

largest part of the out-of-home activity for pre-20th-century Americans.

National surveys reveal a drop in religious participation for recent decades (Lindner, 1998), but still more individuals belong to church-related groups than to any other voluntary grouping. Religious institutions continue to influence many segments of U.S. communities, promoting ethnic as well as theological identity. With outreach programs and social action objectives, many houses of religion now provide social, cultural, and other support for their communities as well as spiritual nurturance for their membership groups. Food pantries, soup kitchens, and drug abuse and family counseling services are all operated by or through religious organizations in thousands of communities. Many care programs are not-for-profit arrangements developed and maintained by local religious organizations, even in the smallest communities. All these features boost the social welfare of communities.

Civic Services.   All communities require fire departments, sanitation programs, and public safety offices. Supported by tax revenues, these services provide for the general stability and safety of the community.

Community services provide an educative function for children. What goes on in those

Children understand the meaning of organized community and the interdependence of community residents when they encounter friendly civic officers.

departments, how the jobs are done, and the problems workers encounter are of interest to all children. Most offices publish materials and have personnel who head information programs for schools and other local groups. Children learn to understand the meaning of organized communities and the interdependence of community residents. They learn how community services affect their lives and perform for them as individuals.

Businesses.   Most communities contain private commercial enterprises linked to daily life in those venues, such as filling stations, newsstands, and mom-and-pop grocery stores that we find in nonindustrialized suburbs. (The so-called hypermarts are both replacing these businesses in many communities and retaining their function as informal links in the lives of community residents.) Other communities contain factories, wharves, large merchandise outlets, and financial and information-processing establishments that employ residents and give a flavor to the community. As children become acquainted with local businesses, they become knowledgeable about economics of their town—where people work, what they produce, and where products go. They also learn of the need for many specialties as they become attuned to the world of work and the effects each institution has on community life and interaction.

In effective communities, commercial establishments cooperate with schools and families. Such cooperation demonstrates commitment to the interdependence of community settings and to the need for mutual support. (Refer to chapters 9 and 11 for discussion of techniques and models for such collaboration.)

Media.   With the explosion and transmission of knowledge in the information age, communities are engulfed with media of all kinds. From standard newspapers through television programs to the Internet, visual and aural messages descend in increasing amounts across the United States. Whether in an isolated prairie town or an urban neighborhood, the impact of media is all-encompassing.

Media affect all other institutions of a community. The type, quality, and amount of information an area receives produce responses from individuals, families, and schools. Effects can be positive or negative, but they are rarely neutral. Since most media are protected under First Amendment provisions, media outlets are largely self-policing, and public acceptance of the products determines the boundaries for individual distributors.

Appropriateness of media products is a significant issue when we consider children's education. Many publications and recordings are adult oriented in topic, format, and relevance, but children are nonetheless exposed to large amounts of them. The V-chip for television and Internet filters such as "KidWatch" will block only a fraction of adult material. Media products that fall outside a community's standard invite thoughts of censorship, and problems always surface when that issue is raised. It is therefore desirable for communities, through public forums, to reach consensus on acceptable quality and then to work for that standard through educational programs and lobbying efforts when required.

Strictly speaking, adults can withhold from children only those materials prohibited by law. This means that all adults working with children must educate them about appropriate and inappropriate materials. Reasonable objectives for media can evolve through the work of churches, civic associations, schools, and neighborhood groups. The effective community is knowledgeable about its media, the effect the media have on residents and the sentiments of its citizens.

Special Interest Groups.   In the late 20th century, the United States witnessed the formation of numerous special interest groups, from the small group of citizens seeking to exert pressure on schools to include or exclude something to the highly organized lobbying groups seeking changes in legislation. In general, a **special interest group** has a particular cause and stance (e.g., antinuclear energy, save the whales, antipornography, pro-choice or pro-life regarding abortion). Many groups disappear after accomplishing their mission; others become entrenched because their cause is ongoing.

Special interest groups are grassroots associations and are very American in concept. Taking as their basis the constitutional amendment protecting association and assembly, citizens come together to work for or against something. In this way, altruistic groups have formed to gain privileges for disenfranchised persons, such as the education for persons with disabilities legislation started in the 1970s, or to highlight a public problem, such as cleaning up the Nashua River (Cherry, 1982). Other groups form to oppose regulations or practices. A nonsmoking lobby is one example; a group censoring local library materials is another.

When a special interest group is headquartered in a particular community or the issue that concerns the group is present in the community, the group's presence is clearly felt. The resulting campaigns will affect many community establishments, in particular, media, political offices, and schools.

How do communities respond to special interest groups? If partnerships are in good working order, we normally find that special interest group pressure can be accommodated and processed in a healthy fashion. All too often this is not the case, and a part of the community bows to the pressure of the campaigning group. For example, one Pennsylvania library contained several volumes on cults and pagan rituals. When a member of a PTA subgroup saw these volumes, the group started a search through the library to identify and condemn all volumes containing information about the occult. Having no agency and little organization to counter the arguments of the

group, library staff quickly acquiesced to the demands and removed all offending materials. This established a dangerous precedent for library materials in this community. The campaign ultimately removed even children's fantasy books featuring ghosts and goblins.

Social Networks.   The informal, everyday contacts of relatives, neighbors, friends, and colleagues produce social networks for adults and children in almost all neighborhoods. These groupings, which can cross gender, age, and socioeconomic status lines, provide enormous support for individuals.

Positive Adult Groups.   Social science research shows the importance of friends and relatives in providing exchanges of goods and services as well as psychological support (Coleman, 1991). Werner and Smith (1992) and Cochran & Davila (1992) indicate that support groups are especially important for at-risk families for providing emotional support to adults for child raising, confronting adversity, and integration into the community. Healthier adult groups mean healthier environments for children. Information about social services, work opportunities, or new resources in a community is often delivered through the social networks of adults, and this benefits children.

Children's Peer Groups.   Children's social networks, often called **peer groups,** are natural and can have desirable results, although at times certain combinations may become destructive (Berndt & Ladd, 1989; Harris, 1998). The effect on a community may be extensive when children associate in groups. Loosely affiliated groups of children often tour malls and parks, visit businesses, and play games with pleasant and positive results. Other groups may harass citizens and damage property.

Children's contacts beyond the home are necessary as children mature, and the emotional support and exchange of information within networks are powerful influences for all

Assessors will find most of the following characteristics in effective communities:

1. A workable health care system available to all income levels
2. Social programs, health facilities, and health offices clustered to maximize usage and cut logistics
3. Community programs designed to educate as well as serve
4. Religious institutions participating in community life and demonstrating concern through social action programs
5. Religious associations that nurture children's ethnic and spiritual identities
6. Municipal service departments that are stable, well maintained, and available for educational visits
7. Commercial enterprises that welcome visits and conduct information sessions
8. Commercial establishments that see adopt-a-school plans as an enhancement to the business
9. Media producers who realize the effects of mass communication and who responsibly produce material appropriate for young children
10. Communication between media outlets, schools, and community agencies regarding available media
11. Special interest groups responsive to community questions about their objectives and policies
12. Positive social networks in evidence (social gatherings, block parties, community clubs)
13. Social clubs for children (sports programs, scout programs, 4-H clubs, seasonal recreational facilities)
14. A populace interested in community schools, in neighborhoods, and in individual children

Figure 12–3 Assessing the Competent Community.

children (Cochran & Davila, 1992). When conducted in supervised and constructive ways, peer groups are essential for adequate socialization and maturation and offer opportunity for many educational insights. Through networks, children learn physical skills for games, such as baseball, hopscotch, or jump rope, and develop negotiating skills when settling disputes.

Healthy communities recognize the presence of social networks and endorse the formation and continuation of groups of individuals. Effective communities also have ways to monitor children's social networks and to steer them in constructive ways (see Figure 12–3).

EFFECTIVE PARTNERSHIPS

Schools as Brokers for Social Settings

When viewing the three major social settings in children's lives, we can see the overlap and interlocking nature of curricula for any one

child. One sees areas of effectiveness in each setting and their relation to outcomes for children's lives. These connections, however, do not necessarily form the three settings into a partnership or any type of collaborative venture. No requirement exists in any community for collaboration, and institutions do not collaborate unless an agent appears and serves as catalyst.

Groups and communities should not wait for the fortuitous appearance of persons who will engineer collaborations. We have one institution now that can provide the incentive and stimulus, and that has the position and requisite skills to best solicit effective social settings in which children prosper. That institution is the school.

This position means that schools must prepare themselves with information and background, establish a plan for making connections among the social settings, and implement that plan. It is hard and extensive work,

Children learn physical skills in games but also develop negotiating ability when settling disputes with their peers.

involving the commitment of instructional staff and administrators who must redefine their own roles and work piecemeal to get consensus among all forces in the community.

One required change is in thinking about what schools are for. The traditional view of teaching has been remediative, that is, filling in the knowledge gaps and developing skills. For too long, schools have thought of the communities and the families with which they work as possessing "deficits" that must be overcome or accommodated. Schools can no longer consider themselves as compensating for inherited faults and inabilities. Schools must now articulate the roles that communities and families can and should bear and devise ways to steer, guide, and collaborate with them to best accomplish these roles.

What would it take to effect such a plan? First, school personnel must be educated in the ways of collaboration, and teachers must work hard at "figuring out" the community served to discern steps and approaches necessary to accomplish the job. Schools may then use their broker position to farm out responsi-

bilities and then address the findings that concern the in-school lives of children served. To start a true collaborative plan is a major effort for most communities. Leadership is essential, and the steps will most likely be taken slowly. But involving families and the community must begin somewhere (see the Implications for Professionals section for a beginning step).

Programs for Teacher Preparation

Empowered school staffs are needed for any plan based on partnerships and collaborations, but we have too many unprepared for the challenges. First, present staff members in most schools will need to rethink their role. New teacher programs must include work in sociology of education, work with volunteers, work with adult learners, collaboration as a skill, and internships with social agencies or community organizations. This implies a very different teacher preparation program and emphasis, and universities must attract the most talented candidates for these roles. Collaborating schools of the future will require fewer teachers, but the core staff must be skilled as-sessment people who are able to program and unite efforts. Few courses exist for this partic-ular focus. One effort was started a few years ago at Wayne State University (Kaplan, 1992).

IMPLICATIONS FOR PROFESSIONALS

Think of yourself filling a new niche in the home-school-community matrix. Then think about how it would unfold.

When approaching the classroom, newly empowered teachers will think of themselves as "at-home" Peace Corps workers who ana-lyze situations and then figure out how best to serve the population with which they find themselves. For example, starting with the lit-eracy skills, teachers will ask themselves, "Where are students in their reading and writ-ing development?" When that assessment/di-agnosis is accomplished, they will meet with parents or others, conduct demonstration lessons, and confer on objectives and ways to attain them. They will use suggestions and ideas that people present about resources in the community that can be used beneficially to enhance or illuminate any subject matter, proj-ect, or skill area. For instance, a teacher's class might accept an invitation to the area water treatment plant to learn about its operation and effect on the community. The group of helpers would plan the trip and study the site as a place for learning. Then later, the teacher would use cooperative learning and coaching skills to help students reason out the benefits of the treatment plant. Finally, the teacher would use literacy skills to describe the treat-ment plant for parents, other school students, and community members.

This is one simple collaboration on a so-cial science project, but this partnership ac-tivity would be followed by others as the school becomes a refocused institution with new teaching strategies. The partnership no-tion replaces the school where teachers wel-come groups of children and teach by distrib-uting books, conducting a reading lesson, as-signing a writing lesson, then proceeding to the next subject. As we pointed out in chapter 8, students and teachers in traditional schools consume large amounts of time in classroom protocols, for example, lining up, moving to and fro, collecting papers, and distributing and collecting books while focusing on one item. Ritual-filled classrooms exist all over and teach little beyond what each child is motivated to seek. The time has arrived to move beyond these time-consuming, tightly structured schools.

SUMMARY AND REVIEW

We have defined effective families, schools, and communities as those entities in which children have maximum opportunities to grow, develop, and prosper. We have dis-cussed effective social settings and provided examples of effective settings working well.

General guidelines exist by which you may examine families, schools, and communi-ties, assess the social settings you encounter, and ascertain how each measures up to stan-dards of effectiveness. Imperfect settings exist for different reasons, many beyond the reach of educators acting alone. Providing individ-ual support in areas where deficits exist is an option, and some professionals have at times been able to give that support. The best resolu-tion for most deficits lies in linking the strengths of all social settings.

The road to stronger relationships is made easier when each social setting is effective in itself. When this is not the case, professionals look for ways to pull together to help children. Each setting affects the others, and the strength of one always bolsters another. The school must be the place where such interac-tions are coordinated. Schools need to become the brokers for new learning communities, which can thrive in the contributions of all three institutions.

SUGGESTED ACTIVITIES AND QUESTIONS

1. Relate the assessment lists in Figures 12–1, 12–2, and 12–3 to, (1) a home you are acquainted with, (2) a school you know well, and (3) the community in which you live or work or attend school. What profiles do you find? Which setting seems strongest?

2. Assume now that you are to be the director of a new collaboration involving the three settings. As the school administrator, what will be your three greatest challenges in establishing a collaborative effort?

3. Describe the hypothetical competent family of a 6-year-old child. Describe a less competent family for another 6-year-old. Speculate how you could use your knowledge of the competent family to assist the less competent one.

4. Imagine that you are working on a new home-school-community collaboration. An official from your state board of education is visiting to view your district's new plan. Develop an outline of your working partnership to show the visitor how the three social settings support each other.

RESOURCES

Books

1. Hart, B., & Risley, T. R. (1995). *Meaningful differences in the everyday experiences of young American children.* Baltimore: Paul Brookes Publishing.

2. Berns, R, M. (1997). *Child, family, school, community: Socialization and support* (4th ed.). Fort Worth: Harcourt Brace.

Films/Videos

1. *Raising healthy kids: Families talk about sexual health.* (1997). [Video, 30 mins]. For parents of young children. Shows importance of parent/child communication and deals with issue of parent as child's primary sexuality educator. Media Works.

2. *Nutrition for infants and children under six.* (1994). [Video, 30 min]. A program on nutritional needs for three specific stages of development. Cambridge Educational.

Organizations

1. Children's Defense Fund (www.childrensdefense. org/) 122 C street, NW, Washington, DC 20001

2. Council for Exceptional Children (www.cec.sped.org/) 1920 Association Drive, Reston, VA 21091

3. Federal Interagency Forum on Child and Family Statistics (http://childstats.gov/) Washington DC 20402

Websites

1. http://www.ncrel.org/sdrs/areas/teOcont.htm. Pathways to School Improvement site gives articles, forums, and links for using up-to-date information on schooling.

2. http://nea.org/ The site presents an overview of the major teacher association plus publications, reports, and statistics on U.S. schools.

Chapter 13

Working Together

If we are to achieve a richer culture, rich in contrasting values, we must recognize the whole gamut of human potentialities, and so weave a less arbitrary social fabric, one in which each diverse human gift will find a fitting place.

(Margaret Mead, 1935, p. 297)

🐦

Much is right with U.S. educational experiences in spite of some glaring and well-publicized problems. Education planners and policy makers in most communities have both a suitable base to build on and numerous models to draw from to bring about improvements and viable partnerships. The future will be positive for children's education if citizens can build on the processes and worthwhile creations already in action. This final chapter addresses the issues for working together. In reading this chapter, you will learn the following:

1. Collaborations among families, schools, and communities entail several levels, or stages, of involvement.

2. Certain conditions enhance the growth of partnerships, and other factors present barriers to forming good working relationships and collaborations.

3. Six particular criteria demonstrate the status of partnerships, and we can use them to design new collaborative ventures.

4. Both bottom-up and top-down approaches can succeed at bringing families, schools, and communities together.

While seldom using the term *collaboration,* residents in rural and urban communities have always had ways of influencing the upbringing of their youngest citizens. In the following vignette, a teacher recalls her childhood years in a poor rural community of the 1930s and indicates directions that would serve us well as we begin a new century.

🐦

A minister, the school principal, and the town's mayor frequently discussed educational problems, recommended solutions, and showed great concern for our community's children. Their efforts were supported by local parents. A party-line telephone system, whereby most families could listen in, aided their communication. For example, one child, late coming home from school on a spring day, was easily found, reprimanded by a passerby, and sent on his way with knowledge that the parents at home would follow through on the reprimand. Children who needed clothes and extra food were identified at school, and with the support of "town fathers," teachers and sometimes others visited the homes. Food, clothing, and other resources were found and delivered, and at times, negligent parents were counseled. Teachers taught formal lessons in the schoolrooms, but they often walked home with us, continuing our education as they pointed out and discussed nature about us. The community was our playground, and adults who were present supervised the children. Older children educated younger ones in many skills and safety rules. One could feel this was a cohesive community and one marked by caring. It was, of course, not an ideal system: A few children didn't reach their potential, and one child didn't even survive. But an overarching support system enhanced opportunities, and of 13 children in my first-grade class, all completed high school, and 7 went on to college.

🐦

The narrator of the preceding vignette demonstrates how parents, schools, and community members all assumed responsibility for children's development. Times were simpler then, and many communities were more closely knit than now, but the lesson of communal caring and the need for shared expectations are still valid today. Author James Comer lived in a close-knit urban community during his childhood, and he tells of a similar collaboration of the social institutions that cared for him. In *Maggie's American Dream: The Life and Times of a Black Family,* Comer (1988) recalls his parents, neighbors, and teachers reinforcing each other's goals for children's engagement in learning. The process in Comer's case wasn't formal, either. Individuals in each social setting seemed to understand each other's roles. In both stories, neighborhood children whose parents were sympathetic to the school's goals were more successful than were children whose parents were out of touch.

Society at the beginning of the 21st century is different from that of several decades earlier. It is harder to establish common objectives where social institutions can work effectively together. Families have new worries and heavier burdens, and children have fewer advocates. In many situations, schools have assumed more of the educative, counseling, and social oversight for children (Kearney, 1999), but from many accounts, it is apparent that schools cannot effectively do the job alone (Benson, 1997; PFIE, 1999). The most disturbing fact in the United States is that our society seems to annually write off as dispensable a large fraction of its youth, condemning them to lives of dysfunction and nonproductiveness (Kotlowitz, 1991; Osofsky, 1998).

Some accounts show that different outlooks have appeared in our nation's communities in recent years. A significant number of professionals and laypersons speak convincingly that education is much more than school buildings, books, and daily schedules. We find a growing recognition that lifestyle diversity and multiculturalism are here to stay and that it makes sense for all residents to pull together in making communities more liveable and schools more productive (Partnership for Family Involvement in Education, 1999).

Amid the high hopes and vision for redoing the educational landscape, practical considerations sober us; we know that change comes slowly. Some workers will have to settle for small victories. But small steps can be beneficial; they represent building blocks. For example, getting cooperation and involving parents and community associations in building playground equipment for a North Carolina school helped hundreds of citizens in that community become familiar with and interested in school functions. Getting local businesses involved in science and math projects for third graders in a rural Michigan town pulled education very close to the lives of many citizens. Small steps do provide a base.

In this chapter, we offer recommendations for working together. We first discuss the levels of involvement in partnerships and then examine experiments that are under way in two different communities. The authors revisited the two communities in 1999 to examine the progress of those family-school-community partnerships that were started in the early 1990s.

LEVELS OF INVOLVEMENT IN COLLABORATIONS

Partnership relations are built on basic premises about leadership, participation, and involvement (Rigsby, 1995). Good collaborative efforts mean that individuals in any group must recognize different levels of involvement. For persons involved in a collaboration, there is always a hierarchy of involvement

(Epstein,1999; Henderson et al., 1986; Wissbrun & Eckart, 1992). Some will participate at a minimum level, others at an associative level, and still others at a decision-making level. Though educators are in the best position for encouraging and establishing partnerships, some teachers, parents, and community members will assume stronger leadership roles while others will contribute at minimum levels.

Understanding Involvement

Laypeople interpret parental and community involvement in school affairs in different ways. Some citizens are proactive and feel naturally connected to their schools. A larger group continues to view teachers as having total control of children's education and either do not seek involvement or feel shut out of the process. This latter group tends to view schools from afar, but its members are often critical when their children don't progress well or they feel that tax dollars are being misspent. This view, of course, contributes very little of substance and generates even more isolation. All educators have a duty to work on attracting this part of the constituency and seeking more participation.

So, how much involvement is productive? Different programs will call for differing amounts of involvement, and generally, participatory intensity varies with level. Most parents and community members can be involved in some school activities; only a few will be present and involved with other in-depth educational matters. The key to successful collaboration is for almost all community citizens to be involved at one level or another, with a few individuals contributing at all levels.

Minimum Level. Teachers and school administrators reach out to parents and community members in various ways, seeking support for school programs. This has been the case for several generations. For example, children have homework that teachers request parents to supervise. The homework might involve interviewing neighbors or finding information about different community businesses. Teachers expect that parents and other community members will respond to these requests and help them with the projects.

The community at large is normally invited to school-sponsored events for which teachers often seek assistance. For example, parents and community members often help make costumes for school plays or props for exhibits. Schools have various fund-raising events, including bake sales, fairs, and sales of particular products. Again, school personnel seek cooperation from parents and others in the community to attend, contribute items to, and support and help with the events. Teachers also seek cooperation from parents and various agencies as they collect materials for children to use in school projects. Calls go out for such items as egg cartons, juice cans, and carpet samples.

The preceding are all examples of minimal involvement, and most readers will recognize and recall similar events from their own childhood. Such minimal involvement is commonplace, it serves a definite purpose, and it is a good foundation from which to start working for more complete participation.

Children benefit from this type of involvement from homes and community. They are drawn into the practical stages of education and often see the application of schoolwork to the real world. The more persons involved, the greater the benefits to children. Successful collaborations mean that a large percentage of parents and community members are involved with their schools at this beginning level.

Associative Level. Some parents and schools seek more than minimal participation. Many teachers request parents and community members to become classroom volunteers on a

Teachers and children benefit when volunteers assist on a regular basis in the classrooms.

regular basis. Volunteers assist teachers in various ways—from making and copying materials for classrooms to reading with children and assisting them in activities. Some volunteers tutor children who have difficulty with assignments, and others assist in the library or school office. Still others become room mothers (or fathers), organizing other community members, helping to supervise children on school trips, or making calls to solicit different kinds of classroom support. Some volunteers become involved in enrichment programs where they offer their special expertise with children in a classroom. In one primary school, a choral director organized the primary-school-age children into a singing group to develop a program of Christmas music that

the children performed at several community functions during the holiday season.

At the associative level, community members also participate in local organizations that support schools. Parent-Teacher Association (PTA) chapters have traditionally supported schools as parents and teachers cooperated in school improvement ventures. At times, PTAs center on fund-raising events; at other times, they may become a political force in the community to improve conditions for children. In one Virginia community, when the school board decided to eliminate some kindergarten positions, make remaining kindergarten classes larger, and transport extra children to nearby schools, the PTAs at these schools banded together to protest the decision. Board members, recognizing the opposition, found other ways to cut their budget.

PTAs and similar organizations have served as advocates for school plans and have at times interpreted curriculum for community members. Still other groups have been responsible for arranging parent education classes and parent support groups. Such actions draw schools closer to their parent and community groups, creating significant communication links.

Children benefit from involvement at the associative level; expectations are clearer, and communication is facilitated. Stronger ties mean stronger programs, and divisiveness is far less likely when schools and communities enjoy this level of interaction. At any point in time, fewer parents will be involved at the associative level than at the minimal level. Comer (1980) notes that if 5% to 10% of parents become actively involved at this associative level, that number makes up an adequate

group as long as it represents a cross-section of the community.

Decision-Making Level.   The third level of parent and community involvement in schools is the decision-making level. At this level, individual parents, businesspersons, professionals, and community leaders assume the right to make decisions for the education of the children.

Parent participation works with little controversy at the minimum and associative levels of involvement. Teachers and school administrators are still in charge of all educational decision making, and parents and community members assist and support the decisions. However, when parents and others become involved in decision making, friction can emerge. Controversy that paralyzes is, of course, not in the best interests of children. Therefore, successful collaboration of parents, teachers, administrators, and community

Figure 13–1   Three Levels of Involvement.

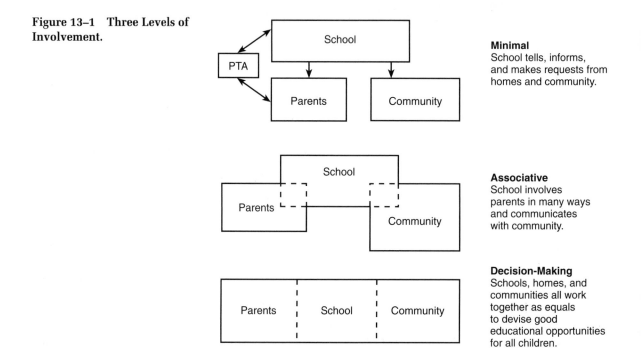

Minimal
School tells, informs, and makes requests from homes and community.

Associative
School involves parents in many ways and communicates with community.

Decision-Making
Schools, homes, and communities all work together as equals to devise good educational opportunities for all children.

members at this level requires mutual respect and a new definition of shared responsibility and accountability (Bloom, 1992; Comer et al., 1996; Wissbrun & Eckart, 1992). Acting at this level requires hard work.

Parents at the decision-making level move beyond being committed advocates for their children into sharing responsibility for providing quality (school) education for their own and other children. They serve on curriculum and other educational committees, identifying goals and objectives and deciding how to achieve them. At this level, parents are expected to serve on committees that hire school staff. They also might assist in forming advocacy groups to secure necessary local, state, or federal funding so that local schools can provide programs important to the community.

Usually, parent and community involvement at this level requires only a small percentage of parents, but these representatives *must* represent the different constituencies within the community. Such involvement dictates changes within the school hierarchy, and such changes can be detrimental unless teachers, administrators, parents, and community members work carefully and with genuine mutual respect to bring gradual change (Comer et al., 1996). Gradual change that steadily enhances school programs is by far the most productive. Figure 13–1 illustrates the collaborative relations of each level of involvement.

ACHIEVING PARTNERSHIPS

In chapter 11, we discussed program models showing that true collaboration does emerge when properly nurtured. These model collaborations took time to build and take even more time to monitor and fine-tune to stay healthy. As such models show, the effort is worthwhile, and the reported educational benefits to children and communities are inspirational. Anyone interested in achieving partnerships for their schools should carefully examine estab-

lished programs. Information about the sustainability of these programs is helpful for beginners developing their particular plans.

In the remainder of this chapter, we consider two communities that are struggling with collaborative efforts. We have adapted Davies's (1993) six criteria for assessing collaborations as a template for viewing the stages of development in each community. These descriptions provide a reasonable guide for the processes that communities move through when forming partnerships with schools and parents. Stated as imperatives, the criteria are as follows:

1. Neutralize bureaucratic resistance to change.
2. Reinvent community.
3. Provide support for families.
4. Integrate educational and social services.
5. Involve those affected by change.
6. Base policy and practice on research.

Woodland: A Rural Situation

This New England community of 4,000 people has a stable population and long traditions. Ethnically, the town is almost totally Anglo-American, but pronounced economic differences appear for the residents. You could say that the community consists of haves, have-nots, and a few have-some-things in between. All citizens use the town's services. Individuals greet each other daily and hire and consult each other but live in quite separate worlds.

Differences have become more intense in recent decades as affluent families continue to send sons and daughters to college, develop land, and generally live pleasant lives. The have-nots have suffered more from a deteriorating local industry and the distress, reduced wages, and anxieties that accompany it. More than those of the haves, their lives are beset

with divorce, substance abuse, single parenting, and diminished living conditions. Lacks
in education nudge almost all young people
from the lower economic level into the limited
service and manual labor jobs in the area. The
result is frequent unemployment, welfare dependence, and substandard housing.

Disparities between the groups appear in
community schools. Little segregation by class
is evident, but the existence of cliques is apparent. Participation in social functions,
sports, and cultural activities is similarly lop-
sided. Teachers adjust to these conditions and
observe protocols for both subgroups but are
candid about the growing school failure rate
for the have-nots.

Woodland, however, has witnessed some
change through grassroots efforts. Several
years ago, reports of lower achievement scores,
students' failing college entrance exams, and
parents' sending children to private schools
became the impetus for several community
groups to take action. Individual groups have
designed various programs for helping to improve conditions for area children. The local
school board authorized a community planning committee to proceed with developing
long-range goals for schools. As need for a new
elementary school building became apparent,
a communitywide committee began to devise
plans. In response to literacy needs, a large
volunteer community group started to serve
children and parents in new ways: delivering
books to infants and toddlers, reading to children at school, providing storytelling hours at
libraries and in homes, offering literacy programs for adults, and assisting children with
homework during after-school programs. One
group of volunteers has for several years offered summer camp experiences for children.
A group of parents who thought their school
was "gloomy" organized to repaint the foyer
and provide bulletin boards for displaying
children's work. When materials for artwork
and dramatic presentations ran out, a local

church group collected and organized art materials for teachers. Organizations with volunteer help now support the school with several
projects, including art appreciation, integrating arts into the curriculum, and special art
classes for gifted and talented students.

For the most part, social services and health
agencies still work separately from the schools,
but several projects now unite social and medical services with school projects. Volunteers
read to children while mothers wait at the local
clinic for medical and social services. Social
services personnel have begun to work with
teachers and community volunteers both during school and in after-school programs. Local
businesses have organized an educational
foundation that solicits and invests money to
fund creative activities. Ironically, Woodland
has high community involvement without any
systematic approach for developing partnerships. No leadership really unites the efforts.

Although this groundswell of concern and
interest exists, lethargy and resistance are still
found in many quarters. Attitudes of parents
and teachers with respect to one another
change slowly. Many parents still feel alienated from the local schools and still avoid contact. Most community officials feel comfortable with the status quo and resist different
ways of operating. To make matters worse,
with so many programs emerging in the
schools, some teachers have started to feel that
the school doesn't belong to them.

The preceding vignette describes a situation several years ago, but the authors have revisited the area to seek updates. While some
good news was shared, on the whole, the vignette description remains in place. Two
things stand out as stimulating growth. First,
the community has received two modest
grants to explore early-education (preschool)
objectives. These again were community efforts, but school personnel have been drawn

into the planning and evaluating of some of the new programs for preschoolers. The second event is the construction of a new consolidated school building. This project has brought nearly 100 people into close working relationships as they have studied and planned educational events to sell the idea of a school, get input on design and new programs, and seek general community support. For the most part, efforts have paid off well in connecting good workers and giving an esprit d'corps for the total community. It is hoped that many community members will remain with the curriculum committee, facilities-use committee, and others. Woodland has not slipped backward. In fact, the town appears to garner positive press coverage for its recent efforts, and working relationships seem in good form for the next several years.

With more leadership from community officials and school administrators, the community could flourish in the bottom-up flow of interest that has begun. Many individuals are now engaged at the associative level of involvement with minimal invitation from school personnel. Using Davies's (1993) criteria, we speculate in the following subsections about outcomes that could evolve for Woodland's budding partnerships.

Neutralize Bureaucratic Resistance to Change. Though only a slender community government exists, resistance to change in Woodland is still difficult to overcome. In any new project, the first task always is convincing school personnel, families, and community that change is needed. Strong leadership is needed to forge ahead, and a school board member or key school administrator could be the pivotal person.

Even without one strong leader, Woodland has made good progress as it grapples with building a new consolidated school to open in 2000. The study groups working for the past 2 years have made good progress in involving school board members, school personnel, and local citizens. The town government has not as yet evidenced enthusiasm for any development,

As community members work to improve schools, an esprit de corps engenders enthusiasm and commitment.

and sentiment still exists for "the typical is good enough." The following are ways of coping with, if not neutralizing, resistance to this change:

- Continue to publish figures on current school statistics, (e.g., achievement scores and needs survey results.)
- Publish alternatives for the present programs by focusing on other emerging school programs.
- Search more vigorously for leaders within the community and solicit ideas and input.
- Continue to notify citizens about ways to get involved.
- Intensify the scheduled information-sharing sessions that have produced positive feedback.
- Sponsor research to portray the weaknesses and strengths of different alternatives.

Reinvent Community. The patterns of past generations are still at work in any community, even though needs do change. In Woodland, an influx of new residents with different experiences and ideas about education has caused differences in expectations. Community study groups have started to redefine inclusiveness in this community, and whereas miscommunication was reinforcing resistance a few years back, much less is evident now.

Rediscovering community may be more appropriate in this case. Different family groups have worked together recently, but their work must move beyond the superficial links if a new sense of community is to emerge. New residents have found a voice in the community's future through new school building work. Their contributions and opinions on community development, school curriculum, and participation in this process have produced some results. But families who have lived in the community for generations must be given a voice; little is observed as yet in this area, and no plan is evident.

Establishing cross-group committees is one way to bring a diverse agenda of desires and hope into the open. The community will need to develop workshops so that the different groups learn strategies for communicating. Establishing common goals will help clarify community beliefs concerning what to teach and how to educate all children. The community must consider seriously the future of all its young citizens, since a large number of them will remain in the town to be future leaders and contributors.

Provide Support for Families. Some families in Woodland desperately need social support. While crime and abject poverty are rare, some families live a hand-to-mouth existence that has become a lifestyle. The results are low aspirations and high dependency. Immediate gratification in the form of fast cars, ATVs, and unhealthy substances dominates the interests of many.

Woodland is making progress through its early-education initiative, but more steps are needed to assist young families to embrace this. Community members must continue to study family needs and then build on their strengths. The early-education grants for coordinating activities to improve confidence and aspirations have been a positive start. Information for determining family needs may be obtained in the following ways:

- Additional anonymous questionnaires (the first is already 3 years old)
- Telephone or home interviews with sample families
- Analysis of local government records
- Small focus groups within the community that have similar particular interests and expectations

Information gathering can be offensive to residents, and volunteer groups working on early education seem to have avoided most pitfalls. Making clear the intention for gather-

Small focus groups within a community share particular interests and expectations.

ing information, being respectful of parents, and demonstrating that their ideas will be heeded will, one would hope, be continued as groups expand their community efforts. Evidence of cultural values and strengths will normally emerge when information is gathered with care. Planners must incorporate these values and strengths into any developing support systems.

Several projects already started in Woodland build on family strengths. A nutritional program demonstrates the value of different foods and how variety in preparation provides interest in healthy eating. Another project, a family reading program, gets quality books into the hands of new parents. The commu-

nity's preschoolers receive gift books as a strategy to inject books into family life, and one criterion for selections is that books reflect the cultural patterns of the community. Offshoots of the plan call for young mothers and their children to gather socially to discuss interests in the books and how they use them. A related objective is to develop a writing program in which young mothers relate stories of their own lives to their children.

Several projects are under way as a result of information gathered through a local Women, Infants, and Children (WIC) program. One is a new regional mental health project that is poised to render support for needy families. Another includes workshops and adult education offerings that have started recently as a result of citizen requests.

Additional support for families, particularly young and struggling families, has emerged through efforts of the projects working on early education. Results are positive, but continued effort is needed to bring all families to participate in the life of their town. The Woodland school district, which continues to stand apart from family connections, must pull its families closer to school operations. The parent education program started by the community group has opened up very positive practices for young families, and this could and should be continued by school personnel. A parent center in the new school would be a logical and very helpful follow-up for the preschool plan already started.

Integrate Educational and Social Services.
In spite of many community activities to enhance children's education, true partnerships do not yet exist in Woodland. The minimal social services presently available have only a small connection with the school and other educational endeavors. The feeling in the community has been that these services must be separate, that there is no logic to combining them. However, researchers now realize that social services linked to schools have much greater chances for success (Dolan, 1995). All communities can strengthen their disparate activities, and Woodland has a small beginning with the medical, dental, and developmental screenings started 2 years ago by the early-education project.

The new building presents a marvelous opportunity for the community to integrate a social services center within the school itself. Social services such as counseling, abuse prevention, GED programs, nutrition, and job training are logically housed in the local educational facilities. Much of the work overlaps and can be coordinated for recipients. In the Woodland school, space has been provided,

but little evidence of plans for staffing or coordinating appears.

In Woodland, some projects are beginning to be linked through a single coordinator. A social services coordinator who works with community people and teachers administers nutrition programs in the schools, the WIC program at the community health center, volunteer reading programs, and a community program for involving children in gardening. Local businesspeople have started to contribute in the area by providing resources and welcoming students for field trips. When services are linked, open decision making follows readily.

Involve Those Affected by Change.
Seemingly, in a small town, most citizens would and could be involved in change. After all, the New England town meeting is the true example of grassroots democracy. Sadly, in Woodland, only about 10% of the residents attend and participate in town government meetings or hearings. Many feel that town affairs are already out of their hands and their voices will not be heard. Community principals must persuade residents to learn about participation.

In Woodland, the immediate goal is to consolidate the work of many people. The first step is to secure strong leadership committed to establishing school, family, and community group links for all the various programs. School personnel should be the arbiters and promoters for developing and supporting this leadership, but that does not seem to be the case. The recent building project was a welcome change for school and community involvement. Progress was made, but more workshops would enhance leadership and communication skills for all persons involved.

A partnership team has not emerged in Woodland, but if it did emerge, it would consolidate so much activity and interest already in progress. One would hope that all members would recognize such a team's authority and be committed to assuming their responsibility, including assisting in communicating to the public the many activities that support community involvement and the benefits accruing to children. When grassroots programs proliferate as they have in Woodland, one great risk is burnout of teachers, parents, and volunteers. A partnership team would serve as a filter to prevent overlap, as different parent, community, and school organizations sponsor new initiatives, and as a support group for fledgling programs, overseeing their assessment and evaluation. The team's final responsibility would be to communicate school successes resulting from collaborations.

Base Policy and Practice on Research.

Often political and educational organizations are estranged from researchers. The irony is that both camps are often looking at the same phenomena, and each has part of the answer to questions that arise. Politicians reason through situations and act on hunches, while educational researchers study circumstances and then experiment. Of course, situations improve best when each agency cooperates and values the viewpoints and findings of the other.

School and community leaders have much to gain by using information gathered by quantitative and qualitative researchers, but in Woodland, outside researchers are viewed with suspicion. Local residents operating on hunches, knowledge of community, and common sense are viewed as more credible than people with charts, calculators, and questionnaires. One can see that educators must move carefully to raise the perceived value of research efforts. In the past two years, Woodland schools have hired well-known speakers to develop brief workshops. The quick-fix objectives were not really accomplished, yet considerable funds were used. So, what is needed is a team to evaluate circumstances first and then to decide how effective consultants can be.

If a true partnership becomes established and the assessment process begins, the Woodland partnership team can easily secure information regarding changes within the schools. Then, as schools in the community seek new methods of assessing their work, it would be logical to conduct other research. We believe that if the first five criteria are met, in all likelihood this last area of a new partnership will emerge.

Big City: An Urban Situation

Little change in physical appearance and demographics (except new expressway development) had come to Big City in the 3 years since the authors last visited. The one major development is in one particular program. This major U.S. city has a varied population, a tradition of strong leadership, and a history of economic ups and downs. As in all large cities, great affluence exists in some areas and abject poverty in others. The ethnic mix varies considerably from one part of the city to another, but overall, the population is typical of most large urban centers today. We focus our discussion on School District 5, which still typifies many large U.S. cities at the turn of the new century.

Big City has a large welfare budget, which is kept completely separated from all school affairs. Different city agencies working with the same family groups in District 5 almost never collaborate. However, Big City has a reputation for moving rapidly on projects, securing funding for experiments, and managing events well. The can-do attitude permeates the city government to a point where schools and other city agencies are brought along as silent partners. While the management shows efficiency, it is a paternalistic style allowing for little involvement of citizens and subgroups, and this always depresses school renewal.

District 5 includes slightly less than 100,000 people, mostly of African American and Anglo-American descent, plus small numbers of recent Hispanic and Asian immigrants. The district is almost totally residential, and family incomes range from below the poverty level to middle income. Some redevelopment has started in two areas, but on the whole the district is made up of older homes in long-established neighborhoods. Most civic associations throughout the area also are traditional in nature. Two new schools have been built recently, four others were done over 12 years ago, and some are still much older establishments. Elementary school curricula throughout the district are traditional, although there is some experimentation, and several schools have attempted closer connections with students' families.

The regional superintendent's office in District 5 now has an interim superintendent, but ideas of the predecessor appear to be continuing. The former superintendent had attempted to move away from traditional curriculum and had championed the cooperative learning ventures at several schools and the school-family partnerships at two others. Other program innovations had received considerable support, and a number of personnel felt that the district was progressing, though most middle-level administrators demonstrated less concern. One interesting new development is the establishment of a Comer School Development Program in Demo School, which had enjoyed several years of success delving into school-family partnerships.

District 5 is in an interesting stage. From prior administrations, most personnel have more than fleeting knowledge of cooperative efforts between homes and schools. In fact, several major studies on school partnerships conducted in the city schools have received national recognition, but many administrators have short terms to serve until retirement and give only lip service to new endeavors. Coupled with a constant battle to maintain adequate school budgets, this has produced slow reform on home-school-community work.

The district population continues to be about 60% African American, but other minorities have pushed the overall minority population for school students to over 75%. The district has a good record in race relations, although schools are segregated by income. Two elementary schools contain over half of all the Anglo-American children in the district, and one of these schools reflects middle-class values. Parts of District 5 have high crime levels; nightly violence and constant police surveillance seem a fact of life in many neighborhoods.

Considerable change has come to Demo School with its dedicated principal. Two years in a Comer plan has intensified activity. And while all agree that progress has come, staff changes have burdened the school's three administrators and the teachers. The principal has installed a parent council that meets to consider school problems and develop community outreach programs. Parent and community representatives are noticeable in the school, and local support for any new program or project is bestowed lavishly. Innovations were applauded by the former regional superintendent and appear to receive continued support from the interim. While middle-level support is ambiguous, the overall effect at Demo School is enthusiasm. One other school has some similarities, but for this one school in District 5, change is noticeable and the effects are promising. For some other parts of the district, old procedures and a stifling bureaucracy remain in place.

We now consider Davies's (1993) criteria for establishing school and home connections with regard to District 5.

Neutralize Bureaucratic Resistance to Change.
Two superintendents in recent decades tried to decentralize management of

schools in Big City, and they fostered new thinking about communication with communities and parents. Modest success appeared in several districts, but headway on site-based management has not been extensive in recent years. Research studies carried out in several schools have kept district personnel cognizant of efforts in partnership. Teachers and administrators are familiar with the language of cooperation, and most are acquainted with positive results in schools that have experimented. However, even with the former regional superintendent's objectives for innovations, bureaucratic resistance continues in many central offices of the district.

Demo School established itself as a partnership model 6 years earlier, showing that change in school-community relationships is possible; the innovation was even transplanted to one other school. The arrival of a Comer plan has produced even greater publicity for the school.

District 5 has always maintained itself adequately, and there is little groundswell for change. Its problems are not as intense as elsewhere in Big City, and many educators feel comfortable with preserving the status quo. The several small projects, like Demo School, that foster cooperative work are heralded as pacesetters. It appears that the district is pleased to have them as representatives but opts out of the work needed to emulate them. District 5 must still be judged as modest in neutralizing resistance to change at present. The district could flourish with cooperative ventures if new leadership continues the process started several years back.

Reinvent Community.   District 5 has made reasonable progress in race relations. Demo School is situated in the poorest section of the district and has succeeded in reinventing a community that now supports school programs, with which citizens collaborate. While still at the stage of minimal to moderate in-

volvement, school personnel have clearly demonstrated how productive work with a community can be in setting up parent groups and gaining confidence of community members.

Mothers, fathers, and extended family members regularly visit the school and participate in supportive ways. Demo School has developed a parent volunteer group to support teaching projects and uses parents as short-term substitutes in classrooms. Area residents, working with the principal, have successfully brought immunization clinics to the school for neighborhood children. Strides have been made in valuing and promoting education, especially among residents of low-income homes. Parent skills are acknowledged in newsletters, on bulletin boards throughout the school, and in school presentations. A feeling of joint purpose pervades this low-income school community. Two near tragedies (shootings at the school, though not connected to the school program), have cast tension on the normally spirited action. Placement of police in the school has resulted in frequent identification checks, and the normal free in-and-out quality is subdued. However, the positive school-community relationships permitted the local violence to be processed in a healthy fashion. In fact, more interest in community safety is evident.

Reinventing community has been a success in Demo School, but a sister school only several blocks away has an almost opposite quality. No parents visit unless summoned, and no joint school-home activities are developed. Most of District 5, in spite of the progress at Demo School, seems locked in a period of partnership stagnation. Community in District 5 has been only partially reinvented when we assess it.

Provide Support for Families.   Supporting families means sustaining them emotionally as well as financially, and these separate objectives rarely come together in Big City. With the

344 Chapter 13 Working Together

exception of families at Demo School, family members in the district keep their social welfare and school affairs far apart. Big City school administration and welfare offices have not established any arrangement to bring two or more city services together.

To focus on children's total "curriculum"—children's experiences at home, in the community, and at school—requires treating all conditions as a single global issue, with the parents at the heart. Supporting parents means uniting services and helping parents make decisions for their children. Most District 5 school personnel know little about the neighborhoods and the children who live there— where they go and what they do after school. Such lack of knowledge is neither helpful nor supportive, and changes must begin within the educational bureaucracy.

In contrast, the principal at Demo School is a strong leader. From the beginning of her tenure she has trained, organized, and supported teachers in the school's new vision for reaching out to families. She initiated a family center in the school and invited parents to join her and other teachers in discussing their children's needs. Early discussions took place over coffee with one or two parents and a teacher. These parents were instrumental in getting other parents involved. At present, we find high parental involvement in the school, and the neighborhood takes great pride in the changes in enthusiasm and skill development of its children.

Integrate Educational and Social Services.
Big City is replete with bureaucracy, extending to all offices and agencies within the urban

Police monitoring in schools subdues enthusiasm, but a stronger community commitment for safety is demonstrated.

boundaries. To bring about even modest change requires reinvention of agency processes. As noted, District 5, except for the few integrated services at Demo School, has little connection to community resources. The gaps among city agencies, even while serving the same populations, keep operations, records, and budgets entirely separate. Each time a service is rendered, both the agency personnel trying to meet family needs and the recipients of benefits must travel to where those services can be found. Misunderstandings abound in these circumstances, and children are left with few advocates.

In Demo School, the parent council succeeded in convincing two city agencies to provide services within the school for community families. The principal found office space and provided a family service coordinator who serves as an advocate for children and families. A computer program, which lists family needs and services provided, helps the coordinator keep up-to-date. This major step has brought considerable publicity to Demo School and has caused exploratory plans in other district schools.

Involve Those Affected by Change.
As noted, the former regional superintendent was committed to change and reinforced collaboration with families and community agencies. However, preserving the status quo is an underlying priority for many in the schools. At Demo School, parents have been involved in deciding about integration of city services and have served as representatives in meetings with other city agencies. All agree that involving the persons affected by change is healthy for this school, but similar concern does not appear elsewhere in the district.

Curriculum matters and assessment procedures are a different matter. In District 5, as elsewhere in Big City, parents and community members are rarely involved in reviewing curriculum, to say nothing of evaluating teachers

or employing new staff members. Demo School, where parents are welcomed into school life and involved as volunteers, has moved only slightly in this area. Only recently has a start been made to validate the input from parents in selection of programs. Most teachers still wish to reserve curriculum decisions for themselves. The final step of giving decision-making power to those affected is moving slowly in District 5.

Most of District 5 has a long way to go in bringing parent and community groups into educational planning and participation. Currently, there are few demands for a community voice in school matters, and this gives educators more time to consider the wisdom of moves to increase outside involvement. But the picture is not completely bleak in the district, and the modest experiments at Demo School and its sister school do provide a positive background. As Davies (1993) notes, "It is much easier to plan, execute, and evaluate programs for [others] than it is to involve the clients or the end-users from the beginning in all aspects of change" (p. 71).

Base Policy and Practice on Research.
District 5 has had numerous funded projects associated with nearby universities that were directed at curriculum study and school organization. Research endeavors are common in most of the area schools, and school personnel are quite sophisticated in accommodating experiments and discussing projects. The district has significant experiences in research and a wealth of information to draw on. Administrative and community attitudes toward research appear positive.

As in other school districts, however, positive attitudes and involvement in research do not necessarily translate to implementing the findings of successful projects. This is the case in most of District 5. Findings from some studies carried on within the district have been published nationally, but with the exception of Demo School, few basic changes have been made. The energy and leadership to push for implementation, particularly at middle levels of school administration, appears to be a prime missing ingredient. A large part of Demo School's success in basing policy and practice on research comes from the interest and strong leadership of the new principal. This is a testament to the fact that leadership undergirds almost all program success in schools today.

Assessing the Partnership Experiments

The two examples described in this chapter show the particular school districts in a state of "becoming." The follow-up visit several years later found only modest changes. The authors found in both cases some progress in each area for bringing schools closer to their natural allies—the home and the community. But complete linkage is yet to be for both Woodland and District 5.

What will it take to bring real change? Both school districts portrayed are typical across the United States. Woodland is an interesting example of bottom-up influences—the agitation for change resides in the community and in homes. Nearly all improvements have come from the population served. Here is a community that has discovered, in a naive fashion, the value of partnership and has started to agitate for more involvement before the school department has discovered its potential. Recent events stemming from community grants and a major building project appear to have harnessed the interest of a significant number of people. The community is poised to make dramatic strides if more pieces fall into place.

In District 5 of Big City, the opposite situation, one of top-down influence, is the norm now and always has been. The leadership by a few administrators initiated and spurred the growth toward collaboration. The community

is placid and has never campaigned for involvement, but some school leaders see the benefits and have started to collaborate with the populations served. One is more pessimistic about the future of District 5, for initiative seems bound with a few charismatic and highly motivated individuals. When these individuals move on, the observer has a feeling that a lot of forward thrust will depart. Comer's assessment on the successes of collaborative ventures seems on target again; that is, one third flourish, another third will fail, and the other third muddles along (O'Neil, 1997).

Individual Responsibility

Even strong leaders cannot accomplish all tasks alone. They require the participation and cooperation of many people. All parents, teachers, and community members have a responsibility to become involved at the different levels of participation if the best rewards are to emerge. At a minimum level, just as some parents are active only in helping children with homework, there will be teachers who will limit their involvement to the traditional ways described in chapter 10. They will take advantage of the community programs that serve children's educational needs. Then some other teachers will seek more involvement as they plan their curriculum for parent and other volunteer support in the classroom. They will participate in workshops with parents and serve on committees with them as equal partners. And a few teachers will campaign hard for parents and community to be involved in decision making and will relish serving with them on partnership teams.

Realizing the dream of partnerships requires more than the effort exhibited in most U.S. school districts today. A spirit for undertaking change has germinated in many areas but seems slow to blossom fully. We all know that change takes time! The recent surge of interest at state and federal levels for partner-

Minimum level of involvement is shown when parents help their children with homework.

ships must be viewed positively. Publications, funding, and legislation all provide a fertile base for more collaboration.

When reading about model programs (refer to chapter 11), we can certify that those programs that included a research and assessment dimension have made great strides in reaching a new level of participation. We find from those model programs that exciting things happen when new ideas are introduced, nurtured carefully, and built as change mecha-

nisms. The results certainly reinforce the desirability of bringing more collaborative work to our nation's schools.

IMPLICATIONS FOR PROFESSIONALS

Partnerships can begin with a single teacher and parent collaborating in a classroom, although possibilities exist for enthusiastic colleagues and parents to expand all sorts of desirable educational programs in any school. When you affiliate with a program that is launching a collaborative venture, you will want to consider the following important steps.

When your team considers collaborations, first define your objectives and agree on what changes are necessary. It's wise also to find out how collaboration has worked for others. Your team will need to locate resources and decide how to assess the progress it makes. Bringing in new helpers and involving them in collaborative ventures always requires finesse. Communication is often a problem as more people become involved in collaborations. You and your teammates must be alert to how you are communicating and how your messages are being interpreted. Finally, you will want to first try out ideas on a small scale—and then expand the experiment.

As you continue planning for moving a larger school unit toward collaboration, other requirements appear. You'll want to keep the following requirements in mind for planning and implementing any larger-scale home-school-community partnership.

1. Community spirit for welcoming new ideas is primary. Success comes naturally when dedicated and committed people are working together to make a difference.

2. Proactive planners, leaders, and researchers must initiate, guide, and polish emerging plans for collaboration.

3. Financial resources, such as grants, must be available to subsidize pilot programs.

4. Interested citizens and community officials must commit to enacting and supporting partnerships. (Such people are often present, for most homes and communities wish for better connections to their schools.)

5. Educators must appreciate public input and want better communications with homes and community agencies.

6. Training and development programs must be available to nourish beginners and provide a background for new leaders. Too many programs erode when a strong leader leaves.

SUMMARY AND REVIEW

When schools are brokers for new learning communities and invest time and energy in forming links with homes and communities, exciting and productive results materialize. We have so much evidence that this is true. The work of James Comer in New Haven, the synthesis of Schorr's (1988) ideas in *Within Our Reach,* and the expansion of the League of Schools Reaching Out, to name but a few, show that we have both reason and compelling need for communities to reach further to obtain better functioning school operations.

New collaborations can mean reaching objectives by somewhat different routes and different rates. These different routes might take more energy, more careful planning, and more financial commitment, but a successful result means a far better and richer product. Even implementing the principles of partnerships in part of a school district eventually enriches the experiences of all district students.

Schools are still the catalysts in most new endeavors. No other social institution in the United States has the oversight or the trained personnel to serve in this capacity. Partnership programs may start with a few small projects, as in Woodland, or may grow from a well-conceived and well-directed program, such as that in District 5's Demo School. However it grows, a plan must call for teachers and administrators to be committed to the new practice. Being committed, gaining knowledge about other programs, devising a plan, establishing means for communicating the plan, and involving others are necessary to the success of any project.

If we are to achieve the type of social and educational change we advocate, we must find and nourish ways to make real the practices behind partnerships. This means setting aside some of the highly competitive stances that our society sponsors and working for the common good. Everyone will benefit, and the least fortunate will win a larger share.

SUGGESTED ACTIVITIES AND QUESTIONS

1. Talk with three teachers about parent involvement in their programs. Have them describe the things parents do when they come to school. To determine the stage of collaboration, relate their statements to the three levels of involvement discussed in this chapter.

2. Interview three parents to learn how they have participated in their children's school programs within the past year. What levels of involvement do you find?

3. Examine a school district with which you are acquainted to ascertain its stage of evolution in collaborative efforts. Does it resemble Woodland or District 5 in Big City? How does your district compare to the two examples in terms of economic status, administrative situation, and problems faced?

RESOURCES

Books

1. Comer, J. P., Haynes, N. M., Joyner, E., & Ben-Avie, M. (1996). *Rallying the whole village: The Comer process for reforming education.* New York: Teachers College Press.
2. Thompson, S. (Ed.). (1993). *Whole child, whole community.* Boston: Institute for Responsive Education.

Films/Videos

1. *Parentmaking Educators Training Program: A comprehensive skills development course to train early childhood parent educators.* (1996). [3 videos, 2 hr each, plus manual]. Focus is on parent educator training. Children's Health Council, Palo Alto, CA.
2. *Rethinking school organization.* (1996). [3 audiocassettes, 1 hr each]. Six authorities on schooling processes, parent involvement, and other educational developments. Agency for Instructional Technology, Bloomington, IN.

Organizations

1. Phi Delta Kappa (http://www.pdkintl.org/) 408 N. Union Street, Bloomington, IN 47402
2. Children's Rights Council (http://www.vix.com/crcl/) 300 I Street NE, Suite 401, Washington DC 20002
3. Council of the Great City Schools (http://www.cgcs.org/) 1301 Pennsylvania Avenue NW, Washington DC 20004

Websites

1. http://www.dac.neu.edu/ire. Institute for Responsive Education website. Contains extensive reports and publications on partnerships and collaborations.
2. http://www.resp-ed.org/html/reaching_out.html League of Schools Reaching Out website. Information on the projects of cluster schools and reform initiation.
3. http://www.cgcs.org. Council of Great City Schools Online. Presents information on the nation's large public school systems and their interschool projects.
4. http://www.classroom.net Classroom Connect has an online magazine for all levels of teachers and features online education programs.

Appendix

===== ❦ ❦ ❦ ❦ ❦ =====

Bibliography of Children's Books

If we are fortunate, we . . . belong to a small, more particular community, defined by ethnicity or kinship, belief system or geography. It is in this intimate circle that we are most "ourselves," where our jokes are best appreciated, our special dishes most enjoyed. These are the people to whom we go first when we need comfort or empathy, for they speak our own brand of cultural shorthand, and always know the correct things to say, the proper things to do.

(Dorris, 1993, p. 1)

❦

The following selected bibliography of children's books portrays a variety of American family structures where individuals are learning together in the home, the school, and the community.

H indicates that the book reveals children learning through the home environment.

S indicates that children from different family structures are learning together at school.

C indicates that different family members are sharing and learning from their community environment.

Different Cultures

Ashley, Bernard. (1991). *Cleversticks*. Illustrated by Derek Brazell. New York: Crown. **S**

Breckler, Rosemary K. (1992). *Hoang Breaks the Lucky Teapot*. Illustrated by Adrian Frankel. Boston: Houghton Mifflin. **H**

Bunting, Eve. (1993). *Someday a Tree*. Illustrated by Ronald Himler. New York: Clarion. **H,C**

Bunting, Eve. (1996). *Going Home*. Illustrated by David Diaz. New York: HarperCollins. **H,C**

Bunting, Eve. (1997). *Moonstick, the Seasons of the Sioux*. Paintings by John Sanford. New York: HarperCollins. **C**

Calhoun, Mary. (1996). *Tonio's Cat*. Illustrated by Diane Stanley. New York: Morrow Junior Books. **C**

Carling, A.L. (1998). *Mama and Papa Have a Store*. New York: Dial Books. **H,C**

Clifton, Lucille. (1974, 1992). *Three Wishes*. Illustrated by Michael Hays (1992). New York: Dell. **C**

Cohen, Miriam. (1989). *See You in Second Grade*. New York: Greenwillow. **S**

Cross, Verda. (1992). *Great Grandma Tells of Threshing Day.* Illustrated by Gail Owens. Morton Grove, IL: Albert Whitman. **H,C**

Crowley, Joy. (1998). *Big Moon Tortilla.* Illustrated by Dyanne Strongbow. Honesdale, PA: Boyd's Mills Press. **H**

Cummings, Pat. (1991). *Clean Your Room, Harvey Moon!* New York: Macmillan. **H**

DeVeaux, Alexis. (1987). *An Enchanted Hair Tale.* Illustrated by Cheryl Hanna. New York: Harper-Collins. **S**

Dooley, Norah. (1991). *Everybody Cooks Rice.* Illustrated by Peter J. Thornton. Minneapolis: Carolrhoda. **H,C**

Fazio, Brenda Lena. (1996). *Grandfather's Story.* Seattle: Sasquatch Books. **H**

Franklin, Kristine L. (1994). *The Shepherd Boy.* Illustrated by Jill Kastner. New York: Atheneum. **C**

Gardella, Tricia. (1993). *Just Like My Dad.* Illustrated by Margot Apple. New York: Harper-Collins. **H**

Garza, Carmen Lomas. (1990). *Cuadros de familia/Family Pictures.* San Francisco: Children's Book Press. **H,C**

Good, Merle. (1993). *Reuben and the Fire.* Illustrated by P. Buckley Moss. Intercourse, PA: Good Books. **C**

Hamm, Diane Johnston. (1991). *Laney's Lost Mama.* Illustrated by Sally G. Ward. Morton Grove, IL: Albert Whitman. **C**

Hartman, Wendy. (1993). *All the Magic in the World.* Illustrated by Niki Daly. New York: Dutton. **C**

Hoyt-Goldsmith, Diane. (1990). *Totem Pole.* Photographs by Lawrence Migdale. New York: Holiday House. **H**

Hu, Dakari. (1993). *Joshua's Masai Mask.* Illustrated by Anna Rich. New York: Lee & Low. **S**

Johnson, Angela. (1990). *Do Like Kyla.* Illustrated by James E. Ransome. New York: Orchard. **H**

Johnson, Angela. (1991). *One of Three.* Illustrated by David Soman. New York: Orchard. **H**

Kendall, Russ. (1992). *Eskimo Boy: Life in an Inupiaq Eskimo Village.* New York: Scholastic. **C**

Ketterman, Helen. (1992). *Not Yet, Yvette.* Illustrated by Irene Trivas. Morton Grove, IL: Albert Whitman. **H**

Kimmelman, Leslie. (1996). *Hooray! It's Passover!* Illustrated by John Himmelmun. **H**

Kroll, Virginia. (1994). *Masai and I.* Illustrated by Nancy Carpenter. New York: Four Winds. **C**

Levy, Janice. (1995). *The Spirit of Tio Fernando.* Illustrated by Morella Fuenmayor, translated by Terens Mlawa. Morton Grove, IL: Albert Whitman. **C**

London, Jonathan. (1997). *Ali, Child of the Desert.* Illustrated by Ted Lewin. **C**

Mandelbaum, Pili. (1990). *You Be Me, I'll Be You.* Brooklyn: Kane-Miller. **H**

Markhun, Patricia Maloney. (1993). *The Little Painter of Sabana Grande.* Illustrated by Robert Casilla. New York: Bradbury/Macmillan. **C**

McCloskey, Robert. (1952). *One Morning in Maine.* New York: Viking. **H,C**

Mac Donald, Suse. (1995). *Nanta's Lion: A Search and Find Adventure.* New York: William Morrow. **C**

McPhail, David. (1993). *Farm Boy's Year.* New York: Atheneum. **H**

Onyefulu, Ifeoma. (1995). *E Meka's Gift: An African Counting Book.* New York: Cobblehill. **C**

Ormerod, Jan. (1991). *When We Went to the Zoo.* New York: Lothrop. **C**

Pinkney, Andrea Davis. (1993). *Seven Candles for Kwanzaa.* Illustrated by Brian Pinkney. New York: Dial. **H**

Pinkney, Brian. (1994). *Max Found Two Sticks.* New York: Simon & Schuster. **C**

Polacco, Patricia. (1990). *Just Plain Fancy.* New York: Simon & Schuster. **C**

Pomerana, Marion. (1998). *The American Wei.* Illustrated by Anne Di Salvo-Ryan. Morton Grove IL: Albert Whitman. **C**

Pryor, Bonnie. (1996). *The Dream Jar.* Illustrated by Mark Graham. New York: Morrow Books. **H**

Quinlan, Patricia. (1987). *My Dad Takes Care of Me.* Illustrated by Vlasta van Kampen. Toronto: Annick. **H**

Saint James, Synthia. (1996). *Sunday.* New York: Albert Whitman. **H**

Smalls, Irene. (1994). *Dawn and the Round To-It.* Illustrated by Tyrone Geter. New York: Simon & Schuster. **H**

Sonneborn, Ruth A. (1970, 1987). *Friday Night Is Papa Night.* Illustrated by Emily Arnold McCully. New York: Puffin. **H**

Soto, Gary. (1993). *Too Many Tamales.* Illustrated by Ed Martinez. New York: G. P. Putnam's Sons. **H**

Stroud, Virginia A. (1994). *Doesn't Fall Off His Horse.* New York: Dial Books. **C**

Surat, Michelle Maria. (1993). *Angel Child, Dragon Child.* Illustrated by Vo-Dinh Mai. New York: Carnival. **S**

Villanueva, Marie. (1993). *Nene and the Horrible Math Monster.* Illustrated by Ria Unson. Chicago: Polychrome. **S**

Walter, Mildred Pitts. (1990). *Two and Too Much.* Illustrated by Pat Cummings. New York: Bradbury. **H**

Watkins, Sherrin. (1994). *White Bead Ceremony.* Illustrated by Kim Doner. Tulsa: Council Oak. **C**

Weiss, Nicki. (1992). *On a Hot, Hot Day.* New York: Putnam. **C**

Wells, Rosemary. (1991). *Max's Dragon Shirt.* New York: Dial. **C**

White Deer of Autumn. (1992). *The Great Change.* Illustrated by Carol Grigg. Hillsboro, OR: Beyond Words. **C**

Williams, Vera. (1990). *More, More, More Said the Baby.* New York: Greenwillow. **H**

Wright, Courtni C. (1994). *Jumping the Broom.* Illustrated by Gershom Griffith. New York: Holiday. **C**

Yamate, Sandra S. (1991). *Char Siu Bao Boy.* Chicago: Polychrome. **S**

Yashima, Taro. (1955). *Crow Boy.* New York: Viking. **S**

Divorced Families

Abercrombie, Barbara. (1995, 1990). *Charlie Anderson.* Upper Saddle River, NJ: Simon & Schuster. **H**

Baum, L. (1986). *One More Time.* Illustrated by Paddy Bouma. New York: Morrow. **H**

Binch, Caroline. (1998). *Since Dad Left.* Brookfield, CT: Millbrook. **H**

Boegehold, Betty. (1985). *Daddy Doesn't Live Here Anymore.* Illustrated by Deborah Borgo. New York: Western. **H**

Bunting, Eve. (1996). *Market Day.* Illustrated by Holly Berry. New York: Joanna Colter Books. **C**

Girard, Linda Walvoord. (1987). *At Daddy's on Saturdays.* Illustrated by Judith Friedman. Morton Grove, IL: Albert Whitman. **H**

Hazen, Barbara Shook. (1983). *Two Homes to Live In: A Child's View of Divorce.* Illustrated by Peggy Luks. New York: Human Sciences. **H**

Helmering, Doris W. (1981). *I Have Two Families.* Illustrated by Heidi Palmer. Nashville: Abington. **H**

Mayle, Peter. (1988). *Why Are We Getting a Divorce?* Illustrated by Arthur Robins. New York: Harmony. **H**

Rush, K. (1994). *Friday's Journey.* New York: Orchard Books. **C**

Stinson, Kathy. (1982). *Mom and Dad Don't Live Together Anymore.* Illustrated by Nancy Lou Reynolds. Toronto: Annick. **H**

Vigna, Judith. (1984). *Grandma Without Me.* Morton Grove, IL: Albert Whitman. **H**

Watson, Jane Werner, Robert E. Switzer, & J. Cotter Hirschberg. (1988). *Sometimes a Family Has to Split Up.* Illustrated by Cat Bowman Smith. New York: Crown. **H**

Weinger, Brigitte. (1995). *Good-bye, Daddy.* Illustrated by Alan Mark. New York: North-South Publications. **H**

Blended Families

Boyd, Lizi. (1987). *The Not-So-Wicked Stepmother.* New York: Viking Penguin. **H,C**

Boyd, Lizi. (1990). *Sam Is My Half-Brother.* New York: Viking Penguin. **H**

Hines, Anna Grossnickle. (1996). *When We Married Gary.* New York: Greenwillow. **H**

Jukes, Mavis. (1984). *Like Jake and Me.* Illustrated by Lloyd Bloom. New York: Alfred A. Knopf (Dragonfly Books). **H**

MacLachlan, Patricia. (1985). *Sarah, Plain and Tall.* New York: Harper & Row. **H,C**

Ransom, Candice F. (1993). *We're Growing Together.* Illustrated by Virginia Wright Frierson. New York: Bradbury. **H,C**

Vigna, Judith. (1980). *She's Not My Real Mother.* Chicago: Albert Whitman. **H,C**

Vigna, Judith. (1982). *Daddy's New Baby.* Morton Grove, IL: Albert Whitman. **H**

Willner-Pardo, Gina. (1994). *What I'll Remember When I Am a Grownup.* Illustrated by Walter Lyon Krudop. New York: Clarion. **H**

Single-Parent Household and Special Relationship With One Parent

Ackerman, Karen. (1994). *By the Dawn's Early Light.* Illustrated by Catherine Stock. New York: Atheneum. **H**

Bang, Molly. (1983). *Ten, Nine, Eight.* New York: Greenwillow. **H**

Bunting, Eve. (1994). *Smoky Night.* Illustrated by David Diaz. San Diego: Harcourt Brace Jovanovich. **C**

Clifton, Lucille. (1977, 1992). *Everett Anderson's 1, 2, 3.* Illustrated by Ann Grifalconi. New York: Holt. **H**

Cooper, Susan. (1993). *Danny and the Kings.* Illustrated by Jos. A. Smith. New York: Margaret K. McElderry. **C**

Greenfield, Eloise. (1988). *Nathaniel Talking.* Illustrated by Jan Spivey Gilchrist. New York: Black Butterfly. **H,S,C**

Haggerty, Mary Elizabeth. (1993). *A Crack in the Wall.* Illustrated by Ruben de Anda. New York: Lee & Low. **H**

Harrison, Troon. (1994). *The Long Weekend.* New York: Harcourt Brace. **C**

Lindsay, Jeanne Warren. (1982, 1991). *Do I Have a Daddy? A Story About a Single-Parent Child* (2nd ed.). Illustrated by Cheryl Boeller. Buena Park, CA: Morning Glory. **H**

Maury, Inez. (1979). *My Mother and I Are Growing Strong.* Illustrated by Sandy Speidel. Translated by Anna Munoz. Berkeley, CA: New Seed. **H,C**

Peterson, Jeanne W. (1994). *My Mama Sings.* Illustrated by Sandra Speidel. New York: HarperCollins. **H**

Rosenberg, Liz. (1993). *Monster Mama.* New York: Putnam Publishing Group. **H**

Saller, Carol (1991). *The Bridge Dancers.* Minneapolis: Carolrhoda. **H**

Say, Allen. (1989). *The Lost Lake.* Boston: Houghton Mifflin. **C**

Sharp, N. L. (1993). *Today I'm Going Fishing With My Dad.* Illustrated by Chris L. Demarest. Honesdale, PA: Boyd's Mill. **C**

Smalls, Irene. (1992). *Jonathan and His Mommy.* Illustrated by Michael Hays. Boston: Little, Brown. **C**

Steptoe, John. (1980). *Daddy Is a Monster . . . Sometimes.* New York: Lippincott. **H**

Tran, Kim-Lan. (1994). *Tet: The New Year.* Illustrated by Mai Vo-Dinh. New York: Simon & Schuster. **C**

Vigna, Judith. (1987). *Mommy and Me by Ourselves Again.* Morton Grove, IL: Albert Whitman. **H**

Waddell, Morton. (1994). *The Big, Big Sea.* Illustrated by Jennifer Eachus. Cambridge, MA: Candlewick. **C**

Adoptive Families

Bang, M.(1996). *Goose.* New York: Blue Sky Press. **H,C**

Banish, Roslyn, with Jennifer Jordan-Wong. (1992). *A Forever Family: A Child's Story About Adoption.* Photographs by Roslyn Banish. New York: HarperTrophy. **H**

Bloom, Suzanne. (1991). *A Family for Jamie: An Adoption Story.* New York: Clarkson N. Potter. **H**

Brodzinsky, Anne Braff. (1996). *The Mulberry Bird: An Adoption Story.* Illustrated by Diane Stanley. Indianapolis: Perspective Press. **H**

Cais, Sheridan. (1998). *Why So Sad, Brown Rabbit?* New York: Dutton. **H**

Cole, Joanna. (1995). *How I Was Adopted: Samantha's Story.* Illustrated by Maxie Chambliss. New York: William Morrow. **H**

Girard, Linda Walvoord. (1986). *Adoption Is for Always.* Illustrated by Judith Friedman. Morton Grove, IL: Albert Whitman. **H**

Girard, Linda Walvoord. (1989). *We Adopted You, Benjamin Koo.* Illustrated by Linda Shute. Morton Grove, IL: Albert Whitman. **H,S**

Kasza, Keiko. (1992). *A Mother for Choco.* New York: Putnam. **H**

Keller, Holly. (1990). *Horace.* New York: Greenwillow. **H**

Koehler, P. (1990, 1997). *The Day We Met You.* Old Tappen, NJ: Simon & Schuster. **H**

Lifton, Betty Jean. (1993). *Tell Me a Real Adoption Story.* Illustrated by Claire Nivola. New York: Alfred A. Knopf. **H**

McCully, Emily Arnold. (1994). *My Real Family.* San Diego: Harcourt. **H,C**

Pellegrini, N. (1991). *Families Are Different.* New York: Holiday House. **H**

Rodgers, Fred. (1995, 1998). *Let's Talk About It: Adoption.* Illustrated by Jim Judkins. New York: Putnam. **H**

Rosenberg, Maxine. (1984). *Being Adopted.* Photographs by George Ancona. New York: Lothrop. **H**

Turner, Ann. (1990). *Through Moon and Stars and Night Skies.* Illustrated by James Graham Hale. New York: Harper & Row. **H,C**

Foster Care and Orphanages

Bemelmans, Ludwig. (1939). *Madeline.* New York: Viking. **C**

Blomquist, G., & P. Blomquist. (1993, 1990). *Zachary's New Home: A Story for Foster and Adoptive Children.* Milwaukee: Gareth Stevens, Inc. **H**

Cannon, Janell. (1994). *Stellaluna.* San Diego: Harcourt. **H,C**

Carlson, Natalie Savage. (1957). *The Happy Orpheline.* Illustrated by Garth Williams. New York: Harper. **C**

Herbert, Stefon. (1991). *I Miss My Foster Parents.* Washington, DC: Child Welfare League of America. **H,C**

MacLachlan, Patricia. (1982). *Mama One, Mama Two.* Illustrated by Ruth Lercher Bornstein. New York: Harper. **H**

Steptoe, John. (1969). *Stevie.* New York: Harper. **H**

Multigenerational Households and Extended Families

Bauer, Marion Dane. (1995). *When I Go Camping With Gramma.* Illustrated by Allen Garns. New York: Bridgewater Books. **C**

Bunting, Eve. (1991). *Sunshine Home.* Illustrated by Diane DeGroat. New York: Clarion. **H**

Burden-Patman, Denise, with Kathryn D. Jones. (1992). *Carnival.* Illustrated by Reynold Ruffins. New York: Simon & Schuster. **H,C**

Casely, Judith. (1986). *When Grandpa Came to Stay.* New York: Greenwillow. **H**

Chiemruom, Sothea. (1994). *Dara's Cambodian New Year.* Illustrated by Dam Nang Pin. New York: Simon & Schuster. **H**

Choi, Sook Nyul. (1993). *Halmoni and the Picnic.* Illustrated by Karen M. Dugan. Boston: Houghton Mifflin. **S**

Coleman, Evelyn. (1996). *White Socks Only.* Illustrated by Tyrone Geter. Morton Grove, IL: Albert Whitman. **H,C**

Crews, Donald. (1991). *Bigmama's.* New York: Greenwillow. **H,C**

Dorros, Arthur. (1991). *Abuela.* Illustrated by Elisa Kleven. New York: Dutton. **C**

Flournoy, Valerie. (1985). *The Patchwork Quilt.* Illustrated by Jerry Pinkney. New York: Dial. **H**

Fox, Mem. (1989, 1994). *Sophie.* Illustrated by Aminah Robinson. New York: Harcourt. **H**

Guback, Georgia. (1994). *Luka's Quilt.* New York: Greenwillow. **H**

Heide, Florence Parry, and Roxanne Heide Pierce. (1998). *Tio Armolo.* New York: Lothrop & Shepard. **H**

Hoffman, Mary. (1991). *Amazing Grace.* Illustrated by Caroline Binch. New York: Dial Books for Young Readers. **H,S**

Howard, Elizabeth F. (1991). *Aunt Flossie's Hats (and) Crab Cakes Later.* New York: Clarion. **H,C**

Jones, Rebecca. (1995). *Great Aunt Martha.* New York: Dutton. **H**

Levine, Arthur. (1995). *Bono and Nonno.* Illustrated by Judy Lanfredi. New York: Tambourine. **C**

Lewin, Ted. (1998). *The Story Tellers.* New York: Lothrop, Lee & Shepard Books. **C**

Mathis, S. B. (1975). *The Hundred Penny Box.* Illustrated by Leo & Diane Dillon. New York: Viking. **H**

McCully, Emily Arnold. (1993). *Grandmas at Bat.* New York: Harper Collins. **C**

McFarlane, Sheryl. (1991, 1993). *Waiting for the Whales.* Illustrated by Ron Lightburn. New York: Philomel. **H,C**

Miles, Miska. (1971). *Annie and the Old One.* Illustrated by Peter Parnall. Boston: Little, Brown. **H**

Moore, Elaine. (1995). *Grandma's Smile.* Illustrated by Dan Andreasen. New York: Lothrop, Lee & Shepard. **H**

Nomura, Takaaki. (1991). *Grandpa's Town.* Translated by Amanda Mayer Stinchecum. Brooklyn: Kane/Miller. **H,C**

Polacco, Patricia. (1990). *Thunder Cake.* New York: Philomel. **H**

Polacco, Patricia. (1992). *Mrs. Katz and Tush.* New York: Bantam (Little Rooster). **C**

Poydar, Nancy. (1994). *Busy Bea.* New York: Macmillan. **H**

Reiser, Lynn. (1998). *Cherry Pies and Lullabies.* New York: Greenwillow. **H**

Rylant, Cynthia. (1985). *The Relatives Came.* Illustrated by Stephen Gammell. New York: Brandbury. **H**

Scheffler, Ursel. (1986). *A Walk in the Rain.* Illustrated by Ulises Wensell. Translated by Andrea Mernan. New York: Putnam. **H,C**

Simon, Francesca. (1998). *Where Are You?* Illustrated by David Melling. Atlanta: Peachtree Publishers. **C**

Swartz, Leslie. (1992, 1994). *A First Passover.* Illustrated by Jacqueline Chwast. New York: Simon & Schuster. **H**

Swentzell, Rita. (1992). *Children of Clay: A Family of Pueblo Potters.* Photographs by Bill Steen. Minneapolis: Lerner. **C**

Wells, Rosemary. (1996). *The Language of Doves.* Illustrated by Greg Shed. New York: Dial. **H**

Wild, Margaret. (1994). *Our Granny.* Illustrated by Julie Vivas. New York: Ticknor & Fields. **H**

Wild, Margaret. (1996). *Old Pig.* New York: Ticknor and Fields. **H,C**

Williams, Vera. (1997). *Lucky Song.* New York: Greenwillow. **H**

Woodruff, Elvira. (1998). *Can You Guess Where We're Going?* Illustrated by Cynthia Fisher. New York: Holiday House. **C**

Zalben, Jane Breskin. (1996). *Papa's Latkes.* New York: Henry Holt. **H**

Zamorano, Ana. (1997). *Let's Eat.* Illustrated by Julie Vivas. New York: Scholastic. **H**

Homeless Families

Barbour, Karen. (1991). *Mr. Bowtie.* San Diego: Harcourt. **C**

Bunting, Eve. (1991). *Fly Away Home.* Illustrated by Ronald Himler. New York: Clarion. **C**

Carlson, Natalie. (1958). *The Family Under the Bridge.* Illustrated by Garth Williams. New York: Harper. **C**

DiSalvo-Ryan, DyAnne. (1991). *Uncle Willie and the Soup Kitchen.* New York: Morrow Junior Books. **C**

Guthrie, D. (2000, 1988). *A Rose for Abby.* Nashville: Abington Press. **C**

Hathorn, Libby. (1994). *Way Home.* Illustrated by Gregory Rogers. New York: Crown. **C**

Sendak, Maurice. (1994). *We're All in the Dumps With Jack and Guy.* New York: HarperCollins. **C**

Weninger, Brigitte. (1997). *Lumina.* Translated by Anthea Bell. Illustrated by Julie Wintz-Litty. New York: North-South Books. **C**

Wolf, Bernard. (1995). *Homeless.* New York: Orchard Books. **H,C**

Migrant Workers and Immigrants

Bunting, Eve. (1988). *How Many Days to America? A Thanksgiving Story.* Illustrated by Beth Peck. New York: Clarion. **C**

Bunting, Eve. (1994). *A Day's Work.* New York: Clarion. **H,C**

Isadora, Rachel, (1991). *At the Crossroads.* New York: Greenwillow. **C**

Rosenberg, Maxine. (1986). *Making a New Home in America.* Photos by George Ancona. New York: Lothrop. **H**

Williams, Sherley Anne. (1992). *Working Cotton.* Illustrated by Carole Byard. San Diego: Harcourt. **C**

Gay and Lesbian Families

Bosche, S. (1983). *Jenny Lives With Eric and Martin.* London: Gay Men's Press. **H**

Brown, Forman. (1991). *Generous Jefferson Bartleby.* Illustrated by Leslie Trawin. Boston: Alyson Wonderland. **H,C**

Elwin, Rosamund, & Michele Paulie. (1990). *Asha's Mums.* Illustrated by Dawn Lee. Toronto: Women's Press. **S**

Heron, Ann, & Meredith Maran. (1991). *How Would You Feel If Your Dad Was Gay?* Illustrated by Kris Kovick. Boston: Alyson Wonderland. **H**

Newman, Leslea. (1989). *Heather Has Two Mommies.* Illustrated by Diane Souza. Boston: Alyson Wonderland. **H**

Newman, Leslea. (1991). *Belinda's Bouquet.* Illustrated by Michael Willhoite. Boston: Alyson Wonderland. **H,C**

Newman, Leslea. (1991). *Gloria Goes to Gay Pride.* Illustrated by Russell Crocker. Boston: Alyson Wonderland. **H,C**

Quinlan, Patricia. (1994). *Tiger Flowers.* Illustrated by Janet Wilson. New York: Dial (Penguin). **H**

Vigna, Judith. (1995). *My Two Uncles.* Morton Grove, IL: Albert Whitman. **H**

Wickens, Elaine. (1994). *Anna Day and the O-Ring.* Los Angeles: Alyson Publications. **H**

Willhoite, Michael. (1990). *Daddy's Roommate.* Boston: Alyson Wonderland. **H**

Willhoite, Michael. (1993). *Uncle What-Is-It Is Coming to Visit!* Boston: Alyson Wonderland. **H**

Children, Family Members, and Friends With Special Needs

Alexander, Sally Hobart. (1990). *Mom Can't See Me.* Photographs by George Ancona. New York: Macmillan. **H**

Alexander, Sally Hobart. (1992). *Mom's Best Friend.* Photographs by George Ancona. New York: Macmillan. **H**

Clifton, Lucille. (1980). *My Friend Jacob.* Illustrated by Thomas Di Grazia. New York: Dutton. **C**

Cohen, Miriam. (1983). *See You Tomorrow, Charles.* Illustrated by Lillian Hoban. New York: Greenwillow. **S**

Cowen-Fletcher, Jane. (1993). *Mama Zooms.* New York: Scholastic. **H**

Day, Shirley. (1995). *Luna and the Big Blur. A Story for Children Who Wear Glasses.* Illustrated by Don Morris. New York: Brunner/Mazel Publishers. **H**

Dugan, Barbara. (1992). *Loop the Loop.* Illustrated by James Stevenson. New York: Greenwillow. **C**

Dwight, Laura. (1998). *We Can Do It.* New York: Starbright Books. **C**

Hines, Anna Grossnickle. (1993). *Gramma's Walk.* New York: Greenwillow. **C**

Kroll, Virginia. (1993). *Naomi Knows It's Springtime.* Illustrated by Jill Kastner. Honesdale, PA: Boyd's Mill. **C**

Lakin, Patricia. (1994). *Dad and Me in the Morning.* Illustrated by Robert O. Steele. Morton Grove, IL: Albert Whitman. **C**

MacLachlan, Patricia. (1980). *Through Grandpa's Eyes.* Illustrated by Deborah Kogan Ray. New York: HarperCollins. **C**

Martin, Bill, Jr., & John Archambault. (1966, 1987). *Knots on a Counting Rope.* Illustrated by Ted Rand. New York: Holt. **C**

Miller, Mary Beth, & George Ancona. (1991). *Handtalk School.* Photographs by George Ancona. New York: Four Winds. **S**

Mohr, Nicholasa. (1995). *Old Lativia and the Mountain of Sorrows.* Illustrated by Rudy Gutierrez. New York: Greenwillow. **H,C**

Muldoon, Kathleen M. (1989). *Princess Pooh.* Illustrated by Linda Shute. Morton Grove, IL: Albert Whitman. **H**

Osofsky, Audrey. (1992). *My Buddy.* Illustrated by Ted Rand. New York: Holt. **H,C**

Rabe, Berniece. (1988). *Where's Chimpy?* Photographs by Diane Schmidt. Morton Grove, IL: Albert Whitman. **H**

Rosenberg, Maxine B. (1988). *Finding a Way: Living With Exceptional Brothers and Sisters.* Photographs by George Ancona. New York: Lothrop. **H**

Stuve-Bodeen, Stephanie. (1998). *We'll Paint the Octopus Red.* Illustrated by Pam DeVito. Bethesda, MD: Woodbine House. **H**

Thompson, Mary. (1992). *My Brother Matthew.* Rockville, MD: Woodbine House. **H**

Waddell, Martin. (1990). *My Great Grandpa.* Illustrated by Dom Mansell. New York: Putnam. **C**

Walker, Lou Ann. (1985). *Amy: The Story of a Deaf Child.* Photographs by Michael Abramson. New York: Lodestar. **S**

Defining Families

Jenness, Aylette. (1990). *Families: A Celebration of Diversity, Commitment, and Love.* Boston: Houghton Mifflin. **H**

Kroll, Virginia. (1994). *Beginnings: How Families Come to Be.* Morton Grove, IL: Albert Whitman. **H**

Leedy, Loreen. F. (1995, 1999). *Who's Who in My Family?* New York: Holiday House. **H**

Morris, Ann. (1990). *Bread, Bread, Bread.* Photographs by Ken Heyman. New York: Lothrop, Lee & Shepard. **H**

Simon, Norma. (1976). *All Kinds of Families.* Illustrated by Joe Lasker. Morton Grove, IL: Albert Whitman. **H**

Strickland, Dorothy S., & Michael S. Strickland. (Eds.). (1994). *Families: Poems Celebrating the African American Experience,* Illustrated by John Ward. Honesdale, PA: Boyd's Mill Press (Wordsong). **H**

Thomas, Marlo. (1987). *Free to Be a Family: A Book About All Kinds of Belonging.* New York: Bantam. **H**

Valentine, Johnny. (1994). *One Dad, Two Dads, Brown Dad, Blue Dads.* Illustrated by Melody Sarecky. Boston: Alyson Wonderland. **H**

Other Books Referred to in Text

Brown, Marcia. (1972). *Three Billy Goats Gruff.* New York: Harcourt. **C**

Cherry, Lynne. (1982). *A River Ran Wild.* San Diego: Harcourt. **C**

Macauley, David. (1998). *The New How Things Work.* Boston: Houghton Mifflin. **C**

Mason, Cherie. (1998). *Everybody's Somebody's Lunch.* Illustrated by Gustav Moore. Gardiner, ME: Tilbury House. **C**

Parnall, Peter. (1987). *Apple Tree.* New York: Greenwillow. **C**

Sendak, Maurice. (1963). *Where the Wild Things Are.* New York: Harper & Row. **H**

Glossary

academic curriculum The objectives, procedures, and materials schools use to ensure children's acquisition of the knowledge and skills affirmed by the community.

academic learning The acquisition of knowledge and skills relating to subject matter disciplines and organized fields of study.

academic rationalism Curriculum focused on education as the pursuit of knowledge in specified study fields and subject matter disciplines to develop the rational mind.

acculturation Modification of an individual's cultural behavior patterns by another cultural group (usually the dominant group).

adoptive family A family unit with at least one legally adopted child.

advocacy The process of publicly supporting a group, person, or cause.

after-school care Care provided for working parents' children (usually 5–10 years of age) during after-school hours.

alternative schools Schools organized with curricula different from and usually in reaction to conventional public school curricula.

assessment Evaluation or determination of extent of learning or change in behavior.

at-risk children (families) Children or families in danger of experiencing developmental gaps and problems due to poverty, abuse, illness, or social disturbance.

authentic assessment Using assessment strategies based on group or individual needs and the kinds of activities undertaken.

authoritarian parenting style Baumrind's term for an autocratic, controlling, and somewhat detached method of raising children.

authoritative parenting style Baumrind's term for a receptive and somewhat democratic, though firm and in control, manner of raising children.

autonomy The ability of persons to regulate and determine their own behavior.

behavioral objectives Intentions of education stated in terms of observable actions.

behaviorism A belief that learning occurs because of a system of rewards, punishments, and reinforcements.

bilingual education Teaching practices designed to encourage fluency in two languages.

biracial families Families in which the racial makeup of the parents is different. Some U.S families claim multiracial makeup because of past generations' biracial marriages.

blended family Two basic family units with children that join together to form a single family unit; often a remarriage, although some partners choose to forego wedlock.

bottom-up Practices and procedures designed to bring about changes or learning through local efforts or individuals' wishes.

charter school An authorized school designed to improve educational opportunities and supported but not regulated by local or state authority.

child care center A facility providing programs (frequently educational) and care for infants to 5-year-old children.

child-centered curriculum Teaching practices and materials focusing on children's interests, needs, and desires, with teachers responding to these interests by providing materials and guidance.

code switching The ability to move easily from one language or dialect to another.

cognitive process A series of actions producing changes in learners' methods of thinking, organizing perceptions, and solving problems.

collaboration Two or more persons or groups working together on joint endeavors for mutually determined objectives.

concrete operational thinking The third stage of Piagetian developmental theory (ages 7–11), characterized by the child's use of logical thought processes applied to real objects or events. At this stage, the child does not yet apply logic to abstract or hypothetical problems.

constructivist curriculum Curriculum based on the premise that the goal of education is for children to learn how to learn; when the individual is active in the learning process and is internally responding to outer stimuli.

criterion-referenced tests Tests designed to examine how well students have mastered a set of materials based on specified instructional goals and predetermined criteria.

cultural background The traditions, customs, knowledge, beliefs, art, mores, and regulations adhered to by a given group of people.

cultural deprivation Used formerly to describe the problems of certain families and groups. The notion that individuals lacked certain skills for productive school learning as a result of gaps in cultural background.

cultural literacy The corpus of knowledge of major historical and literary events all literate persons should know to be considered "educated" by their culture.

cultural pluralism The concept that all cultures have value and contribute to society.

custodial parent The parent to whom a court assigns the primary responsibility of a child's care and upbringing.

day care Programs provided for children whose parents work outside the home.

day care providers The adults who care for a group of children in a day care setting.

departmentalized program School practices in which students are taught different academic subjects by specialists in these academic fields.

Distar A curriculum designed by C. Bereiter and S. Englemann based on behavioral principles of instruction and learning.

drop-in child care A place where parents may find child care services for brief periods of time and with flexible schedules.

dual-income family A family wherein both parents or resident adults have income.

early intervention services Services provided in natural environments to infants and toddlers at risk of developmental delays.

egg-box construction A popular school design of the 1950s and 1960s. The building resembled an egg box, with a central corridor and classrooms on either side.

elaborated language code Syntactically complex speech that requires persons one communicates with to use judgment, imagination, and reason to interpret ambiguities and abstractions.

enculturation The process by which one learns the mores and habits of a particular cultural group.

ethnic orientation Relating to the complex set of characteristics and values, including national origin and linguistic, physical, and religious traits, by which a social group identifies itself.

Even Start Federally funded home-based family literacy program requiring established links to Head Start program.

extended community The area and population beyond the immediate neighborhood or local environment.

extended family The kin of the basic family unit who are economically dependent on and/or emotionally attached to the household.

family Two or more persons living together and linked for emotional and economic support.

family day care Care provided children in a home setting but outside the child's own home.

fixed curriculum The curriculum, often perceived to be mandated by local, state, and national education boards, that has been determined for a particular classroom.

Follow Through U.S. government-sponsored program that supports students after Head Start programs through kindergarten and the primary grades. (*See* Head Start.)

formal community structures The organizations and agencies within a community that support services for that community.

formal curriculum The curriculum, authorized by state and local education boards, that is public, is usually printed, and indicates the objectives, procedures, and materials for student learning.

foster family   A family unit wherein adults offer support to children who are not related by blood or adoption.

gay and lesbian   Persons with a sexual preference for some of their own sex. *Gay* is a generic term; lesbian refers specifically to women.

general equivalency diploma (GED)   A means of acquiring a high school diploma without having graduated from an accredited high school.

Head Start   Comprehensive federally funded program for poor preschool children and their families. It is designed to provide health, nutritional, social, and educational experiences to compensate for the negative effects of poverty.

hidden curriculum   Instructive events in a child's life that influence learning and attitude, often seen as hindering the stated goals of the school.

home care   Care of children by someone other than the parents but provided in the child's home setting.

homelessness   A chronic condition in which a person has no permanent place of residence and thus constantly moves from one place to another.

home schooling   The education of children undertaken completely by parents and done in the home environment.

hyperactivity   Behavior characterized by excessive or abnormal body movements and high expenditure of energy.

inclusion   Instruction for each child is provided, preferably in the regular classroom, with support services from whichever personnel is most appropriate at that moment in the child's schedule.

individualized educational program (IEP)   A program, mandated by law, developed by those responsible for the education of a particular child with special needs.

individualized family service plan (IFSP)   A written plan, mandated by law, that provides appropriate services for at-risk infants and toddlers and their families.

Individuals with Disabilities Education Act (IDEA)   Reauthorization and amendment of the 1975 Education for All Handicapped Students Act that governs how students with disabilities are to be educated in today's schools.

industrial model   A model for educational practice based on the manner in which industry operates.

infant/toddler program   Programs that offer a combination of play activities for infants and toddlers and parent education for the adults.

informal community structures   The personal relationships that families establish with members outside the home or extended family.

informal curriculum   All the events, stimuli, and activities that children undertake outside classrooms from which learning occurs.

interethnic family   A family unit that has more than one ethnic group represented in the unit. Blood parents may be of different groups, but also children of different groups may be adopted by parents of a single group.

itinerant family   A family unit that moves regularly, often following crop harvests or engaged in other limited-time work.

kinesthetic orientation   A manner of human functioning that best produces learning through the sensations of touch or body movement.

latchkey children   Children of school age who return after school to an empty house because all resident adults are at work.

learning modality   Consistent set of behaviors and performances by which an individual approaches tasks to be learned.

literacy development   The process of acquiring meaning from signs and symbols and of transferring meaning to signs and symbols.

literacy events   Activities related to reading and writing that support literacy development.

local educational authority (LEA)   The agency with the obligation and rights to oversee the education of children in its jurisdiction.

locus of control   The perception one has of where responsibility for one's actions lie. May be internal or external.

lower working class   That part of the population, usually consisting of unskilled laborers, who are less secure financially, at risk of unemployment, and at times receiving government assistance with basic living needs.

magnet schools   Schools organized around a particular focus, such as math or drama, and drawing students from a large area (metropolitan or state).

mainstream   Integrating special-needs children into the regular classroom. (*See also* inclusion)

marginalized families (children)   Persons responsible for the welfare of children who are unable or unwilling to provide for basic needs and nurturance.

melting pot thesis   Concept that a single culture will emerge if children are educated for one set of behavior patterns and beliefs.

mentors   Persons serving as guides or teachers to others on a one-to-one basis.

metacognition   The processes one uses in understanding how one gains knowledge.

middle class   That part of the population whose income falls within the median range for the whole. Professionals and businesspersons are often in this class.

migrant family   (*See* itinerant family)

monocultural   Reflecting the beliefs, behavior patterns, and characteristics of a single cultural group.

mores   Those rituals, traditions, customs, and behavior patterns seen as essential for a social group's survival and well-being.

mothers'-day-out programs   Programs that offer to children a few hours of supervised care so that their mothers may take time for themselves.

multicultural   Association with and appreciation of the practices of different cultures, religions, and ethnic groups.

nanny care   Care provided by a specially trained person to care for children in their homes. Au pair care is similar but refers to foreign students who care for young children in exchange for room and board.

National Council for the Accreditation of Teacher Education (NCATE)   National organization that sets standards for and evaluates teacher education programs.

networking   A system of making connections with individuals and groups that allows communication and involvement as a unit.

norm-referenced testing   Assessment whereby evaluation is based on comparison to a predetermined control group, often peers of the individual being tested.

nuclear family   A family unit consisting of two parents and their biological children.

nursery school   Program, usually private, designed for 2- to 5- year-olds. Often a half-day program but may have a full-day schedule.

open-space schools   Schools with large open spaces or "pods" in which several teachers organize the space to fit the needs of their particular students.

out-of-home care   Regular care provided to young children outside of the home setting.

parent center   Specific location, usually within a school, where parents can work and socialize and feel a part of the school.

parent cooperatives   Private nursery schools where parents share both the teaching and the administrative decision making.

parent empowerment   A process whereby parents become decision makers, often in collaboration with school personnel, for the education of their children.

partnerships   Relationships among different groups in which each group has equal influence on decision making.

perceptual field   Human range of recognition and organization of sensory input.

permissive parenting style   Baumrind's term for a manner of raising children that is nondemanding and noncontrolling that allows children to develop according to their natural instincts.

personal relevance curriculum   Curriculum based on the belief that the goal of education is to support personally satisfying experiences for each student.

person-oriented family   Manner of behaving in which the family unit focuses on the future development of individual children.

phonics   The letter-sound relationships of a language.

play school or group   Program designed, usually for toddlers, to focus on the importance of children engaging in play as a means of enhancing development.

position-oriented family   Manner of family functioning that is present oriented and object oriented and that assigns roles according to position in the family.

postmodern family   Family of today that views parenting as a shared responsibility of father, mother, and care provider.

power brokers   Members of a community or group with enough influence and power to become major decision makers for that community or group.

preoperational thinking   The second stage of Piagetian developmental theory (ages 2–7) characterized by symbolic functions. The child moves from functioning as a result of sensorimotor stimuli to developing the ability to internally represent events and act on this memory.

proof of equivalency   A requirement that home schoolers have proof that the education they provide for their children is equivalent to what children would receive in the formal school.

resilient   Demonstrating ability to cope and manage in spite of debilitating environmental circumstances.

restricted language code   A manner of speaking that is syntactically simple and direct and that has concrete meanings.

role expectations   Behavioral expectations for an individual depending on status or function within the family, peer group, school, or community.

Scholastic Aptitude Test (SAT)   Norm-referenced exams for high school students. Often used by colleges and scholarship boards to determine ability for advanced study.

scope and sequence charts   Lists of important skills for children's achievement, arranged on two dimensions: (1) the broad extent of the skill, (2) the order in which a skill or set of related skills is learned.

secular education   Education in which there is no religious or spiritual training.

secular humanism   Belief that the goals of education are to develop children's sense of personal growth, integrity, and autonomy but should not encompass the religious or spiritual part of the person.

self-fulfilling prophecy   A concept that expectations of others shape and reinforce one's behavior such that the expectations are eventually met. Also known as the "Pygmalion Effect."

sensory mode   The manner of receiving information through the five senses.

service agencies   Organizations within a community that provide those health, educational, transportation, protection, and communication services necessary to that community's citizens.

significant adults   The adults in a child's life who are particularly important to the child. This relationship exists independently of any biological or formal social relation between child and adult.

single-parent family   A family unit consisting of one parent, either mother or father, and children, and no other adults.

site-based management   A procedure for managing schools in which organizational and educational decisions for children at a particular school should be made by persons at that school.

social capital   The amount of human connections and relationships resulting in learning.

social climate   The attitudes, feelings, and relationships that people within a community maintain toward one another.

social networks   Parallel relationships developed among individuals in a community that foster communication and a sense of belonging.

social reconstructionist curriculum   Curriculum based on the thesis that the goals of education are to effect social change. Students learn social needs and values and how to use these concepts in critical thought processes.

social setting   A place, such as home, school, or community, wherein interactive events between or among individuals happen naturally.

socialization skills   The acquired ability to interact within the norms, values, and mores of a social group.

socioeconomic status (SES)   The economic and social level to which one belongs because of wealth, occupation, and educational background.

special interest groups   Groups with a narrow purpose or agenda organized to influence others to their point of view.

sponsored independence parenting style   Clark's term, similar to Baumrind's *authoritative style,* describing a manner of raising children. Indicates a rational, receptive, and warm but demanding style.

stages of development   Distinct steps in the growth process that individuals pass through from infancy through adulthood.

standardized tests   Tests with scientifically chosen items, given under similar conditions, that enable persons to be compared to a group standard. Tests may be either criterion referenced or norm referenced.

Structural English Immersion (SEI)   Programs where bilingual children are taught all subjects in English, receiving special English language assistance as needed and using their own language only to clarify concepts.

subfamily   A family cluster living with other adults or families in which the parent in the cluster is not the central family figure in the household.

technologist curriculum   A curriculum based on the notion that the primary goal of education is for students to master the basic skills of reading and computing in order to function in present society.

theme-focused programs   A phase of curriculum, based on a particular theme, wherein important objectives are identified and activities are prepared so that students acquire knowledge and skills relating to that theme.

three-group rotation   A technique for schooling that organizes a class of children into three groups and then rotates groups throughout the day into different learning centers or events.

time on task   The actual amount of time a student is engaged in or attending to a particular assigned task.

top-down   Practices and procedures designed to didactically bring about changes or learning. Typically, changes are initiated at the administrative or supervisory level and imposed on groups, classrooms, or schools.

traditional curriculum   Curriculum based on the notion that the objective of education is for students to acquire knowledge in subject matter disciplines and specified fields of study. Similar to *academic curriculum.*

transactional process of development   The process whereby multiple facets of the environment (people, objects, symbols) unleash the child's genetic potential to produce varied behaviors. Children's reactions and behaviors in turn affect new actions or movements from the environment.

underclass   That part of the population limited in opportunity and resources and locked into a cycle of poverty and despair.

units of study   Part of a curriculum based on a particular theme, around which learning activities are organized. Similar to *theme-focused programs.*

unstructured learning   Learning resulting from incidental and self-selected experiences in which children become interested and involved.

upper class   The most economically advantaged group of a population; often wealth is inherited.

upper working class   That population group represented by skilled laborers who are financially able to cope but severely affected by economic conditions.

voucher plans   Plans whereby parents receive certificates indicating the financial support for their children's education. Parents have the right to select a school and use the certificate to pay the cost of education.

well-baby clinic   Health clinics or hospital programs where parents can, without cost, bring their children for regular checkups and discussions regarding ways to provide a healthy environment.

whole language programs   Curriculum practice emphasizing the totality of language, presuming that children should learn to read the same way they learn to speak, that is, holistically with respect to their environment. Reading, writing, speaking, and listening are all aspects of language learned in conjunction.

Woman, Infants, and Children (WIC)   Federally funded program to supply nutritional and health support for lower income or welfare families.

writing-to-read   A strategy for teaching reading in combination with teaching writing.

References

Adams, M. J. (1990). *Beginning to read: Thinking and learning about print.* Cambridge, MA: MIT Press.

American Academy of Pediatrics, Task Force on Children and Television. (1990). *Children, adolescents and television.* Elk Grove Village, IL: Author.

American Association of School Administrators. (1986). *Religion in the public schools.* Arlington, VA: Author.

American Civil Liberties Union. (1995). *Religion in the public schools: A joint statement of current laws.* New York: Author.

An Ounce of Prevention Fund. (1994). *Head start on Head Start: An Ounce of Prevention Fund paper.* Chicago: Author. (ERIC Document Reproduction Service No. ED 368 475)

Anderson, J., & Suntken, J. (1989). The me-museum. In D. Strickland & L. M. Morrow (Eds.), *Emerging literacy: Young children learn to read and write* (pp. 42–55). Newark, DE. International Reading Association.

Anderson, J. W. (1972). Attachment behavior out of doors. In N. Blurton Jones (Ed.), *Ethological studies of child behavior* (pp. 199–225). New York: Cambridge University Press.

Annie E. Casey Foundation. (1998). *Kids Count data book: State profiles of child well-being.* Baltimore, MD: Author.

Apple, M. W. (1995). *Eduction and power* (2nd ed.). New York: Routledge.

Applebee, A. N. (1989). *Child's concept of story. Ages 2–17.* Chicago: University of Chicago Press.

Applebee, A. N. (1996). *Curriculum as conversation.* Chicago: University of Chicago Press.

Arendell, T. (1997). A social constructionist approach to parenting. In T. Arendell (Ed.), *Contemporary parenting: Challenges and issues Vol. 9. Understanding families* (pp. 1–45). Thousand Oaks, CA: Sage.

Argulewicz, E. N. (1983). Effects of ethnic membership, socioeconomic status, and home language on LD, EMR, and EH placements. *Learning Disabilities Quarterly, 6*(2), 195–200.

Babbitt, G. (1999). Interview, Director of the Growing Up Reading Program, Deer Isle, ME.

Bailyn, B., Dalleck, R., Davis, D. B., Donald, D. H., Thomas, J. L., & Wood, G. S. (1997). *The great American republic: A history of the American people* (5th ed.). Lexington, MA: D. C. Heath

Baker, K. (1998). Structural English immersion: Breakthrough in teaching limited English proficient students. *Phi Delta Kappan, 80*(3), 199–204.

Ball, S., & Bogatz, G. (1970). *The first year of Sesame Street: An evaluation.* Princeton, NJ: Educational Testing Service.

Banks, J. A. (1996). *Multicultural education, transformative knowledge, and action: Historical and contemporary perspectives.* New York: Teachers College Press.

Banks, J.A. (1998). *An introduction to multicultural education* (2nd Ed.). Boston: Allyn & Bacon.

Barbour, N. H., & Seefeldt, C. (1993). *Developmental continuity across preschool and primary grades.* Wheaton, MD: Association for Childhood Education International.

Barker, P. (1990). The home schooled teenager grows up. In A. Pedersen & P. O'Mara (Eds.), *Schooling at home: Parents, kids, and learning* (pp. 203–208). Santa Fe, NM: John Muir Publications.

Barth, R. (1983). Social support network in services for adolescents and their families. In J. K. Whittaker & J. Garbarino (Eds.), *Social support networks* (pp. 289–331). New York: Aldine.

Bauch, J. F. (1989). The TransParent school model: New technology for parent involvement. *Educational Leadership, 47*(2), 32–34.

Baumrind, D. (1966). Effects of authoritative parental control on child behavior. *Child Development, 37,* 387–407.

Baumrind, D. (1968). Authoritarian vs. authoritative parental control. *Adolescence, 3,* 255–272.

Baumrind, D. (1971). Current patterns of parental authority. *Developmental Psychology Monograph, 75,* 43–88.

Begley, S. (1996, February 19). I am your child. *Newsweek,* 100, 55–61.

Bell, T. H. (1993). Reflections one decade after a nation at risk. *Phi Delta Kappan, 75*(8), 593–597.

Belmont, L., & Marolla, F. A. (1973). Birth order, family size and intelligence, *Science, 182,* 1096–1101.

Bennett, K. P., & LeCompte, M. D. (1990). *How schools work: A sociological analysis of education.* New York: Longman.

Bennett, W. (1998). *A nation still at risk.* Policy Review, No 90 23–29.

Benson, P. (1997). *All kids are our kids.* San Francisco: Jossey-Bass.

Berger, E. H. (2000). *Parents as partners in education: Families and schools working together* (4th ed.). Englewood Cliffs, NJ: Merrill/Prentice Hall.

Berlin, I. (1998). *Many thousands gone: The first two centuries of slavery in North America.* Cambridge: Bleknap/Harvard.

Berndt, T. J. (1979). Developmental changes in conformity to peers and parents. *Developmental psychology, 15,* 608–616.

Berndt, T. J., & Ladd, G. W. (1989). *Peer relationships in child development.* New York: Wiley.

Berns, R. M. (1997). *Child, family, school, community: Socialization and support* (4th ed.). New York: Harcourt Brace Jovanovich.

Bernstein, B. (1972). A sociolinguistic approach to socialization with some reference to educability. In J. Gumperz & D. Hymes (Eds.), *Directions in sociolinguistics* (pp. 465–497). New York: Holt, Rinehart & Winston.

Bettelheim, B. (1976). *The uses of enchantment.* New York: Knopf.

Bianchi, S. M. (1990). America's children: Missed prospects. *Population Bulletin, 45*(1), 7–10.

Bianchi, S. M., & Spain, D. (1996). Women, work and family in America. *Population Bulletin, 47*(2), 2–47.

Bigner, J. J. (1998). *Parent-child relations: An introduction to parenting* (5th Ed.). Columbus, OH: Merrill.

Binford, V. M., & Newell, J. M. (1991). Richmond, Virginia's two decades of experience with Ira Gordon's approach to parent education. *Elementary School Journal, 91*(3), 233–237.

Black, J. K., Puckett, & M. B. (1996). *The young child: Development from prebirth through age eight* (2nd ed.). Englewood Cliffs, NJ: Merrill/Prentice Hall.

Blank, H. (1997). Child care in the context of welfare form. In S. B. Kamerman & A. J. Kahn (Eds.), *Child care in the context of welfare "reform" (pp. 1–44).* New York: Cross-National Studies Research Program, Columbia University School of Social Work.

Blau, J. (1992). *The visible poor: Homelessness in the United States.* New York: Oxford University Press.

Bloom, B. S., Englehart, M. D., Furst, E. J., Hill, W. H., & Krathwohl, D. R. (1956). *Taxonomy of educational objectives, Handbook I: Cognitive domain.* New York: McKay.

Bloom, J. (1992). *Parenting our schools: A hands-on guide to education reform.* Boston: Little, Brown.

Bornstein, M. H. (1995). Parenting infants. In M. H. Bornstein (Ed.), *Handbook of parenting Vol. 1: Children and Parenting* (pp. 3–4). Mahwah, NJ: Lawrence Erlbaum.

Bossard, J., & Boll, E. (1949). Ritual in family living. *American Sociological Review, 14,* 526–530.

Bradley, R. H. (1995). Environments and parenting. In M. H. Bornstein (Ed.), *Handbook of parenting Vol. 2:* Biology & Ecology of Parenting (pp. 236–256). Mahwah, NJ: Lawrence Erlbaum.

Bredekamp, S., & Rosegrant, T. (1995). *Reaching potential: Appropriate curriculum and assessment for young children* (Vol. 2). Washington, DC: National Association of the Education for Young Children.

Bronfenbrenner, U. (1979). *The ecology of human development: Experiment by nature and design.* Cambridge: Harvard University Press.

Bronfenbrenner, U. (1986). Ecology of the family as a context of human development: Research perspectives. *Developmental Psychology, 22,* 723–742.

Bronfenbrenner, U. (1995). Developmental ecology through space and time: A future perspective. In P. Moen, G. H. Elder, & K. Luscher (Eds.), *Examining lives in context* (pp. 619–648). Washington, DC: American Psychological Association.

Bronfenbrenner, U., & Crouter, A. (1982). Work and family through time and space. In S. B. Kammerman & C. D. Hayes (Eds.), *Families that work: Children in a changing world* (pp. 39–83). Washington, DC: National Academy Press.

Bronfenbrenner, U., Moen, P., & Garbarino, J. (1984). Child, family, and community. In R. D. Parke (Ed.), *Review of child development research Vol. 7: The family* (pp. 283–328). Chicago: University of Chicago Press.

Bronfenbrenner, U., & Weiss, H. (1983). *Beyond policies without people: An ecological perspective on child and family policy.* New York: Cambridge University Press.

Brophy, B. (1989, August 7). Spock had it right: Studies suggest that kids thrive when parents set firm limits. *U. S. News & World Report,* 49–51

Bruer, J. T. (1998). Brain science: Brain fiction. *Educational Leadership, 56*(3), 8–18.

Buchwald, A. (1994). *Leaving home: A memoir.* New York: Putnam.

Bullivant, B. M. (1993). Culture: Its nature and meaning for educators. In J. A. Banks & C. A. M. Banks (Eds.), *Multicultural education: Issues and perspectives* (2nd ed.) (pp. 29–47). Boston: Allyn & Bacon.

Bullock, H. A. (1967). *A history of Negro education in the South from 1619 to the present.* Cambridge, MA: Harvard University Press.

Bumstead, R. A. (1979). Educating your child at home: The Perchemlides case. *Phi Delta Kappan, 61*(2), 97–100.

Burnette, S. (1998). Book 'em! Cops and librarians working together. *American Libraries, 29*(2), 48–50.

Bus, A. G., & Van Ijzendoorn, M. H. (1995). Mothers reading to their 3 year olds. The role of mother-child attachment security in becoming literate. *Reading Research Journal Quarterly, 30*(4), 998–1014.

Bush, J. (1997). *Youth and Family Centers: Evaluation of an Integrated School-Based Health Care Program.* (ERIC Document Reproduction Service No. ED 406 439)

Butler, R. D. (1976). Black children's racial preference: A selected review of literature. *Journal of Afro-American Issues, 4*(2), 168–171.

Calderone, M. S., & Johnson, E. W. (1989). *The family book about sexuality.* New York: Harper & Row.

Calvery, R., Bell, D., & Vaupal, C. (1992). *The difference in achievement between home schooled and public schooled students for grades four, seven, and ten in Arkansas.* Paper presented at the annual meeting of the Mid-South Educational Research Association, Knoxville, TN. (ERIC Document Reproduction Service No. ED 354 248)

Carnegie Corporation. (1994.) *Starting points. Meeting the needs of our youngest.* New York: Author. http://www.carnegie.org/starting_points/startpt1.html.

Carnegie Forum on Education and the Economy. (1986). *A nation prepared: Teachers for the 21st century.* New York: Carnegie Corporation.

Carter, D. A. (1993). Community and parent involvement: A road to school improvement. *ERS Spectrum, 11*(1), 39–45.

Casper, L. M. (1996). *Who's minding our preschoolers.* Washington, DC: U.S. Bureau of the Census.

Ceci, S. J., & Hembrooke, H. A. (1995). A bioecological model of intellectual development. In P. Moen, G. Elder, & K. Luscher (Eds.), *Examining lives in context. Perspective on the ecology of human development* (pp. 303–306). Washington, DC: American Psychological Association.

Center for the Study of Social Policy. (1992). *The challenge of change: What the 1990 census tells us about children.* Washington, DC: Author.

Cherry, L. (1982). *A river ran wild.* San Diego: Harcourt Brace.

Child Welfare League of America. (1994). *Kinship care: A natural bridge.* Washington DC: Author.

Children's Defense Fund. (1990). *S.O.S. America: A children's defense budget.* Washington, DC: Author.

Children's Defense Fund. (1997). *Key facts about child care and early education: A briefing book.* Washington, DC: Author.

Children's Defense Fund. (1998). *The state of America's children: A report from the Children's Defense Fund.* Boston: Beacon Press.

Clark, R. M. (1983). *Family life and school achievement: Why poor black children succeed or fail.* Chicago: University of Chicago Press.

Clarke-Stewart, K. A. (1993). *Daycare* (Rev. ed). Cambridge, MA: Harvard University Press.

Clarke-Stewart, K. A., Allhusen, V. D., and Clements, D. C. (1995). Nonparenting caregiving. In M. H. Bornstein (Ed.), *Handbook of parenting Vol. 3. Status and social conditions of parenting* (pp.141–175). Mahwah, NJ: Lawrence Erlbaum.

Clawson, B. (1992). Preparing for successful children. In L. Kaplan (Ed.), *Education and the family* (pp. xix—xxii). Boston: Allyn & Bacon.

Clay, J. W. (1990). Working with lesbian and gay parents and their children. *Young Children, 45*(3), 31–35.

Clay, M. M. (1991). *Becoming literate: The construction of inner control.* Portsmouth, NH: Heinemann.

Clinchy, E. (1993). Building an extended family in East Harlem. In S. Thompson (Ed.), *Whole child, whole community* (pp. 28–34). Boston: Institute for Responsive Education.

Cochran, M. (1990). The network as an environment for human development. In M. Cochran, M. Larner, D. Riley, L. Gunnarsson, & C. R. Henderson, Jr. (Eds.), *Extending families: The social networks of parents and their children* (pp. 265–277). New York: Cambridge University Press.

Cochran, M., & Davila, V. (1992). Societal influences on children's peer relationships. In R. D. Parke & G. W. Ladd (Eds.), *Family-peer relationships: Modes of linkage* (pp. 191–214) Hillsdale, NJ: Lawrence Erlbaum Associates.

Cochran, M., & Niegro, S. (1995). Parenting and social networks. In M. H. Bornstein (Ed.), *Handbook of parenting Vol. 3: Status and social conditions of parenting* (pp. 393–418). Mahwah, NJ: Lawrence Erlbaum.

Cochran, M., & Riley, D. (1990). The social networks of six-year-olds: Context, content, and consequence. In M. Cochran, M. Larner, D. Riley, L. Gunnarsson, & C. R. Henderson, Jr. (Eds.), *Extending families: The social networks of parents and their children* (pp. 154–179). New York: Cambridge University Press.

Cohen, D. L. (1992). Children without "traditional family" support are posing complex challenges for schools. *Education Week, 12*(15), 5.

Cohen, D. L. (1994). Carnegie Corporation presses early-years policies. *Education Week, 13*(29), 1, 13.

Cohen, S. (1974). *A history of colonial education, 1607–1776.* New York: Wiley.

Coleman, J. S. (1966). *Equality of educational opportunity.* Washington, DC: U.S. Government Printing Office.

Coleman, J. S. (1990). *Foundations of social theory.* Cambridge, MA: Harvard University Press.

Coleman, J. S. (1991). *Policy perspectives: Parental involvement in education.* Washington, DC: U.S. Department of Education, Office of Educational Research and Improvement.

Coleman, J. S. (1996). *Parents, their children and schools.* Boulder, CO: Westview Press.

Coles, R. (1997). *The moral intelligence of children.* New York: Random House.

Colfax, J. D., & Colfax, M. (1992). *Hard times in paradise.* New York: Warren.

Collins, R. C. (1984, April). *Head Start: A review of research with implications for practice in early childhood education.* Paper presented at the annual meeting of the American Educational Research Association, New Orleans. (ERIC Document Reproduction Service No. ED 245 833)

Comer, J. P. (1980). *School power: Implications of an intervention project.* New York: The Free Press.

Comer, J. P. (1988). *Maggie's American dream: The life and times of a black family.* New York: New American Library.

Comer, J. P. (1997). *Waiting for a miracle: Why schools can't solve our problems and how we can.* New York: Penguin Putnam.

Comer, J. P., Ben-Avie, M., Haynes, N., & Joyner, E. T. (Eds.). (1999). *Child by child: The Comer process for change in education.* New York: Teachers College Press.

Comer, J. P., & Haynes, N. M. (1991). Parent involvement in schools: An ecological approach. *Elementary School Journal, 91*(3), 271–277.

Comer, J. P., Haynes, N. M., & Joyner, E. T. (1996). The School Development Program. In J. P. Comer, N. M. Haynes, E. T. Joyner, & M. Ben-Avie (Eds.), *Rallying the whole village: The Comer process for reforming education* (pp. 1–27). New York: Teachers College Press.

Comstock, G., & Paik, H. (1991). *Television and the American child.* San Diego: Academic Press.

Cook, T., Appleton, H., Conner, R., Shaffer, A., Tamkin, G., & Weber, S. (1975). *"Sesame Street" revisited.* New York: Russell Sage Foundation.

Coontz, S. (1997). *The way we really are: Coming to terms with America's changing families.* New York: Basic Books.

Cornell, C. E. (1993). Language and culture monsters that lurk in our traditional rhymes and folktales. *Young Children, 48*(6), 40–46.

Cremin, L. A. (1961). *The transformation of the school: Progressivism in American education, 1876–1957.* New York: Alfred A. Knopf.

Cremin, L. A. (1982). *American education: The national experience, 1783–1876.* New York: Harper & Row.

Cross, W. E. (1987). Black identity: Rediscovering the distinction between personal identity and reference group orientation. In M. B. Spencer, G. Brookins, & W. Allen (Eds.), *Beginnings: The social and affective development of black children* (pp. 155–171). Mahwah, NJ: Lawrence Erlbaum.

Cruickshank, D. (1990). *Research that informs teachers and teacher educators.* Bloomington, IN: Phi Delta Kappa Educational Foundation.

Crump. J. (1999, May 4). CyberEducation report sparks nationwide response. *Forbes Digital* (www.forbes.com).

Culatta, R. A. & Tompkins, J. R. (1999). *Fundamentals of special education.* Upper Saddle River, NJ: Merrill.

Curran, D. (1983). *Traits of a healthy family.* Minneapolis: Winston.

Damon, W. (1988). *The moral child: Nurturing children's natural moral growth.* New York: The Free Press.

D'Angelo, D. A., & Adler, C. R. (1991). Chapter 1: A catalyst for improving parent involvement. *Phi Delta Kappan, 72*(5), 350–355.

Danzberger, J. P., & Gruskin, S. J. (1993). *Project abstracts: Educational Partnerships Program. Programs for the improvement of practice.* Washington, DC: Office of Educational Research and Improvement.

Dash, J. (1992). *Daughters of the dust.* New York: New Press.

Dash, L. (1996). *Rosa Lee: A mother and her family in urban America.* New York: Basic Books.

Davies, D. (1990). Shall we wait for the revolution?: A few lessons from the Schools Reaching Out Project. *Equality and Choice, 6*(3), 68–73.

Davies, D. (1993). Looking backward. In S. Thompson (Ed.), *Whole child, whole community* (pp. 67–72). Boston: Institute for Responsive Education.

Davies, D. (1995). Commentary: Collaboration and family empowerment as strategies to achieve comprehensive services. In L. C. Rigsby, M. C. Reynolds, & M. C. Wang (Eds.), *School-community connections* (pp. 411–430). San Francisco: Jossey-Bass.

Davies, D., Burch, P., & Johnson, V. R. (1992). *A portrait of Schools Reaching Out. Report of a survey of practices and policies of family-community-school collaboration.* Boston: Center on Families, Communities, Schools, and Children's Learning.

Davies, D., Burch, P., & Palanki, A. (1993). *Fitting policy to family needs: Delivering comprehensive services through collaboration and family empowerment.* Boston: Center on Families, Communities, Schools, and Children's Learning.

Davies, D., Palanki, A., & Burch, P. (1993). The whole school for the whole child. In S. Thompson (Ed.), *Whole child, whole community* (pp. 18–23). Boston: Institute for Responsive Education.

Davis, P. (1995). *A journey through the lives of the underclass.* New York: Wiley.

Debaryshe, B. B. (1993, March). Maternal reading, related beliefs and reading socialization practices in low SES homes. In M. E. Evans (Chair), *Adult and child influences on early literacy interactions.* Biennial meeting of the Society of Research in Child Development, New Orleans.

Deckard, S.(1996). *Home schooling laws and resource guide for all fifty states* (9th ed). Ramona, CA: Vision Publishing.

Deiner, P. L. (1997). *Infants and toddlers: Development and program planning.* New York: Harcourt Brace.

DeVita, C. J. (1995). The United States at mid-decade. *Population Bulletin, 50*(4), 2–42.

Dewey, J. (1913, 1975). *Interest and effort in education.* Edwardsville: Southern Illinois University Press.

Dighe, J. (1993). Children and the earth. *Young Children, 48*(3), 58–63.

Dinkmeyer, D., & McKay, G. D. (1983). *Systematic training for effective parenting.* Circle Pines, MN: American Guidance Service.

Dolan, L. J. (1995). An evaluation of family support and integrated services in six elementary schools. In L. C. Rigsby, M. C. Reynolds, & M. C. Wang (Eds.), *School-community connections* (pp. 395–420). San Francisco: Jossey-Bass.

Doll, R. C. (1995). *Curriculum improvement: Decision making and process* (9th ed.). Boston: Allyn & Bacon.

Dornbusch, S., Ritter, P. L., Leiderman, P. H., Roberts, D. F., & Fraleigh, M. J. (1987). The relation of parenting style to adolescent school performance. *Child Development, 58*(5), 1244–1257.

Dorris, M. (1993). Foreword. In M. Roesell, *Kinaalda: A Navajo girl grows up* (pp. 1–2). Minneapolis: Lerner.

Dreeben, R. (1970). Schooling and authority: Comments on the unstudied curriculum. In N. V. Overly (Ed.), *The unstudied curriculum: Its impact on children* (pp. 85–103). Washington, DC: ASCD.

Duffey, J. (1998). Home schooling: A controversial alternative. *Principal 77*(5), 23–26.

Dunn, K., & Frazier, E. R. (1990). *Teaching styles.* Reston, VA: National Association of Secondary School Principals.

Dunn, R. (1999). *Complete guide to the Learning Styles Inservice Program.* Upper Saddle River, NJ: Prentice Hall.

Durkin, D. D. (1966). *Children who read early.* New York: Teachers College Press.

Dworetzky, J. P. (1990). *Introduction to child development* (4th ed.). New York: West.

Dyson, A. H. (1986). Transitions and tensions: Interrelationships between the drawing, talking and dictating of young children. *Research in the Teaching of English, 20*(4), 379–409.

Ecksel, I. B. (1992). Schools as socializing agents in children's lives. In L. Kaplan (Ed.), *Education and the family* (pp. 86–99). Boston: Allyn & Bacon.

Eddowes, E. A., & Hranitz, J. R. (1989). Educating children of the homeless. *Childhood Education, 65*(4), 197–200.

Edelsky, C. (1996). *With literacy and justice for all: Rethinking the social in language and education* (2nd ed.). Bristol, PA: Taylor & Francis.

Edin K,.& Lein, L.(1997). *Making ends meet: How single mothers survive welfare and low wages.* New York: Russell Sage Foundation.

Education Commission of the States. (1996). *Bridging the gap between neuroscience and education. Summary of the workshop cosponsored by Education Commission of the States and the Charles A. Dana Foundation.* Denver: Author.

Educational Research Service. (1992). Children with disabilities: Educational status and trends. *ERS Research Digest, 18,* 1–4.

Eisner, E. W. (1994). *The educational imagination: On the design and evaluation of school programs* (3rd ed.). Englewood Cliffs, NJ: Merrill/Prentice Hall.

Eitzen, D. S. (1992). Problem students: The sociocultural roots. *Phi Delta Kappan, 73*(8), 584–590.

Elgin, C. Z. (1990). Representation, comprehension and competence. In V. A. Howard (Ed.), *Varieties of thinking* (pp. 62–75). New York: Routledge, Chapman & Hall.

Elkin, F., & Handel, G. (1989). *The child and society* (5th ed.). New York: Random House.

Elkind, D. (1988). *The hurried child* (Rev. ed.). Reading, MA: Addison-Wesley.

Elkind, D. (1994). *Ties that stress: The new family imbalance.* Cambridge: Harvard University Press.

Elkind, D. (1995). School and family in the postmodern world. *Phi Delta Kappan 77*(1), 8–14.

Emery, R. E. (1988). *Marriage, divorce, and children's adjustment.* Beverly Hills, CA: Sage.

Epstein, J. (1999). *School and family partnerships: Preparing educators and improving schools.* Boulder, CO: Westview Press.

Epstein, J. L. (1992). School and family partnerships. In A. Alkin (Ed.), *Encyclopedia of educational research* (pp. 1139–1151). Englewood Cliffs, NJ: Merrill/Prentice Hall.

Erikson, E. (1963). *Childhood and society.* New York: Norton.

Essa, E. L., & Murray, C. I. (1999). Sexual play: When should you be concerned? *Childhood Education, 75*(4), 231–234.

Evans, E. (1975). *Contemporary influences in early childhood education* (2nd ed.). New York: Holt, Rinehart & Winston.

Even Start (1999). Even Start. (available on website: http://www.ed.gov/legislation/ESEA/sec1201.html)

Farenga, P. (1990). Methodologies and curricula. In A. Pedersen & P. O'Mara (Eds.), *Schooling at home: Parents, kids, and learning* (pp. 95–104). Santa Fe, NM: John Muir Publications.

Federal Interagency Forum on Child & Family Statistics. (1998). *America's children: Key national indicators of well-being.* Washington DC: The Forum.

Fine, M. J. (1993). Current approaches to understanding family diversity. *Family Relations, 43*(3), 235–237.

Fitzgerald, J., Spiegel, D. L., & Cunningham, J. W. (1991). The relationship between parental literacy level and perceptions of emergent literacy. *Journal of Reading Behavior, 23,* 191–214.

Fitzpatrick, M. A., & Vangelisti, A. (1995). *Explaining family interactions.* Thousand Oaks, CA: Sage.

Florida State Department of Education. (1992). *Florida's First Start Program planning and implementation.* Tallahassee, FL: Author. (ERIC Document Reproduction Service No. ED 374 859)

Fordham Foundation. (1998). *A nation "still" at risk: An education manifesto.* (ERIC Document Reproduction No. ED 422 455

Fox, R. A., Anderson, R. C., Fox, T. A., & Rodriguez, M. A. (1991). STAR parenting: A model for helping parents effectively deal with behavioral difficulties. *Young Children, 46*(4), 54–61.

Frost, S. E., Jr. (1966). *Historical and philosophical foundations of Western education.* Englewood Cliffs, NJ: Merrill/Prentice Hall.

Fuchs, D., & Fuchs, L.S. (1998). Inclusion versus full inclusion. *Childhood Education, 74*(5), 309–320.

Fuller, M. L. (1986). Teacher's perceptions of children from intact and single parent families. *School Counselor, 33*(7), 365–374.

Gadsden, V. L. (1998). Family cultures and literacy learning. In J. Osborn & F. Lehr (Eds.), *Literacy for all: Issues in teaching and learning* (pp. 32–51). New York: Guilford Press.

Galinsky, E. (1987). *The six stages of parenthood.* Reading, MA: Addison-Wesley.

Galinsky, E., Howes, C., Kontos, S., & Shinn, M. (1994). *The study of children in family child care and relative care: Highlights of the findings.* New York: Families and Work Institute.

Galle, O., Gove, W., & McPherson, J. (1972). Population density and pathology: What are the relationships for men? *Science, 176,* 23–30.

Gandini, L. (1993). Fundamentals of the Reggio Emilia approach to early childhood education. *Young Children, 49*(1), 4–8.

Garbarino, J., & Abramowitz, R. H. (1992). The family as a social system. In J. Garbarino (Ed.), *Children and families in the social environment* (2nd ed.) (pp. 71–98). New York: Aldine de Gruyer.

Garbarino, J., Dubrow, N., Kostelny, K., & Pardo, C. (1998). *Children in danger: Coping with the consequences of community violence (2nd ed.).* San Francisco: Jossey-Bass.

Garbarino, J., Kostelny, K., & Dubrow, N. (1998). *No place to be a child: Growing up in a war zone* (2nd ed.). Lexington, MA: D. C. Heath.

Garcia, J. (1993). The changing image of ethnic groups in textbooks. *Phi Delta Kappan, 75*(1), 29–35.

Gardner, H. (1983). *Frames of mind. The theory of multiple intelligences.* New York: Basic Books.

Gardner, H. (1999). *The disciplined mind: What all students should understand.* Upper Saddle River, NJ: Simon & Schuster.

Gardner, S. (1993). Failure by fragmentation. In S. Thompson (Ed.), *Whole child, whole community* (pp. 11–17). Boston: Institute for Responsive Education.

Garn, G. (1998). The thinking behind Arizona's charter movement. *Educational Leadership, 56*(2), 48–50.

Gearheart, B. R., Weishahn, M., & Gearheart, C. J. (1996). *The exceptional student in the regular classroom* (6th ed.). Upper Saddle River, NJ: Merrill/Prentice Hall.

Gelfer, J. I. (1991). Teacher-parent partnerships: Enhancing communications. *Childhood Education, 67*(3), 164–167.

Gersten, J. C. (1992). Families in poverty. In M. E. Procidano & C. B. Fisher (Eds.), *Contemporary families: A handbook for school professionals* (pp. 137–158). New York: Teachers College Press.

Giroux, H. A. (1978). Developing educational programs: Overcoming the hidden curriculum. *The Clearing House, 52*(4), 148–152.

Goffman, E. (1967). *Interaction ritual: Essays on face-to-face behavior.* New York: Harper & Row.

Goleman, D. (1995). *Emotional intelligence.* New York: Bantam Books.

Gonzales-Mena, J. (1998). *The child in the family and the community* (2nd ed.). Upper Saddle River, NJ: Merrill/Prentice Hall.

Good, T. L., & Brophy, J. E. (1972). Behavioral expression of teacher attitudes. *Journal of Educational Psychology, 63,* 617–624.

Good, T. L., & Brophy, J. E. (1986). School effects. In M. C. Wittrock (Ed.), *Handbook of research on teaching* (3rd ed.) (pp. 570–604). Upper Saddle River, NJ: Merrill/Prentice Hall.

Good, T. L., & Brophy, J. E. (1996). *Looking in classrooms* (7th ed.). Boston: Addison-Wesley.

Goodman, A. E. (1993). *A brief history of the future: The United States in a changing world order.* Boulder, CO: Westview Press.

Gorder, C. (1996). *Home schools: An alternative. You do have a choice!* (4th ed.). Tempe, AZ: Blue Bird.

Gordon, I. J. (1969). *Reaching the child through parent education: The Florida approach.* Gainsville, FL: Gainesville Institute for Development of Human Resources. (ERIC Document Reproduction Service No. ED 057 880)

Gordon, I. J., Guinagh, B. J., & Jester, R. F. (1977). The Florida Parent Education Infant and Toddler Program. In M. C. Day & R. K. Parker (Eds.), *The preschool in action* (2nd ed.) (pp. 95–127). Boston: Allyn & Bacon.

Gordon, T. (1975). *Parent effectiveness training.* New York: Peter H. Wyden.

Gorsuch, R. L. (1976). Religion as a major prediction of significant human behavior. In W. J. Donaldson, Jr. (Ed.), *Research in mental health and religious behavior* (pp. 206–221). Atlanta: Psychological Studies Institute.

Gorter-Reu, M. S., & Anderson, J. M. (1998). Home Kits, Home Visits, and More! *Young Children, 53*(3), 71–75.

Gouvis, C. (1995). *Special report on children and violence: Maryland KIDS COUNT.* Baltimore: The Urban Institute.

Graham, P. A. (1993). What America has expected of its schools over the past century. *American Journal of Education, 101*(2), 83–98.

Graue, M. E., Weinstein, T., & Walberg, H. J. (1983). School-based home instruction and learning: A quantitative analysis. *Journal of Educational Research, 76,* 351–360.

Gray, P., & Chanoff, D. (1984). When play is learning: A school for self-directed education. *Phi Delta Kappan, 65*(9), 608–611.

Greenberg, P. (1990). Head Start—Part of a multipronged antipoverty effort for children and their families. Before the beginning: A participant's view. *Young Children, 45*(6), 40–73.

Griffel, G. (1991). Walking on a tightrope: Parents shouldn't have to walk it alone. *Young Children, 46*(3), 40–42.

Groves, B., Zuckerman, B., & Marans, S. (1993). Silent victims: Children who witness violence. *Journal of American Medical Association, 269*(2), 262–265.

Grumbine, E. (1988). The university of the wilderness. *Journal of Environmental Education, 19*(4), 3–7.

Gunter, B., & McAleer, J. (1997). Children and television (2nd ed.). New York: Routledge

Gustafson, C. (1998). Phone home. *Educational Leadership, 56*(2), 31–33.

Gutek, G. L. (1996). *Historical and philosophical foundations.* Columbus, OH: Prentice Hall.

Guterson, D. (1992). *Family matters: Why homeschooling makes sense.* New York: Harcourt.

Haberman, M. (1992). Creating community contexts that educate: An agenda for improving education in inner cities. In L. Kaplan (Ed.), *Education and the family* (pp. 27–40). Boston: Allyn & Bacon.

Hagan, J. L. (1998). The new welfare law is tough on work. *Families in Society, 79*(6), 596–605.

Haley, A. (1976). *Roots.* Garden City, New York: Doubleday.

Hamblett, E. (1994). Personal communication.

Hampton, F. M., Mumford, D. A., Bond, L., (1998). Parent involvement in inner-city schools. The project FAST extended family approach to success. *Urban Education, 33*(3), 410–427.

Hansberry, L. (1959). *Raisin in the Sun.* New York: Random House.

Harrington-Lueker, D. (1994). Charter "profit": Will Michigan heap money on an electronic charter school? *American School Board, 181*(9), 27–29.

Harris, J. R. (1995). Where is the child's environment? A group socializing theory of development. *Psychological Review, 102*(3), 458–489.

Harris, J. R. (1998). *The nurture assumption.* New York: The Free Press.

Hart, B., & Risley, T. R. (1995). *Meaningful differences in the everyday experience of young American children.* Baltimore: Paul Brookes Publishing.

Hart, C. H., DeWolf, M., & Burts, D. C. (1993). Parental disciplinary strategies and preschool behavior in playground settings. In C. H. Hart (Ed.), *Children on playgrounds: Reserach perspectives and applications* (pp. 271–340). Albany: State University of New York Press.

Hartup, W. W. (1983). Peer relations. In P. H. Mussen (Ed.), *Handbook of child psychology: Vol. 4. Socialization, personality, and social development* (pp. 103–196). New York: Wiley.

Head Start Bureau. (1980). *A Handbook for involving parents in Head Start* (DHHS Publication No. OHDS 88–331187). Washington, DC: U.S. Government Printing Office.

Heath, S. D. (1983). *Ways with words: Language, life, and work in communities and classrooms.* New York: Cambridge University Press.

Heath, S. D., & MacLaughlin, M. W. (1989). A child resource policy. Moving beyond dependence on school and family. *Phi Delta Kappan, 68*(8), 576–581.

Heaverside, S., & Farris, E. (1989). *Educational partnership in public elementary and secondary schools.* Washington, DC: Office of Educational Research and Improvement.

Helburn, S. (1995). *Cost, quality and child outcomes in child care centers: Technical Report.* Denver: Department of Economics, Center for Research in Economic and Social Policy, University of Colorado.

Helburn, S. W., & Howes, C. (1996). Child care cost and quality. *The Future of Children, 6,* 62–82.

Heleen, O. (1990). Schools reaching out: An introduction. *Equity and Choice, 6*(3), 5–9.

Helm, J. (1994). Family theme bags: An innovative approach to family involvement in the school. *Young Children, 49*(4), 48–52.

Henderson, A. T. (1987). *The evidence continues to grow: Parent involvement improves student achievement.* Columbia, MD: National Committee for Citizens in Education.

Henderson, A. T., Marburger, C. L., & Ooms, T. (1986). *Beyond the bake sale: An educator's guide to working with parents.* Columbia, MD: National Committee for Citizens in Education.

Hendrick, J. (Ed.). (1997). *First steps toward teaching the Reggio way.* Upper Saddle River, NJ: Merrill/Prentice Hall.

Hess, R. D., & Holloway, S. D. (1984). Family and school as educational institutions. In R. D. Parke (Ed.), *Review of child development research: Vol. 7. The family* (pp. 179–222). Chicago: University of Chicago Press.

Hetherington, E. M. (1988). Parents, children and siblings six years after divorce. In R. A. Hinde & J. Stevenson-Hinde (Eds.), *Relationships within families* (pp. 311–331). Oxford: Oxford University Press.

Hetherington, E. M., & Camara, K. A. (1984). Families in transition: The processes of dissolution and reconstitution. In R. D. Parke (Ed.), *Review of child development research: Vol. 7. The family* (pp. 179–222). Chicago: University of Chicago Press.

Hetherington, E. M. & Stanley-Hagan, M. M. (1995). Parenting in divorced and remarried families. In M. Bornstein (Ed.), *Handbook of parenting Vol 3. Status and social conditions of parenting* (pp. 230–262). Mahwah, NJ: Lawrence Erlbaum.

Hewison, J., & Tizard, J. (1980). Parent involvement and reading attainment. *British Journal of Educational Psychology, 50*(3), 209–215.

Hildebrand, V., Phenice, L. A., Gray, M. M., & Hines, R. P. (1996). *Knowing and serving diverse families.* Columbus, OH: Merrill/Prentice Hall.

Hill, E. (1967). *Evan's Corner.* New York: Holt.

Hillis, M. R.(1996). Allison Davis and the study of race, social class, and schooling. In J. A. Banks

(Ed.), *Multicultural education, transformative knowledge and action: Historical and contemporary perspectives.* New York: Teachers College Press.

Hinde, R. A. (1995). Foreword. In M. Bornstein (Ed.), *Handbook of parenting Vol. 1: Children and Parenting.* Mahwah, NJ: Lawrence Erlbaum.

Hodges, E.V.E., Boivin, M., Vitaro, F., & Bukowski, W. M. (1999). The power of friendship: Protection against an escalating cycle of peer victimization. *Developmental Psychology, 35*(1), 94–101.

Hoffer, T. B., & Coleman, J. S. (1990). Changing families and communities: Implications for schools. In B. Mitchell & L. L. Cunningham (Eds.), *Educational leadership and changing contexts of families, communities and schools: Eighty-ninth Yearbook of the NSSE, Part II* (pp. 118–134). Chicago: National Society for the Study of Education.

Hofferth, S. L.(1996). Child care in the United States today. *The future of children, 6,* 41–61.

Hofferth, S. L. (1991). National child care survey, 1990. Washington, D.C.: The Urban Institute.

Hoge, D. R. (1996). Religion in America: The demographics of belief and affiliation. In E. P. Shafranske (Ed.). *Religion and the clinical practice of psychology* (pp. 21–41). Washington, DC: American Psychological Association.

Holmbeck, G. N., Paikoff, R., & Brooks-Gunn, J. (1995). Parenting adolescents. In M. Bornstein (Ed.), *Handbook of Parenting Vol. 1: Children and parenting* (pp. 91–118). Mahwah, NJ: Lawrence Erlbaum.

Holt, J. C. (1964). *How children fail.* New York: Pitman.

Honig, A.S. (1993). Mental health for babies: What do theory and research teach us? *Young Children, 48*(3), 69–76.

Hrabowski, F. A., Maton, K. I., & Greif, G. L. (1998). *Beating the odds: Raising academically successful African American males.* New York: Oxford University Press.

Hunt, J. M. (1961). *Intelligence and experience.* New York: Ronald Press.

Hurd, T. L., Lerner, R. M., & Barton, C. E. (1999). Integrated services: Expanding partnerships to meet the needs of today's children and families. *Young Children, 54*(2), 74–81.

Hurst, C. O. (1993). Teaching in the library: Dark and stormy reading. *Teaching Pre K–8, 23*(5), 92–94.

Intergroup married couples 1998. (February 1999) *Population today, 27*(2): 6.

Jacobson, S. K., & Padua, S. M. (1992). Pupils and parks: Environmental education in national parks of developing countries. *Childhood Education, 68*(5), 290–294.

Janosik, E., & Green, E. (1992). *Family life: Process and practice.* Boston: Jones & Bartlett.

Jencks, C., Smith, M. S., Acland, H., Bane, M. J., Cohen, I., Gintis, H., Heyns, B., & Michaelson, S. (1972). *Inequality: A reassessment of family and schooling in America.* New York: Harper & Row.

Jenkins, E. J., & Bell, C. C. (1997). Exposure and response to community violence among children and adolescents. In J. Osofsky (Ed.), *Children in a violent society* (pp. 9–31). New York: Guilford Press.

Jeub, C. (1994). Why parents choose home schooling. *Educational Leadership, 52*(1), 50–52.

Johnson, V. R. (1990). Schools reaching out: Changing the message to "good news." *Equity and Choice, 6*(3), 20–24.

Jones, K. (1988). *Interactive learning events: A guide for facilitators.* New York: Nichols.

Joyce, B., & Weil. M., (1996). *Models of teaching* (5th ed.). Boston: Allyn & Bacon.

Kagan, S. L. (1993). Home-school linkages. In S. L. Kagan, D. R. Powell, B. Weisbourd, & E. F. Zigler (Eds.), *America's family support programs: Perspectives and prospects* (pp. 160–181). New Haven, CT: Yale University Press.

Kagan, S. L. (1994, March). *Families and children: Who is responsible?* Paper presented at the annual meeting of the Association of Childhood International, New Orleans.

Kagan, S. L. & Neuman, M. J. (1997). Highlights of the quality 2000 initiative: Not by chance. *Young Children, 50*(6), 54–62.

Kaplan, L. (1992). Parent education in home school and society: A course description. In L. Kaplan (Ed.), *Education and the family* (pp. 273–278). Boston: Allyn & Bacon.

Katz, P. A. (1976). The acquisition of racial attitudes in children. In P. A. Katz (Ed.), *Towards the elimination of racism* (pp. 125–154). New York: Pergamon.

Kearney, M. (1999). The role of teachers in helping children of domestic violence. *Childhood Education, 75*(5), 290–296.

Kelly, K. (1993, November). Shock wave (anti) warrior. *Wired,* 4– 6.

Kerman, K. (1990). Home schooling day by day. In A. Pedersen & P. O'Mara (Eds.), *Schooling at home: Parents, kids, and learning* (pp. 175–182). Santa Fe, NM: John Muir Publications.

Keyersling, M. D. (1972). *Windows on day care.* New York: National Council of Jewish Women.

Kidder, T. (1989). *Among schoolchildren.* Boston: Houghton Mifflin.

Kidwell, C. S., & Swift, D. W. (1976). Indian education. In D. W. Swift (Ed.), *American education: A sociological view* (pp. 329–- 390). Boston: Houghton Mifflin.

Kinch, A. F., & Schweinhart, L. J. (1999). Making child care work for everyone. *Young Children, 54*(1), 68–73.

Knowles, J. G. (1989). Cooperating with home school parents: A new agenda for public schools? *Urban Education, 23*(4), 392–411.

Kontos, S., Howes, C., Shinn, M., & Galinsky, E. (1995). *Quality in family child care and relative care.* New York: Teachers College Press.

Koran, J., Longino, S., & Shafer, L. (1983). A framework for conceptualizing research in natural history museums and science centers. *Journal of Research in Science Teaching, 20*(4), 325–339.

Kotlowitz, A. (1991). *There are no children here: The story of two boys growing up in the other America.* New York: Doubleday.

Kozol, J. (1967). *Death at an early age.* Boston: Houghton Mifflin.

Kozol, J. (1991). *Savage inequalities: Children in America's schools.* New York: Crown.

Kumove, L. (1966). *A preliminary study of the social implications of high density living conditions.* Toronto: Social Planning Council of Metropolitan Toronto.

Ladd, G. W., and LeSieur, K. D. (1995). Parents and children's peer relationships. In M. Bornstein (Eds.), *Handbook of Parenting Vol. 4: Applied and practical parenting* (pp. 419–545). Mahwah, NJ: Lawrence Erlbaum.

Lancy, D. F., & Nattiv, A. (1992). Parents as volunteers: Storybook readers/listeners. *Childhood Education, 68*(4), 208–212.

Larner, M., & Halpern, R. (1987). Lay home visiting: Strengths, tensions, and challenges. *Zero to Three, 8,* 1–7.

Lazar, I. (1977). *The persistence of preschool effects: A long-term follow up of fourteen infant and preschool experiments.* Washington, DC: Administration for Children, Youth, and Families.

Leach, P. (1994). *Children first: What our society must do—and is not doing—for our children today.* New York: Alfred Knopf.

Lefcourt, H. M. (1984). *Research with the locus of control construct.* New York: Academic Press.

Leibert, R. M., & Sprafkin, J. (1988). *The early window: Effects of television on children and youth* (3rd ed.). New York: Pergamon.

Lerner, R. M., & Simon, L.A.K. (1998). Directions for the American outreach university in the twenty-first century. In R. M. Lerner & L.A.K. Simon (Eds.), *Creating a new outreach university for America's youth and families: Building university-community collaborations for the twenty-first century* (pp. 461–81). New York: Garland.

Letiecq, B. L., Anderson, E. A., & Koblinsky, A. (1998). Social support of homeless and house mothers: A comparison of temporary and permanent housing arrangements. *Family Relations, 47*(4), 415–421.

Levenstein, P. (1977). The mother-child home program. In M. C. Day & R. K. Parker (Eds.), *The preschool in action* (2nd ed.) (pp. 27–49). Boston: Allyn & Bacon.

Levin, H. M. (1991). Cost benefit and cost effectiveness analyses of interactions for children in poverty. In A. C. Huston (Ed.), *Children in poverty: Child development and public policy* (pp. 222–240). New York: Cambridge University Press.

Levine, J. A., & Pittinsky, T.L.(1997). *Working fathers: New strategies for balancing work and family.* Reading, MA: Addison Wesley.

Levy, D. E. (1992). Teaching family ritual: Sunday, sausage, and solidarity. *Teaching Sociology, 20*(4), 311–313.

Lewis, R., & Morris, J. (1998). Communities for children. *Educational Leadership, 55*(8), 34–36.

Lightfoot, S. L. (1978). *Worlds apart: Relationships between schools and families.* New York: Basic Books.

Lindner, E. W. (Ed.). (1998). *Yearbook of American and Canadian Churches 1998.* Nashville: Abingdon Press.

Lindsey, E.W. (1998). The impact of homelessness and shelter life on family relationships. *Family Relations, 47*(3), 243–252.

Lines, P. (1995). Home schooling. *ERIC Digest, No. 95.* (Gov Doc. ED 1.310/2:381849)

Lines, P. M. (1991). *Estimating the home schooled population* (Report No. OR 91–-537). Washington, DC: Office of Educational Research and Improvement. (GPO ED 1.310/2:337903)

Louv, C. (1990). *Childhood's future.* Boston: Houghton Mifflin.

Lund, L., & Wild, C. (1993). *Ten years after a nation at risk.* New York: The Conference Board.

Macaulay, D.(1998). *The new how things work.* Boston: Houghton Mifflin.

Maccoby, E. E., & Martin, J. (1983). Socialization in the context of family: Parent-child interaction. In P. H. Mussen (Ed.), *Handbook of child psychology: Socialization, personality and social development* (4th ed.) (pp. 1–102). New York: Wiley.

Maeroff, G. I. (1998). Altered destinies: Making life better for schoolchildren in need. *Phi Delta Kappan, 79*(6), 424–432.

Mallett, D. (1995). *Inch by inch: The garden song.* New York: HarperCollins.

Marx, E., Wooley, S. F., & Northup, D. (Eds.). (1998). *Health is academic: A guide to coordinated school health programs.* New York: Teachers College Press.

Maslow, A. H. (1970). *Motivation and personality* (Rev. ed.). New York: Norton.

Mason, C. (1998). *Everybody is somebody's lunch.* Gardner, ME: Tilbury House.

Mason, M. A. (1998). The modern American stepfamily: Problems and possibilities. In M. A. Mason, A. Skolnick, & S. D. Sugarman (Eds.),

All our families: New policies for a new century (pp. 95–116). New York: Oxford University Press.

Mayberry, M., Knowles, J. G., Ray, B., & Marlow, S. (1995). *Home schooling: Parents as educators.* Thousand Oaks, CA: Corwin.

Mayer, S. (1997). *What money can't buy: Family income and children's life chances.* Cambridge, MA : Harvard University Press.

McCormick, L., & Holden, R. (1992). Homeless children: A special challenge. *Young Children, 57*(6), 61–67.

McFalls, J. A. Jr. (1998). Population: A lively introduction. *Population Bulletin, 53*(3), 3–47.

McGoldrick, M. (1993). Ethnicity, cultural diversity and normality. In F. Walsh, (Ed.), *Normal Family Process* (2nd ed.) (pp. 331–360). New York: Guilford Press.

McNeil, J. D. (1996). *Curriculum: A comprehensive introduction* (5th ed.). Reading, MA: Addison Wesley.

Mead, M. (1935). *Sex and temperament in three primitive societies.* New York: Knopf.

Meadows, S. (1996). *Understanding child development: Psychological perspectives in an interdisciplinary field of inquiry.* London: Hutchinson.

Meier, D. (1995). *The power of their ideas: Lessons for America from a small school in Harlem.* Boston: Beacon Press.

Merenda, D. W. (1989). Partners in education: An old tradition renamed. *Educational Leadership, 47*(2A), 4–7.

Meringoff, L. K. (1980). Influence of the medium on children's story apprehension. *Journal of Educational Psychology, 72,* 240–249.

Metz, E. G. (1993). The camouflaged at-risk student: White and wealthy. *Momentum, 24*(2), 40–44.

Meyers, J., & Kyle, J. E. (1996). *Critical needs, critical choices: A survey on children and families in America's cities.* Washington, DC: National League of Cities.

Miles, J. (1986/1987). Wilderness as a learning place. *Journal of Environmental Education, 18*(2), 33–40.

Miller, A. C. (1987). *Maternal health and infant survival.* Washington, DC: National Center for Clinical Infant Programs.

Miller, M. S. (1991). *The school book: Everything parents should know about their child's education, from preschool through eighth grade.* New York: St. Martin's Press.

Minuchin, P. P., & Shapiro, E. K. (1983). The school as a context for social development. In P. H. Mussen (Ed.), *Handbook of child psychology: Vol. 4. Socialization, personality, and social development* (pp. 197–274). New York: Wiley.

Mitchell, B., & Cunningham, L. L. (Eds.). (1990). *Educational leadership and changing contexts of families, communities and schools. Eighty-ninth yearbook of the NSSE, part II.* Chicago: National Society for the Study of Education.

Mitchell. C. J. & Spencer, L. M. (1997). *21st century community learning centers program.* Washington, DC: U.S. Department of Education, Office of Educational Research and Improvement.

Monroe, L. (1997). *Nothing's impossible: Leadership lessons and stories from the front.* New York: Time Books.

Moore, G. T. (1985). State of the art in play environment. In J. L. Frost & S. Sunderlin (Eds.), *When children play* (pp. 171–192). Wheaton, MD: Association for Childhood Education International.

Morse, S. C. (1997). *Unschooled migrant youth: Characteristics and strategies to serve them.* (Gov. Doc: ED 1.310/2:405158) Washington, DC: Superintendent of Documents.

Moyer, M., Pate, D. J., & Simons, J. V. (1998, November). *Public-private collaborations to provide support for at-risk families and their children, birth to 4 years old.* Paper presented at the annual conference of the National Association for the Education of Young Children, Toronto, Canada.

Murray, J. P. (1997). Media violence and youth. In J. D. Osofsky (Ed.), *Children in a violent society* (pp.72–97). New York: Guilford Press.

NICHD Early Child Care Research Network (1997). Child care in the first year of life. *Merrill-Palmer Quarterly, 43,* 340–360.

Nash, M. (1997, September 3). Fertile minds. *Time,* 152:48–56.

National Association for the Education for Young Children. (1990). *How to choose a good early childhood program.* Washington, DC: Author.

National Association for the Education of Young Children. (1998). *Accreditation criteria and procedures of the National Association for the Education of Young Children.* Washington, DC: Author.

National Center for Educational Statistics. (1992). What young children do at home: Reading and TV watching are among the most common family activities for 3- to 8-year-olds. *Principal, 72*(2), 21–24.

National Center for Educational Statistics (1996). *National household education survey.* Washington, DC: U.S. Department of Education.

National Commission of Excellence in Education. (1983). *A nation at risk: The imperative for educational reform.* Washington, DC: U.S. Government Printing Office.

National Commission on Migrant Children. (1992). *Invisible children: A portrait of migrant education in the United States* (Stock No. 022–003–01173–1, Supt. of Documents). Washington, DC: Author.

National Education Goals. (1993). (ED 1.2:G 53/5)

Neill, A. S. (1960). *Summerhill.* New York: Hart.

Nelson, E. (1986). *Home schooling* (Report No. R-86–0003). Washington, DC: Office of Educational Research and Improvement. (ERIC Document Reproduction Service No. ED 282 348)

Neuman, S. B. (1995). *Myth of the TV effect.* Norwood, NJ: Ablex.

Neuman, S. B., & Roskos, K. (1994). Bridging home and school with a culturally responsive approach. *Childhood Education, 70*(4), 210–214.

Newberger, J. J. (1997). New brain development research: A wonderful window of opportunities to build public support for early childhood education. *Young Children, 52*(4), 4–10.

Newman, R. (1998). Making time for family. *Childhood Education, 74*(3), 174–175.

Nichelason, M. G. (1994). *Homeless or hopeless.* Minneapolis: Lerner.

Noddings, N. (1992). *The challenge to care in schools: An alternative approach to education.* New York: Teachers College Press.

Notar, E. E. (1989). Children and TV commercials: Wave after wave of exploitation. *Childhood Education, 66*(2), 66–67.

Notar, E. E. (1992). They come with stories. *Childhood Education, 68*(3), 131–133.

O'Hare, W. P. (1992). America's minorities: The demographics of diversity. *Population Bulletin, 47*(4), 2–40.

O'Hare, W. P. (1996). A new look at poverty in America. *Population Bulletin, 51*(2), 1–42.

Oladele, F. (1999). Passing the spirit. *Educational Leadership, 56*(4), 62–65.

Olson, M. R., & Haynes, J. A. (1993). Successful single parents. *Families in Society, 74*(5), 259–267.

O'Neil, J. (1997). Building schools as communities: A conversation with James Comer. *Educational Leadership, 54*(8), 6–10.

Opie, I. A., & Opie, P. (1969). *Children's games in street and playground: Chasing, catching, seeking, hunting, racing, duelling, exerting, daring, guessing, acting, pretending.* Oxford: Clarendon.

O'Reilly, R. C., & Green, E. T. (1992). *School law for the 1990s: A handbook* (2nd ed.). New York: Greenwood.

Osofsky, J. D. (1997). Children and youth violence: An overview of the issue. In J. D. Osofsky (Ed.), *Children in a violent society* (pp. 3–8). New York: Guilford Press.

Osofsky, J. D.(1998). Children as invisible victims of domestic and community violence. In G. W. Holden, R. Geffner, & E. N. Jouriles (Eds.), *Children exposed to marital violence* (pp. 95–120). Washington DC: American Psychological Association.

Owens, K. (1993). *The world of the child.* Englewood Cliffs, NJ: Merrill/Prentice Hall.

Page, S., & Rosenthal, R. (1990). Sex and expectations of teachers and sex and race of students as determinants of teaching behavior and student performance. *Journal of School Psychology, 28,* 119–131.

Papert, S. (1993). *The children's machine: Rethinking school in the age of the computer.* New York: Basic Books.

Papert, S. (1996). *The connected family: Bridging the digital generation gap.* Marietta, GA: Longstreet Press.

Pardeck, J. T. (1990). An analysis of the deep social structure preventing the development of a national policy for children and families in the United States. *Early Child Development and Care, 57,* 23–30.

Parke, R. D. (1990, Fall). *Family-peer systems: In search of a linking process.* Newsletter. Developmental Psychology, American Psychological Association, Division 7.

Partnership for Family Involvement in Education. (1999). *Excelencia en educacion.* Washington, DC: U.S. Office of Education.

People v. DeJonge, 501 N.W. 2d 127 (Mich. 1993).

Perchemlides v. Frizzle, no. 16641 (Mass. Hampshire County Superior Court, 1978).

Permanent Judical Commission on Justice for Children. (n.d.). *Children's Centers in the New York State Courts.* Albany, NY: Communications Office of the New York State Unified Court System.

Perry, B. (1997). Incubated in terror: Neurodevelopmental factors in the "cycle of violence." In J. D. Osofsky (Ed.), *Children in a violent society* (pp. 121–149). New York: Guilford Press.

Perry, D. G. (1987, Fall). How is aggression learned? *School Safety,* 23–25.

PFIE (1999). What is the partnership for involvement in education? (Available on website: http://www.pfie.ed.gov./about_main.htm)

Pipher, M. (1996). *The shelter of each other: Rebuilding our families.* New York: Ballantine Books.

Piaget, J. (1952). *The origins of intelligence.* New York: International Universities Press.

Piaget, J. (1967). *Six psychological studies.* New York: Random House.

Pierce, S. H., Alfonso, E. M. & Garrison, M. E. B. (1998). Examining proximal processes in young children's home environments: A preliminary report. *Family Relations, 27*(1). 3–35.

Polakow, V. (1993). *Lives on the edge: Single mothers and their children in the other America.* Chicago: University of Chicago Press.

Popin, M. (1990). *The active parenting discussion program.* Marietta, GA: Active Parenting.

Postman, N. (1983). Engaging children in the great conversation. *Phi Delta Kappan, 64*(5), 310–317.

Powell, D. R. (1990). Home visiting in the early years: Policy and program design decisions. *Young Children, 45*(6), 65–73.

Prescott, A. B. (1994). Personal communication.

Priesnitz, H. (1990). First day of school at thirteen. In A. Pedersen & P. O'Mara (Eds.), *Schooling at home: Parents, kids, and learning* (pp. 200–202). Santa Fe, NM: John Muir Publications.

Proctor, P. (1984). Teacher expectations: A model for school improvement. *Elementary School Journal, 84*(4), 469–481.

Quality Education for Minorities Project. (1990). *Education that works: An action plan for the education of minorities.* Cambridge, MA: Quality Education for Minorities Project, Massachussetts Institute of Technology.

Quint, S. (1994). *Schooling homeless children: A working model for America's public schools.* New York: Teachers College Press.

Ramirez-Smith, C. (1995). Stopping the cycle of failure: The Comer model. *Educational Leadership, 52*(5), 14–19.

Ramsey, P. G. (1987). Young children's thinking about ethnic differences. In J. S. Phinney & M. J. Rotheram (Eds.), *Childrens ethnic socialization: Pluralism and development* (pp. 56–72). Newbury Park, CA: Sage.

Ramsey, P.G. (1998). *Teaching and learning in a diverse world: Multicultural education for young children* (2nd ed.). New York: Teachers College Press.

Randolph, S. M., Koblinsky, S. A., and Roberts, D. D. (1998). Studying the role of family and school in the development of African American preschoolers in violent neighborhoods. *Journal of Negro Education, 65*(3), 282–294.

Ray, B. (1997, May/June). Home education across the United States. *Home School Court Report, 13*(3), 11–16.

Raywid, M. A. (1995). The struggles and joys of trail-blazing: A tale of two charter schools. *Phi Delta Kappan, 76*(7), 555–560.

Reid, W. J., & Crisafulli, A. (1990). Marital discord and child behavior problems: A meta-analysis. *Journal of Abnormal Child Psychology, 18*(1), 105–117.

Rice, M. L., Huston, A. C., Truglio, R., & Wright, J. C. (1990). Words from *Sesame Street:* Learning vocabulary while viewing. *Developmental Psychology, 26*(3), 421–428.

Rich, D. (1987). *Teachers and parents: An adult to adult approach.* Washington, DC: National Education Association.

Rich, D. (1992). *Megaskills: In school and life—The best gift you can give your child.* Boston: Houghton Mifflin.

Rich, J. M. (1992). *Foundations of education: Perspectives on American education.* Englewood Cliffs, NJ: Merrill/Prentice Hall.

Richards, M. H., & Duckett, E. (1994). The relationship of maternal employment to early adolescent daily experience with and without parents. *Child Development, 65*(1), 225–236.

Richardson, S., & Zirkel, P. (1991). Home schooling law. In J. A. Van Galen & M. A. Pitman (Eds.), *Home schooling: Political, historical, and pedagogical perspectives* (pp. 159–210). Norwood, NJ: Ablex.

Rigsby, L. C. (1995). Introduction: The need for new strategies. In L. C. Rigsby, M. C. Reynolds, and M. C. Wang (Eds.), *School-community connections* (pp. 1–20). San Francisco: Jossey-Bass.

Riley, R. W. (1995). Reflections on Goals 2000. *Teachers College Record, 96*(3), 380–389.

Rissi, A. S. (1993). The future in the making: Recent trends in the work-family interface. *American Journal of Orthopsychiatry, 63*(2), 166–176.

Robinson, J. D., & Godbey, G. (1997). *Time for life: The surprising way Americans use their time.* University, PA: Penn State University Press.

Rodriguez, J. (1997). "At risk": A measure of school failure in American education. (ERIC Document Reproduction Service No. ED 412 220)

Rose, L. C., & Gallup, A. M. (1998). The 30th annual Phi Delta Kappan Gallup poll: The public attitude toward the public schools. *Phi Delta Kappan, 80*(1), 41–56.

Rosenthal, R., & Jacobson, L. (1968). *Pygmalion in the classroom.* New York: Holt, Rinehart & Winston.

Rotter, J. C. (1987). *Parent-teacher conferencing: What research says to the teacher* (2nd ed.). Washington, DC: National Education Association.

Sadker, D., Lerner, P., & Sadker, M. (1999). *Teachers, schools, and society* (5th ed.). New York: Mc-Graw-Hill.

Sadker, D., & Sadker, M. (1995). *Failing at fairness: How America's schools cheat girls.* New York: Touchstone.

Salzstein, H. D. (1976). Social influence and moral development: A perspective on the role of parents and peers. In T. Lickona (Ed.), *Moral development and behavior: Theory, research, and social issues* (pp. 241–252). New York: Holt, Rinehart & Winston.

Sameroff, A. J. (1993). Models of development and developmental risk. In C. H. Zeanah, J. (Ed.), *Handbook of infant and mental health* (pp. 3–13). New York: Guilford Press.

Sameroff, A. J. (1996). *The five to seven year shift: The age of reason or responsibility.* Chicago: University of Chicago Press.

Sameroff, A., Seifer, R., Barocas, R., Zax, M., & Greenspan, S. (1987). Intelligence quotient scores of 4–year-old children: Social-environmental risk factors. *Pediatrics, 79,* 343–350.

Sanderson, S. K. (1995). *Social Transformations: A general theory of historical development.* Cambridge, MA: Blackwell Publishers.

Saul, W., & Newman, A. R. (1986). *Science fare: An illustrated guide and catalog of toys, books, and activities for kids.* New York: Harper & Row.

Scarf, M. (1995). *Intimate worlds: Life inside the family.* New York: Random House.

Scarf, M. (1997). *Intimate worlds: How families thrive and why they fail.* New York: Ballantine Books.

Scarr, S. (1998). American child care today. *American Psychologist, 53,* 95–108.

Scarr, S., & Eisenberg, M. (1998). Child care research: Issues perspective and results. *Annual Review of Psychology, 44,* 613– 644.

Scarr, S., Phillips, D., & McCartney, K. (1990). Facts, fantasies, and the future of child care in the United States. *Psychological Science, 1,* 26–35.

Schiamberg, L. B. (1988). *Child and adolsecent development.* Englewood Cliffs, NJ: Merrill/Prentice Hall.

Schlossman, S. (1976). Before Home Start: Notes towards a history of parent education in America, 1897–1929. *Harvard Educational Review, 46*(3), 436–467.

Schorr, L. (1988). *Within our reach: Breaking the cycle of disadvantage.* New York: Anchor.

Schott, J. C. (1989). Holy wars in education. *Educational Leadership, 47*(2), 61–66.

Schwartz, L. L., & Kaslow, F. W. (1997). *Painful partings: Divorce and its aftermath.* New York: Wiley.

Schwartz, P. (1995, February 16). The silent family: Together, but apart. *The New York Times,* p. C6.

Schweinhart, L. J., & Weikart, D. P. (1993). Success by empowerment: The High/Scope Perry preschool study through age 27. *Young Children, 49*(1), 54–58.

Schweinhart, L. J., & Weikart, D. P. (1997). *Lasting differences: The HighScope preschool curriculum comparison study through age 23.* (Monographs of the High/Scope Educational Research Foundation, 12). Ypsilanti, MI: High/Scope Press.

Seefeldt, C., & Barbour, N. (1998). *Early childhood education: An introduction* (4th ed.). Englewood Cliffs, NJ: Merrill/Prentice Hall.

Shames, S. (1991). *Outside the dream: Child poverty in America.* Washington, DC: Children's Defense Fund.

Shoop, R. J., & Dunklee, D. R. (1992). *School law for the principal: A handbook for practitioners.* Boston: Allyn & Bacon.

Sigel, I. E., Dreyer, A. S., & McGillicuddy-DeLisi, A. V. (1984). Psychological perspectives of the family. In R. D. Parke (Ed.), *Review of child development research Vol. 7: The family* (pp. 42–79). Chicago: University of Chicago Press.

Sigel, I. E., McGillicuddy-DeLisi, A. V., & Goodnow, J. J. (Eds.) (1992). *Parental belief systems: The psychological consequences for children,* 2nd edition. Hillsdale, NJ: Lawrence Erlbaum Associates.

Silber, J. (1989). *Straight shooting: What's wrong with America and how to fix it.* New York: Harper & Row.

Singer, J. L., & Singer, D. G. (1990). *Television, imagination, and aggression: A study of preschoolers.* Hillsdale, NJ: Lawrence Erlbaum Associates.

Singer, J. L., & Singer, D. G. (1992). *The house of make believe: Children's play and the developing imagination.* Cambridge, MA: Harvard University Press.

Slaby, R. G., Roedell, W. C., Arezzo, D., & Hendrix, K. (1995). *Early violence prevention: Tools for teachers of young children.* Washington, DC: National Association for the Education of Young Children.

Smilansky, S., & Shefatya, L. (1990). *Facilitating play: A medium for promoting cognitive socioemotional and academic development in young children.* Gaithersburg, MD: Psychosocial-Educational Publications.

Smith, T. B. (1994). *Home-based family literacy mentoring: A guide for Head Start teachers.* (ERIC Document Reproduction Service No. ED 372 290)

Smrekar, C. E. (1993). Rethinking family—School interactions: A prologue to linking schools and social services. *Education and Urban Society, 25*(2), 175–186.

Spewock, T. S. (1991). Teaching parents of young children through learning packets. *Young Children, 47*(1), 28–30.

Spitz, R. (1946). Hospitalism: An inquiry into the genesis of psychiatric conditioning in early childhood. In D. Fenschel et al. (Eds.), *Psychoanalytical studies of the child* (Vol. 1) 102–122. New York: International Universities Press.

Sprafkin, C., Serbin, L. A., Dernier, C., & Connor, J. M. (1983). Sex-differentiated play: Cognitive consequences and early interventions. In M. B. Liss (Ed.), *Social and cognitive skills: Sex roles and children's play* (pp. 168–192). New York: Academic Press.

Stallings, J. (1980). Allocated academic learning time revisited, or beyond time on task. *Educational Researcher, 9*(11), 11–16.

Stein, C. B. Jr. (1986). *Sink or swim: The politics of bilingual education.* Westport, CT: Greenwood Publishing Group.

Steinberg, L. (1991). Authoritative parenting and adolescent adjustment across various ecological niches. *Journal of Research in Adolesence, 1*, 19–36.

Stiggins, R. J. (1997). *Student-centered classroom assessment* (2nd ed.). Upper Saddle River, NJ: Merrill/Prentice Hall.

Stille, Alexander. (1998, September). The betrayal of history. *New York Review of Books.* Available www.nybooks.com.

Stinnett, N., & DeFrain, J. (1986). *Secrets of strong families.* Boston: Little, Brown.

Stone, S. J. (1999). Epilogue. *Childhood Education, 75*(5), 304.

Studer, J. R. (1993/1994). Listen so that parents will speak. *Childhood Education, 70*(2), 74–76.

Sutherland, Z., & Arbuthnot, M. H. (1991). *Children and books* (8th ed.). New York: HarperCollins.

Swap, S. M. (1993). *Developing home-school partnerships: From concepts to practice.* New York: Teacher's College Press.

Swick, K. J. (1999). Empowering homeless and transient children and families: An ecological framework for early childhood teachers. *Early Childhood Education Journal, 26*(3), 195–201.

Szasz, M. C. (1977). *Education and the American Indian.* Albuquerque: University of New Mexico Press.

Szasz, M. C. (1988). *Indian education in the American colonies, 1607–1783.* Albuquerque: University of New Mexico Press.

Tao, F., Khan, S., & Arriola, C. (1997). *Special analysis of migrant education: Even Start Projects 1995–1996 program year.* (ERIC Document Reproduction Service No. ED 417 921)

Tao, F., Khan, S., Gamse, B., St. Pierre, R., & Tarr, H. (1996). *Evaluation of the Even Start Family Literacy Program: Interim Report, 1996.* (ERIC Document Reproduction Service No. ED 418 815)

Tapscott, D. (1999). Educating the net generation. *Educational Leadership, 56*(5), 6–11.

Taylor, K. W. (1981). *Parents and children learn together.* New York: Teachers College Press.

Taylor, R. L. (1997). Who's parenting?: Trends and patterns. In T. Arendell (Ed.), *Contemporary parenting: Challenges and Issues* (pp. 68–91). Thousand Oaks, CA: Sage.

Teale, W. H. (1986). Home background and young children's literacy development. In W. H. Teale & E. Sulzby (Eds.), *Emergent literacy: Writing and reading* (pp. 173–206). Norwood, NJ: Ablex.

Terpstra, M. (1994). A home/school school district partnership. *Educational Leadership, 52*(1), 57–58.

Thompson, S. (1993). Whole child, whole community. In S. Thompson (Ed.), *Whole child, whole community* (p. 1–4). Boston: Institute for Responsive Education.

Tiedt, P. L., & Tiedt, I. M. (1998). *Multicultural teaching: A handbook of activities, information and resources.* Reading, MA: Allyn & Bacon.

Tittle, C. K. (1986). Gender research and education. *American Psychologist, 41*(10), 1161–1168.

Travers, P. D., & Rebore, R. W. (1995). *Foundations of education: Becoming a teacher* (3rd ed.). Reading, MA: Allyn & Bacon.

Turnbull, A., Turnbull, R., Shank, M., & Leal, D. (1999). *Exceptional lives: Special education in today's schools* (2nd ed.). Upper Saddle River, NJ: Merrill/Prentice Hall.

Tushnet, N. C. (1993, April). *Educational Partnerships Program as a force for educational change: Findings for a national study.* Paper presented at the meeting of the American Educational Research Association, Atlanta, GA. (ERIC Document Reproduction Service No. ED 360 731)

Tyson, H. (1999). A load off the teachers' backs: Coordinated School Health Programs. *Phi Delta Kappan, 80*(5), (K1–K8).

Uphoff, J. K. (1993). Religious diversity and education. In J. A. Banks & C. A. McGee-Banks (Eds.), *Multicultural education: Issues and perspectives* (2nd ed.) (pp. 90–107). Boston: Allyn & Bacon.

U.S. Bureau of the Census. (1998a). *Statistical abstract of the United States: 1998* (118th ed.). Washington, DC: Author

U. S. Bureau of the Census. (1998b). *Current population report: P20–497–1998.* Washington, DC: Author.

U. S. Department of Education. (1986). *What works: Research about teaching and learning.* Washington, DC: Author.

U.S. Department of Education. (1991). *America 2000: An education strategy.* Washington, DC: Author.

U.S. Department of Education. (1993). *Goals 2000: Educate America.* Washington, DC: Author.

U.S. Department of Education. (1994). *Strong families, strong schools.* Washington, DC: Author.

Valente, W. D. (1998). *Law in the schools* (4th ed.). Upper Saddle River, NJ: Merrill/Prentice Hall.

Van Evra, J. (1998). *Television and child development* (2nd Ed). Mahwah, NJ.: Lawrence Erlbaum.

Van Galen, J. A. (1988). Becoming home schoolers. *Urban Education, 23*(1), 89–106.

Van Galen, J. A., & Pitman, M. A. (1991). *Home schooling: Political, historical, and pedagogical perspectives.* Norwood, NJ: Ablex.

Vosler, N. R. (1996). *New approaches to family practice: Confronting economic stress.* Thousand Oaks, CA: Sage Publications.

Voss, M. M. (1993). "I just watched": Family influences on one child's learning. *Language Arts, 70,* 632–641.

Wagner, M. (1995). *Contributions of poverty and ethnic background to the participation of secondary school students in special education.*

Washington, DC: U.S. Department of Education.

Wagner, N. J. (1995). *Into the woods.* Unpublished master's thesis, University of Maryland, Baltimore.

Wagstaff, L. H., & Gallagher, K. S. (1990). Schools, families and communities: Idealized images and new realities. In B. Mitchell & L. L. Cunningham (Eds.), *Educational leadership and changing contexts of families, communities, and schools: Eighty-ninth Yearbook of NSSE, Part II* (pp. 91–117). Chicago: National Society for the Study of Education.

Walberg, H. J. (1984). Improving the productivity of America's Schools. *Educational Leadership, 41*(8), 19–27.

Walker, L. J., & Taylor, J. H. (1991). Family interaction and the development of moral reasoning. *Child Development, 62,* 264– 283.

Wallace, N. (1990). Home schooling's unique structure. In A. Pedersen & P. O'Mara (Eds.), *Schooling at home: Parents, kids, and learning* (pp. 183–190). Santa Fe, NM: John Muir Publications.

Wallerstein, J. S., Corbin, S. B., & Lewis, J. H. (1988). Children of divorce: A ten-year study. In E. M. Hetherington and J. D. Arasteh (Eds.), *Impact of divorce, single parenting and step parenting on children* (pp. 197–214). Hillsdale, NJ: Lawrence Erlbaum Associates.

Webb, L. D., Metha, A., & Jordan, K. F. (1999). *Foundations of American education* (3rd ed.). Upper Saddle River, NJ: Merrill/Prentice Hall.

Weber, E. (1969). *The kindergarten.* New York: Teachers College Press.

Weikhart, D. P., & Schweinhart, L. J. (1991). Disadvantaged children and curriculum effects. In L. Rescorla, M. C. Hyson, & K. Hirsch-Pasek (Eds.), *Academic instruction in early childhood: Challenge or pressure?* (No. 53) (pp. 57–64). San Francisco: Jossey-Bass.

Weinberg, M. (1977). *A chance to learn: A history of race and education in the United States.* New York: Cambridge University Press.

Weiss, A. R. (1997). *Going it alone: A study of Massachusetts charter schools.* Boston: Institute for Responsive Education.

Weldin, D. J., & Tumarkin, S. R. (1999). More power in the portfolio process. *Childhood Education, 75*(2), 90–96.

Wells, S. S. (1998). Charter school reform in California: Does it meet expectations? *Phi Delta Kappan, 80*(2), 305–312.

Werner, E. E., & Smith, R. S. (1992). *Overcoming the odds: High risk children from birth to adulthood.* Ithaca: Cornell University Press.

Werner, E. E., & Smith, R. S. (1998). *Vulnerable but invincible: A longitudinal study of resilient children and youth.* New York: McGraw-Hill.

Westinghouse Learning Corporation—Ohio University. (1969). *The impact of Head Start.* Springfield, VA: Clearinghouse for Federal Scientific and Technical Information, U.S. Department of Commerce.

White, B. L. (1971, October). *Fundamental early environmental influences on the development of competence.* Paper presented at the Third Western Symposium on Learning, Cognitive Learning, Washington State College, Bellingham.

White, B. L., & Watts, J. C. (1973). *Experience and environment: Major influences on the development of the young child* (Vol. 1). Upper Saddle River, NJ: Prentice Hall.

Whitman, W. (1855). *Leaves of grass.* Brooklyn: Andrew & James Rome.

Williams, L. R. (1992). Determining the curriculum. In C. Seefeldt (Ed.), *The early childhood curriculum: A review of current research* (2nd ed.) (pp. 1–15). New York: Teachers College Press.

Williams, M. R. (1997). *The parent centered early school.* New York: Garland Publishing.

Williams, W. L. (1998). Social acceptance of same-sex relationships in families: Models from other cultures. In C. J. Patterson & A. R. D'Augelli (Eds.), *Lesbian, gay, and bisexual identities in families: Psychological perspectives* (pp. 53–75). New York: Oxford University Press.

Wisconsin v. Yoder, 406 U.S. 205 (1972).

Wissbrun, D., & Eckart, J. A. (1992). Hierarchy of parental involvement in schools. In L. Kaplan (Ed.), *Education and the family* (pp. 119–132). Boston: Allyn & Bacon.

Wohl, Faith. (1997). A panoramic view of work and family. In S. Parasuraman & J. H. Greenhaus (Eds.), *Integrating work and family: Challenges and choices for a changing world* (pp. 15–24). Westport, CT: Quorum Books.

Woolfolk, A. E. (1998). *Educational psychology* (7th ed.). Boston: Allyn & Bacon.

Wright, J. & Huston, A. (1995). *Effects of educational TV viewing of lower income preschoolers on academic skills, school readiness, and school adjustment one to three years later.* Lawrence, KS: Center for Research on the Influence of Television on Children.

Yamaguchi, B. J. Strawser, S., & Higgins, K. (1997). Children who are homeless: Implications for educators. *Intervention in School and Clinic, 33*(2), 90–97.

Yell, M. L. (1998). The legal bases of inclusion. *Educational Leadership, 56*(2), 70–71.

Young, K. T., Marsland, K. W., & Zigler, E. (1997). The regulatory status of center-based infant and toddler child care. *American Journal of Orthopsychiatry, 67*(4), 541–560.

Zeanah, C. H. & Scheeringa, M. S. (1997). The experiences and effects of violence in infancy. In J. S. Osofsky (Ed.), *Children in a violent society* (pp. 97–123). New York: Guilford Press.

Zelizer, V. A. (1994). *Pricing the priceless child: The changing social value of children.* Princeton, NJ: Princeton University Press.

Index

⸙⸙⸙⸙⸙